AdvancED ActionScript 3.0 Animation

Keith Peters

friendsof

DESIGNER TO DESIGNER™

an Apress® company

AdvancED ActionScript 3.0 Animation

ISBN-13 (pbk): 978-1-4302-1608-7

ISBN-13 (electronic): 978-1-4302-1608-7

Printed and bound in the United States of America 9 8 7 6 5 4 3 2 1

Trademarked names may appear in this book. Rather than use a trademark symbol with every occurrence of a trademarked name, we use the names only in an editorial fashion and to the benefit of the trademark owner, with no intention of infringement of the trademark.

Distributed to the book trade worldwide by Springer-Verlag New York, Inc., 233 Spring Street, 6th Floor, New York, NY 10013. Phone 1-800-SPRINGER, fax 201-348-4505, e-mail orders-ny@springer-sbm.com, or visit www.springeronline.com.

For information on translations, please contact Apress directly at 2855 Telegraph Avenue, Suite 600, Berkeley, CA 94705. Phone 510-549-5930, fax 510-549-5939, e-mail info@apress.com, or visit www.apress.com.

Apress and friends of ED books may be purchased in bulk for academic, corporate, or promotional use. eBook versions and licenses are also available for most titles. For more information, reference our Special Bulk Sales–eBook Licensing web page at http://www.apress.com/info/bulksales.

The information in this book is distributed on an "as is" basis, without warranty. Although every precaution has been taken in the preparation of this work, neither the author(s) nor Apress shall have any liability to any person or entity with respect to any loss or damage caused or alleged to be caused directly or indirectly by the information contained in this work.

The source code for this book is freely available to readers at www.friendsofed.com in the Downloads section.

Credits

Lead Editor	**Production Editor**
Ben Renow-Clarke	Janet Vail
Technical Reviewer	**Compositor**
Seb Lee-Delisle	Lynn L'Heureux
Editorial Board	**Proofreader**
Clay Andres, Steve Anglin, Mark Beckner,	Nancy Bell
Ewan Buckingham, Tony Campbell,	
Gary Cornell, Jonathan Gennick,	**Indexer**
Michelle Lowman, Matthew Moodie,	Carol Burbo
Jeffrey Pepper, Frank Pohlmann,	
Ben Renow-Clarke, Dominic Shakeshaft,	**Artist**
Matt Wade, Tom Welsh	Kinetic Publishing Services, LLC
Project Manager	**Cover Image Designer**
Sofia Marchant	Bruce Tang
Copy Editor	**Interior and Cover Designer**
Nancy Sixsmith	Kurt Krames
Associate Production Director	**Manufacturing Director**
Kari Brooks-Copony	Tom Debolski

To Miranda and Kristine, for their patience and support, once again.

CONTENTS AT A GLANCE

CONTENTS

ABOUT THE AUTHOR

Keith Peters is a non-recovering Flash addict, author of several books on Flash and ActionScript, speaker at Flash conferences around the world, and owner of various Flash-related web sites (www.bit-101.com, www.artfromcode.com, and www.wickedpissahgames.com).

Keith lives in Wellesley, Massachusetts with his wife Miranda and daughter Kristine, in a house that Flash helped pay for. He works as a senior Flash programmer at Infrared5 in Boston.

ABOUT THE TECHNICAL REVIEWER

Seb Lee-Delisle has been working in digital media for more than 15 years and is one of the founding partners of UK Flash specialists Plug-in Media (http://pluginmedia.net), working with clients such as BBC, Sony, Philips, Unilever, and Barclays. He is also one of the developers of Papervision3D, the highly successful open source, real time 3D ActionScript library. Seb's work with Plug-in Media has pushed the boundaries of 3D and gaming in Flash. He has recently completed the live 3D GameDay visualizations for Major League Baseball and a real time 3D website for the BBC kids' show Big and Small.

ABOUT THE COVER IMAGE DESIGNER

Bruce Tang is a freelance web designer, visual programmer, and author from Hong Kong. His main creative interest is generating stunning visual effects using Flash or Processing.

Bruce has been an avid Flash user since Flash 4, when he began using Flash to create games, websites, and other multimedia content. After several years of ActionScripting, he found himself increasingly drawn toward visual programming and computational art. He likes to integrate math and physics into his work, simulating 3D and other real-life experiences onscreen. His first Flash book was published in October 2005. Bruce's folio, featuring Flash and Processing pieces, can be found at www.betaruce.com, and his blog at www.betaruce.com/blog.

The cover image uses a high-resolution Henon phase diagram generated by Bruce with Processing, which he feels is an ideal tool for such experiments. Henon is a strange attractor created by iterating through some equations to calculate the coordinates of millions of points. The points are then plotted with an assigned color.

$$x_{n+1} = x_n \cos(a) - (y_n - x_n^p) \sin(a)$$

$$y_{n+1} = x_n \sin(a) + (y_n - x_n^p) \cos(a)$$

ACKNOWLEDGMENTS

Little—if any—of the material in this book is stuff I dreamed up in my own head. Thanks to the hundreds of programmers, developers, scientists, mathematicians, and physicists who studied, researched, programmed, translated, and made their work available for others to benefit from.

Layout conventions

To keep this book as clear and easy to follow as possible, the following text conventions are used throughout.

- Important words or concepts are normally highlighted on the first appearance in *italics*.

- Code is presented in `fixed-width` font.

- New or changed code is normally presented in **`bold fixed-width font`**.

- Pseudo-code and variable input are written in *`italic fixed-width font`*.

- Menu commands are written in the form Menu ➤ Submenu ➤ Submenu.

- Where I want to draw your attention to something, I've highlighted it like this:

    Ahem, don't say we didn't warn you.

- Sometimes code won't fit on a single line in a book. Where this happens, I use an arrow like this: ➡

    ```
    This is a very, very long section of code that should be written all ➡
    on the same line without a break.
    ```

Chapter 1

ADVANCED COLLISION DETECTION

Collision detection is the math, art, science, or general guesswork used to determine whether some object has hit another object. This sounds pretty simple, but when you are dealing with objects that exist only in a computer's memory and are represented by a collection of various properties, some complexities can arrive.

The basic methods of collision detection are covered in *Foundation ActionScript 3.0 Animation: Making Things Move!* (hereafter referred to as *Making Things Move*). This chapter looks at one method of collision detection that wasn't covered in that book and a strategy to handle collisions between large amounts of objects.

Note that the subject of collision detection does not delve into what you do *after* you detect a collision. If you are making a game, you might want the colliding objects to blow up, change color, or simply disappear. One rather complex method of handling the results of a collision was covered in the "Conservation of Momentum" chapter of *Making Things Move*. But ultimately it's up to you (and the specs of the application or game you are building) to determine how to respond when a collision is detected.

Hit Testing Irregularly Shaped Objects

Making Things Move covered a few basic methods of collision detection, including the built-in hitTestObject and hitTestPoint methods, as well as distance-based collision detection. Each of these methods has its uses in terms of the shapes of objects on which you are doing collision detection. The hitTestObject method is great for detecting collisions between two rectangular-shaped objects, but will often generate false positives for other shapes. The hitTestPoint method is suitable for finding out whether the mouse is over a particular object or whether a very small point-like object has collided with any other shaped object, but it is rather useless for two larger objects. Distance-based collision detection is great for circular objects, but will often miss collisions on other shaped objects.

The Holy Grail of collision detection in Flash has been to test two irregularly shaped objects against each other and accurately know whether or not they are touching. Although it wasn't covered in *Making Things Move*, a method has existed for doing this via the BitmapData class since Flash 8. In fact, the method is even called hitTest.

First, a note on terminology. ActionScript contains a BitmapData class, which holds the actual bitmap image being displayed, and a Bitmap class, which is a display object that contains a BitmapData and allows it to be added to the display list. If I am referring to either one of these classes specifically, or an instance of either class, I will use the capitalized version. But often I might casually use the term **bitmap** in lowercase to more informally refer to a bitmap image. Do not confuse it with the Bitmap class.

BitmapData.hitTest compares two BitmapData objects and tells you whether any of their pixels are overlapping. Again, this sounds simple, but complexities arise once you start to think about it. Bitmaps are rectangular grids of pixels, so taken in its simplest form, this method would be no more complex (or useful) than the hitTestObject method on a display object. Where it really starts to get useful is when you have a transparent bitmap with a shape drawn in it.

When you create a BitmapData object, you specify whether it will support transparency right in the constructor:

```
new BitmapData(width, height, transparent, color);
```

That third parameter is a Boolean value (true/false) that sets the transparency option. If you set it to false, the bitmap will be completely opaque. Initially, it will appear as a rectangle filled with the specified background color. You can use the various BitmapData methods to change any of the pixels in the bitmap, but they will always be fully opaque and cover anything behind that BitmapData. Color values for each pixel will be 24-bit numbers in the form 0xRRGGBB. This is a 6-digit hexadecimal number, where the first pair of numbers specifies the value for the red channel from 00 (0) to FF (255), the second pair sets the green channel, and the third sets the blue channel. For example, 0xFFFFFF would be white, 0xFF0000 would be red, and 0xFF9900 would be orange. For setting and getting values of individual pixels, you would use the methods setPixel and getPixel, which use 24-bit color values.

However, when you specify true for the transparency option in a BitmapData class, each pixel now supports an alpha channel, using a 32-bit number in the format 0xAARRGGBB. Here, the first 2 digits represent the level of transparency for a pixel, where 00 would be completely transparent, and FF would be fully opaque. In a transparent BitmapData, you would use setPixel32 and getPixel32 to set and read colors of individual pixels. These methods take 32-bit numbers. Note that if you pass in a 24-bit number to one of these methods, the alpha channel will be evaluated as being 0, or fully transparent.

To see the exact difference between the two, let's create one of each. You can use the following class as the main class in a Flex Builder 3 or 4 ActionScript Project, or as the document class in Flash CS3 or CS4. This class, BitmapCompare, is available at this book's download site at www.friendsofed.com.

```actionscript
package
{
    import flash.display.Bitmap;
    import flash.display.BitmapData;
    import flash.display.Sprite;
    import flash.display.StageAlign;
    import flash.display.StageScaleMode;
    import flash.geom.Rectangle;

    public class BitmapCompare extends Sprite
    {
        public function BitmapCompare()
        {
            stage.align = StageAlign.TOP_LEFT;
            stage.scaleMode = StageScaleMode.NO_SCALE;

            // draw a bunch of random lines
            graphics.lineStyle(0);
            for(var i:int = 0; i < 100; i++)
            {
                graphics.lineTo(Math.random() * 300,
                                Math.random() * 400);
            }

            // create an opaque bitmap
            var bmpd1:BitmapData = new BitmapData(300, 200,
                                                  false, 0xffffff);
            bmpd1.fillRect(new Rectangle(100, 50, 100, 100), 0xff0000);
            var bmp1:Bitmap = new Bitmap(bmpd1);
            addChild(bmp1);

            // create a transparent bitmap
            var bmpd2:BitmapData = new BitmapData(300, 200,
                                                  true, 0x00ffffff);
            bmpd2.fillRect(new Rectangle(100, 50, 100, 100),
                           0xffff0000);
            var bmp2:Bitmap = new Bitmap(bmpd2);
            bmp2.y = 200;
            addChild(bmp2);
        }
    }
}
```

This code first draws a bunch of random lines on the stage, just so you can tell the difference between the stage and the bitmaps. It then creates two bitmaps and draws red squares in the center of each. The top bitmap is opaque and covers the lines completely. The bottom bitmap is transparent, so only the red square covers the lines on the stage. You can see the result in Figure 1-1.

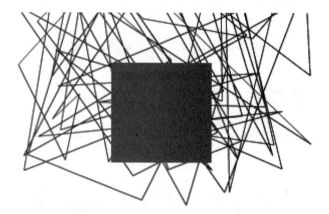

Figure 1-1. An opaque bitmap on top, transparent below

Furthermore, with a transparent bitmap you can use partial transparency. Change the second `fillRect` statement in the last code sample to the following:

```
bmpd2.fillRect(new Rectangle(100, 50, 100, 100), 0x80FF0000);
```

Note that we used a 32-bit AARRGGBB color value for the fill, and the alpha value has been halved to 0x80, or 128 in decimal. This makes the red square semitransparent, as seen in Figure 1-2.

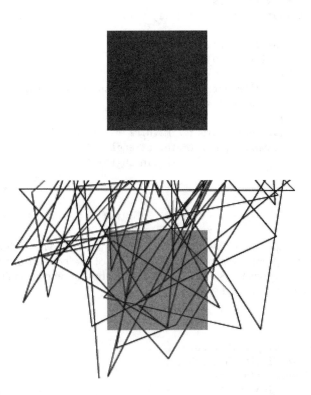

Figure 1-2. A semitransparent square

Bitmaps for collision detection

So now let's take a look at how to use bitmaps to achieve collision detection. First, we'll need a nice irregular shape to test with. A five-pointed star will do nicely. Why not make it into its very own class so we can reuse it? Here's the Star class, also available at the book's download site:

```
package
{
    import flash.display.Sprite;

    public class Star extends Sprite
    {
        public function Star(radius:Number, color:uint = 0xFFFF00):void
        {
            graphics.lineStyle(0);
            graphics.moveTo(radius, 0);
```

```
            graphics.beginFill(color);
            // draw 10 lines
            for(var i:int = 1; i < 11; i++)
            {
                var radius2:Number = radius;
                if(i % 2 > 0)
                {
                 // alternate radius to make spikes every other line
                    radius2 = radius / 2;
                }
                var angle:Number = Math.PI * 2 / 10 * i;
                graphics.lineTo(Math.cos(angle) * radius2,
                                Math.sin(angle) * radius2);
            }
        }
    }
}
```

This just draws a series of lines at increasing angles and alternate radii, which cleverly form a star. And here is the class that does the hit testing. Again, like most of the code in this book, it can be used either as a document class in Flash CS3 or CS4, or as a main application class in Flex Builder 3 or 4, and is available from the book's download site.

```
    package
    {
        import flash.display.Bitmap;
        import flash.display.BitmapData;
        import flash.display.Sprite;
        import flash.display.StageAlign;
        import flash.display.StageScaleMode;
        import flash.events.MouseEvent;
        import flash.filters.GlowFilter;
        import flash.geom.Matrix;
        import flash.geom.Point;

        public class BitmapCollision1 extends Sprite
        {
            private var bmpd1:BitmapData;
            private var bmp1:Bitmap;
            private var bmpd2:BitmapData;
            private var bmp2:Bitmap;

            public function BitmapCollision1()
            {
                stage.align = StageAlign.TOP_LEFT;
                stage.scaleMode = StageScaleMode.NO_SCALE;

                // make a star
                var star:Star = new Star(50);
```

```
        // make a fixed bitmap, draw the star into it
        bmpd1 = new BitmapData(100, 100, true, 0);
        bmpd1.draw(star, new Matrix(1, 0, 0, 1, 50, 50));
        bmp1 = new Bitmap(bmpd1);
        bmp1.x = 200;
        bmp1.y = 200;
        addChild(bmp1);

        // make a moveable bitmap, draw the star into it, too
        bmpd2 = new BitmapData(100, 100, true, 0);
        bmpd2.draw(star, new Matrix(1, 0, 0, 1, 50, 50));
        bmp2 = new Bitmap(bmpd2);
        addChild(bmp2);

        stage.addEventListener(MouseEvent.MOUSE_MOVE,
                                onMouseMoving);
    }

    private function onMouseMoving(event:MouseEvent):void
    {
        // move bmp2 to the mouse position (centered).
        bmp2.x = mouseX - 50;
        bmp2.y = mouseY - 50;

        // the hit test itself.
        if(bmpd1.hitTest(new Point(bmp1.x, bmp1.y), 255, bmpd2,
                        new Point(bmp2.x, bmp2.y), 255))
        {
            bmp1.filters = [new GlowFilter()];
            bmp2.filters = [new GlowFilter()];
        }
        else
        {
            bmp1.filters = [];
            bmp2.filters = [];
        }
    }
    }
}
```

Here we create a star using the Star class and draw it into two bitmaps. We use a matrix to offset the star during drawing by 50 pixels on each axis because the registration point of the star is in its center, and the registration point of the bitmap is at the top left. We offset it so we can see the whole star.

One of these bitmaps (bmp1) is in a fixed position on the stage; the other (bmp2) is set to follow the mouse around. The key line comes here:

```
if(bmpd1.hitTest(new Point(bmp1.x, bmp1.y), 255, bmpd2,
                new Point(bmp2.x, bmp2.y), 255))
```

This is what actually determines if the two bitmaps are touching. The signature for the BitmapData.hitTest method looks like this:

```
hitTest(firstPoint:Point,
        firstAlphaThreshold:uint,
        secondObject:Object,
        secondPoint:Point,
        secondAlphaThreshold:uint);
```

You'll notice that the parameters are broken down into two groups: first and second. You supply a point value for each. This corresponds to the top-left corner of BitmapData. The reason for doing this is that each bitmap might be nested within another symbol or deeply nested within multiple symbols. In such a case, they might be in totally different coordinate systems. Specifying an arbitrary point lets you align the two coordinate systems if necessary, perhaps through using the DisplayObject.localToGlobal method. In this example, however, both bitmaps will be right on the stage, so we can use their local position directly to construct the point for each.

The next first/last parameters are for the alpha threshold. As you saw earlier, in a transparent BitmapData, each pixel's transparency can range from 0 (fully transparent) to 255 (fully opaque). The alpha threshold parameters specify how opaque a pixel must be in order to register a hit. In this example, we set both of these to 255, meaning that for a pixel in either bitmap to be considered for a hit test, it must be fully opaque. We'll do another example later that shows the use of a lower threshold.

Finally, there is the secondObject parameter. Note that it is typed to an object. Here you can use a Point, a Rectangle, or another BitmapData as the object to test against. If you are using a Point or Rectangle, you do not need to use the final two parameters. Testing against a Point is useful if you want to test whether the mouse is touching a bitmap. A quick example follows:

```
if(myBitmapData.hitTest(new Point(myBitmapData.x, myBitmapData.y),
                        255,
                        new Point(mouseX, mouseY)))
{
    // mouse is touching bitmap
}
```

I can't think of a particularly useful example for testing a bitmap against a rectangle, but it's good to know that if the need arises, it's there!

In our example, however, we are using another BitmapData object, so we pass that in along with the second Point and alpha threshold.

Finally, if there is a hit, we give each star a red glow through the use of a default glow filter. If no hit, we remove any filter. You can see the results in Figures 1-3 and 1-4.

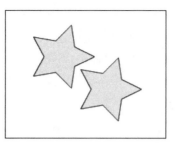

Figure 1-3. Stars are not touching.

Figure 1-4. And now they are.

Play with this for awhile, and you'll see that it truly is pixel-to-pixel collision detection.

Hit testing with semitransparent shapes

In the preceding example, we drew a star that was totally opaque into each bitmap. We were thus testing against fully opaque pixels in each bitmap and therefore we set the alpha threshold to 255 in each one. (We actually could have set the alpha threshold to anything above zero and had the same effect.)

Now let's look at hit testing with a shape that *isn't* fully opaque. We'll alter the BitmapCollsion1 class slightly, naming it BitmapCollision2 (available for download on the book's site):

```
package
{
    import flash.display.Bitmap;
    import flash.display.BitmapData;
    import flash.display.GradientType;
    import flash.display.Sprite;
    import flash.display.StageAlign;
    import flash.display.StageScaleMode;
    import flash.events.MouseEvent;
    import flash.filters.GlowFilter;
    import flash.geom.Matrix;
    import flash.geom.Point;

    public class BitmapCollision2 extends Sprite
    {
        private var bmpd1:BitmapData;
        private var bmp1:Bitmap;
        private var bmpd2:BitmapData;
        private var bmp2:Bitmap;
```

```
public function BitmapCollision2()
{
    stage.align = StageAlign.TOP_LEFT;
    stage.scaleMode = StageScaleMode.NO_SCALE;

    // make a star
    var star:Star = new Star(50);

    // make a gradient circle
    var matrix:Matrix = new Matrix();
    matrix.createGradientBox(100, 100, 0, -50, -50);
    var circle:Sprite = new Sprite();
    circle.graphics.beginGradientFill(GradientType.RADIAL,
                                [0, 0], [1, 0]
                                [0, 255], matrix);
    circle.graphics.drawCircle(0, 0, 50);
    circle.graphics.endFill();

    // make a fixed bitmap, draw the star into it
    bmpd1 = new BitmapData(100, 100, true, 0);
    bmpd1.draw(star, new Matrix(1, 0, 0, 1, 50, 50));
    bmp1 = new Bitmap(bmpd1);
    bmp1.x = 200;
    bmp1.y = 200;
    addChild(bmp1);

    // make a moveable bitmap, draw the star into it, too
    bmpd2 = new BitmapData(100, 100, true, 0);
    bmpd2.draw(circle, new Matrix(1, 0, 0, 1, 50, 50));
    bmp2 = new Bitmap(bmpd2);
    addChild(bmp2);

    stage.addEventListener(MouseEvent.MOUSE_MOVE,
                        onMouseMoving);
}

private function onMouseMoving(event:MouseEvent):void
{
    // move bmp2 to the mouse position (centered).
    bmp2.x = mouseX - 50;
    bmp2.y = mouseY - 50;

    // the hit test itself.
    if(bmpd1.hitTest(new Point(bmp1.x, bmp1.y), 255, bmpd2,
                    new Point(bmp2.x, bmp2.y), 255))
    {
        bmp1.filters = [new GlowFilter()];
        bmp2.filters = [new GlowFilter()];
    }
```

```
        else
        {
            bmp1.filters = [];
            bmp2.filters = [];
        }
      }
    }
}
```

Here we make a new Sprite named circle and draw a radial gradient-filled circle shape in it. We draw this to bmpd2 instead of the star. If you test this, you'll see that no hit will be registered until the very center of the circle touches the star because only at the center is the circle fully opaque. You can see the results in Figures 1-5 and 1-6.

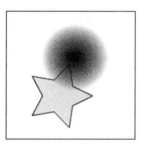

Figure 1-5. The star is touching the circle, but not a pixel that has the required alpha threshold.

Figure 1-6. Only the center of the circle has an alpha of 255, so you get a hit.

Change the hit test line to make the second alpha threshold a lower value like so:

```
if(bmpd1.hitTest(new Point(bmp1.x, bmp1.y), 255, bmpd2,
                 new Point(bmp2.x, bmp2.y), 128))
```

Now you have to move the circle only part way onto the square, just so it hits a pixel whose alpha is at least 128. Try setting that second alpha threshold to different values to see the effects. Note that if you set it to zero, you might get a hit even before the circle touches the star because it will successfully hit test even against the fully transparent pixels in the very corner of the bitmap. Remember that the bitmap itself is still a rectangle, even if you can't see it all. Also note that changing the first alpha threshold (to anything other than 0) won't change anything because the star doesn't. have any semitransparent pixels—they are either fully transparent or fully opaque.

Using BitmapData.hitTest for nonbitmaps

In the examples so far, we've been using Bitmap objects directly as the display objects we are moving around and testing against. But in many (if not most) cases, you'll actually be moving around different types of display objects such as MovieClip, Sprite, or Shape objects. Because you can't do this type of hit testing on these types of objects, you'll need to revise the setup a bit. The strategy is to keep a couple of offline BitmapData objects around, but not on the display list. Each time you want to check a collision between two of your actual display objects, draw one to each bitmap and perform your hit test on the bitmaps.

Realize that this is not the only way, or necessarily the best possible way, of using bitmaps for collision detection. There are probably dozens of possible methods, and this one works fine. Feel free to use it as is or improve on it.

Here's the class, BitmapCollision3 (download it from the book's site):

```
package
{
    import flash.display.BitmapData;
    import flash.display.Sprite;
    import flash.display.StageAlign;
    import flash.display.StageScaleMode;
    import flash.events.MouseEvent;
    import flash.filters.GlowFilter;
    import flash.geom.Matrix;
    import flash.geom.Point;

    public class BitmapCollision3 extends Sprite
    {
        private var bmpd1:BitmapData;
        private var bmpd2:BitmapData;
        private var star1:Star;
        private var star2:Star;

        public function BitmapCollision3()
        {
            stage.align = StageAlign.TOP_LEFT;
            stage.scaleMode = StageScaleMode.NO_SCALE;

            // make two stars, add to stage
            star1 = new Star(50);
            addChild(star1);

            star2 = new Star(50);
            star2.x = 200;
            star2.y = 200;
            addChild(star2);

            // make two bitmaps, not on stage
            bmpd1 = new BitmapData(stage.stageWidth, stage.stageHeight, true, 0);
            bmpd2 = bmpd1.clone();

            stage.addEventListener(MouseEvent.MOUSE_MOVE,
                            onMouseMoving);
        }
```

```
private function onMouseMoving(event:MouseEvent):void
{
    // move star1 to the mouse position
    star1.x = mouseX;
    star1.y = mouseY;

    // clear the bitmaps
    bmpd1.fillRect(bmpd1.rect, 0);
    bmpd2.fillRect(bmpd2.rect, 0);

    // draw one star to each bitmap
    bmpd1.draw(star1,
            new Matrix(1, 0, 0, 1, star1.x, star1.y));
    bmpd2.draw(star2,
            new Matrix(1, 0, 0, 1, star2.x, star2.y));

    // the hit test itself.
    if(bmpd1.hitTest(new Point(), 255, bmpd2, new Point(), 255))
    {
        star1.filters = [new GlowFilter()];
        star2.filters = [new GlowFilter()];
    }
    else
    {
        star1.filters = [];
        star2.filters = [];
    }
}
```

In the constructor this time, we make two BitmapData objects and two stars. There's no need to put the BitmapData objects in Bitmaps, as they are not going on the display list. The stars, on the other hand, do get added to the display list. The first star, star1, gets moved around with the mouse. Each time the mouse is moved, both bitmaps are cleared by using fillRect, passing in a color value of zero. Remember that if the alpha channel is not specified, it is taken as zero, so this has the result of making all pixels completely transparent. Then each star is drawn to its corresponding bitmap:

```
bmpd1.draw(star1, new Matrix(1, 0, 0, 1, star1.x, star1.y));
bmpd2.draw(star2, new Matrix(1, 0, 0, 1, star2.x, star2.y));
```

The matrix uses the stars' x and y positions as translation values, resulting in each star being drawn in the same position it is in on the stage. Now we can do the hit test:

```
if(bmpd1.hitTest(new Point(), 255, bmpd2, new Point(), 255))
```

Because `BitmapData` is not on the display list or even in a `Bitmap` wrapper, and because both stars are in the same coordinate space and have been drawn to each `BitmapData` in their relative positions, we don't need to do any correction of coordinate spaces. We just pass in a new default `Point` (which will have x and y both zero) to each of the `Point` arguments. We'll leave the alpha thresholds at 255 because both stars are fully opaque.

Although this example doesn't look any different from the others, it's actually completely inverted, with the bitmaps invisible and the stars visible. Yet it works exactly the same way.

These are just a few examples of using `BitmapData.hitTest` to do collision detection on noncircle, rectangle, or point-shaped objects. I'm sure once you get how it all works, you can think up some cool variations for it.

Next up, we'll look at how to do collision detection on a large scale.

Hit Testing with a Large Number of Objects

ActionScript in Flash Player 10 runs faster than ever before and it lets us do more stuff at once and move more objects at the same time. But there are still limits. If you start moving lots of objects on the screen, sooner or later things will start to bog down. Collision detection among large numbers of objects compounds the problem because each object needs to be compared against every other object. This is not limited to collision detection only; any particle system or game in which a lot of objects need to interact with each other, such as via gravity or flocking (see Chapter 2), will run into the same problems.

If you have just six objects interacting with each other, each object needs to pair up with every other object and do its hit test, gravitational attraction, or whatever action it needs to do with that other object. At first glance, this means 6 times 6, or 36 individual comparisons. But, as described in *Making Things Move*, it's actually fewer than half of that: 15 to be precise. Given objects A, B, C, D, E, F, you need to do the following pairings:

AB, AC, AD, AE, AF

BC, BD, BE, BF

CD, CE, CF

DE, DF

EF

Notice that B does not have to check with A because A has already checked with B. By the time you get to E, it's already been checked against everything but F. And after that, F has been checked by all the others. The formula for how many comparisons need to occur is as follows, where N is the number of objects:

$(N^2 - N)/2$

For 6 objects, that's $(36 - 6)/2$ or 15.

For 10 objects, that's (100 – 10)/2 or 45 checks.

20 objects means 190 checks, and 30 objects is 435!

You see that this goes up very quickly, and you need to do something to limit it. One hundred objects aren't really hard to move around the screen in ActionScript 3.0, but when you start doing collision detection or some other interobject comparisons, that's 4,950 separate checks to do! If you are using distance-based collision detection, that's 4,950 times calculating the distance between two objects. If you're using bitmap collision, as described earlier in the chapter, that's 4,950 times clearing two bitmaps, drawing two objects, and calling the hitTest method. On every frame! That's bound to slow your SWF file down.

Fortunately, there is a trick to limit the number of checks you need to do. Think about this: if two relatively small objects are on opposite sides of the screen, there's no way they could possibly be colliding. But to discover that, we need to calculate the distance between them, right? So we are back to square one. But maybe there's another way.

Suppose that we break down the screen into a grid of square cells, in which each cell is at least as large as the largest object, and then we assign each object to one of the cells in that grid—based on where the center of that object is located. If we set it up just right, an object in a given cell can collide only with the objects in the eight other cells surrounding it. Look at Figure 1-7, for example.

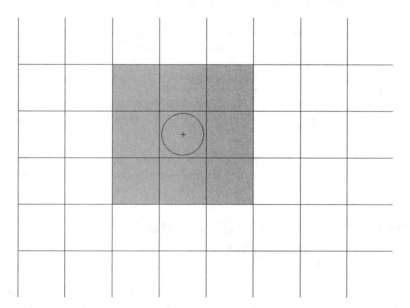

Figure 1-7. The ball can collide only with objects in the shaded cells.

The ball shown is assigned to a cell based on its center point. The only objects it can hit are those in the shaded cells. There is no way it can collide with an object in any of the white cells. Even if the ball were on the very edge of that cell, and another ball were on the very edge of a white cell, they could not touch each other (see Figure 1-8).

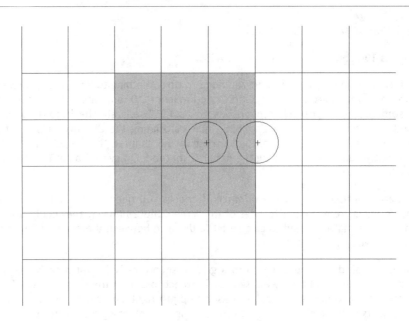

Figure 1-8. There's no way the two balls can collide.

Again, this scenario depends on the size of the cells being at least as large as the largest object you will be comparing. If either of the balls were larger than the cells, it would be possible for them to hit each other in the above scenario.

Okay, that's the basic setup. Knowing that, there are probably a number of ways to proceed. I'm not sure there is a single best way, but the goal is to test each object against all the other objects it could possibly reach and make sure that you never test any two objects against each other twice. That's where things get a bit tricky.

I'll outline the method I came up with, which will seem pretty abstract. Just try to get an idea of which areas of the grid we'll be doing collision detection with. Exactly how we'll do all that will be discussed next.

Implementing grid-based collision detection

We'll start in the upper-left corner. I'll reduce the grid size a bit to make things simpler. See Figure 1-9.

You'll want to test all the objects in that first darker cell with all the objects in all the surrounding cells. Of course, there are no cells to the left or above it, so you just need to check the three light gray cells. Again, there is no way that an object in that dark gray cell can possibly hit anything in any of the white cells.

When that's done, we move on to the next cell. See Figure 1-10.

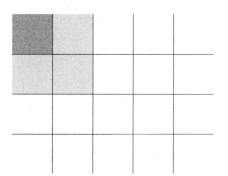

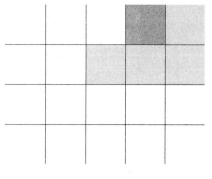

Figure 1-9. Test all the objects in the first cell with all the objects in the surrounding cells.

Figure 1-10. Continuing with the next cell

With this one, there are a couple more available cells surrounding it, but remember that we already compared all the objects in that first cell with all the objects in the three surrounding cells, which includes the one being tested now. So there is no need to test anything with the first cell again.

We continue across the first row in the same fashion. We only need to test the current cell, the cell to its right, and the three cells below it. See Figures 1-11, 1-12, and 1-13.

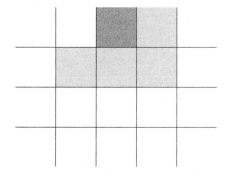

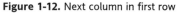

Figure 1-11. Continuing across the first row

Figure 1-12. Next column in first row

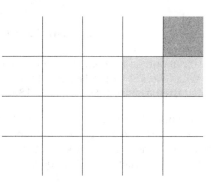

Figure 1-13. Final column in first row

Of course, when we get to the last cell in the row, there is nothing to the right, so it's just the two below it.

We then start row two. See Figures 1-14 and 1-15.

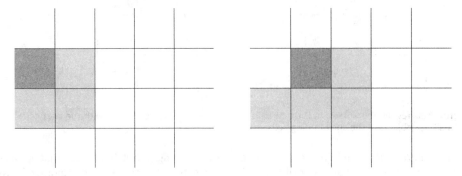

Figure 1-14. Starting the second row   **Figure 1-15.** Next column in second row

We begin to have all of the surrounding cells available, but the top row has already been completely checked against anything in the second row. So we can ignore that. It winds up being no different from the first row. It's always nice when you can reuse your code.

Finally, we get to the last row. See Figures 1-16 and 1-17.

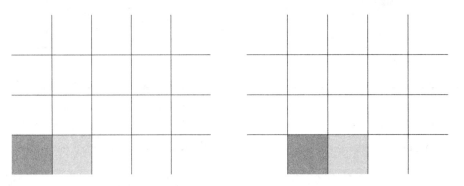

Figure 1-16. The last row   **Figure 1-17.** Second column, last row

Here, there is no lower row to worry about, and the upper row is done. So we just have to test each cell against the cell to the right. When we get to the last cell, there is nothing to even test against because all other cells have already tested against it. See Figure 1-18.

Okay, that's what we have to do. Now how do we do it? Well, at most, we are going to have five cells to deal with: the main cell we are examining, the one to the right, and the three below. Each of these "cells" is actually an array of objects. Call these arrays cell0, cell1, cell2, cell3, cell4, and cell5. And to keep it simple, we'll assume that each cell contains only Ball objects.

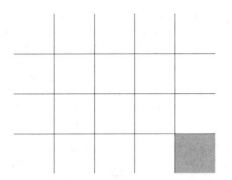

Figure 1-18. Nothing to do here

Let's take cell0, the first array of ball objects. Any of the balls in this cell might be hitting any of the others, so we need to test them all against each other. We do that via a double loop, as described in *Making Things Move*. Here's a rough pass at the code for it:

```
for(var i:int = 0; i < cell0.length - 1; i++)
{
    var ballA:Ball = cell0[i] as Ball;
    for(var j:int = i + 1; j < cell0.length; j++)
    {
        var ballB:Ball = cell0[j] as Ball;
        // hit test or other reaction between ballA and ballB
    }
}
```

This tests each ball against every other ball, in a way that no ball is ever tested against itself, and no pair is ever tested twice. That does it for all collision detection between the balls in cell0. Now we move on to testing cell0 against cell1. This is a bit different: we take each ball in cell0 and test them, one by one, against each ball in cell1. Again, this winds up as a double loop:

```
for(var i:int = 0; i < cell0.length; i++)
{
    var ballA:Ball = cell0[i] as Ball;
    for(var j:int = 0; j < cell1.length; j++)
    {
        var ballB:Ball = cell1[j] as Ball;
        // hit test or other reaction between ballA and ballB
    }
}
```

Note that this code iterates fully through all the elements of both arrays, unlike the first comparison, which did some fancy tricks to avoid double-checking. We don't have to worry about that here because we're dealing with two arrays that contain completely different elements.

We can repeat this last type of check to compare cell0 with cell2, cell3, cell4, and cell5. At that point, cell0 would be complete, and we would move on to the next cell, which would then become cell0. Of course, there will be fewer than four surrounding cells for all the cells on the left, right, or bottom edge, so we have to take that into account.

Now, if your brain is like mine, it's hard to read all this and see how that complexity could possibly be more efficient than just comparing all the objects to each other. But let's do the math. Remember that if we compared 100 objects with each other, we would do 4,950 checks. In the examples that follow, we'll be keeping track of exactly how many comparisons actually occur. The numbers will vary based on the size of the screen, the size of the objects, the number of objects, the size of the grid, and the random distribution of the objects. In my tests, 100 objects were averaging between 100 and 200 individual hit tests. That's a saving of about 4,800 checks! Because each hit test consists of several lines of code, including a fairly expensive square root calculation, the CPU savings can be significant.

Of course, there is significant overhead in creating and updating the grid, assigning all the objects to it, and looping through all those arrays, which is something you'll usually do on every frame. In the case of a large number of objects, the savings you get from the reduced number of calculations will far outweigh that overhead. But in a system with fewer objects, it will be more efficient to just check each object against all the others. We'll discuss how to gauge the benefits of both methods to decide when to use each later in the chapter.

Coding the grid

Okay, our first go at this will be purely for clarity's sake. We'll break down each function so you can see what's happening as we go through it. Then we'll go clean it up and make it a reusable class.

Before we dive into the collision detection itself, let's get something to detect collisions: the Ball class, which you can download at this book's site at www.friendsofed.com:

```
package
{
    import flash.display.Sprite;

    public class Ball extends Sprite
    {
        private var _color:uint;
        private var _radius:Number;
        private var _vx:Number = 0;
        private var _vy:Number = 0;


        public function Ball(radius:Number, color:uint = 0xffffff)
        {
            _radius = radius;
            _color = color;
            draw();
        }

        private function draw():void
        {
            // draw a circle with a dot in the center
            graphics.clear();
            graphics.lineStyle(0);
```

```
        graphics.beginFill(_color, .5);
        graphics.drawCircle(0, 0, _radius);
        graphics.endFill();
        graphics.drawCircle(0, 0, 1);
}

public function update():void
{
    // add velocity to position
    x += _vx;
    y += _vy;
}

public function set color(value:uint):void
{
    _color = value;
    draw();
}

public function get color():uint
{
    return _color;
}

public function set radius(value:Number):void
{
    _radius = value;
    draw();
}

public function get radius():Number
{
    return _radius;
}

public function set vx(value:Number):void
{
    _vx = value;
}

public function get vx():Number
{
    return _vx;
}

public function set vy(value:Number):void
{
    _vy = value;
}
```

```
        public function get vy():Number
        {
            return _vy;
        }

    }
}
```

There's no rocket science here. It takes a radius and a color and then draws a circle. Each circle keeps track of its x and y velocity and adds them to its position when told to update. Good enough.

Now here's the start of the application class, which you can use as your main class in Flex Builder or your document class in Flash CS3 or CS4. Make sure that the Ball class is in the same location as this class. I'll keep everything in the default package for now, again for clarity. Feel free to organize the classes into a package structure that works for you. This is the GridCollision class, which you can download from this book's download page.

```
package {
    import flash.display.Sprite;
    import flash.display.StageAlign;
    import flash.display.StageScaleMode;

    public class GridCollision extends Sprite
    {
        private const GRID_SIZE:Number = 50;
        private const RADIUS:Number = 25;

        private var _balls:Array;
        private var _grid:Array;
        private var _numBalls:int = 100;
        private var _numChecks:int = 0;

        public function GridCollision()
        {
            stage.align = StageAlign.TOP_LEFT;
            stage.scaleMode = StageScaleMode.NO_SCALE;

            makeBalls();
            makeGrid();
            drawGrid();
            assignBallsToGrid();
            checkGrid();
            trace(_numChecks);
        }

    // the rest of the methods described in this section will go here
    }
}
```

Here we have some constants for the grid size and the radius of the balls. Remember that the grid size should be at least the size of the largest object, which for a circle would be twice its radius. So we satisfied that requirement.

Then we have an array for the balls and another array to serve as the grid. We'll be testing with 100 balls and we have a variable to hold the cumulative number of hit tests we're doing.

The constructor calls a number of methods: to create the balls, make the grid, draw the grid, assign the balls to the grid, and check the grid for collisions. Finally it traces out how many hit tests were done.

Now let's start in on the other methods of the class. First is makeBalls:

```
private function makeBalls():void
{
    _balls = new Array();
    for(var i:int = 0; i < _numBalls; i++)
    {
        // create a Ball and add it to the display list
        // and the _balls array
        var ball:Ball = new Ball(RADIUS);
        ball.x = Math.random() * stage.stageWidth;
        ball.y = Math.random() * stage.stageHeight;
        addChild(ball);
        _balls.push(ball);
    }
}
```

Again, nothing too complex here. This makes an array, runs a loop creating a bunch of instances of Ball, randomly scatters them around the stage, adds them to the display list, and pushes them in the _balls array.

Next is the makeGrid() method:

```
private function makeGrid():void
{
    _grid = new Array();
    // stage width / grid size = number of columns
    for(var i:int = 0; i < stage.stageWidth / GRID_SIZE; i++)
    {
        _grid[i] = new Array();
        // stage height / grid size = number of rows
        for(var j:int = 0; j < stage.stageHeight / GRID_SIZE; j++)
        {
            _grid[i][j] = new Array();
        }
    }
}
```

Here we create a two-dimensional array in which each element represents a square portion of the screen. Each element of the two-dimensional array contains yet another array. (You could call this a three-dimensional array, but it doesn't really fit our paradigm.) These final arrays will be used to hold the objects assigned to each area of the grid.

The next method, drawGrid(), is for your eyes only. It doesn't do anything useful in terms of collision detection; it just helps you visualize where each grid element is. In a final game or application, you would most likely not draw the grid.

```
private function drawGrid():void
{
    // draw lines to indicate rows and columns
    graphics.lineStyle(0, .5);
    for(var i:int = 0; i <= stage.stageWidth; i += GRID_SIZE)
    {
        graphics.moveTo(i, 0);
        graphics.lineTo(i, stage.stageHeight);
    }
    for(i = 0; i <= stage.stageHeight; i += GRID_SIZE)
    {
        graphics.moveTo(0, i);
        graphics.lineTo(stage.stageWidth, i);
    }
}
```

On to one of the most important methods, assignBallsToGrid:

```
private function assignBallsToGrid():void
{
    for(var i:int = 0; i < _numBalls; i++)
    {
        // dividing position by grid size
        // tells us which row and column each ball is in
        var ball:Ball = _balls[i] as Ball;
        var xpos:int = Math.floor(ball.x / GRID_SIZE);
        var ypos:int = Math.floor(ball.y / GRID_SIZE);
        _grid[xpos][ypos].push(ball);
    }
}
```

This code might need a bit of explanation. The first part is pretty obvious: loop through the array, getting a reference to each Ball object in it. We then divide that ball's x position by the grid size and round the result down to the nearest integer value. This tells us in which column of the grid that ball should be. We do the same thing for the y position, which gives us the row of the grid to put it in. See Figure 1-19.

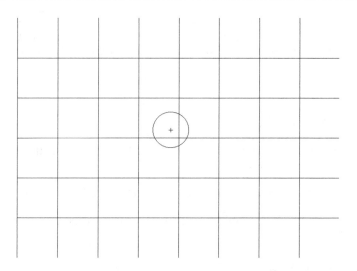

Figure 1-19. Figuring out which grid element a ball belongs to

In this example, let's say that the grid elements are 100×100. The ball you see there is at a position of 380 on the x-axis and 280 on the y-axis. We divide 380 by 100 and get 3.8. Round that down to get 3, which tells us that the ball goes in column 3 of the grid. Remember that arrays are zero-indexed, so an index of 3 is actually the fourth column. Doing the same thing for y tells us that it's in row 2 (the third row). You can easily validate the math by looking at the diagram and seeing that the center point of the ball is indeed in the fourth column, third row of the grid (counting from the top left).

Going back to the code, we assign the results of these calculations to xpos and ypos and use them to index the two-dimensional grid. Because each element of that two-dimensional array is an array itself, we push the object onto the array in that element.

When the loop is finished, each object will be in a specific element in the grid. Some grid elements will contain a single object; some will contain multiple objects; many will be empty. Now we are ready to do our hit testing.

The checkGrid() method does all the heavy lifting. In fact, it relies on a few other methods that you'll soon see as well. Let's jump in:

```
private function checkGrid():void
{
    // loop through each row and column of grid
    for(var i:int = 0; i < _grid.length; i++)
    {
        for(var j:int = 0; j < _grid[i].length; j++)
        {
            // examine all the objects in the first cell
            // against each other
            checkOneCell(i, j);
```

```
            checkTwoCells(i, j, i + 1, j);     // cell to the right
            checkTwoCells(i, j, i - 1, j + 1); // below to the left
            checkTwoCells(i, j, i, j + 1);     // directly below
            checkTwoCells(i, j, i + 1, j + 1); // below to the right
        }
    }
}
```

We use a double loop to loop through each column and row of the grid. The indexes i and j represent the cell we are currently examining. The first thing we do is compare all the objects in that cell to each other via the checkOneCell() method:

```
private function checkOneCell(x:int, y:int):void
{
    // check all the balls in a single cell against each other
    var cell:Array = _grid[x][y] as Array;

    for(var i:int = 0; i < cell.length - 1; i++)
    {
        var ballA:Ball = cell[i] as Ball;
        for(var j:int = i + 1; j < cell.length; j++)
        {
            var ballB:Ball = cell[j] as Ball;
            checkCollision(ballA, ballB);
        }
    }
}
```

This code does a double loop through the array, as described in *Making Things Move*, which results in every object in the cell compared with every other object exactly one time.

We then call the checkTwoCells() method four times:

```
checkTwoCells(i, j, i + 1, j);     // cell to the right
checkTwoCells(i, j, i - 1, j + 1); // cell below to the left
checkTwoCells(i, j, i, j + 1);     // cell directly below
checkTwoCells(i, j, i + 1, j + 1); // cell below to the right
```

The indexes i and j still refer to the main cell we are checking. Then i + 1, j refers to the cell to the right; i -1, j + 1 is the cell to the lower left; i, j + 1 is directly below; and i + 1, j + 1 is the lower right, exactly as shown in Figures 1-9 through 1-18. Here is checkTwoCells():

```
private function checkTwoCells(x1:int, y1:int, x2:int, y2:int):void
{
    // make sure the second cell really exists
    if(x2 < 0) return;
    if(x2 >= _grid.length) return;
    if(y2 >= _grid[x2].length) return;
```

```
var cell0:Array = _grid[x1][y1] as Array;
var cell1:Array = _grid[x2][y2] as Array;

// check all the balls in one cell against all in the other
for(var i:int = 0; i < cell0.length; i++)
{
    var ballA:Ball = cell0[i] as Ball;
    for(var j:int = 0; j < cell1.length; j++)
    {
        var ballB:Ball = cell1[j] as Ball;
        checkCollision(ballA, ballB);
    }
}
}
```

Here, i and j have become x1 and y1. These variables are used to get a reference to the first cell. The next two parameters have become x2 and y2. We need to make sure that they are in range. If x2 is less than zero, or greater than or equal to _grid.length, _grid[x2] will be null. This will occur if the main cell is in the first or last column. (See Figures 1-9 and 1-13.) Similarly, if y2 is greater than the number of cells in that column, it will be out of range, and _grid[x2][y2] will be null (See Figures 1-16 through 1-18.) If any of these conditions occur, we just exit out of the method because there is no valid second cell to check against.

However, if we make it past that, we can successfully get references to the two cells to check. We use a double loop to loop through all the elements of the first cell and compare them with all the elements of the second cell, exactly as described earlier.

Last but not least is the collision detection itself. We've gotten all the way down to the point where we have two objects to test against each other. We call checkCollision(), passing in a reference to each of them. That method looks like this:

```
private function checkCollision(ballA:Ball, ballB:Ball):void
{
    // if distance is less than sum of radii, collision
    _numChecks++;
    var dx:Number = ballB.x - ballA.x;
    var dy:Number = ballB.y - ballA.y;
    var dist:Number = Math.sqrt(dx * dx + dy * dy);
    if(dist < ballA.radius + ballB.radius)
    {
        ballA.color = 0xff0000;
        ballB.color = 0xff0000;
    }
}
```

Because we are actually down to the point of performing real live collision detection between two objects, we update the _numChecks property. Then we do a standard distance-based, collision-detection method using the square of the distances between the two balls on the x-axis and y-axis. If it is less than the sum of their radii, we color them both red. We could actually do even more optimization by getting rid of the square root, squaring the sum of the radii, and comparing them. Any time you can avoid a Math function, you can save some CPU time.

Whew. That's a lot of work, but remember that you are avoiding executing the last method possibly thousands of times. If all goes well, you should wind up with something like Figure 1-20.

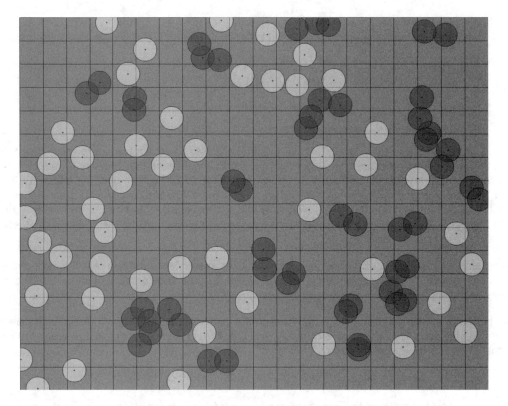

Figure 1-20. One hundred objects, successfully hit-tested

Verify that all the balls that are touching are red, and those that are not touching are white. If that's not the case, there's an error somewhere. Find it and fix it before moving on. The most important part of a collision-detection routine is, of course, accurately detecting collisions.

Testing and tuning the grid

Each time you run this application, you should get a trace of how many collision checks were done. On my computer, with a screen resolution of 1440×900 and running the SWF in a maximized browser, I get anywhere from 80 to 130 hit tests occurring for the exact code described previously: 100 balls of radius 25 and a grid size of 50. A smaller stage size will generate more hit tests. Run it a few times to see what range of numbers you get. Because the only thing changing in consecutive runs is the random distribution of the balls, you will get an idea of the average you are getting.

Now try increasing the size of the grid by setting it to 100, for example. You'll notice that you will get a significantly higher number of hit tests because there are more balls in each cell. This sounds bad, but it also decreases the number of cells and the number of arrays you have to loop through, which can be a benefit, as you'll soon see.

Now try reducing the grid size to 40—or even 30. There are fewer hit tests, but look closely at the results. You'll probably see an occasional missed hit—two objects touching that have not been marked as hitting (that is, they are still white). This is not good, but it should serve to remind you of the importance of the grid size being at least as large as the largest object. You could take this a step further and dynamically set the size of the grid based on the largest object in the simulation.

Set the grid size back to 50 and change the line that creates each ball in makeBalls to this:

```
var ball:Ball = new Ball(Math.random() * RADIUS);
```

This change shouldn't have any effect on the number of checks; it works fine. It just points out that the system still works when the objects are of different sizes—keeping in mind the rule about grid size, of course.

Now let's do some serious tuning and see how we're actually doing in terms of performance, particularly in comparison with the "test each object against every other object" method.

To do this, we'll need another method to test against. Well call this method basicCheck(). Here it is:

```
private function basicCheck():void
{
    for(var i:int = 0; i < _balls.length - 1; i++)
    {
        var ballA:Ball = _balls[i] as Ball;
        for(var j:int = i + 1; j < _balls.length; j++)
        {
            var ballB:Ball = _balls[j] as Ball;
            checkCollision(ballA, ballB);
        }
    }
}
```

This is the code that will generate 4,950 hit tests for 100 objects. We know we are beating that in terms of raw number of checks, but there is a heck of a lot less overhead than all that grid stuff. How do the two methods stack up against each other? Are we really seeing any benefit?

Well, obviously we must be seeing some benefit or this chapter wouldn't be here, but instead of taking my word for it, I'll let you see for yourself. What we'll do is do run our grid-based code ten times and then run this method ten times, and see which takes less time to run. This will happen in the constructor, which I've changed to look like this:

```
public function GridCollision()
{
    stage.align = StageAlign.TOP_LEFT;
    stage.scaleMode = StageScaleMode.NO_SCALE;

    makeBalls();
    drawGrid();
```

```
var startTime:int;
var elapsed:int;
var i:int;

// get initial time
startTime = getTimer();
// do this 10 times
for(i = 0; i < 10; i++)
{
    makeGrid();
    assignBallsToGrid();
    checkGrid();
}
// subtract current time from start time
elapsed = getTimer() - startTime;
trace("Grid-based:", elapsed);

// do again for basic check
startTime = getTimer();
for(i = 0; i < 10; i++)
{
    basicCheck();
}
elapsed = getTimer() - startTime;
trace("Basic check", elapsed);
}
```

Here we create variables for the start time and elapsed time of each test. Set the start time to the result of getTimer() and run the following three methods ten times:

```
makeGrid();
assignBallsToGrid();
checkGrid();
```

Subtract the start time from the current time to see how long that took. Do it again with basicCheck() run ten times.

What kind of results does that give you? For my setup, I'm seeing that the grid-based method runs almost 2.5 times faster than the basic check. Not as dramatic as I would have expected, considering we're doing away with 4,800 hit tests, which shows that the grid method does have considerable overhead. But still, a 2.5 times increase in speed is a good thing, right?

Furthermore, the more objects you have, the better savings you're going to see. If I increase the _numBalls property to 1000, the grid-based method handles it in less than a second, whereas the basic check takes more than 13 seconds. (Of course, one frame per second is not an acceptable frame rate, but it's better than 13 seconds per frame!) On the other hand, if I reduce the number of balls down to 50, the basic check is actually faster. So there is a make/break point where the overhead starts to outweigh the savings in the hit testing you're getting, and it's better to switch over to a simple test. Where that point is depends on your application and needs to be tested for.

Set _numBalls back to 100 and run it a few times just to get an idea how long the grid-based method is taking. On my machine, I'm averaging about 55 milliseconds for the 10 runs. Now change the grid size from 50 to 75. My average goes down to about 37 milliseconds. I found that a grid size of between 85 to 100 averages about 32 milliseconds, which is more than 4 times faster than the basic check! Note that all these numbers are just examples to serve as a basic guide. You might get very different results. The important fact to take away is that by tweaking the grid size you can find a setting that gives you optimal results for your application. There are a lot of variables here: stage size, number of objects, size of objects, grid size, and the hit testing algorithm you are using (not to mention individual computer performance). I haven't come up with a magic formula that will give you the best parameters to use.

Making it a reusable class

Hopefully, going through the GridCollision class has helped you get a good grasp of the concepts behind grid-based collision detection and proven its worthiness. But there are quite a few problems with it. First of all, it's all wrapped up in the main document class, so it would require copying and pasting to use it in another application. It's also heavily coupled with the Ball class. If you wanted to use it with another class of object, you'd have to change all references to that class. Furthermore, the hit testing algorithm is coded into it as a distance-based collision detection. You might want to use a simple hitTestObject or even a bitmap-based hit test instead. So let's create a new class that handles all these issues and is about as optimized as I could make it. We'll call it CollisionGrid, which is among this book's downloads at www.friendsofed.com:

```
package
{
    import flash.display.DisplayObject;
    import flash.display.Graphics;
    import flash.events.EventDispatcher;

    public class CollisionGrid extends EventDispatcher
    {
        private var _checks:Vector.<DisplayObject>;
        private var _grid:Vector.<Vector.<DisplayObject>>;
        private var _gridSize:Number;
        private var _height:Number;
        private var _numCells:int;
        private var _numCols:int;
        private var _numRows:int;
        private var _width:Number;


        public function CollisionGrid(width:Number,
                                      height:Number,
                                      gridSize:Number)
        {
            _width = width;
            _height = height;
            _gridSize = gridSize;
            _numCols = Math.ceil(_width / _gridSize);
```

```
        _numRows = Math.ceil(_height / _gridSize);
        _numCells = _numCols * _numRows;
}

public function drawGrid(graphics:Graphics):void
{
    // make lines to represent grid
    graphics.lineStyle(0, .5);
    for(var i:int = 0; i <= _width; i += _gridSize)
    {
        graphics.moveTo(i, 0);
        graphics.lineTo(i, _height);
    }
    for(i = 0; i <= _height; i += _gridSize)
    {
        graphics.moveTo(0, i);
        graphics.lineTo(_width, i);
    }
}

public function check(objects:Vector.<DisplayObject>):void
{
    var numObjects:int = objects.length;
    _grid = new Vector.<Vector.<DisplayObject>>(_numCells);
    _checks = new Vector.<Vector.<DisplayObject>>();
    // loop through all objects
    for(var i:int = 0; i < numObjects; i++)
    {
        var obj:DisplayObject = objects[i];
        // use a single index to represent positon in
        // one dimensional grid
        var index:int = Math.floor(obj.y / _gridSize) *
                    _numCols + Math.floor(obj.x / _gridSize);
        // only create cell here if an object is assigned to i
        if(_grid[index] == null)
        {
            _grid[index] = new Vector.<DisplayObject>;
        }
        // put the object in the cell
        _grid[index].push(obj);
    }

    checkGrid();
}

private function checkGrid():void
{
    // loop through each cell of grid
    for(var i:int = 0; i < _numCols; i++)
```

```
    {
        for(var j:int = 0; j < _numRows; j++)
        {
            // all the objects in the first cell
            // against each other
            checkOneCell(i, j);
            checkTwoCells(i, j, i + 1, j);     // right
            checkTwoCells(i, j, i - 1, j + 1); // lower left
            checkTwoCells(i, j, i,     j + 1); // lower
            checkTwoCells(i, j, i + 1, j + 1); // lower right
        }
    }
}

private function checkOneCell(x:int, y:int):void
{
    // get cell represented by x, y
    var cell:Vector.<DisplayObject> = _grid[y * _numCols + x];
    if(cell == null) return;

    // how many objects in cell
    var cellLength:int = cell.length;

    // compare all objects to each other
    for(var i:int = 0; i < cellLength - 1; i++)
    {
        var objA:DisplayObject = cell[i];
        for(var j:int = i + 1; j < cellLength; j++)
        {
            var objB:DisplayObject = cell[j];
            _checks.push(objA, objB);
        }
    }
}

private function checkTwoCells(x1:int, y1:int,
                               x2:int, y2:int):void
{
    // make sure cell exists in grid
    if(x2 >= _numCols || x2 < 0 || y2 >= _numRows) return;
    // get each cell, make sure there are objects in each
    var cellA:Vector.<DisplayObject> =
                _grid[y1 * _numCols + x1];
    var cellB:Vector.<DisplayObject> =
                _grid[y2 * _numCols + x2];
    if(cellA == null || cellB == null) return;
```

```
            var cellALength:int = cellA.length;
            var cellBLength:int = cellB.length;

            // compare all objs in one cell to all in the other
            for(var i:int = 0; i < cellALength; i++)
            {
                var objA:DisplayObject = cellA[i];
                for(var j:int = 0; j < cellBLength; j++)
                {
                    var objB:DisplayObject = cellB[j];
                    _checks.push(objA, objB);
                }
            }
        }

        public function get checks():Array
        {
            return _checks;
        }
    }
}
```

Most of this code should be familiar from the previous example. A lot has been done to make it as optimized as possible, especially the use of vectors. Vectors are new to Flash 10, and are essentially typed arrays. Because the compiler knows that every element in the vector is going to be the same type, it can create much more efficient byte code that executes faster at run time. Switching from arrays to vectors nearly doubles the performance of this application!

The drawGrid() method is no different from what you saw earlier. It draws a grid!

The check() method is the main public method you will interact with in this class. You pass it a vector of DisplayObjects. I chose DisplayObject because objects used for collision detection are usually sprites, movie clips, shapes, or bitmaps, which are all defined by classes that inherit from DisplayObject. DisplayObjects also all have x and y properties, which we need to determine their position and hence their location in the grid. If you are using a custom class that does not inherit from DisplayObject, be sure to change the type in the class.

The check() method creates a vector called _grid, and another called _checks. You are familiar with _grid, but it is implemented a bit differently here—as a one-dimensional vector with some tricky indexing instead of a two-dimensional array. This is done because it is quicker and uses fewer resources to loop through a single array than to loop through two. We'll go through it in more detail very shortly. The _checks vector will be used to hold a list of objects that need to be hit tested. Note that the CollisionGrid class does not do the hit testing itself. It makes the grid, assigns the objects to it, and generates a list of objects that could potentially be colliding. It's up to you, the user of the class, to go through this array and do the actual collision detection.

Next, it loops through the vector of DisplayObjects passed to it and assigns each one to the grid. This bit of code might need some explanation:

```
for(var i:int = 0; i < numObjects; i++)
{
    var obj:DisplayObject = objects[i];
    // use a single index to represent positon in
    // one dimensional grid
    var index:int = Math.floor(obj.y / _gridSize) * _numCols +
                    Math.floor(obj.x / _gridSize);
    // only create cell here if an object is assigned to i
    if(_grid[index] == null)
    {
        _grid[index] = new Vector.<DisplayObject>;
    }
    // put the object in the cell
    _grid[index].push(obj);
}
```

Again, we are using a one-dimensional vector instead of a two-dimensional array. The index variable figures out what element of that vector corresponds to a specific row and column. The basic formula is the following, where x and y are the integer column and row indexes:

    index = y * numColumns + x

Figure 1-21 should help to explain.

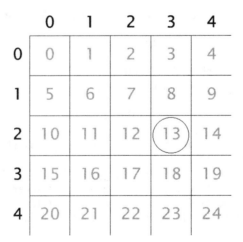

Figure 1-21. Using a single flat array as a grid

There are five columns and five rows. The object is in column 3 and row 2, so x = 3, and y = 2. Thus the index is 2 * 5 + 3, or 13, and that's exactly where you see it in the grid.

In the code, we are getting the column and row index the same way we were before:

    Math.floor(obj.x / _gridSize)

and

```
Math.floor(obj.y / _gridSize)
```

The only difference is that we are doing the whole thing in one line:

```
index = Math.floor(obj.y / _gridSize) * _numCols +
        Math.floor(obj.x / _gridSize);
```

The next statement is another optimization trick. Instead of looping through and creating a vector for each grid cell, many of which will never be used, we just check whether or not a vector exists there. If not, we create it. This is a form of lazy instantiation. In this case "lazy" isn't a derogatory term; it just refers to the decision to hold off creating something until you actually need it. There are cases when it makes sense and other times when it doesn't. Here, it seems to be a good idea:

```
if(_grid[index] == null)
{
    _grid[index] = new Vector.<DisplayObject>;
}
```

When we get to the final line of this loop, we know that the vector exists and we push the object onto it:

```
_grid[index].push(obj);
```

The final line of the check() method calls checkGrid(), which I'll repeat here:

```
private function checkGrid():void
{
    // loop through each cell of grid
    for(var i:int = 0; i < _numCols; i++)
    {
        for(var j:int = 0; j < _numRows; j++)
        {
            // all the objects in the first cell against each other
            checkOneCell(i, j);
            checkTwoCells(i, j, i + 1, j);       // right
            checkTwoCells(i, j, i - 1, j + 1); // lower left
            checkTwoCells(i, j, i,     j + 1); // lower
            checkTwoCells(i, j, i + 1, j + 1); // lower right
        }
    }
}
```

This doesn't do anything different from the earlier example.

The checkOneCell() and checkTwoCells90() methods work essentially the same as well. Of course, they use one-dimensional vectors instead of two-dimensional arrays, and because vectors are created only for a cell when actually needed, they first check to see whether the cell is null. Also notice that instead of doing collision detection, they simply push the two objects they are checking onto the _checks vector.

At the end of it all, _checks will contain a list of objects that need to be checked against each other. This is a simple list in which each 2 consecutive elements need to be checked (that is, check element 0 with element 1, element 2 with 3, 4 with 5, and so on). Finally, we provide a public getter called checks to access this list.

Using the class

Okay, we have this lovely class, so let's see it in action. Here, I've altered the main class, naming it GridCollision2. Like everything else, it's downloadable from www.friendsofed.com.

```
package {
    import flash.display.Sprite;
    import flash.display.StageAlign;
    import flash.display.StageScaleMode;
    import flash.utils.getTimer;
    import flash.display.DisplayObject;

    public class GridCollision2 extends Sprite
    {
        private const GRID_SIZE:Number = 80;
        private const RADIUS:Number = 25;

        private var _balls:Vector.<DisplayObject>;
        private var _grid:CollisionGrid;
        private var _numBalls:int = 100;

        public function GridCollision2()
        {
            stage.align = StageAlign.TOP_LEFT;
            stage.scaleMode = StageScaleMode.NO_SCALE;

            _grid = new CollisionGrid(stage.stageWidth,
                                      stage.stageHeight,
                                      GRID_SIZE);
            _grid.drawGrid(graphics);

            makeBalls();

            var startTime:int;
            var elapsed:int;

            // loop 10 times and measure elapsed time
            startTime = getTimer();
            for(var i:int = 0; i < 10; i++)
            {
                _grid.check(_balls);
                var numChecks:int = _grid.checks.length;
                for(var j:int = 0; j < numChecks; j += 2)
```

```
                        {
                            checkCollision(_grid.checks[j] as Ball,
                                           _grid.checks[j + 1] as Ball);
                        }
                    }
                    elapsed = getTimer() - startTime;
                    trace("Elapsed:", elapsed);
                }


                private function makeBalls():void
                {
                    // create balls, add to display list and _balls list
                    _balls = new Vector.<DisplayObject>(_numBalls);
                    for(var i:int = 0; i < _numBalls; i++)
                    {
                        var ball:Ball = new Ball(RADIUS);
                        ball.x = Math.random() * stage.stageWidth;
                        ball.y = Math.random() * stage.stageHeight;
                        ball.vx = Math.random() * 4 - 2;
                        ball.vy = Math.random() * 4 - 2;
                        addChild(ball);
                        _balls[i] = ball;
                    }
                }


                private function checkCollision(ballA:Ball, ballB:Ball):void
                {
                    // perform collision ctest between two individual balls
                    var dx:Number = ballB.x - ballA.x;
                    var dy:Number = ballB.y - ballA.y;
                    var dist:Number = Math.sqrt(dx * dx + dy * dy);
                    if(dist < ballA.radius + ballB.radius)
                    {
                        ballA.color = 0xff0000;
                        ballB.color = 0xff0000;
                    }
                }
            }
        }
    }
```

The main changes are in the constructor. Because making and drawing the grid are encapsulated in the CollisionGrid class and just take a single line of code each, I removed the separate methods for makeGrid() and drawGrid() and just do those things directly in the constructor.

The makeBalls() method is called next. It is nearly identical to the earlier example, except that it uses a vector instead of an array.

There's a single timer loop because I was interested only in testing this new class. You can certainly add another timer loop for the basic check to compare that as well, but you should already have an idea of how long that takes. In that loop, we call `_grid.check(_balls)`. We've already looked at that in depth. When that is finished, we know that `_grids.checks` contains a vector of objects to compare. The next for loop shows how to use it:

```
for(var j:int = 0; j < numChecks; j += 2)
{
    checkCollision(_grid.checks[j] as Ball,
                    _grid.checks[j + 1] as Ball);
}
```

Here we loop through that vector, incrementing by 2 each time; then we get references to the next 2 items with the indexes j and j + 1. We cast these as Balls and send them to the checkCollision() method, which hasn't changed at all.

In my tests, this application runs almost twice as fast as the first example, owing mainly to the use of vectors and probably to the fact that we create vectors for cells only when we actually need them (lazy instantiation). We're ready for prime time with this, which means we can start to animate it.

Animating is really not much different from the single hit test; you just do it more often. Also, because we've presumably tuned the engine to the stage size and number of objects and have figured out our ideal grid size, we can get rid of the timing loop. But remember that when using this type of collision grid again in a new project or changing the parameters of this application, you'll want to do some timing tests again to get it tuned.

Our main class becomes this, which you can find on this book's download page:

```
package {
    import flash.display.Sprite;
    import flash.display.StageAlign;
    import flash.display.StageScaleMode;
    import flash.display.DisplayObject;
    import flash.events.Event;

    public class GridCollision3 extends Sprite
    {
        private const GRID_SIZE:Number = 80;
        private const RADIUS:Number = 25;

        private var _balls:Vector.<DisplayObject>;
        private var _grid:CollisionGrid;
        private var _numBalls:int = 100;

        public function GridCollision3()
        {
            stage.align = StageAlign.TOP_LEFT;
            stage.scaleMode = StageScaleMode.NO_SCALE;

            _grid = new CollisionGrid(stage.stageWidth,
                                        stage.stageHeight,
                                        GRID_SIZE);
```

```
        _grid.drawGrid(graphics);

        makeBalls();
        addEventListener(Event.ENTER_FRAME, onEnterFrame);
    }

    function onEnterFrame(event:Event):void
    {
        // add velocity to position of each ball
        updateBalls();
        // determine which balls need to be checked
        _grid.check(_balls);
        var numChecks:int = _grid.checks.length;
        for(var j:int = 0; j < numChecks; j += 2)
        {
            // check each pair
            checkCollision(_grid.checks[j] as Ball,
                           _grid.checks[j + 1] as Ball);
        }
    }

    private function makeBalls():void
    {
        // create all the balls
        _balls = new Vector.<DisplayObject>(_numBalls);
        for(var i:int = 0; i < _numBalls; i++)
        {
            var ball:Ball = new Ball(RADIUS);
            ball.x = Math.random() * stage.stageWidth;
            ball.y = Math.random() * stage.stageHeight;
            ball.vx = Math.random() * 4 - 2;
            ball.vy = Math.random() * 4 - 2;
            addChild(ball);
            _balls[i] = ball;
        }
    }

    private function updateBalls():void
    {
        for(var i:int = 0; i < _numBalls; i++)
        {
            // move each ball, bounce off walls
            var ball:Ball = _balls[i] as Ball;
            ball.update();
            if(ball.x < RADIUS)
            {
                ball.x = RADIUS;
                ball.vx *= -1;
            }
```

```
            else if(ball.x > stage.stageWidth - RADIUS)
            {
                ball.x = stage.stageWidth - RADIUS;
                ball.vx *= -1;
            }
            if(ball.y < RADIUS)
            {
                ball.y = RADIUS;
                ball.vy *= -1;
            }
            else if(ball.y > stage.stageHeight - RADIUS)
            {
                ball.y = stage.stageHeight - RADIUS;
                ball.vy *= -1;
            }
            ball.color = 0xffffff;
        }
    }

    private function checkCollision(ballA:Ball, ballB:Ball):void
    {
        // perform check between two individual balls
        var dx:Number = ballB.x - ballA.x;
        var dy:Number = ballB.y - ballA.y;
        var dist:Number = Math.sqrt(dx * dx + dy * dy);
        if(dist < ballA.radius + ballB.radius)
        {
            ballA.color = 0xff0000;
            ballB.color = 0xff0000;
        }
    }
  }
}
```

The main changes are the addition of the onEnterFrame() method and updateBalls() method. The constructor now just creates the grid and balls and sets up the ENTER_FRAME listener. The onEnterFrame() method updates each ball's position via the updateBalls() method and then does the grid-based collision detection exactly as before. The updateBalls() method just moves things around, wrapping them around the screen and changes the color of each ball back to white at the beginning of each frame. Only if they collide in the checkCollision() method are they reset to red.

Of course, you can use a different type of collision reaction here now to get something that looks like the balls actually bouncing off of each other. This is covered extensively in the "Conservation of Momentum" chapter of *Making Things Move*.

This method of collision detection should increase the number of things you can have moving around the stage at one time and reacting with each other by several times. Just remember the tuning tips and test, test, test to make sure that you are getting the best performance *and* accurate detection.

Collision detection: Not just for collisions

When you think of the term **collision detection**, it's natural to think only about two objects hitting each other. But particularly when you are using a distance-based method, it's sometimes better to think about it terms of the spatial relationship between two objects. Maybe you are not only interested in collisions, per se, but also in whether two objects are within a certain distance of each other. Perhaps in a game, the enemy has to be within so many pixels of a "good guy" in order to see him, for example.

For this, we can still use a grid-based collision detection setup, but instead of the size of the objects determining the grid size, it's the critical distance between two objects that would be important instead. In *Making Things Move*, I showed an example of particles interacting that was inspired by Jared Tarbell's Node Garden (at www.levitated.net). I realized that this would be a perfect example to convert to a grid-based setup, so I did just that. First let's take a look at the original code:

```
package {
    import flash.display.Sprite;
    import flash.display.StageScaleMode;
    import flash.display.StageAlign;
    import flash.events.Event;
    import flash.geom.Point;

    [SWF(backgroundColor=0x000000)]
    public class NodeGardenLines extends Sprite
    {
        private var particles:Array;
        private var numParticles:uint = 30;
        private var minDist:Number = 100;
        private var springAmount:Number = .001;

        public function NodeGardenLines()
        {
            init();
        }

        private function init():void
        {
            stage.scaleMode = StageScaleMode.NO_SCALE;
            stage.align = StageAlign.TOP_LEFT;
            particles = new Array();
            for(var i:uint = 0; i < numParticles; i++)
            {
                // create all the particles
                var particle:Ball = new Ball(3, 0xffffff);
                particle.x = Math.random() * stage.stageWidth;
                particle.y = Math.random() * stage.stageHeight;
```

```
            particle.vx = Math.random() * 6 - 3;
            particle.vy = Math.random() * 6 - 3;
            addChild(particle);
            particles.push(particle);
        }

        addEventListener(Event.ENTER_FRAME, onEnterFrame);
    }

    private function onEnterFrame(event:Event):void
    {
        graphics.clear();
        for(var i:uint = 0; i < numParticles; i++)
        {
            // update each particle wrap around screen
            var particle:Ball = particles[i];
            particle.x += particle.vx;
            particle.y += particle.vy;
            if(particle.x > stage.stageWidth)
            {
                particle.x = 0;
            }
            else if(particle.x < 0)
            {
                particle.x = stage.stageWidth;
            }
            if(particle.y > stage.stageHeight)
            {
                particle.y = 0;
            }
            else if(particle.y < 0)
            {
                particle.y = stage.stageHeight;
            }
        }

        for(i=0; i < numParticles - 1; i++)
        {
            var partA:Ball = particles[i];
            for(var j:uint = i + 1; j < numParticles; j++)
            {
                // spring each particle to each other particle
                var partB:Ball = particles[j];
                spring(partA, partB);
            }
        }
    }
```

```
        private function spring(partA:Ball, partB:Ball):void
        {
            var dx:Number = partB.x - partA.x;
            var dy:Number = partB.y - partA.y;
            var dist:Number = Math.sqrt(dx * dx + dy * dy);
            if(dist < minDist)
            {
                // if particles are close enough, draw a line
                // and spring them toward each other
                graphics.lineStyle(1, 0xffffff, 1 - dist / minDist);
                graphics.moveTo(partA.x, partA.y);
                graphics.lineTo(partB.x, partB.y);
                // acceleration is proportional to distance
                var ax:Number = dx * springAmount;
                var ay:Number = dy * springAmount;
                // add accel to each particle, in opposite directions
                partA.vx += ax;
                partA.vy += ay;
                partB.vx -= ax;
                partB.vy -= ay;
            }
        }
    }
}
```

I won't go into explaining this code in depth. It basically creates a number of particles and moves them around. If two particles are less than a specific distance from each other, they will spring toward each other, and a line will be drawn between them. The closer the particles, the stronger the force between them, and the brighter the line. Notice also that the stage color has been set to black with SWF metadata at the top of the class:

```
[SWF(backgroundColor=0x000000)]
```

This metadata will work in Flex Builder or Flash CS4, but Flash CS3 will ignore it, requiring you to set the background color in the Properties Inspector instead. But because we'll soon be using Flash 10–specific features (vectors), I'll assume that you are using Flash CS4.

This file also uses a class called Ball, which is slightly different from the Ball class we've used so far in this chapter. The one we've been using will look slightly different, but will work just fine.

This example uses 30 particles, with a distance of 100 pixels or less for particles to react to each other. As is, this works just fine and doesn't need any improvement. But let's push it beyond its comfort zone by changing a couple of parameters:

```
private var numParticles:uint = 500;
private var minDist:Number = 50;
```

We'll increase the number of particles to 500, and the distance will go down to 50. If you are using the Flash authoring environment, you'll probably want to make the stage size a bit larger to handle all the particles without crowding them—say 1000×800. When you run the file now, you'll see that it is struggling significantly, achieving maybe a few frames per second.

Now let's see how implementing grid-based collision detection can help. The loop that does the checking between all the particles is in bold. That's the part we need to replace with the grid. We'll also probably see some improvement simply by changing the arrays into vectors. If you are curious, first try changing each instance of Array to Vector.<DisplayObject> and see how much that improves things. You'll also need to import the flash.display.DisplayObject class and cast the objects to the Ball class when you access them, like so:

```
var particle:Ball = particles[i] as Ball;
```

In my tests, although there seemed to be some improvement, it was slight. A double loop with 500 elements results in 124,750 checks on every frame. It's vital to get that number down because only a small percent of them are potential collisions. Implementing grid-based collision detection will bring that down to fewer than 10,000 checks. Here's the code in a new class called NodeGardenGrid (the lines in bold are the only ones that have changed from the original):

```
package {
    import flash.display.DisplayObject;
    import flash.display.Sprite;
    import flash.display.StageScaleMode;
    import flash.display.StageAlign;
    import flash.events.Event;
    import flash.geom.Point;

    [SWF(backgroundColor=0x000000)]
    public class NodeGardenGrid extends Sprite
    {
        private var particles:Vector.<DisplayObject>;
        private var numParticles:uint = 500;
        private var minDist:Number = 50;
        private var springAmount:Number = .001;
        private var grid:CollisionGrid;

        public function NodeGardenGrid()
        {
            init();
        }

        private function init():void
        {
            stage.scaleMode = StageScaleMode.NO_SCALE;
            stage.align = StageAlign.TOP_LEFT;

            grid = new CollisionGrid(stage.stageWidth,
                                     stage.stageHeight, 50);
            particles = new Vector.<DisplayObject>();
            for(var i:uint = 0; i < numParticles; i++)
            {
                // create all particles
                var particle:Ball = new Ball(3, 0xffffff);
                particle.x = Math.random() * stage.stageWidth;
```

```
            particle.y = Math.random() * stage.stageHeight;
            particle.vx = Math.random() * 6 - 3;
            particle.vy = Math.random() * 6 - 3;
            addChild(particle);
            particles.push(particle);
        }

        addEventListener(Event.ENTER_FRAME, onEnterFrame);
    }

    private function onEnterFrame(event:Event):void
    {
        graphics.clear();
        for(var i:uint = 0; i < numParticles; i++)
        {
            // update particles, wrap around stage
            var particle:Ball = particles[i] as Ball;
            particle.x += particle.vx;
            particle.y += particle.vy;
            if(particle.x > stage.stageWidth)
            {
                particle.x = 0;
            }
            else if(particle.x < 0)
            {
                particle.x = stage.stageWidth;
            }
            if(particle.y > stage.stageHeight)
            {
                particle.y = 0;
            }
            else if(particle.y < 0)
            {
                particle.y = stage.stageHeight;
            }
        }
        // determine which particles need to be checked
        grid.check(particles);
        var checks:Vector.<DisplayObject> = grid.checks;
        trace(checks.length);
        var numChecks:int = checks.length;
        for(i=0; i < numChecks; i += 2)
        {
            // spring each pair toward each other
            var partA:Ball = checks[i] as Ball;
            var partB:Ball = checks[i + 1] as Ball;
            spring(partA, partB);
        }
    }
```

```
private function spring(partA:Ball, partB:Ball):void
{
    var dx:Number = partB.x - partA.x;
    var dy:Number = partB.y - partA.y;
    var dist:Number = Math.sqrt(dx * dx + dy * dy);
    if(dist < minDist)
    {
        graphics.lineStyle(1, 0xffffff, 1 - dist / minDist);
        graphics.moveTo(partA.x, partA.y);
        graphics.lineTo(partB.x, partB.y);
        var ax:Number = dx * springAmount;
        var ay:Number = dy * springAmount;
        partA.vx += ax;
        partA.vy += ay;
        partB.vx -= ax;
        partB.vy -= ay;
    }
}
```

Ensure that your movie is set to publish to the Flash 10 format and that the CollisionGrid.as file is in your class path. In my tests, this resulted in about 6,500 checks per frame. Note that the grid is created with a grid size of 50, which is the same value as minDist. This particular code does not rely on the radii of the particles, only the distance between them. Remember that you'd probably want to do some actual timing tests and adjust the grid size for best performance, however. A larger grid size will give you more checks to do, but will result in less looping through arrays. Somewhere you'll hit a sweet spot of best performance. But even at the minimal value of 50, the performance is appreciably better.

Summary

So that covers our discussion of advanced collision detection. There are many ways these two techniques (bitmap- and grid-based collision checking) can be used, and the examples here were just a few ideas to get you started. Again, the most important thing to take away from this, particularly in the grid-based system, is to test, test, test; measure performance; and tune the collision engine for the best results. And remember that it excels in high numbers of objects, but the overhead outweighs any benefits for a smaller number of objects.

Next up is a very different subject, steering behaviors. We'll also get into a bit of artificial intelligence.

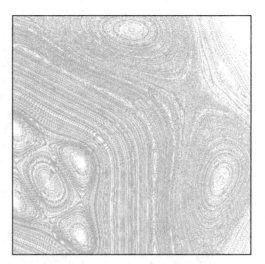

Chapter 2

STEERING BEHAVIORS

The term **steering behaviors** refers to a set of algorithms that allows objects to move around in a seemingly intelligent manner. These behaviors, which fall under the headings of **artificial intelligence** and **artificial life**, enable characters to seemingly take on a life of their own—deciding where, when, and how to move in order to achieve goals, chase or run from other characters, avoid obstacles, follow paths, and so on.

The term was coined by Craig Reynolds in a paper titled "Steering Behaviors for Autonomous Characters," published in 1999 for the Game Developers' Conference. It describes a number of algorithms that create a system of forces that are applied to characters used in games and simulations. These forces are used to affect the characters' movements to carry out various things the characters need or want to do. They also encompass various group dynamics such as flocking. In fact, Reynolds was already known for his "boids" simulation of flocking birds (see Figure 2-1).

Figure 2-1. Craig Reynolds' "boids"

As of this writing, you can find Reynolds' paper at www.red3d.com/cwr/steer/, but a quick search for the title will also give you multiple download locations. In the paper itself, Reynolds doesn't go into the implementations of the algorithms in much depth, although the page just mentioned does link to an open source, C++ version of the behaviors: OpenSteer (http://opensteer.sourceforge.net/). Nevertheless, the system he describes in that paper has been at the foundation of many, if not most, artificial intelligence movement engines created after that point. This chapter will follow in those footsteps, creating an ActionScript 3.0–based version of most of the behaviors described in the paper.

Before we dive in, let me say that the goal of this chapter is to introduce the behaviors, give an understanding of them, and show a framework with some basic implementations of each. Some of the later more-involved behaviors can be implemented in many different ways, with vastly different degrees of complexity. There isn't necessarily a "standard" or "correct" way of doing all the behaviors, and the implementations I give are very much on the simple end of the spectrum. In other words, consider this an introduction and launching-off point. For use in a production-level application, the code presented here will need quite a bit of refinement as well as tailoring to your specific needs.

Behaviors

First, let's get a broad overview of the basic behaviors—what each one does and what it's used for:

- *seek*: The character attempts to move to a specific point. This can be a fixed point or a moving target, such as another character.

- *flee*: The exact opposite of seek. The character attempts to move as far away as possible from the given point. Again, the point can be either fixed or moving.

- *arrive*: Identical to seek except that the character's speed will slow down once it gets close enough to the point, performing an easing motion to eventually stop right at the target point.

- *pursue*: An improvement on seek because the target's velocity is taken into account. Instead of seeking the point where the target is now, the character predicts where it is going and then moves to that point. Obviously, this applies only to a moving target because a fixed point has no velocity.

- *evade*: The opposite of pursue. The character predicts where the point will be based on its velocity and tries to get as far away from that point as possible.

- *wander*: A random but smooth and realistic motion.

- *object avoidance*: The character can perceive objects in its path and steers to avoid them.

- *path following*: The character does its best to stay on a given path, but does so in a way that continues to be realistic in terms of physics and any other behaviors being applied.

In addition to these behaviors, the complex compound behavior known as **flocking** simulates group behavior of similar characters and is generally created by applying three other simple behaviors:

- *separation*: Each character in the flock tries to maintain an acceptable distance from its neighbors.

- *cohesion*: Each character attempts to not stray too far from its flockmates.

- *alignment*: Each character tries to steer in the same direction as its neighbors.

Although these three behaviors are relatively simple, when combined they can produce some amazing group dynamics that really make you feel that you are dealing with flocks of birds or groups of other creatures. Adjusting various parameters on each of the three sub-behaviors can alter the character of the group, resulting in a loose group that breaks up often, a tight-knit clump, a column following a single leader, and many other variations.

Before we can get to work on the behavior of moving objects, however, we need to first work out a method of moving them.

Vector2D Class

The steering behaviors as just described have been implemented numerous times in different languages (probably once or twice in ActionScript, too). The way they were originally described (and in most implementations you will find it so) is with vectors. (If you want to learn more about vectors, refer to Chapter 5 of *Foundation ActionScript 3.0 Animation: Making Things Move!*, in which I describe them in more detail.)

In brief, a **vector** describes something that has both direction and magnitude. For example, the velocity of a moving object consists of which way it is moving (direction) and its speed (magnitude). Thus, velocity is best expressed as a vector. Acceleration—any force that acts to change the velocity of an object—also consists of the magnitude of the force and its direction (another vector). Vectors are also good for expressing the relative positions between two objects where the magnitude is the distance between them and the direction is the angle from one to the other.

Furthermore, you can use a vector to describe a character's heading or the way it is facing. In this case, there is no magnitude involved, only direction, so you can set the magnitude to 1.0. Such a vector is called a **unit vector**, and the fact that it's only one unit long makes it capable of performing highly optimized vector math calculations.

All these vector properties are very useful for steering behaviors because they make extensive use of velocities, directional forces, distances between objects, and object headings. So a vector class in ActionScript 3.0 would be very useful for creating steering behaviors. And, being the nice guy I am, I went ahead and created one for you. Of course, I later found out that Flash CS4 ships with its own Vector3D class, so you might want to eventually migrate over to it. But I find that the extra dimension brings quite a bit more complexity, so I decided to stick with my own Vector2D class as a more lightweight alternative for this chapter. I won't explain it in depth, but it contains most of the useful methods you'll find in similar classes in other languages, specifically those used in creating steering behaviors. I'll present it here in its entirety because it will be good as a reference. As you use individual methods of the class, I'll explain them a bit more in detail. You can download the class as the Vector2D.as file from this book's download page at www.friendsofed.com.

```
package com.foed
{
    import flash.display.Graphics;

    /**
     * A basic 2-dimensional vector class.
     */
    public class Vector2D
    {
        private var _x:Number;
        private var _y:Number;

        /**
         * Constructor.
         */
        public function Vector2D(x:Number = 0, y:Number = 0)
        {
            _x = x;
            _y = y;
        }

        /**
         * Can be used to visualize the vector.
         * Generally used for debug purposes only.
         * @param graphics The Graphics instance to draw the vector on.
         * @param color The color of the line used to for the vector.
         */
```

```
public function draw(graphics:Graphics, color:uint = 0):void
{
    graphics.lineStyle(0, color);
    graphics.moveTo(0, 0);
    graphics.lineTo(_x, _y);
}

/**
 * Generates a copy of this vector.
 * @return Vector2D A copy of this vector.
 */
public function clone():Vector2D
{
    return new Vector2D(x, y);
}

/**
 * Sets this vector's x and y values, and thus length, to zero.
 * @return Vector2D A reference to this vector.
 */
public function zero():Vector2D
{
    _x = 0;
    _y = 0;
    return this;
}

/**
 * Whether or not this vector is equal to zero,
 * i.e. its x, y, and length are zero.
 * @return Boolean True if vector is zero, otherwise false.
 */
public function isZero():Boolean
{
    return _x == 0 && _y == 0;
}

/**
 * Sets / gets the length or magnitude of this vector.
 * Changing the length will change the x and y but not
 * the angle of this vector.
 */
public function set length(value:Number):void
{
    var a:Number = angle;
    _x = Math.cos(a) * value;
    _y = Math.sin(a) * value;
}
public function get length():Number
```

```
{
    return Math.sqrt(lengthSQ);
}

/**
 * Gets the length of this vector, squared.
 */
public function get lengthSQ():Number
{
    return _x * _x + _y * _y;
}

/**
 * Gets / sets the angle of this vector.
 * Changing the angle changes the x and y but retains the
 * same length.
 */
public function set angle(value:Number):void
{
    var len:Number = length;
    _x = Math.cos(value) * len;
    _y = Math.sin(value) * len;
}
public function get angle():Number
{
    return Math.atan2(_y, _x);
}

/**
 * Normalizes this vector. Equivalent to setting
 * the length to one, but more efficient.
 * @return Vector2D A reference to this vector.
 */
public function normalize():Vector2D
{
    if(length == 0)
    {
        _x = 1;
        return this;
    }
    var len:Number = length;
    _x /= len;
    _y /= len;
    return this;
}

/**
 * Ensures the length of the vector is no longer
 * than the given value.
 * @param max The maximum value this vector should be.
```

```
 * If length is larger than max, it will be truncated
 * to this value.
 * @return Vector2D A reference to this vector.
 */
public function truncate(max:Number):Vector2D
{
    length = Math.min(max, length);
    return this;
}

/**
 * Reverses the direction of this vector.
 * @return Vector2D A reference to this vector.
 */
public function reverse():Vector2D
{
    _x = -_x;
    _y = -_y;
    return this;
}

/**
 * Whether or not this vector is normalized,
 * i.e. its length is equal to one.
 * @return Boolean True if length is one, otherwise false.
 */
public function isNormalized():Boolean
{
    return length == 1.0;
}

/**
 * Calculates the dot product of this vector and
 * another given vector.
 * @param v2 Another Vector2D instance.
 * @return Number The dot product of this vector and
 * the one passed in as a parameter.
 */
public function dotProd(v2:Vector2D):Number
{
    return _x * v2.x + _y * v2.y;
}

/**
 * Calculates the angle between two vectors.
 * @param v1 The first Vector2D instance.
 * @param v2 The second Vector2D instance.
 * @return Number the angle between the two given vectors.
 */
public static function angleBetween(v1:Vector2D,
                                    v2:Vector2D):Number
```

```
{
    if(!v1.isNormalized()) v1 = v1.clone().normalize();
    if(!v2.isNormalized()) v2 = v2.clone().normalize();
    return Math.acos(v1.dotProd(v2));
}

/**
 * Determines if a given vector is to the right or left
 * of this vector.
 * @return int If to the left, returns -1. If to the right, +1.
 */
public function sign(v2:Vector2D):int
{
    return perp.dotProd(v2) < 0 ? -1 : 1;
}

/**
 * Finds a vector that is perpendicular to this vector.
 * @return Vector2D A vector perpendicular to this vector.
 */
public function get perp():Vector2D
{
    return new Vector2D(-y, x);
}

/**
 * Calculates the distance from this vector to another
 * given vector.
 * @param v2 A Vector2D instance.
 * @return Number The distance from this vector to the
 * vector passed as a parameter.
 */
public function dist(v2:Vector2D):Number
{
    return Math.sqrt(distSQ(v2));
}

/**
 * Calculates the distance squared from this vector to
 * another given vector.
 * @param v2 A Vector2D instance.
 * @return Number The distance squared from this vector
 * to the vector passed as a parameter.
 */
public function distSQ(v2:Vector2D):Number
{
    var dx:Number = v2.x - x;
    var dy:Number = v2.y - y;
    return dx * dx + dy * dy;
}
```

```
/**
 * Adds a vector to this vector, creating a new
 * Vector2D instance to hold the result.
 * @param v2 A Vector2D instance.
 * @return Vector2D A new vector containing the
 * results of the addition.
 */
public function add(v2:Vector2D):Vector2D
{
    return new Vector2D(_x + v2.x, _y + v2.y);
}


/**
 * Subtracts a vector from this vector, creating a
 * new Vector2D instance to hold the result.
 * @param v2 A Vector2D instance.
 * @return Vector2D A new vector containing the
 * results of the subtraction.
 */
public function subtract(v2:Vector2D):Vector2D
{
    return new Vector2D(_x - v2.x, _y - v2.y);
}


/**
 * Multiplies this vector by a value, creating a
 * new Vector2D instance to hold the result.
 * @param v2 A Vector2D instance.
 * @return Vector2D A new vector containing the
 * results of the multiplication.
 */
public function multiply(value:Number):Vector2D
{
    return new Vector2D(_x * value, _y * value);
}


/**
 * Divides this vector by a value, creating a new
 * Vector2D instance to hold the result.
 * @param v2 A Vector2D instance.
 * @return Vector2D A new vector containing the
 * results of the division.
 */
public function divide(value:Number):Vector2D
{
    return new Vector2D(_x / value, _y / value);
}
```

```
/**
 * Indicates whether this vector and another
 * Vector2D instance are equal in value.
 * @param v2 A Vector2D instance.
 * @return Boolean True if the other vector is
 * equal to this one, false if not.
 */
public function equals(v2:Vector2D):Boolean
{
    return _x == v2.x && _y == v2.y;
}

/**
 * Sets / gets the x value of this vector.
 */
public function set x(value:Number):void
{
    _x = value;
}
public function get x():Number
{
    return _x;
}

/**
 * Sets / gets the y value of this vector.
 */
public function set y(value:Number):void
{
    _y = value;
}
public function get y():Number
{
    return _y;
}

/**
 * Generates a string representation of this vector.
 * @return String A description of this vector.
 */
public function toString():String
{
    return "[Vector2D (x:" + _x + ", y:" + _y + ")]";
}
        }
    }
```

Languages such as C or C++ have a neat feature called **operator overloading**, which enables you to map a built-in operator of the language, such as + or -, to a method of a class. So instead of vectorC = vectorA.add(vectorB), you could write vectorC = vectorA + vectorB.

Although operator overloading makes your classes look much more like native types and become easier to work with, ActionScript does not yet support it, so we are stuck with using slightly more wordy implementations.

Closely related to the implementation issue, one of the challenges of architecting a class like this is to determine how certain class methods should work when called on an instance—in this case, methods such as truncate, normalize, reverse, add, subtract, multiply, and divide. There are two possibilities: a method such as add can directly alter the internal state of the object it is called on or it can return a new object that is a result of the vector add operation.

For example, suppose that you had vectorA as (3, 2), meaning that its x value is 3 and y value is 2, and vectorB as (4, 5). Then you ran the following code:

```
vectorA.add(vectorB);
```

According to the first school of thought, vectorB would remain unchanged, but vectorA would be altered to equal (7, 7).

The other possibility would look something like this:

```
vectorC = vectorA.add(vectorB);
```

Here, vectorA and vectorB would both maintain their original values (3, 2) and (4, 5), and a newly created vectorC would be equal to (7, 7).

So which of these is the correct way for the add method to work? I went back and forth on this a few times while creating the class and eventually realized that there are many cases in which you need to grab a vector from an object, such as its position or velocity, and do some mathematical manipulation on that value without changing the object itself. So add, subtract, multiply, and divide leave the original object untouched.

However, operations such as truncate, reverse, and normalize strongly imply that they are doing something to the object itself. So they do alter the internal values as well as return an instance of the object itself, which will be useful.

It's not too hard to do the opposite of these behaviors. If you want to add vectorB to vectorA, for example, and have vectorA get the result of the add operation, just do this:

```
vectorA = vectorA.add(vectorB);
```

And if you need to get the truncated, reversed, or normalized value of a vector without changing the original, use the clone method like so:

```
normalizedA = vectorA.clone().normalize();
```

This method creates a copy of vectorA and normalizes it, leaving the original vectorA untouched.

As Seb Lee-Delisle pointed out while doing the technical review of this book, creating copies of objects like this can result in a situation in which you might have many objects being created, used briefly, and then discarded. One of the side effects is that the garbage collector in the Flash Player has to track all these dead objects and remove them, which leads to performance issues. I opted to leave things the way they are for clarity's sake, but realize that this is an area for fine-tuning.

Now that we have a vector class to represent a character's position, velocity, and various forces, we'll need a base class to represent a character.

Vehicle Class

The Vehicle class is the base class for the steered characters, but it does not have any steering behaviors. It merely handles basic motion: position, velocity, mass, and what happens when the character hits the edge of the screen (it can either bounce off or reappear on the opposite edge of the screen). The SteeredVehicle class extends Vehicle, adding the steering behaviors themselves. Using this kind of architecture allows the Vehicle class to potentially be used for other types of objects that need to move around but do not require steering behaviors. It also allows The SteeredVehicle class to concentrate solely on the implementation of the steering functionality without worrying about the details of basic motion.

So far, we've been referring to **characters** as the things moving around and having behaviors. From here on out, I'll be using the terms **character** and **vehicle** somewhat interchangeably. If it helps, think of a character as the thing riding around in a vehicle, even if that "vehicle" is the character's own body. If that doesn't help, read the "Locomotion" section of the "Steering Behaviors for Autonomous Characters" article referenced at the beginning of the chapter, which explains it quite nicely.

So without further ado, here's the class, which you can download as the Vehicle.as file from the book's download site:

```
package com.foed
{
    import flash.display.Sprite;

    /**
     * Base class for moving characters.
     */
    public class Vehicle extends Sprite
    {
        protected var _edgeBehavior:String = WRAP;
        protected var _mass:Number = 1.0;
        protected var _maxSpeed:Number = 10;
        protected var _position:Vector2D;
        protected var _velocity:Vector2D;

        // potential edge behaviors
        public static const WRAP:String = "wrap";
        public static const BOUNCE:String = "bounce";
```

```
/**
 * Constructor.
 */
public function Vehicle()
{
    _position = new Vector2D();
    _velocity = new Vector2D();
    draw();
}

/**
 * Default graphics for vehicle. Can be overridden in subclass.
 */
protected function draw():void
{
    graphics.clear();
    graphics.lineStyle(0);
    graphics.moveTo(10, 0);
    graphics.lineTo(-10, 5);
    graphics.lineTo(-10, -5);
    graphics.lineTo(10, 0);
}

/**
 * Handles all basic motion.
 * Should be called on each frame / timer interval.
 */
public function update():void
{
    // make sure velocity stays within max speed.
    _velocity.truncate(_maxSpeed);

    // add velocity to position
    _position = _position.add(_velocity);

    // handle any edge behavior
    if(_edgeBehavior == WRAP)
    {
        wrap();
    }
    else if(_edgeBehavior == BOUNCE)
    {
        bounce();
    }

    // update position of sprite
    x = position.x;
    y = position.y;
```

```
        // rotate heading to match velocity
        // convert radians to degrees: degrees = radians * 180 / PI
        rotation = _velocity.angle * 180 / Math.PI;
    }

    /**
     * Causes character to bounce off edge if edge is hit.
     */
    private function bounce():void
    {
        if(stage != null)
        {
            if(position.x > stage.stageWidth)
            {
                position.x = stage.stageWidth;
                velocity.x *= -1;
            }
            else if(position.x < 0)
            {
                position.x = 0;
                velocity.x *= -1;
            }

            if(position.y > stage.stageHeight)
            {
                position.y = stage.stageHeight;
                velocity.y *= -1;
            }
            else if(position.y < 0)
            {
                position.y = 0;
                velocity.y *= -1;
            }
        }
    }

    /**
     * Causes character to wrap to opposite edge if edge is hit.
     */
    private function wrap():void
    {
        if(stage != null)
        {
            if(position.x > stage.stageWidth) position.x = 0;
            if(position.x < 0) position.x = stage.stageWidth;
            if(position.y > stage.stageHeight) position.y = 0;
            if(position.y < 0) position.y = stage.stageHeight;
        }
    }
```

```
/**
 * Sets / gets what will happen if character hits edge.
 */
public function set edgeBehavior(value:String):void
{
    _edgeBehavior = value;
}
public function get edgeBehavior():String
{
    return _edgeBehavior;
}

/**
 * Sets / gets mass of character.
 */
public function set mass(value:Number):void
{
    _mass = value;
}
public function get mass():Number
{
    return _mass;
}

/**
 * Sets / gets maximum speed of character.
 */
public function set maxSpeed(value:Number):void
{
    _maxSpeed = value;
}
public function get maxSpeed():Number
{
    return _maxSpeed;
}

/**
 * Sets / gets position of character as a Vector2D.
 */
public function set position(value:Vector2D):void
{
    _position = value;
    x = _position.x;
    y = _position.y;
}
public function get position():Vector2D
{
    return _position;
}
```

```
/**
 * Sets / gets velocity of character as a Vector2D.
 */
public function set velocity(value:Vector2D):void
{
    _velocity = value;
}
public function get velocity():Vector2D
{
    return _velocity;
}

/**
 * Sets x position of character.
 * Overrides Sprite.x to set internal Vector2D position.
 */
override public function set x(value:Number):void
{
    super.x = value;
    _position.x = x;
}

/**
 * Sets y position of character.
 * Overrides Sprite.y to set internal Vector2D position.
 */
override public function set y(value:Number):void
{
    super.y = value;
    _position.y = y;
}

    }
}
```

If you are familiar with some of the basic concepts in *Making Things Move*, there are not any really new concepts here, but things are handled differently. First, instead of representing position and velocity as x and y values—for example, x, y, vx, vy—it uses a single Vector2D for each: _position and _velocity.

Most of the work happens in the update method. First it truncates the velocity to ensure that it does not exceed _maxSpeed; then it adds the velocity to the position. In *Making Things Move*, we would have done something like the following:

```
x += _vx;
y += _vx;
```

We can do it in a single line with vectors:

```
_position = _position.add(_velocity);
```

Then the method checks the edges and calls either the wrap or the bounce method. Finally, it updates the screen position of the Sprite to match the x and y values of _position and then adjusts the rotation so the character is pointed in the direction it is moving:

```
x = position.x;
y = position.y;
rotation = _velocity.angle * 180 / Math.PI;
```

Most of the rest of the code consists of getters and setters for the various protected properties. I did include a default draw method that gets called when the class is instantiated. This can be overridden in subclasses to create proper graphics for your characters, but it allows something to be visible onscreen until the graphics are all set to go.

As a quick test of the Vehicle class, create a new document class named VehicleTest, available as the VehicleTest.as file from the book's download page:

```
package
{
    import com.foed.Vector2D;
    import com.foed.Vehicle;

    import flash.display.Sprite;
    import flash.display.StageAlign;
    import flash.display.StageScaleMode;
    import flash.events.Event;

    public class VehicleTest extends Sprite
    {
        private var _vehicle:Vehicle;

        public function VehicleTest()
        {
            stage.align = StageAlign.TOP_LEFT;
            stage.scaleMode = StageScaleMode.NO_SCALE;

            _vehicle = new Vehicle();
            addChild(_vehicle);

            _vehicle.position = new Vector2D(100, 100);

            _vehicle.velocity.length = 5;
            _vehicle.velocity.angle = Math.PI / 4;

            addEventListener(Event.ENTER_FRAME, onEnterFrame);
        }
```

```
        private function onEnterFrame(event:Event):void
        {
            _vehicle.update();
        }
    }
}
```

This creates a new Vehicle and adds it to the display list. It sets the position as a new Vector2D instance:

```
_vehicle.position = new Vector2D(100, 100);
```

Another way of doing the same thing is to set the x and y values of the position directly:

```
_vehicle.position.x = 100;
_vehicle.position.y = 100;
```

Or with the overridden setters for x and y, you could even just set the x and y of the vehicle itself directly, and the position vector would still get the values:

```
_vehicle.x = 100;
_vehicle.y = 100;
```

The class uses yet another tactic in setting the velocity: setting the length and angle of the velocity property, which demonstrates the flexibility available in using vectors:

```
_vehicle.velocity.length = 5;
_vehicle.velocity.angle = Math.PI / 4;
```

Here the length will be the speed, and the angle will be the direction. Don't forget that the angle is in radians, so Math.PI / 4 is equal to 45 degrees. Again, if you knew the x and y velocity at which you wanted the vehicle to move, you could assign a new Vector2D with those values or set the velocity's x and y properties directly, as was done with the position.

Finally, it sets a listener to the ENTER_FRAME event and calls update on the vehicle each frame. This will cause the vehicle to move in the assigned direction. When it hits the edge of the screen, it will wrap around to the opposite side. You can see how this looks in Figure 2-2.

Good enough for a test of the Vehicle class. Let's move on to bigger and better things—steering behaviors, which is what this chapter is all about.

Figure 2-2. A moving vehicle

SteeredVehicle Class

The SteeredVehicle class extends the Vehicle class and adds the steering behaviors to it. Each behavior will be defined in a public method that can be called on each frame or timer interval to apply that type of steering force. Usually all steering forces would be applied and then the vehicle's update method would be called.

For example, if we wanted to create a vehicle that simply wandered, we would call its wander method, followed by its update method on each frame:

```
private function onEnterFrame(event:Event):void
{
    _vehicle.wander();
    _vehicle.update();
}
```

Here's how steering methods work: whenever a steering method is called, it calculates a **steering force**, which is a force that will cause the vehicle to turn clockwise or counterclockwise. For example, the seek method would calculate a force that would be exactly enough to turn the vehicle from wherever it is currently facing to head directly at the point it is seeking. There could be more than one steering behavior active on any given vehicle—it might be seeking one point, but fleeing or evading another vehicle at the same time. So these forces add up. When the update method is finally called, the vehicle takes the sum total of all the steering behaviors applied to it and uses it to change its velocity (its direction and speed).

Here's the core of the SteeredVehicle without any behaviors coded yet (the file is SteeredVehicle. as, downloadable from this book's site):

```
package com.foed
{
    import flash.display.Sprite;

    public class SteeredVehicle extends Vehicle
    {
        private var _maxForce:Number = 1;
        private var _steeringForce:Vector2D;

        public function SteeredVehicle()
        {
            _steeringForce = new Vector2D();
            super();
        }

        public function set maxForce(value:Number):void
        {
            _maxForce = value;
        }
        public function get maxForce():Number
        {
            return _maxForce;
        }

        override public function update():void
        {
            _steeringForce.truncate(_maxForce);
            _steeringForce = _steeringForce.divide(_mass);
            _velocity = _velocity.add(_steeringForce);
            _steeringForce = new Vector2D();
            super.update();
        }
    }
}
```

You can see immediately that there's a _steeringForce property, which is a Vector2D. This property keeps track of the total steering force that is added to by each behavior (note that there is also a _maxForce property). You don't see vehicles or characters turning "on a dime" in real life, so we limit how much turning force can actually occur on a single frame. Public access to this value is given via the maxForce getter/setter pair. By adjusting maxForce, you can make a vehicle that makes sharp turns and moves quickly and accurately to where it's going, or one that makes large lazy loops.

Now let's jump to the update method. Imagine that there are some steering behavior methods and one or more of them has been called, so the _steeringForce property contains a meaningful vector. The method first truncates _steeringForce so it is no larger than the maximum possible steering force. It then divides _steeringForce by the vehicle's mass. Just as in real life, a heavy vehicle has more momentum and needs to turn in a wider arc, whereas a lighter vehicle can turn more quickly. Then the steering force is added to the vehicle's current velocity, and the _steeringForce variable is reset to a zero vector so it can be added up the next time around. Finally, the super class' update method is called, doing all the basic motion stuff that is already in the Vehicle class.

Now let's take a look at the implementation of behaviors, starting with seek. Each one will be a new public method of the SteeredVehicle class. Some of the behaviors will require new class properties or additional methods, and they will be shown as they become necessary.

Seek behavior

As described before, seek merely causes the vehicle to move to a specific spot. Here's how it looks:

```
public function seek(target:Vector2D):void
{
    var desiredVelocity:Vector2D = target.subtract(_position);
    desiredVelocity.normalize();
    desiredVelocity = desiredVelocity.multiply(_maxSpeed);
    var force:Vector2D = desiredVelocity.subtract(_velocity);
    _steeringForce = _steeringForce.add(force);
}
```

First, we calculate a desired velocity, which is the exact velocity that would put the vehicle at the target now. We get that velocity by subtracting the vehicle's position from the target position. This gives us a vector that says, "If you moved this far, in this direction, you'd be where you want to be." See Figure 2-3.

Of course, you can't always get what you want. But if you try sometime, you'll find you can come up with an algorithm that looks pretty good. Here, we'll normalize the desired velocity and multiply it by the maximum speed. This will give us a vector that still points at the target, but whose magnitude is equal to the fastest the vehicle can possibly travel, which is equivalent to saying, "You can't get there instantaneously, but go in this direction as fast as you can, and you'll get there as soon as you can."

This is still just a desired velocity, however; the vehicle already has an existing velocity. By subtracting it from the desired velocity, we now have a vector that says, "Add this vector to your current velocity, and you'll be doing the best you possibly can, heading in the right direction at maximum speed."

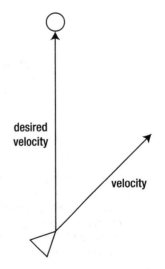

desired velocity

velocity

Figure 2-3. The desired velocity to reach the target right now

69

This vector is then added to the overall steering force. Remember that in the update method, _steeringForce is then truncated to _maxForce, however. So we still will not wind up going exactly where we want, but we'll be doing the best we possibly can within the constraints of _maxForce and _maxSpeed. Figure 2-4 shows this.

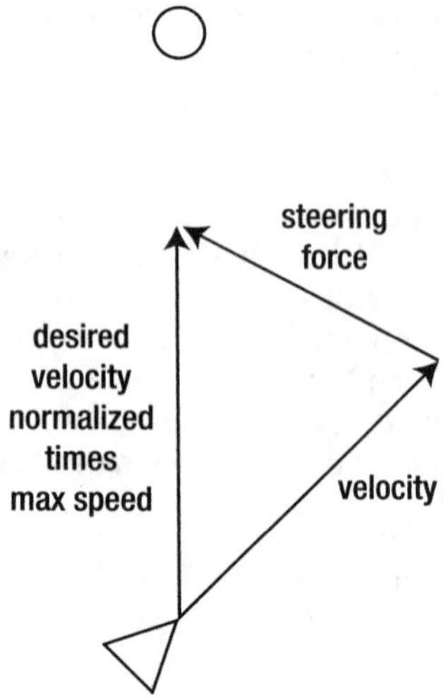

Now let's see an example of the seek behavior in action:

```
package
{
    import com.foed.SteeredVehicle;
    import com.foed.Vector2D;

    import flash.display.Sprite;
    import flash.display.StageAlign;
    import flash.display.StageScaleMode;
    import flash.events.Event;

    public class SeekTest extends Sprite
    {
        private var _vehicle:SteeredVehicle;

        public function SeekTest()
        {
            stage.align = StageAlign.TOP_LEFT;
            stage.scaleMode = StageScaleMode.NO_SCALE;

            _vehicle = new SteeredVehicle();
            addChild(_vehicle);

            addEventListener(Event.ENTER_FRAME, onEnterFrame);
        }

        private function onEnterFrame(event:Event):void
        {
            _vehicle.seek(new Vector2D(mouseX, mouseY));
            _vehicle.update();
        }
    }
}
```

Figure 2-4. Best possible desired velocity, and the force required to change current velocity to that

This is a pretty simple example. It merely creates a new steered vehicle, puts it on stage, and then on every frame the vehicle seeks the mouse and updates. Try changing the values for maxSpeed and maxForce on the vehicle, or even try changing its mass to get a good feel for how all those things change the steering behavior. You can also cause it to seek to a fixed point instead of the mouse. Or if you are feeling adventurous, create another Vehicle and have the steered vehicle seek it. It might look something like this in the onEnterFrame method:

```
_vehicle.seek(_targetVehicle.position);
```

You might even try having one steered vehicle seek the mouse and another steered vehicle seek the first one. When you've got a good feel for how that all works, we'll move on to the next behavior: flee.

Flee behavior

The flee behavior is the complete, total, and absolute opposite of seek. In fact, it is the exact same implementation in all but the last line, which subtracts the calculated force from _steeringForce instead of adding it:

```
public function flee(target:Vector2D):void
{
    var desiredVelocity:Vector2D = target.subtract(_position);
    desiredVelocity.normalize();
    desiredVelocity = desiredVelocity.multiply(_maxSpeed);
    var force:Vector2D = desiredVelocity.subtract(_velocity);
    _steeringForce = _steeringForce.subtract(force);
}
```

There's no need to cover this one in much detail because it's all exactly the same as seek. The last line says, "OK, you've figured out exactly what you need to do to hit that target. Now turn around and go the exact opposite way." Here's a simple test of flee (you can download the FleeTest.as file from the book's download site):

```
package
{
    import com.foed.SteeredVehicle;
    import com.foed.Vector2D;
    import com.foed.Vehicle;

    import flash.display.Sprite;
    import flash.display.StageAlign;
    import flash.display.StageScaleMode;
    import flash.events.Event;

    public class FleeTest extends Sprite
    {
        private var _vehicle:SteeredVehicle;

        public function FleeTest()
        {
            stage.align = StageAlign.TOP_LEFT;
            stage.scaleMode = StageScaleMode.NO_SCALE;

            _vehicle = new SteeredVehicle();
            _vehicle.position = new Vector2D(200, 200);
            _vehicle.edgeBehavior = Vehicle.BOUNCE;
            addChild(_vehicle);

            addEventListener(Event.ENTER_FRAME, onEnterFrame);
        }
```

```
                private function onEnterFrame(event:Event):void
                {
                    _vehicle.flee(new Vector2D(mouseX, mouseY));
                    _vehicle.update();
                }
            }
        }
```

The major differences here, apart from the obvious one of calling flee instead of seek, are that I positioned the vehicle out on the stage a bit and told it to bounce when it hits the edges. If you remove those two lines, you'll see why I added them. The vehicle will try to avoid the mouse by sticking itself in the corners, and you might not even see it.

Now that we have a couple of diametrically opposed behaviors, the obvious next thing to do is to create a couple of vehicles with each type of behavior and then see what they do with each other. The next example does just that, available as the SeekFleeTest1.as file from the download site:

```
    package
    {
        import com.foed.SteeredVehicle;
        import com.foed.Vector2D;
        import com.foed.Vehicle;

        import flash.display.Sprite;
        import flash.display.StageAlign;
        import flash.display.StageScaleMode;
        import flash.events.Event;

        public class SeekFleeTest1 extends Sprite
        {
            private var _seeker:SteeredVehicle;
            private var _fleer:SteeredVehicle;

            public function SeekFleeTest1()
            {
                stage.align = StageAlign.TOP_LEFT;
                stage.scaleMode = StageScaleMode.NO_SCALE;

                _seeker = new SteeredVehicle();
                _seeker.position = new Vector2D(200, 200);
                _seeker.edgeBehavior = Vehicle.BOUNCE;
                addChild(_seeker);

                _fleer = new SteeredVehicle();
                _fleer.position = new Vector2D(400, 300);
                _fleer.edgeBehavior = Vehicle.BOUNCE;
                addChild(_fleer);

                addEventListener(Event.ENTER_FRAME, onEnterFrame);
            }
```

```
            private function onEnterFrame(event:Event):void
            {
                _seeker.seek(_fleer.position);
                _fleer.flee(_seeker.position);
                _seeker.update();
                _fleer.update();
            }
        }
    }
```

Here we have a couple of vehicles: _seeker and _fleer. I'm sure I don't have to explain that the seeker seeks the fleer, and the fleer flees the seeker (try saying that ten times quickly!). Let this one run for awhile to see the two interacting on their own. Then try changing various parameters and see what happens.

Now that we have more than one behavior, we can apply multiple behaviors to a single vehicle. In the next example, vehicle A will seek vehicle B, B will seek C, and C will seek A. Each vehicle will also flee the one that is seeking it, and the three of them will chase each other around in circles. This example is found in the SeekFleeTest2.as file, and shown in Figure 2-5:

```
package
{
    import com.foed.SteeredVehicle;
    import com.foed.Vector2D;
    import com.foed.Vehicle;

    import flash.display.Sprite;
    import flash.display.StageAlign;
    import flash.display.StageScaleMode;
    import flash.events.Event;

    public class SeekFleeTest2 extends Sprite
    {
        private var _vehicleA:SteeredVehicle;
        private var _vehicleB:SteeredVehicle;
        private var _vehicleC:SteeredVehicle;

        public function SeekFleeTest2()
        {
            stage.align = StageAlign.TOP_LEFT;
            stage.scaleMode = StageScaleMode.NO_SCALE;

            _vehicleA = new SteeredVehicle();
            _vehicleA.position = new Vector2D(200, 200);
            _vehicleA.edgeBehavior = Vehicle.BOUNCE;
            addChild(_vehicleA);

            _vehicleB = new SteeredVehicle();
            _vehicleB.position = new Vector2D(400, 200);
            _vehicleB.edgeBehavior = Vehicle.BOUNCE;
            addChild(_vehicleB);
```

```
            _vehicleC = new SteeredVehicle();
            _vehicleC.position = new Vector2D(300, 260);
            _vehicleC.edgeBehavior = Vehicle.BOUNCE;
            addChild(_vehicleC);

            addEventListener(Event.ENTER_FRAME, onEnterFrame);
        }

        private function onEnterFrame(event:Event):void
        {
            _vehicleA.seek(_vehicleB.position);
            _vehicleA.flee(_vehicleC.position);

            _vehicleB.seek(_vehicleC.position);
            _vehicleB.flee(_vehicleA.position);

            _vehicleC.seek(_vehicleA.position);
            _vehicleC.flee(_vehicleB.position);

            _vehicleA.update();
            _vehicleB.update();
            _vehicleC.update();
        }
    }
}
```

Figure 2-5. A chases B, B chases C, and C chases A.

Again, play with the parameters, mix it up, and see what kind of situations you can create. When you are ready, we'll move on to the arrive behavior.

Arrive behavior

The arrive behavior is, in many respects, exactly the same as the seek behavior. In fact, they usually use the same algorithm and operate exactly the same way. The difference is that when a vehicle gets within a certain distance of its target in arrive mode, it switches into a kind of precision mode where it eases in to the target point, slowing down as it gets closer and closer.

To see why the arrive behavior is sometimes necessary, run the SeekTest class shown earlier. Move the mouse to a position away from the vehicle and let go and allow the vehicle to "catch" it. You'll see that the vehicle zooms right past the target; then it seems to realize its mistake, flips around, and heads back. This process continues indefinitely because the vehicle will always attempt to head toward its target at maximum speed, even if it's only a few pixels away.

The arrive behavior fixes this problem by slowing things down as the vehicle approaches the target:

```
public function arrive(target:Vector2D):void
{
    var desiredVelocity:Vector2D = target.subtract(_position);
    desiredVelocity.normalize();

    var dist:Number = _position.dist(target);
    if(dist > _arrivalThreshold)
    {
        desiredVelocity = desiredVelocity.multiply(_maxSpeed);
    }
    else
    {
        desiredVelocity = desiredVelocity.multiply(_maxSpeed * dist
                                            / _arrivalThreshold);
    }

    var force:Vector2D = desiredVelocity.subtract(_velocity);
    _steeringForce = _steeringForce.add(force);
}
```

The first couple of lines are the same as the seek behavior method. But before multiplying the desired velocity by maximum speed, we check the distance to the target. If the distance is greater than a certain threshold, we multiply as usual. After exiting the if statement, we continue the method exactly the same as the seek method.

However, if the distance is less than this threshold, we have to do something else altogether. Instead of multiplying by _maxSpeed, we multiply by _maxSpeed * dist / _arriveThreshold. If the distance is just a bit less than the threshold, dist / _arriveThreshold will be a number very close to 1.0, such as 0.99. Thus, desiredVelocity will be very close to (but somewhat less than) _maxSpeed. As the distance approaches zero, however, that ratio gets smaller and smaller, as does the resulting magnitude of desiredVelocity. So the resulting velocity also goes to zero (assuming that's the only behavior or force working on the vehicle). This is shown in Figure 2-6.

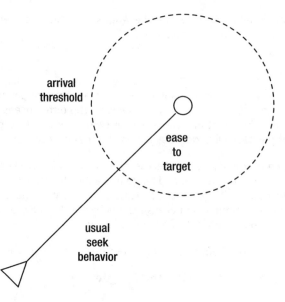

Figure 2-6. If within the arrival threshold, ease to target. Otherwise, just use seek.

Of course, the SteeredVehicle class now needs this new threshold property, so we'll add it to the top of the class:

```
package com.foed
{
    import flash.display.Sprite;

    public class SteeredVehicle extends Vehicle
    {
        private var _maxForce:Number = 1;
        private var _steeringForce:Vector2D;
        private var _arrivalThreshold:Number = 100;
        ...
    }
}
```

And we'll add a setter and getter for arrivalThreshold so you can tweak the value:

```
public function set arriveThreshold(value:Number):void
{
    _arrivalThreshold = value;
}
public function get arriveThreshold():Number
{
    return _arrivalThreshold;
}
```

You can see this in action in the following test class:

```
package
{
    import com.foed.SteeredVehicle;
    import com.foed.Vector2D;

    import flash.display.Sprite;
    import flash.display.StageAlign;
    import flash.display.StageScaleMode;
    import flash.events.Event;

    public class ArriveTest extends Sprite
    {
        private var _vehicle:SteeredVehicle;

        public function ArriveTest()
        {
            stage.align = StageAlign.TOP_LEFT;
            stage.scaleMode = StageScaleMode.NO_SCALE;

            _vehicle = new SteeredVehicle();
            addChild(_vehicle);

            addEventListener(Event.ENTER_FRAME, onEnterFrame);
        }

        private function onEnterFrame(event:Event):void
        {
            _vehicle.arrive(new Vector2D(mouseX, mouseY));
            _vehicle.update();
        }
    }
}
```

The only difference between this class and the SeekTest class is that one line in onEnterFrame where it calls arrive instead of seek. You'll see that if you move the mouse around, the vehicle behaves just as it would if it were seeking, but if you leave the mouse alone and let the vehicle approach it, it will ease in to a perfect stop right at the mouse cursor. Move the mouse again and it goes back to seek mode. By adjusting arriveThreshold on the vehicle, you can change how close it gets to the target before it switches into arrive mode.

Feel free to add some other vehicles and play around with this one if you want. Otherwise, we'll move on to pursue.

Pursue behavior

Once again, I get to say something along the lines of "this is very similar to the seek behavior." And it's true. In fact, pursue makes a call to seek as its last action. The essence of pursue is prediction of where the target will be in the future. This implies that the target is a moving object, so it has a position and velocity. Therefore, we can say that the target is a Vehicle. In fact, it might be another SteeredVehicle, but it is still a Vehicle by inheritance.

So, how do we predict where the target will be? We take its current velocity, extend it into the future, and then use that predicted point as the target for seek. But how far in the future do we calculate? Very good question! We'll call this the **look ahead time**. If you calculate too far into the future (high look ahead time) you'll overshoot the target. Not far enough into the future (low look ahead time) and you'll still be lagging behind. In fact, the seek behavior could be defined as pursue with a look ahead time of zero. (Where is it zero seconds in the future? Right where it is.)

One strategy is to base the look ahead time on the distance between the two vehicles. If you are far from your target, it will take you awhile to get there, so predict further into the future. If you are very close, you'll be there very soon, so the look ahead time should be much smaller. This is the technique that SteeredVehicle uses. Let's take a look:

```
public function pursue(target:Vehicle):void
{
    var lookAheadTime:Number = position.dist(target.position) /
                               _maxSpeed;
    var predictedTarget:Vector2D =
        target.position.add(target.velocity.multiply(lookAheadTime));
    seek(predictedTarget);
}
```

The first thing we do is calculate the look ahead time, based on the distance between the two divided by the maximum speed. This gives the number of frames or timer intervals it would take to reach the target if it were not moving. We can then predict the target's position that many frames in the future by taking its current position and adding its velocity times the look ahead time. Finally, we just seek to this new predicted target. See Figure 2-7.

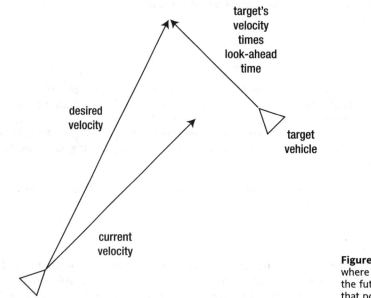

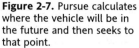

Figure 2-7. Pursue calculates where the vehicle will be in the future and then seeks to that point.

Again, this method will result only in a rough estimate because everything is in motion. But it's good enough to make it more accurate than just seeking. It's also pretty simple and fast. There are more accurate (and more complex) algorithms out there for pursue, and you are welcome to research and implement them as you wish. But this will at least get you started.

Now let's see it in action. We'll create three vehicles this time. One is a simple moving Vehicle that serves as the target. Each of the other two is a SteeredVehicle, one seeking the target's position and the other pursuing the target. If all goes well, the pursuer should win, thanks to its superior algorithm. You can download the PursueTest.as file from this book's site.

```
package
{
    import com.foed.SteeredVehicle;
    import com.foed.Vector2D;
    import com.foed.Vehicle;

    import flash.display.Sprite;
    import flash.display.StageAlign;
    import flash.display.StageScaleMode;
    import flash.events.Event;

    public class PursueTest extends Sprite
    {
        private var _seeker:SteeredVehicle;
        private var _pursuer:SteeredVehicle;
        private var _target:Vehicle;

        public function PursueTest()
        {
            stage.align = StageAlign.TOP_LEFT;
            stage.scaleMode = StageScaleMode.NO_SCALE;

            _seeker = new SteeredVehicle();
            _seeker.x = 400;
            addChild(_seeker);

            _pursuer = new SteeredVehicle();
            _pursuer.x = 400;
            addChild(_pursuer);

            _target = new Vehicle();
            _target.position = new Vector2D(200, 300);
            _target.velocity.length = 15;
            addChild(_target);

            addEventListener(Event.ENTER_FRAME, onEnterFrame);
        }
```

```
        private function onEnterFrame(event:Event):void
        {
            _seeker.seek(_target.position);
            _seeker.update();

            _pursuer.pursue(_target);
            _pursuer.update();

            _target.update();
        }
    }
}
```

Note that the two steered vehicles start out at the same position, but although the seeker moves to where the target is at any given moment, the pursuer immediately heads out in front of the target and intercepts it.

Definitely experiment with this one—there are a lot of potential parameters and values to mess around with. Next up is evade.

Evade behavior

As you might already have guessed, evade is the exact opposite of pursue. And as pursue was analogous to (and used) seek, evade is analogous to flee and will make use of it.

Essentially, evade predicts where the vehicle that it is trying to avoid will be in the future and goes directly away from that point. All the same principles discussed in the pursue section apply here. In fact, it's really the same method as pursue, but its last line calls flee instead of seek:

```
public function evade(target:Vehicle):void
{
    var lookAheadTime:Number = position.dist(target.position) /
                               _maxSpeed;
    var predictedTarget:Vector2D =
     target.position.subtract(target.velocity.multiply(lookAheadTime));
    flee(predictedTarget);
}
```

Not much more needs to be said about it. Here's a quick test of the pursue and evade methods, available as the PursueEvadeTest.as file:

```
package
{
    import com.foed.SteeredVehicle;
    import com.foed.Vector2D;
    import com.foed.Vehicle;

    import flash.display.Sprite;
    import flash.display.StageAlign;
    import flash.display.StageScaleMode;
    import flash.events.Event;
```

```
public class PursueEvadeTest extends Sprite
{
    private var _pursuer:SteeredVehicle;
    private var _evader:SteeredVehicle;

    public function PursueEvadeTest()
    {
        stage.align = StageAlign.TOP_LEFT;
        stage.scaleMode = StageScaleMode.NO_SCALE;

        _pursuer = new SteeredVehicle();
        _pursuer.position = new Vector2D(200, 200);
        _pursuer.edgeBehavior = Vehicle.BOUNCE;
        addChild(_pursuer);

        _evader = new SteeredVehicle();
        _evader.position = new Vector2D(400, 300);
        _evader.edgeBehavior = Vehicle.BOUNCE;
        addChild(_evader);

        addEventListener(Event.ENTER_FRAME, onEnterFrame);
    }

    private function onEnterFrame(event:Event):void
    {
        _pursuer.pursue(_evader);
        _evader.evade(_pursuer);
        _pursuer.update();
        _evader.update();
    }
}
```

As you can see, this example is essentially the same test as SeekFleeTest1, but it uses pursue and evade instead. Because both vehicles use the more advanced methods, neither winds up with any particular added advantage, so it's hard to see the difference between it and the seek/flee test. But play with it a bit, swap out some methods, and see what you can discover. Next, we move away from the seek/flee type of behaviors into the more random wander behavior.

Wander behavior

The wander behavior is pretty much just what it sounds like. The character just moves about the screen rather aimlessly. It's often used to simulate searching or foraging in games or simulations—or simply just wandering.

As simple as it sounds, the wander behavior turns out to be a bit more complex. You could simply apply some random, Brownian motion to a character, but it would wind up looking rather jittery or jerky. We're looking for something smoother and more natural. The way this is usually done is by placing an imaginary circle in front of the character, picking a random spot on that circle and using that as a target. On each frame or update, that random point is randomly moved somewhat. But because that target point is always on that imaginary circle, the resulting steering force never varies hugely from one frame to the next. You can see this behavior in Figure 2-8.

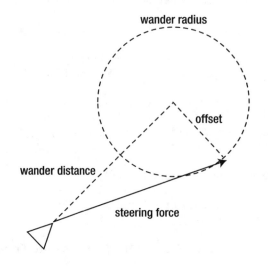

Figure 2-8. Wander's use of distance, radius, and offset to produce a steering force

A few factors can vary to give a range of different flavors of wandering: the size of the circle, how far out in front of the character the circle is placed, and how much the target point can randomly move on each frame.

Here's the wander method:

```
public function wander():void
{
    var center:Vector2D =
                velocity.clone().normalize().multiply(_wanderDistance);
    var offset:Vector2D = new Vector2D(0);
    offset.length = _wanderRadius;
    offset.angle = _wanderAngle;
    _wanderAngle += Math.random() * _wanderRange - _wanderRange * .5;
    var force:Vector2D = center.add(offset);
    _steeringForce = _steeringForce.add(force);
}
```

First we find the center of the circle. The velocity vector will point directly in front of the vehicle. By normalizing this vector and multiplying it by _wanderDistance, we get where the circle will be. From there, we add another vector called offset, which is the random point on the circle. So the length of offset is the _wanderRadius, and the angle is _wanderAngle. We'll then randomly change _wanderAngle within the range of _wanderRange. The center plus offset gives a vector that is the steering force for this behavior. We'll add this to the overall steering force and we'll be done.

Note that there are new variables for the SteeredVehicle class. We'll define these at the start of the class and initialize them with some default values:

```
private var _wanderAngle:Number = 0;
private var _wanderDistance:Number = 10;
private var _wanderRadius:Number = 5;
private var _wanderRange:Number = 1;
```

And then we'll provide some accessors for most of them so they can be changed on an individual vehicle (_wanderAngle is completely random and should not need to be set explicitly):

```
public function set wanderDistance(value:Number):void
{
    _wanderDistance = value;
}
public function get wanderDistance():Number
{
    return _wanderDistance;
}

public function set wanderRadius(value:Number):void
{
    _wanderRadius = value;
}
public function get wanderRadius():Number
{
    return _wanderRadius;
}

public function set wanderRange(value:Number):void
{
    _wanderRange = value;
}
public function get wanderRange():Number
{
    return _wanderRange;
}
```

Finally, of course, an example to see how it looks, as in the WanderTest.as file:

```
package
{
    import com.foed.SteeredVehicle;
    import com.foed.Vector2D;

    import flash.display.Sprite;
    import flash.display.StageAlign;
    import flash.display.StageScaleMode;
    import flash.events.Event;
```

```
public class WanderTest extends Sprite
{
    private var _vehicle:SteeredVehicle;

    public function WanderTest()
    {
        stage.align = StageAlign.TOP_LEFT;
        stage.scaleMode = StageScaleMode.NO_SCALE;

        _vehicle = new SteeredVehicle();
        _vehicle.position = new Vector2D(200, 200);
        addChild(_vehicle);

        addEventListener(Event.ENTER_FRAME, onEnterFrame);
    }

    private function onEnterFrame(event:Event):void
    {
        _vehicle.wander();
        _vehicle.update();
    }
}
```

You can experiment with various new wander variables to see what they do. And don't forget to see how the other properties (for example, mass, maxSpeed, and maxForce) affect wandering as well. You might want to retry some of the earlier seek or pursue tests and have the seeker/pursuer chase a wandering vehicle.

Things are starting to get interesting and will become even more so as we go on. We're through with the simpler behaviors. The remaining ones get more complex, starting with object avoidance.

Object avoidance

Unlike some of the behaviors you've looked at so far, not only is object avoidance much more complicated but it also seems that everyone who has implemented it has a slightly different take on it—from relatively simple methods to extremely intricate solutions. Because there isn't a universally accepted standard for this behavior, I'll get you started with a very basic implementation and encourage you to improve upon it as you wish.

The whole subject of **object avoidance** means that something is in a vehicle's path, and the vehicle has to steer one way or the other to avoid being hit. So it's somewhat related to collision detection, but it throws a prediction factor into the mix: "At my current velocity, I will hit this object in the future."

Of course, once a collision is predicted, some intelligent action needs to be taken to ensure that the collision doesn't occur. Naively, you could just stop or turn around, but remember that multiple behaviors might be in play. If you are attempting to flee from or evade a predator, stopping or turning back when you see a tree in your path isn't a very intelligent option. Ideally, you should take whatever action is necessary to avoid the obstacle while continuing to flee or evade. And the predator itself will most likely also need to avoid the obstacle while continuing to pursue you.

Furthermore, you can imagine that the closer you are to an object you need to avoid, the more you have to alter your path to avoid it. If you were walking through the desert and saw a pyramid a few miles off, you could just turn a degree or two either way and then walk right by it. But if you waited until it was directly in front of you, you'd need to turn almost 90 degrees to avoid it.

So, you see how complex this can get and why there are so many different solutions. The first simplification that most solutions make is to treat obstacles as circles (or spheres in 3D). The obstacle might not actually be a circle, but if you imagine it as a center point with a radius, calculations are a lot easier and generally workable. Remember that you're usually not looking for pixel-perfect collision detection; just to know where something is and roughly how big it is, so you can get the heck out of the way. So here is the Circle class that will represent obstacles to avoid:

```
package com.foed
{
    import flash.display.Sprite;

    public class Circle extends Sprite
    {
        private var _radius:Number;
        private var _color:uint;

        public function Circle(radius:Number, color:uint = 0x000000)
        {
            _radius = radius;
            _color = color;
            graphics.lineStyle(0, _color);
            graphics.drawCircle(0, 0, _radius);
        }

        public function get radius():Number
        {
            return _radius;
        }

        public function get position():Vector2D
        {
            return new Vector2D(x, y);
        }
    }
}
```

This class simply takes a radius and a color and then draws a circle at that radius. It has a getter for the radius and one for position, which returns a Vector2D to make things fit in well with all the vector-based code. Now on to the implementation of the avoid behavior.

Because there usually will be more than a single object to avoid, the avoid method takes an array of circles, loops through them, and sees whether they need to be avoided. If so, it calculates a steering force to do so. This code gets pretty complex, and because there are so many variations on how to do object avoidance, I'll merely present this as an example without much detailed explanation.

The code to predict the collision is very roughly based on the example found in *AI for Game Developers* by David M. Bourg and Glenn Seemann (O'Reilly), but greatly simplified. The steering force is calculated based on a conglomeration of multiple sources and ideas and a bit of my own imagination. I'll leave the comments to explain the code (and Figure 2-9 shows what's happening):

```
public function avoid(circles:Array):void
{
    for(var i:int = 0; i < circles.length; i++)
    {
        var circle:Circle = circles[i] as Circle;
        var heading:Vector2D = _velocity.clone().normalize();

        // vector between circle and vehicle:
        var difference:Vector2D = circle.position.subtract(_position);
        var dotProd:Number = difference.dotProd(heading);

        // if circle is in front of vehicle...
        if(dotProd > 0)
        {
            // vector to represent "feeler" arm
            var feeler:Vector2D = heading.multiply(_avoidDistance);
            // project difference vector onto feeler
            var projection:Vector2D = heading.multiply(dotProd);
            // distance from circle to feeler
            var dist:Number = projection.subtract(difference).length;

            // if feeler intersects circle (plus buffer),
            //and projection is less than feeler length,
            // we will collide, so need to steer
            if(dist < circle.radius + _avoidBuffer &&
                projection.length < feeler.length)
            {
                // calculate a force +/- 90 degrees
                // from vector to circle
                var force:Vector2D = heading.multiply(_maxSpeed);
                force.angle += difference.sign(_velocity) *
                            Math.PI / 2;

                // scale this force by distance to circle.
                // the farther away, the smaller the force
                force = force.multiply(1.0 - projection.length /
                                        feeler.length);

                // add to steering force
                _steeringForce = _steeringForce.add(force);
```

```
                        // braking force - slows vehicle down so it has
                        // time to turn. The closer it is, the harder it brakes
                        _velocity = _velocity.multiply(projection.length /
                                                       feeler.length);

                    }
                }
            }
        }
```

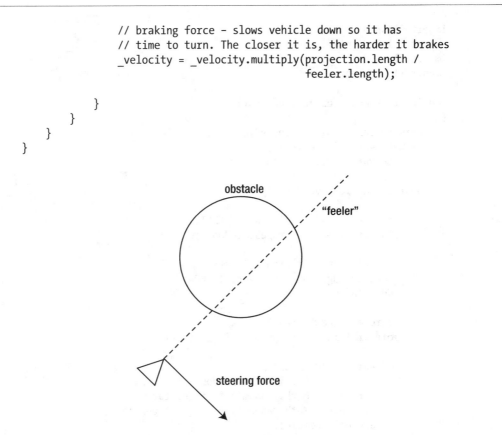

Figure 2-9. When a collision with an object is detected, a steering force is applied.

Note that there are a couple of additional properties you have to add to the class:

```
    private var _avoidDistance:Number = 300;
    private var _avoidBuffer:Number = 20;
```

The avoid distance is how far into the distance a vehicle will look for obstacles. The avoid buffer is the amount of space the vehicle will try to leave between itself and an object as it passes by.

This code isn't perfect, but it performs relatively well and doesn't hit the CPU all that hard. Use it as is or feel free to improve upon it or start from scratch. Here's an example of it in use, as seen in the AvoidTest.as file:

```
    package
    {
        import com.foed.Circle;
        import com.foed.SteeredVehicle;
        import com.foed.Vector2D;
        import com.foed.Vehicle;
```

```
import flash.display.Sprite;
import flash.display.StageAlign;
import flash.display.StageScaleMode;
import flash.events.Event;

public class AvoidTest extends Sprite
{
    private var _vehicle:SteeredVehicle;
    private var _circles:Array;
    private var _numCircles:int = 10;

    public function AvoidTest()
    {
        stage.align = StageAlign.TOP_LEFT;
        stage.scaleMode = StageScaleMode.NO_SCALE;

        _vehicle = new SteeredVehicle();
        _vehicle.edgeBehavior = Vehicle.BOUNCE;
        addChild(_vehicle);

        _circles = new Array();
        for(var i:int = 0; i < _numCircles; i++)
        {
            var circle:Circle =
                    new Circle(Math.random() * 50 + 50);
            circle.x = Math.random() * stage.stageWidth;
            circle.y = Math.random() * stage.stageHeight;
            addChild(circle);
            _circles.push(circle);
        }

        addEventListener(Event.ENTER_FRAME, onEnterFrame);
    }

    private function onEnterFrame(event:Event):void
    {
        _vehicle.wander();
        _vehicle.avoid(_circles);
        _vehicle.update();
    }
}
```

An array of circles is created, and the vehicle wanders around while trying to avoid the circles. It's pretty simple to implement, but works well. This implementation can handle wandering or straight motion, but it gets a bit rough used in combination with seeking as the vehicle attempts to seek straight through an object while simultaneously trying to avoid it. This kind of behavior might be better attempted with path finding, as covered in Chapter 4. Next we'll move on to another behavior that works well with path finding: path following.

Path following

Path following is pretty much what it sounds like: the vehicle follows a predefined path. Although paths can be represented graphically in a map or game world, for steering behaviors they are generally represented as a series of waypoints. In an ActionScript 3.0 implementation, it can be as simple as an array of Vector2D objects.

The strategy is amazingly simple. You take the first waypoint and seek to it as a target. When the vehicle is within a certain distance from that waypoint, you consider that it has reached that waypoint and move on to the next waypoint. And so on until the last waypoint is reached. You can have a looping path; in that case, it starts over again from the first waypoint when the last waypoint is reached. See Figure 2-10.

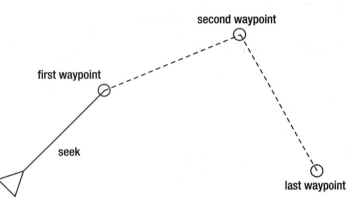

Figure 2-10. Seek to the first waypoint. When you get close enough, seek to the next one. And so on.

There are two new properties that have to be added to the class:

```
private var _pathIndex:int = 0;
private var _pathThreshold:Number = 20;
```

And let's provide some accessors to these properties:

```
public function set pathIndex(value:int):void
{
    _pathIndex = value;
}
public function get pathIndex():int
{
    return _pathIndex;
}

public function set pathThreshold(value:Number):void
{
    _pathThreshold = value;
}
```

```
public function get pathThreshold():Number
{
    return _pathThreshold;
}
```

The first accessor, _pathIndex, holds the index in the array that points to the next waypoint. The _pathThreshold accessor defines how close you must get to a waypoint before considering it "done."

Here's the implementation:

```
public function followPath(path:Array, loop:Boolean = false):void
{
    var wayPoint:Vector2D = path[_pathIndex];
    if(wayPoint == null) return;
    if(_position.dist(wayPoint) < _pathThreshold)
    {
        if(_pathIndex >= path.length - 1)
        {
            if(loop)
            {
                _pathIndex = 0;
            }
        }
        else
        {
            _pathIndex++;
        }
    }
    if(_pathIndex >= path.length - 1 && !loop)
    {
        arrive(wayPoint);
    }
    else
    {
        seek(wayPoint);
    }
}
```

It's a bit of a tangle of conditionals. First, we grab the first waypoint off the path array that is passed in. If for any reason this is not a valid Vector2D object, we simply return. This allows for an empty array to be passed in without an error.

If it's valid, we check to see whether it's within the threshold distance. If so, we check to see whether it's the last waypoint of the path. If so, and if we are looping, we loop back to the first waypoint. If it's not the last waypoint, we move to the next one. A bit complicated to write, but if you draw out a series of waypoints with a path running through them on a piece of paper and then step through the logic, you'll see that it's really pretty straightforward.

At this point, we have the waypoint we're moving to. We could just execute that last line here—seek(wayPoint)—and it would work relatively well. But we can make it a bit more elegant by allowing for one special case: if we're moving to the last waypoint in the path and we're *not* looping, let's perform an arrive behavior instead of seeking. This lets the vehicle ease nicely into the last point of the path instead of doing that flipping-back-and-forth thing.

That's all there is to it. Of course, we need an example of it in action (the PathTest.as file):

```
package
{
    import com.foed.SteeredVehicle;
    import com.foed.Vector2D;

    import flash.display.Sprite;
    import flash.display.StageAlign;
    import flash.display.StageScaleMode;
    import flash.events.Event;
    import flash.events.MouseEvent;

    public class PathTest extends Sprite
    {
        private var _vehicle:SteeredVehicle;
        private var _path:Array;

        public function PathTest()
        {
            stage.align = StageAlign.TOP_LEFT;
            stage.scaleMode = StageScaleMode.NO_SCALE;

            _vehicle = new SteeredVehicle();
            addChild(_vehicle);

            _path = new Array();

            stage.addEventListener(MouseEvent.CLICK, onClick);
            addEventListener(Event.ENTER_FRAME, onEnterFrame);
        }

        private function onEnterFrame(event:Event):void
        {
            _vehicle.followPath(_path, true);
            _vehicle.update();
        }

        private function onClick(event:MouseEvent):void
        {
            graphics.lineStyle(0, 0, .25);
            if(_path.length == 0)
            {
                graphics.moveTo(mouseX, mouseY);
            }
            graphics.lineTo(mouseX, mouseY);
```

```
            graphics.drawCircle(mouseX, mouseY, 10);
            graphics.moveTo(mouseX, mouseY);
            _path.push(new Vector2D(mouseX, mouseY));
        }
    }
}
```

Pretty basic, I'm sure you'll agree. Most of the class is concerned with drawing the path so you can see it. There's a _path array and the vehicle is set to follow it in the onEnterFrame method. Initially, it will be an empty array—no waypoints—so the vehicle won't move. But each time you click the mouse, a new waypoint will be added to the path, based on where you clicked. Again, most of the code in the onClick method is simply there to make the path visible.

As soon as you start clicking, the vehicle will start following the path you created. Because the loop parameter is specified as true, it will go around the path in a circuit. Note that the vehicle isn't mechanically sticking to the path; it's moving naturally—overshooting sharp turns and cutting corners a bit here and there. By changing the threshold value, you can affect how it handles corners. Other properties of SteeredVehicle—such as mass, maxSpeed and maxForce—will also affect the turning behavior. So you have plenty of values to tweak to get the exact look and feel you want.

Path following is often used in conjunction with path finding (covered in Chapter 4). Path finding is concerned with finding the best path between two points. It takes into account areas that a character can't travel on and potentially factors in situations like rough terrain versus easy terrain. It is usually grid-based, so the result is an array of grid cells for the character to move through to reach the goal. This array can then be used as the path for the path following steering behavior, to give it a more natural feel.

Finally I'll discuss the last behavior, flocking, which is really a complex behavior composed of three sub-behaviors.

Flocking

You can hardly mention flocking behaviors without referring to Craig Reynolds and his "boids" simulation. Reynolds did an amazing job of breaking down a seemingly incredibly complex process into a few simple behaviors.

If you think about a flock of birds, it has three main characteristics:

- First, the birds stay in the same general area. If one bird moves too far away from its flock, it will soon return. This is known as **cohesion** (see Figure 2-11).

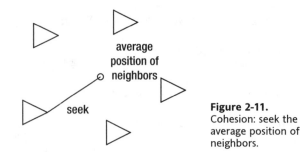

Figure 2-11.
Cohesion: seek the average position of neighbors.

- Second, the birds, despite sticking together, somehow manage to avoid hitting each other. They have an individual sense of personal space and avoid getting too close to other birds or allowing another bird to get too close. This is known as **separation** (see Figure 2-12).

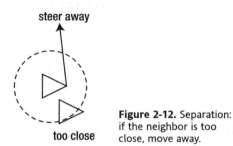

Figure 2-12. Separation: if the neighbor is too close, move away.

- Third, the birds move in the same general direction. Yes, there is a bit of individual variation, but in general, the flock flies in this direction or that, with each individual bird eventually falling into line. This is known as **alignment** (see Figure 2-13).

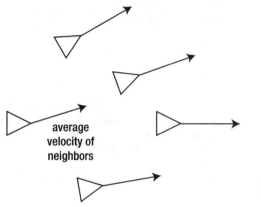

Figure 2-13. Alignment: adjust to the average velocity of neighbors.

These three behaviors—cohesion, separation, and alignment—make up complex flocking behavior.

When considering the complex behavior of a flock of birds, some tend to imagine some single intelligence controlling the flock as a whole, or assume that each bird has complete awareness of every other bird and the flock as a whole. I won't argue against either of these things, but I will say that when you start understanding the three behaviors that make up flocking, you'll find that there is no need for each bird to be all-knowing, nor is there any need for an overall "hive-mind" controlling the flock. In fact, each bird just needs to be able to see the few other birds in its immediate vicinity. If it steers to be close to them, but not too close, and aligns its direction with the way they are heading, the seemingly mystical flocking behavior will emerge all by itself.

Although flocking technically consists of three sub-behaviors, these three are almost exclusively used together. You'll normally not want your characters to exhibit only one or two of these behaviors, so all three will be coded into a single method. This implementation will also be more efficient because there will be lots of looping going on and it will be good if we can accomplish everything in a single loop instead of three. Okay, here's the method:

```
public function flock(vehicles:Array):void
{
    var averageVelocity:Vector2D = _velocity.clone();
    var averagePosition:Vector2D = new Vector2D();
    var inSightCount:int = 0;
    for(var i:int = 0; i < vehicles.length; i++)
    {
        var vehicle:Vehicle = vehicles[i] as Vehicle;
        if(vehicle != this && inSight(vehicle))
        {
            averageVelocity = averageVelocity.add(vehicle.velocity);
            averagePosition = averagePosition.add(vehicle.position);
            if(tooClose(vehicle)) flee(vehicle.position);
            inSightCount++;
        }
    }
    if(inSightCount > 0)
    {
        averageVelocity = averageVelocity.divide(inSightCount);
        averagePosition = averagePosition.divide(inSightCount);
        seek(averagePosition);
        _steeringForce.add(averageVelocity.subtract(_velocity));
    }
}
```

First, we pass in an array of vehicles. The strategy is to loop through this array and see which vehicles are within the sight of the current vehicle. If a vehicle is within sight, we add its velocity and position each to a running total. We also keep track of how many vehicles are within sight so that we can calculate an average. Notice also that if the vehicle we are processing is the current vehicle, we ignore it.

If a vehicle is too close, we execute a flee behavior away from it, which allows for the separation aspect.

Once we've gone through the whole array, if any were found in range, we calculate the average position and velocity. We seek to the average position and we add steering force toward the average velocity.

Not too painful, but you might notice that there are a couple of calls to methods we haven't seen yet: inSight and tooClose:

```
public function inSight(vehicle:Vehicle):Boolean
{
    if(_position.dist(vehicle.position) > _inSightDist) return false;
    var heading:Vector2D = _velocity.clone().normalize();
    var difference:Vector2D = vehicle.position.subtract(_position);
    var dotProd:Number = difference.dotProd(heading);
    if(dotProd < 0) return false;
    return true;
}
```

```
public function tooClose(vehicle:Vehicle):Boolean
{
    return _position.dist(vehicle.position) < _tooCloseDist;
}
```

The inSight method determines whether a vehicle can see another vehicle. To do this, it first checks whether the distance to that vehicle is within a certain range. If not, it returns false. Then it does some fancy vector math to determine whether the vehicle is in front of or behind it. If the other vehicle is in front, the first vehicle can see that vehicle; if behind, it can't. This is actually a rather rigid implementation because it allows only for an 180-degree field of vision. It works well enough for demonstration purposes, but if you want to improve upon this behavior, one of the first things you can do is allow for a variable field of vision. A narrower field of vision would mean that the character could see only what is directly in front of it and less to the sides. A wider field would mean that the character could see somewhat behind itself. These variations in the field of vision would result in different patterns of flocking.

Next is the tooClose method, which returns true if the vehicle is within a certain range; false if not.

You'll see that these two methods rely on a couple of other class variables. So we'll add those as well as some accessors:

```
private var _inSightDist:Number = 200;
private var _tooCloseDist:Number = 60;

public function set inSightDist(value:Number):void
{
    _inSightDist = value;
}
public function get inSightDist():Number
{
    return _inSightDist;
}

public function set tooCloseDist(value:Number):void
{
    _tooCloseDist = value;
}
public function get tooCloseDist():Number
{
    return _tooCloseDist;
}
```

Finally, we'll need a class to test it with (you can find this in the FlockTest.as file):

```
package
{
    import com.foed.SteeredVehicle;
    import com.foed.Vector2D;
    import com.foed.Vehicle;
```

```
import flash.display.Sprite;
import flash.display.StageAlign;
import flash.display.StageScaleMode;
import flash.events.Event;

public class FlockTest extends Sprite
{
    private var _vehicles:Array;
    private var _numVehicles:int = 30;

    public function FlockTest()
    {
        stage.align = StageAlign.TOP_LEFT;
        stage.scaleMode = StageScaleMode.NO_SCALE;

        _vehicles = new Array();
        for(var i:int = 0; i < _numVehicles; i++)
        {
            var vehicle:SteeredVehicle = new SteeredVehicle();
            vehicle.position = new Vector2D(Math.random() *
                                            stage.stageWidth,
                                            Math.random() *
                                            stage.stageHeight);
            vehicle.velocity =
                        new Vector2D(Math.random() * 20 - 10,
                                     Math.random() * 20 - 10);
            vehicle.edgeBehavior = Vehicle.BOUNCE;
            _vehicles.push(vehicle);
            addChild(vehicle);
        }
        addEventListener(Event.ENTER_FRAME, onEnterFrame);
    }

    private function onEnterFrame(event:Event):void
    {
        for(var i:int = 0; i < _numVehicles; i++)
        {
            _vehicles[i].flock(_vehicles);
            _vehicles[i].update();
        }
    }
}
}
```

Here we simply make a whole bunch of steered vehicles, scatter them about on stage, and add them to an array. On each frame, we loop through the array, running the flock behavior on each, and then update it. You'll see that although each vehicle is moving around on its own, it has an awareness of those around it, and a group dynamic sets in. Play around with the variables, number of vehicles, and so on to get an idea about how it all works.

Another candidate for improvement is optimization of the array handling. Each vehicle currently checks the entire array of other vehicles, which can be pretty inefficient. You might want to try to refactor it to use a double loop or even a grid-based approach, as described in Chapter 1. However, this would require moving some of the flocking code outside of the `SteeredVehicle` class, either to the main document class or perhaps to some other flock manager class. I'll leave that to you.

Summary

This chapter covered the basics of steering behaviors, from simple seek and flee to far more complex obstacle avoidance and flocking. The fun comes from combining these behaviors to create even more complex dynamics. And again, this chapter is a mere introduction to the subject. There is a huge amount of material online and in other books related to steering, often under the heading of artificial intelligence. If nothing else, I hope you are at least inspired to start digging up that data and putting it to use in your own ActionScript 3.0 applications and games.

The next chapter discusses isometric worlds and path finding. Combine them with steering behaviors (and maybe some advanced collision detection), and you'll have a blockbuster game on your hands.

Chapter 3

ISOMETRIC PROJECTION

Isometric projection is a technique that has been used in computer games since at least the early '80s. It's a quick and efficient way of simulating a three-dimensional space, giving you the illusion of depth without a lot of the costly perspective calculations you have to do in "real 3D." In the early days, most video games were top-down or side-scrolling. Zaxxon (see Figure 3-1) and Qbert (see Figure 3-2) were the first commercial isometric games.

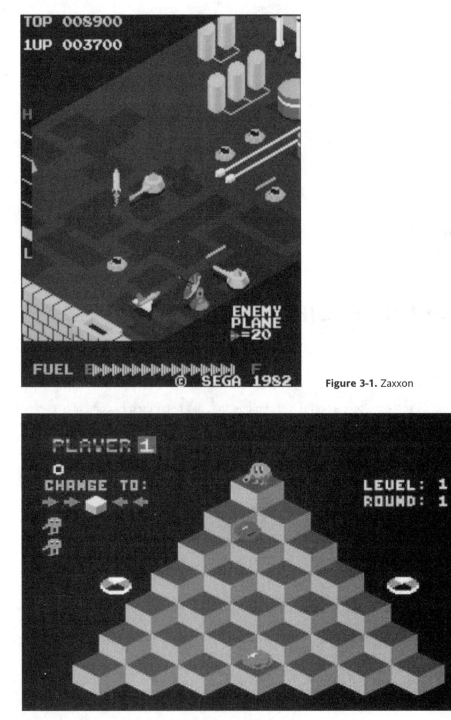

Figure 3-1. Zaxxon

Figure 3-2. Qbert

These days, despite the cutting-edge 3D technology in first-person shooter games such as Halo, isometric games are still very popular, particularly in role-playing or strategy games.

To understand isometric projection, first let's take a look at projection is and how isometric projection differs from other methods of visualizing 3D.

Projection refers to the representation of a three-dimensional object or scene on a two-dimensional surface, whether a sheet of paper or a computer screen. A camera uses its lens to create a projection of the objects in front of it onto a sheet of film or electronic sensor. Even your eyes do the same thing, projecting an image onto your retina.

When we move to paper and computer screens, there are many different types of projection available. The type you are probably most used to is **perspective projection**. In this type of projection, objects that are farther away from the viewpoint are rendered smaller and closer to a vanishing point. This is the type of projection described in the 3D chapters of *Making Things Move*, what is used by default in 3D frameworks such as Papervision3D and other 3D software, how cameras render their images, and most imitates what you perceive with your own eyes.

Isometric projection, on the other hand, is a type of axonometric projection. In this type of projection, the scale of objects does not change as their distance from the camera changes.

The word *isometric* means "equal measure." It refers to the fact that the angles between each of the x-, y-, and z-axis lines in this projection are the same: 120 degrees. You can see this in Figure 3-3.

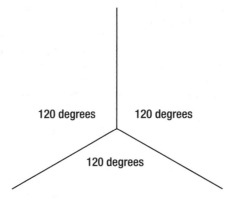

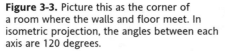

Figure 3-3. Picture this as the corner of a room where the walls and floor meet. In isometric projection, the angles between each axis are 120 degrees.

Isometric worlds in games are almost always tile-based worlds, so you have a floor that is composed of individual tiles instead of a continuous, seamless environment. Objects in the world are tiles themselves or are placed on tiles. In most cases, tiles are reused numerous times, so a single tile can be used multiple times to create an entire floor (see Figure 3-4), or a relatively small number of tiles can be used to create quite a varied environment (as in Zaxxon, shown in Figure 3-1).

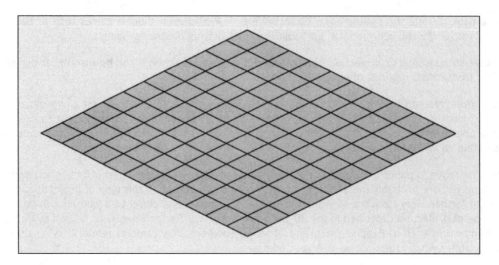

Figure 3-4. A single tile used to create a whole floor

Isometric versus Dimetric

Okay, here's a dirty little secret, a little tidbit you can drop into conversations at cocktail parties to make yourself sound more intelligent (or just really geeky): almost every game, engine, art, and so on labeled as *isometric* is not really isometric; they are *dimetric*, meaning that there are two different angles used between the three axes (see Figure 3-5). Note that **dimetric** simply means "two measures." (There is a third type of axonometric projection, called **trimetric**, in which each axis has a different angle.) Dimetric projection doesn't have to use the angles shown in this example, but these are the angles most used in computer games, isometric artwork, and so on.

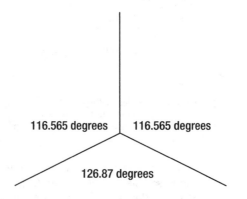

Figure 3-5. Dimetric projection uses two angles.

Now, those seem rather odd angles to use instead of the nice round 120s. But there are several very good reasons for using these angles when you are working with pixels. Let's take a single tile rendered in true isometric and in dimetric (see Figure 3-6).

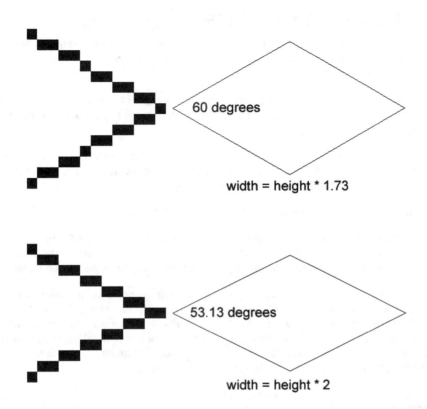

60 degrees

width = height * 1.73

53.13 degrees

width = height * 2

Figure 3-6. A single tile in true isometric and in dimetric projections

The top tile is rendered in isometric. The angle labeled is 60 degrees. The proportions of the tile's width to its height end up being 1.73:1. The bottom tile is dimetric. Although the angle is not a nice whole number, the ratio of width to height is 2:1. This makes creating artwork for such systems far easier. Instead of creating 173×100 pixel graphics for your tiles, for example, you create 200×100 tiles. Positioning the tiles is similarly much more straightforward.

And if that weren't important enough, the dimetric tile just looks a whole lot better. You can see it in the full-sized tiles on the right—the dimetric one has nice smooth lines, whereas the isometric tile edges look a little jagged. In the enlarged version to the left, you can see why that is. In isometric, for every pixel you move vertically, you need to move 1.73 pixels horizontally. Because you can't move a partial pixel, sometimes you move two pixels; sometimes one. That's what gives it the jagged look. However, in the dimetric version, you move up or down one pixel and over two, every time, nice and smooth.

Because it makes things easier to code and easier to design, and because that's what everyone else does, we'll go with the dimetric system. And now that you have a thorough understanding of what's what and what's not, we'll relax a bit and even though we know it's not *really* isometric, we're going to go ahead and call it that (because everyone else does).

Creating Isometric Graphics

Although it's not coding, it's useful to know how to create graphics for isometric systems. (And I'm really talking about 2:1 ratio, 26.565 degree, dimetric systems, but this will be the last clarification.) Specifically, let's make a single tile.

First, go into Flash, Fireworks, PhotoShop, or whatever program in which you want to make your graphics in. Make a square. A real square with all four sides equal, not an almost-square rectangle. Make it 100×100.

Now rotate it 45 degrees. Again, use a tool that allows you to rotate it exactly 45 degrees, not roughly 45 degrees. Many tools allow you to hold down the Shift key to draw squares and snap rotations to 45 and 90 degrees. You should have a diamond shape now.

Finally, scale it by 50% vertically, keeping it at 100% horizontal scale.

You should wind up with the exact shape shown in the bottom half of Figure 3-6. The size of this shape will now be roughly 141.4×70.7, which is a 2:1 ratio. Fireworks will round off to the nearest pixel, so you'll get 141×71, which is good enough for government work, as my stepdad used to say.

Now, if you tell your designers they have to make all their graphics some weird dimensions like 141.4×70.7, they won't be too happy with you. So select the object and change its height to 100. Then if it doesn't do it automatically, change the width to 200. The shape is now 200×100, which will make your designers very happy. You can, of course, go with smaller or larger tile sizes, as long as they retain that 2:1 ratio. In practice, you'll probably wind up making your tiles smaller than this to allow for more detail and better collision detection (covered later in the chapter).

Now you can fill this diamond with whatever graphics you want: grass, rocks, water, dirt, wood, stone, and so on. Ideally the graphics will tile so they can be placed together seamlessly. (That's why they're called tiles!) If you want to give the tile some height, just move everything up a bit, draw some lines down from the corners, and connect them like you see in Figure 3-7.

You'll be able to dig up all kinds of good tutorials on how to create isometric graphics online—how to do color, shading, smooth tiling, and so on. Just search for "isometric art tutorials" or "isometric pixel art". As for this chapter, we'll get back to coding.

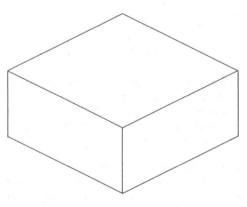

Figure 3-7. An isometric box

Isometric Transformations

One of the most important (and possibly the least understood, most confused, and most asked about) subjects in creating isometric worlds is how to take isometric world x, y, z coordinates and transform them into screen x, y, z coordinates, and vice versa.

I've seen this done at least five or six different ways, all quite different. Some were very accurate but somewhat inefficient. Others were quick and worked well, but didn't really reflect the actual 3D transformations involved with an isometric view. And one or two were . . . well, I don't know what they were or where the authors came up with the ideas, and maybe they even worked, but they didn't have any logic I could understand.

Transforming world coordinates to screen coordinates

First, let's look at the actual 3D transformation that goes on in viewing something in an isometric view, which will enable you to understand the accurate method and the shortcuts that go into the quick method. I created a SWF file that demonstrates the transformations. It's called `IsoProjection.swf` and can be found with the files available from this book's download page.

When you open the SWF, you'll see a cube rendered in top, front, and side views, as shown in Figure 3-8.

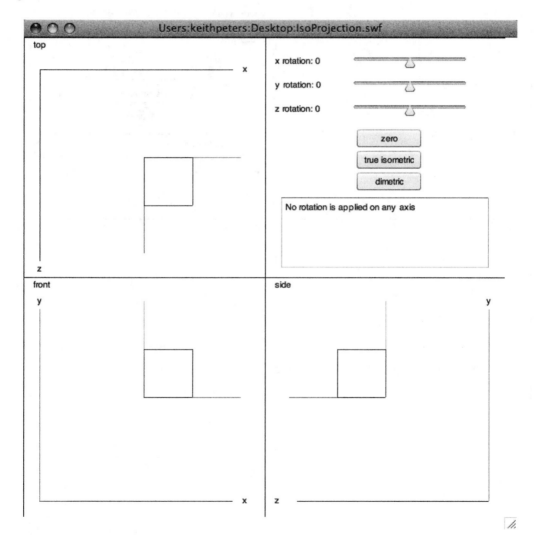

Figure 3-8. Three views of an unrotated cube

This SWF also shows the coordinate system we'll use, which is the same 3D coordinate system we would use in most Flash-based 3D systems: the x-axis goes left to right, the y-axis goes up and down, and the z-axis goes "in and out" of the screen, representing depth.

The first transformation is rotating the world 45 degrees on the y-axis. You can go ahead and do this with the y-rotation slider. Use the left and right arrow keys to make it exactly 45 degrees, which gives the picture shown in Figure 3-9.

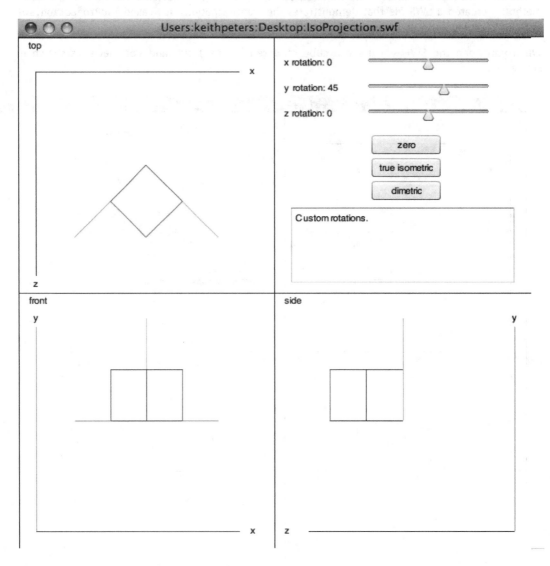

Figure 3-9. First rotation: 45 degrees on y-axis

The second transformation will be a –30 degree rotation on the x-axis. Again, use the x-rotation slider and keyboard. You can see the results in Figure 3-10.

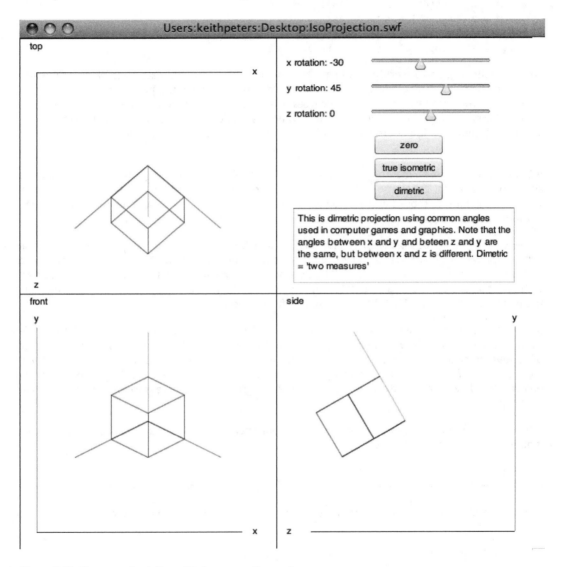

Figure 3-10. The second rotation: –30 degrees on the x-axis

You'll see now that the top and bottom faces of the cube are the same shape displayed in the bottom half of Figure 3-6. These shapes will be twice as wide as they are tall and will have the smooth 2:1 slope edges described earlier.

You can also create these same transformations by clicking the dimetric button, and you can see "true isometric projection" by clicking that button as well.

The pseudocode for creating these transformations is as follows:

```
sX = x * cos(45) - z * sin(45);
z1 = z * cos(45) + x * sin(45);
sY = y *  cos(-30) - z1 * sin(-30);
z2 = z1 * cos(-30) + y *  sin(-30);
```

This takes the x, y, and z world coordinates of a point in 3D space and calculates sX and sY, which refer to a point that can be plotted onscreen. This represents rotating the point around the y-axis 45 degrees and then around the x-axis -30 degrees. (See the chapter on coordinate rotation in *Making Things Move*.) Actually, the second-to-last line, which calculates z2, is not even needed here but was included to show the full coordinate rotation. It will be needed later, however, when we do depth sorting.

Although you can code a method like this and use it safely with the knowledge that you are following all the rules of math, geometry, and trigonometry, there are a few problems with it from a practical viewpoint. First are all those calls to trigonometry functions. Actually, you could do quite a bit of optimization with this, so the trig wouldn't be too much of a problem in the long run.

However, a more serious problem is that this method favors those odd tile sizes. Remember that 100×100 square we made in the preceding graphics creation section? And how when we rotated and scaled it, it came out to 141.4×70.7? Well that's exactly what we are doing here in code. So if you start with four points that made up a 100×100 square and use the formulas just shown to rotate them, in the end they will form a 141.4×70.7 diamond. So far, so good.

But remember that we then resized that diamond tile to 200×100. This amounts to multiplying the width and height by 1.414, which is the square root of 2. That's not a bizarre coincidence; it's because of various trigonometric relationships of angles of 45 degrees. I'll leave you to work that out if you are interested. If we are scaling our graphics like this, we need to do the same thing in our code, or objects placed by code will be out of alignment with the graphics. And here is where something rather cool happens.

When we factor in that square root of two to the coordinates in the isometric transform and simplify it all down, you get the following:

```
sx = x - z;
sy = y * 1.2247 + (x + z) * .5;
```

If you are interested in how we do that simplification, it follows here. If you trust me, feel free to jump to the next section.

We start off with the straight up coordinate rotation formula:

```
x1 = x * cos(45) - z * sin(45)
z1 = z * cos(45) + x * sin(45)
y1 = y  * cos(-30) - z1 * sin(30)
z2 = z1 * cos(-30) + y  * sin(30)
```

Throw in some rough approximations for the trig:

```
x1 = x * .707 - z * .707
z1 = z * .707 + x * .707
y1 = y  * .866 - z1 * -.5
z2 = z1 * .866 + y  * -.5
```

Simplify:

```
x1 = (x - z) * .707
z1 = (x + z) * .707
y1 = y  * .866 - z1 * -.5
z2 = z1 * .866 + y  * -.5
```

Get rid of z1, expanding it in the formula for y1 and z2:

```
x1 = (x - z) * .707
y1 = y  * .866 - ((x + z) * .707) * -.5
z2 = ((x + z) * .707) * .866 + y  * -.5
```

Multiply x1, y1, and z2 by the square root of 2 (1.414). It turns out that .707 * 1.414 = 1, which simplifies a lot:

```
x1 = x - z
y1 = y * 1.2247 + (x + z) * .5
z2 = (x + z) * .866 - y  * .707
```

We'll use this z2 calculation again when we get to depth sorting.

So, whether you followed all that explanation or not, we now have a function that is quite a bit simpler than the original function. All you have to remember is that a 100×100 square in the isometric world equals a 200×100 diamond-shaped tile in the final 2D rendering. Of course, you're not stuck with using 200×100. If you start with a 50×50 square in world coordinates, you'll get a 100×50 diamond. To simplify it, the height of that diamond shape is equal to the size of the square that tile represents. Simple!

Many implementations simply drop the 1.2247 and say the following:

```
x1 = x - z
y1 = y + (x + z) * .5
```

This will work fine when all the objects in the scene are at the same height. In simple systems, all tiles are simply put at a y of zero. In this case, you could reduce it to the following:

```
x1 = x - z
y1 = (x + z) * .5
```

But in cases in which objects might be at different heights, that 1.2247 is required for correct screen placement of objects. You can still get away without it, but any object placed at a height other than zero will not really be at its proper height and can give the whole scene a feeling of being squashed.

Transforming screen coordinates to world coordinates

Now we'll need a way to go the other way as well: screen coordinates to isometric 3D coordinates. There's a little problem here because screen coordinates represent only two dimensions, and we need three. Most of the time, the use case for such a transformation is to translate a mouse click position to a location somewhere on the floor or ground of the world. Therefore, what we really want to do is translate screen x, y coordinates to world x, z coordinates; and leave the y, or height, as zero. So, if we take the isometric to screen algorithm, we get the following:

```
sx = x - z;
sy = y * 1.2247 + (x + z) * .5;
```

Set y to zero, solve for x and z, and simplify—we get the following pseudocode:

```
x = sy + sx / 2
y = 0
z = sy - sx / 2
```

That's straight algebra, nothing I dreamed up on my own. You start with screen coordinates, sx and sy, and get back an x, y, and z that represents a 3D point in the world space.

IsoUtils class

Enough theory and enough pseudocode. Let's see some real code and see it in action. First, we'll need a structure to hold a 3D point. As with all the code in this book, it's available on this book's download page at www.friendsofed.com. You'll find it as the Point3D.as file.

```
package com.friendsofed.isometric
{
    public class Point3D
    {
        public var x:Number;
        public var y:Number;
        public var z:Number;

        public function Point3D(x:Number = 0,
                                y:Number = 0,
                                z:Number = 0)
        {
            this.x = x;
            this.y = y;
            this.z = z;
        }
    }
}
```

Now, here's the IsoUtils class, available for download as IsoUtls.as, which handles the conversion from world to screen coordinates, and vice versa, as we just covered:

```
package com.friendsofed.isometric
{
    import flash.geom.Point;

    public class IsoUtils
    {
        // a more accurate version of 1.2247...
        public static const Y_CORRECT:Number = Math.cos(-Math.PI / 6) *
                                          Math.SQRT2;

        /**
         * Converts a 3D point in iso space to a 2D screen position.
         * @arg pos the 3D point.
         */
        public static function isoToScreen(pos:Point3D):Point
        {
            var screenX:Number = pos.x - pos.z;
            var screenY:Number = pos.y * Y_CORRECT +
                               (pos.x + pos.z) * .5;
            return new Point(screenX, screenY);
        }

        /**
         * Converts a 2D screen position to a 3D point in iso space,
         * assuming y = 0.
         * @arg point the 2D point.
         */
        public static function screenToIso(point:Point):Point3D
        {
            var xpos:Number = point.y + point.x * .5;
            var ypos:Number = 0;
            var zpos:Number = point.y - point.x * .5;
            return new Point3D(xpos, ypos, zpos);
        }
    }
}
```

Note that the magic number, 1.2247, has been created as a static const and calculated with trig. This will result in it being a precise value instead of the rounded-off version, and it will be calculated only once. Accuracy *and* efficiency!

And now a rough idea of how these methods would be used:

```
package
{
    import com.friendsofed.isometric.IsoUtils;
    import com.friendsofed.isometric.Point3D;
```

```
import flash.display.Sprite;
import flash.display.StageAlign;
import flash.display.StageScaleMode;
import flash.geom.Point;

public class IsoTransformTest extends Sprite
{
    public function IsoTransformTest()
    {
        stage.align = StageAlign.TOP_LEFT;
        stage.scaleMode = StageScaleMode.NO_SCALE;

        var p0:Point3D = new Point3D(0, 0, 0);
        var p1:Point3D = new Point3D(100, 0, 0);
        var p2:Point3D = new Point3D(100, 0, 100);
        var p3:Point3D = new Point3D(0, 0, 100);

        var sp0:Point = IsoUtils.isoToScreen(p0);
        var sp1:Point = IsoUtils.isoToScreen(p1);
        var sp2:Point = IsoUtils.isoToScreen(p2);
        var sp3:Point = IsoUtils.isoToScreen(p3);

        var tile:Sprite = new Sprite();
        tile.x = 200;
        tile.y = 200;
        addChild(tile);

        tile.graphics.lineStyle(0);
        tile.graphics.moveTo(sp0.x, sp0.y);
        tile.graphics.lineTo(sp1.x, sp1.y);
        tile.graphics.lineTo(sp2.x, sp2.y);
        tile.graphics.lineTo(sp3.x, sp3.y);
        tile.graphics.lineTo(sp0.x, sp0.y);
    }
}
}
```

You can find this class in the IsoTransformTest.as file. It first creates four instances of Point3D, forming a square on the x-z plane. It then uses IsoUtils.isoToScreen to convert them to four two-dimensional points, which are drawn to the screen—offset by 200 on the x- and y-axis so it's not jammed in the corner.

Running this class will result in the good old familiar diamond shape. If you were to throw the line trace(width, height) in at the end of the class, you'd see that the diamond is exactly 200×100, as you would expect.

Of course, plotting 3D points and drawing individual lines is no way to create a rich isometric world. These utility methods are mainly used for positioning isometric objects in the world. Our next step is to create a class to represent an isometric object.

Isometric Objects

In general, the objects that make up your world will be created by graphic artists (or by yourself, assuming the graphic artist role) in a graphics program such as Fireworks, Photoshop, or even Flash itself. These objects include various tiles decorated with grass, trees, dirt, water, buildings, and so on—or various characters, perhaps even animated ones. It will be your job (back in the programmer role if you are a one-person shop) to get these graphics into the 3D world, to correctly place them, and to move some of them around. This gives the concept of a graphical object that needs to be positioned and moved in isometric space. Sounds like a good candidate for a class. Here's an introduction to the IsoObject class, available for download as the IsoObject.as file:

```
package com.friendsofed.isometric
{
    import flash.display.Sprite;
    import flash.geom.Point;
    import flash.geom.Rectangle;

    public class IsoObject extends Sprite
    {
        protected var _position:Point3D;
        protected var _size:Number;
        protected var _walkable:Boolean = false;

        // a more accurate version of 1.2247...
        public static const Y_CORRECT:Number = Math.cos(-Math.PI / 6) *
                                                Math.SQRT2;

        public function IsoObject(size:Number)
        {
            _size = size;
            _position = new Point3D();
            updateScreenPosition();
        }

        /**
         * Converts current 3d position to a screen position
         * and places this display object at that position.
         */
        protected function updateScreenPosition():void
        {
            var screenPos:Point = IsoUtils.isoToScreen(_position);
            super.x = screenPos.x;
            super.y = screenPos.y;
        }
```

```
/**
 * String representation of this object.
 */
override public function toString():String
{
    return "[IsoObject (x:" + _position.x + ",
            y:" + _position.y + ", z:" + _position.z + ")]";
}

/**
 * Sets / gets the x position in 3D space.
 */
override public function set x(value:Number):void
{
    _position.x = value;
    updateScreenPosition();
}
override public function get x():Number
{
    return _position.x;
}

/**
 * Sets / gets the y position in 3D space.
 */
override public function set y(value:Number):void
{
    _position.y = value;
    updateScreenPosition();
}
override public function get y():Number
{
    return _position.y;
}

/**
 * Sets / gets the z position in 3D space.
 */
public function set z(value:Number):void
{
    _position.z = value;
    updateScreenPosition();
}
public function get z():Number
{
    return _position.z;
}
```

```
/**
 * Sets / gets the position in 3D space as a Point3D.
 */
public function set position(value:Point3D):void
{
    _position = value;
    updateScreenPosition();
}
public function get position():Point3D
{
    return _position;
}


/**
 * Returns the transformed 3D depth of this object.
 */
public function get depth():Number
{
    return (_position.x + _position.z) * .866 -
            _position.y * .707;
}


/**
 * Indicates whether the space occupied by this object
 * can be occupied by another object.
 */
public function set walkable(value:Boolean):void
{
    _walkable = value;
}
public function get walkable():Boolean
{
    return _walkable;
}


/**
 * Returns the size of this object.
 */
public function get size():Number
{
    return _size;
}


/**
 * Returns the square area on the x-z plane
 * that this object takes up.
 */
```

```
        public function get rect():Rectangle
        {
            return new Rectangle(x - size / 2, z - size / 2,
                                 size, size);
        }

    }
}
```

Most of this class deals with getting and setting the 3D position of the object and calculating its screen position based on it. Because the class extends Sprite, the screen position can be set by assigning values to super.x and super.y. (The super is necessary because the getters and setters for x and y have been overridden to refer to the 3D positions, not the screen positions.) Notice that the update-ScreenPosition method makes use of the IsoUtils.isoToScreen method you just saw.

If you'll be using this class extensively, here's a suggestion you might want to implement. As it stands, updateScreenPosition will be called three times if you set x, y, and z, which is rather inefficient. It is often handled by having an invalidate method that marks the object as needing updating and sets an enterFrame listener to update it once on the next frame. That way, you could update x, y, and z 100 times in succession, and the screen position would be calculated only a single time when you're done.

The other methods—such as the getters and setters for depth, walkable, and rect—mainly have to do with depth sorting and collision detection, which we will cover later in the chapter.

Note that the constructor takes a single parameter, size. All IsoObjects have a size property that determines their footprint, or how much space they take up on the x-z plane. This footprint is always considered to be a square, which makes sense in a tile-based world. You'll see more of this when we start drawing tiles in the next section and when we enter the collision detection phase later on.

Now, this IsoObject class has no graphics in it yet. We could draw some manually, but let's just create a new class or a drawn isometric tile, the DrawnIsoTile class in the DrawnIsoTile.as file:

```
package com.friendsofed.isometric
{
    public class DrawnIsoTile extends IsoObject
    {
        protected var _height:Number;
        protected var _color:uint;

        public function DrawnIsoTile(size:Number,
                                     color:uint,
                                     height:Number = 0)
        {
            super(size);
            _color = color;
            _height = height;
            draw();
        }
```

```
/**
 * Draws the tile.
 */
protected function draw():void
{
    graphics.clear();
    graphics.beginFill(_color);
    graphics.lineStyle(0, 0, .5);
    graphics.moveTo(-size, 0);
    graphics.lineTo(0, -size * .5);
    graphics.lineTo(size, 0);
    graphics.lineTo(0, size * .5);
    graphics.lineTo(-size, 0);
}

/**
 * Sets / gets the height of this object.
 * Not used in this class, but can be used in subclasses.
 */
override public function set height(value:Number):void
{
    _height = value;
    draw();
}
override public function get height():Number
{
    return _height;
}

/**
 * Sets / gets the color of this tile.
 */
public function set color(value:uint):void
{
    _color = value;
    draw();
}
public function get color():uint
{
    return _color;
}
        }
    }
```

As you can see, this class adds color and height values to the constructor, which get passed to class properties. There are also getters and setters for these two values. Although the height value is not used in this class, it can be used in subclasses that draw solid blocks instead of just flat tiles.

The draw method is called by the constructor and any time the height or color is changed. It draws the 2:1 diamond shape that keeps reappearing in this chapter, using the specified color. Pretty simple, but it allows you to start creating larger isometric areas composed of multiple tiles, as seen in the following example, which you can find in the TileTest.as file:

```
package
{
    import com.friendsofed.isometric.DrawnIsoTile;
    import com.friendsofed.isometric.Point3D;

    import flash.display.Sprite;
    import flash.display.StageAlign;
    import flash.display.StageScaleMode;

    public class TileTest extends Sprite
    {
        public function TileTest()
        {
            stage.align = StageAlign.TOP_LEFT;
            stage.scaleMode = StageScaleMode.NO_SCALE;

            var world:Sprite = new Sprite();
            world.x = stage.stageWidth / 2;
            world.y = 100;
            addChild(world);

            for(var i:int = 0; i < 20; i++)
            {
                for(var j:int = 0; j < 20; j++)
                {
                    var tile:DrawnIsoTile =
                                new DrawnIsoTile(20, 0xcccccc);
                    tile.position = new Point3D(i * 20, 0, j * 20);
                    world.addChild(tile);
                }
            }
        }
    }
}
```

This code first creates a sprite called world, which acts as a holder for all the tiles, and allows us to position them all as a group. This is moved to the center of the screen horizontally and down somewhat from the top edge.

Then a double loop is run. In the body of the inner loop, a new DrawnIsoTile is created with a size of 20 and a default color. Its position is set on the x- and z-axis, as a multiple of the loop variables, and the tile is added to the world. When you run this, you should get something like Figure 3-11.

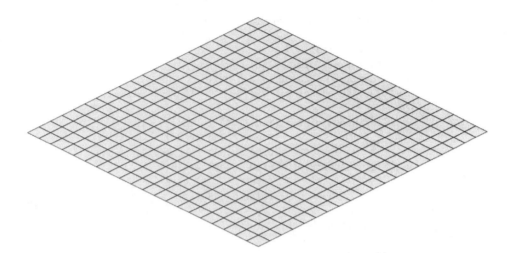

Figure 3-11. DrawnIsoTiles laid out in a grid

This is the basic setup for a tiled isometric world. You should experiment with this one a bit. Note that changing the length of the two loops controls the size of the resulting grid. Because the tiles' sizes are all 20, and they are each placed 20 units apart on the x- and z-axis, they line up perfectly. Try changing either of these values; you'll see that the tiles either overlap or are left with gaps between them. Normally you want them to tile seamlessly, of course, but it's good to know how to change it if you need to. You can also try fiddling with the y position. In the example, all tiles are set with a y of zero, so they form a flat surface. Try different methods of changing the y to see what you can come up with. Another thing to try is varying the colors somehow.

There's no need even to use the double loop and create a grid. Try arranging tiles by placing each one individually or coming up with some other algorithm to arrange them.

Tiles are good, but let's go a bit further and create a 3D isometric block with a variable height. When you get into 3D forms, you have to start thinking about lighting. An isometric block will have three visible faces, each pointing in a different direction. To enhance the illusion of space, each one should be shaded a bit differently. Usually there's a light source to the top left or top right, which makes the top surface the brightest, and the left or right faces each a bit less bright, depending on whether the light is to the left or right. In the DrawnIsoBox class (see the DrawnIsoBox.as file), I assume that the light source is off to the right, so the right face is medium brightness and the left face is a bit darker:

```
package com.friendsofed.isometric
{
    public class DrawnIsoBox extends DrawnIsoTile
    {

        public function DrawnIsoBox(size:Number,
                                    color:uint,
                                    height:Number)
        {
            super(size, color, height);
        }
```

```
override protected function draw():void
{
    graphics.clear();
    var red:int = _color >> 16;
    var green:int = _color >> 8 & 0xff;
    var blue:int = _color & 0xff;

    var leftShadow:uint = (red * .5) << 16 |
                          (green * .5) << 8 |
                          (blue * .5);
    var rightShadow:uint = (red * .75) << 16 |
                           (green * .75) << 8 |
                           (blue * .75);

    var h:Number = _height * Y_CORRECT;

    // draw top
    graphics.beginFill(_color);
    graphics.lineStyle(0, 0, .5);
    graphics.moveTo(-_size, -h);
    graphics.lineTo(0, -_size * .5 - h);
    graphics.lineTo(_size, -h);
    graphics.lineTo(0, _size * .5  - h);
    graphics.lineTo(-_size, -h);
    graphics.endFill();

    // draw left
    graphics.beginFill(leftShadow);
    graphics.lineStyle(0, 0, .5);
    graphics.moveTo(-_size, -h);
    graphics.lineTo(0, _size * .5 - h);
    graphics.lineTo(0, _size * .5);
    graphics.lineTo(-_size, 0);
    graphics.lineTo(-_size, -h);
    graphics.endFill();

    // draw right
    graphics.beginFill(rightShadow);
    graphics.lineStyle(0, 0, .5);
    graphics.moveTo(_size, -h);
    graphics.lineTo(0, _size * .5 - h);
    graphics.lineTo(0, _size * .5);
    graphics.lineTo(_size, 0);
    graphics.lineTo(_size, -h);
    graphics.endFill();
    }
  }
}
```

Because we pass in only a single color, the class separates the color into its component red, green, and blue values; reduces each component by a certain percentage; and recombines them into darker colors for the left and right faces. Another possibility is to draw each face in its own sprite or shape, and then adjust the color transformation values on the shapes used for the right and left panels. It can be even more flexible when allowing for dynamic lighting, but I'll leave that as an exercise for you and go on with this isometric stuff.

Another important thing to notice is the following line:

```
var h:Number = _height * Y_CORRECT;
```

This line takes the height that is passed in and converts it to an accurate transformed isometric height. Remember when we derived the isometric transformation formulas, we were left with this:

```
sx = x - z;
sy = y * 1.2247 + (x + z) * .5;
```

I mentioned that some implementations dropped that 1.2247, which works to a degree but leaves things a bit squashed. Well, because height is a y value, we need to apply that correction here, too, or the box will look squashed, too. This will mostly show up when attempting to create a cube. You make both the size and height the same value: 20, for example. You expect to see a cube, but it looks more like a cake box. Correcting the value allows you to make cube that looks like a cube.

Of course, now we need an example using the DrawnIsoBox class. It would be easy to convert the TileTest class by just changing the name of the class when the object is created, but this wouldn't be too interesting because the height is still defaulting to zero, so it would just look like a tile. You can change the height, but you'll just have a thick plane instead of a flat plane. Instead, let's do something a bit more interesting: using the screenToIso method of the IsoUtils class to capture mouse clicks and dynamically add boxes where we click. The next example can be downloaded as BoxTest.as:

```
package
{
    import com.friendsofed.isometric.DrawnIsoBox;
    import com.friendsofed.isometric.DrawnIsoTile;
    import com.friendsofed.isometric.IsoUtils;
    import com.friendsofed.isometric.Point3D;

    import flash.display.Sprite;
    import flash.display.StageAlign;
    import flash.display.StageScaleMode;
    import flash.events.MouseEvent;
    import flash.geom.Point;

    [SWF(backgroundColor=0xffffff)]
    public class BoxTest extends Sprite
    {
        private var world:Sprite;
        public function BoxTest()
```

```
                {
                    stage.align = StageAlign.TOP_LEFT;
                    stage.scaleMode = StageScaleMode.NO_SCALE;

                    world = new Sprite();
                    world.x = stage.stageWidth / 2;
                    world.y = 100;
                    addChild(world);

                    for(var i:int = 0; i < 20; i++)
                    {
                        for(var j:int = 0; j < 20; j++)
                        {
                            var tile:DrawnIsoTile =
                                        new DrawnIsoTile(20, 0xcccccc);
                            tile.position = new Point3D(i * 20, 0, j * 20);
                            world.addChild(tile);
                        }
                    }

                    world.addEventListener(MouseEvent.CLICK, onWorldClick);
                }

                private function onWorldClick(event:MouseEvent):void
                {
                    var box:DrawnIsoBox = new DrawnIsoBox(20, Math.random() *
                                                            0xffffff, 20);
                    var pos:Point3D =
                        IsoUtils.screenToIso(new Point(world.mouseX,
                                                        world.mouseY));
                    box.position = pos;
                    world.addChild(box);
                }

            }
        }
```

Most of the class is exactly the same as the TileTest class. After we create the grid of tiles, we add a mouse click event listener to the world sprite. When the world is clicked on, we create a new box, giving it a random color. Then we get the mouse coordinates from the world sprite and convert them to an isometric point and use it to set the box's position. Finally, we add the box to the world.

This class allows for a free form placement of the boxes. It might be good to align the new boxes with the existing tiles by rounding the x, y, and z values to the nearest multiple of 20:

```
private function onWorldClick(event:MouseEvent):void
{
    var box:DrawnIsoBox = new DrawnIsoBox(20, Math.random() *
                                     0xffffff, 20);
    var pos:Point3D = IsoUtils.screenToIso(new Point(world.mouseX,
                                     world.mouseY));
    pos.x = Math.round(pos.x / 20) * 20;
    pos.y = Math.round(pos.y / 20) * 20;
    pos.z = Math.round(pos.z / 20) * 20;
    box.position = pos;
    world.addChild(box);
}
```

Now when you click, the box that is created will snap to the grid created by the tiles, giving you something like Figure 3-12.

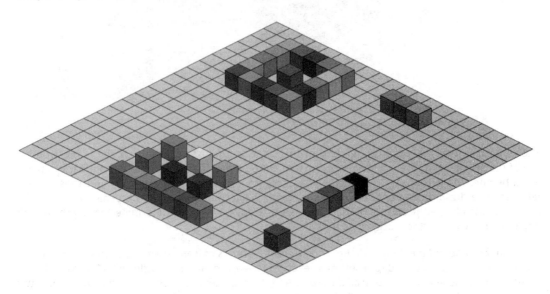

Figure 3-12. DrawnIsoBoxes on a grid of tiles

You've probably already noticed some problems as you experimented with this one. Most likely these problems had to do with depth sorting, which is exactly what will be covered next.

Depth Sorting

No doubt that as you clicked around in the last demo, you saw that boxes that should have been behind other boxes were occasionally incorrectly placed in front. An example can be seen in Figure 3-13.

Figure 3-13. Oops! Depth problem.

The problem is that the addChild method of the world sprite just puts the new child object on the top of the display list above everything else that might be there. If you draw boxes from back to front, you'll be fine. The two boxes on the right side of Figure 3-13 were drawn this way. But those on the left side were drawn from front to back, so although the second box should be behind the first one, addChild just plopped it on top. To handle this situation, we need to determine the depth of each object in the world and sort according to that.

Earlier in the chapter I mentioned that many different methods of isometric projection were out there. The situation with isometric depth sorting is even worse—everyone has a little "trick" to sort objects. I must have found at least a dozen, all different. And the arguments on various forums over which was the proper way to do it—epic battles! Many of these methods worked fairly well if all objects were on the same y value. But many also broke down as soon as you started dealing with objects at different heights.

I didn't want to just pass on some semiworkable "trick" that I didn't really understand. It seemed to me that the problem could be solved in a pretty straightforward mathematical manner.

Back when we discussed the rotational transforms that go into creating an isometric view (45 degrees on the y-axis, −30 degrees on the x-axis), we boiled it down to the following:

```
x1 = x - z
y1 = y * 1.2247 + (x + z) * .5
z2 = (x + z) * .866 - y  * .707
```

x1 and y1 were the transformed x and y coordinates and were used to determine the screen position of the point or object. z2 is the transformed z-axis coordinate. Although we brushed it aside at the time, we can now use it for depth sorting because it is what gives us the distance from the viewpoint. This is what all those tricks are trying to do, with various degrees of success. But this is the exact mathematical value and it will sort things perfectly, no matter where they are on any axis.

So this is what I used. If you take another look at the `IsoObject` class, you'll see this method:

```
/**
 * Returns the transformed 3D depth of this object.
 */
public function get depth():Number
{
    return (_position.x + _position.z) * .866 - _position.y * .707;
}
```

As you can see, this method calculates the transformed z value. I could have used more accurate values here, but because this method isn't actually used to visually render anything, only to compare two objects, these rounded-off values seemed adequate and quick.

The strategy is to put all the IsoObjects in an array and then sort the array based on the depth property. We can then rearrange the display list based on the order of the array. We'll have to sort the array and rearrange the display list every time an object is added. We'll do that in the next demo (available for download as the `DepthTest.as` file):

```
package
{
    import com.friendsofed.isometric.DrawnIsoBox;
    import com.friendsofed.isometric.DrawnIsoTile;
    import com.friendsofed.isometric.IsoUtils;
    import com.friendsofed.isometric.Point3D;

    import flash.display.Sprite;
    import flash.display.StageAlign;
    import flash.display.StageScaleMode;
    import flash.events.MouseEvent;
    import flash.geom.Point;

    [SWF(backgroundColor=0xffffff)]
    public class DepthTest extends Sprite
    {
        private var world:Sprite;
        private var objectList:Array;

        public function DepthTest()
        {
            stage.align = StageAlign.TOP_LEFT;
            stage.scaleMode = StageScaleMode.NO_SCALE;
```

```
                    world = new Sprite();
                    world.x = stage.stageWidth / 2;
                    world.y = 100;
                    addChild(world);

                    objectList = new Array();

                    for(var i:int = 0; i < 20; i++)
                    {
                        for(var j:int = 0; j < 20; j++)
                        {
                            var tile:DrawnIsoTile =
                                        new DrawnIsoTile(20, 0xcccccc);
                            tile.position = new Point3D(i * 20, 0, j * 20);
                            world.addChild(tile);
                            objectList.push(tile);
                        }
                    }
                    sortList();
                    world.addEventListener(MouseEvent.CLICK, onWorldClick);
                }

                private function onWorldClick(event:MouseEvent):void
                {
                    var box:DrawnIsoBox = new DrawnIsoBox(20, Math.random() *
                                                    0xffffff, 20);
                    var pos:Point3D =
                                IsoUtils.screenToIso(new Point(world.mouseX,
                                                        world.mouseY));
                    pos.x = Math.round(pos.x / 20) * 20;
                    pos.y = Math.round(pos.y / 20) * 20;
                    pos.z = Math.round(pos.z / 20) * 20;
                    box.position = pos;
                    world.addChild(box);
                    objectList.push(box);
                    sortList();
                }

                private function sortList():void
                {
                    objectList.sortOn("depth", Array.NUMERIC);
                    for(var i:int = 0; i < objectList.length; i++)
                    {
                        world.setChildIndex(objectList[i], i);
                    }
                }
            }
        }
    }
```

Here, we create an array called objectList. Each tile and each box are added to the array, and the sortList method is run. This method sorts the array on the depth property. Don't forget to specify Array.NUMERIC or it will sort the array as string values, evaluating "70" as greater than "100". (I'm embarrassed to say how many hours I wasted trying to debug that one!)

One caveat for isometric depth sorting is that it relies on objects in the world being the same size (by *size* I mean the size property of the IsoObject class that defines the object's square footprint on the x-z plane). Objects can be any height without causing a problem, but should not be wider or deeper than other objects in the world. You can usually get away with making one or two character objects being smaller than the rest of the tiles, but you should usually choose a standard object size and stick with it. I've seen a few attempts to make an isometric world with varying object sizes. They usually result in fantastically complex depth sorting that nobody other than the original programmer really understands and is usually quite error prone. Or they wind up imposing additional complex restrictions on object shapes and positions to make up for the standard tile size restriction. The better way to make large objects is to split them up into multiple objects, each one the standard size.

This last example results in the boxes being perfectly sorted, no matter where you place them. However, it seems that occasionally the tiles appear on top of the boxes. This is because when boxes are placed "on top of" a tile, they actually have the exact same x, y, z position—meaning that their transformed depths are also exactly the same. So from a sorting viewpoint, it doesn't really matter which goes first. There are two ways to handle it: put the tiles slightly lower or put the boxes slightly higher. It doesn't have to be much—not enough to be visible, but enough to affect the depth calculation. You can do that in the line that creates the tiles:

```
tile.position = new Point3D(i * 20, 0.1, j * 20);
```

Setting the y of each tile to 0.1 is enough to put it below the boxes, but not move it visibly.

Another somewhat more complex (but more efficient) way is to have two different world sprites—one for the tiles and one for the boxes. You don't really need to sort all those 400 tiles every time. They aren't moving, and you always want all the tiles to be under all the boxes. So put them in their own sprite and put that sprite under the sprite that holds the boxes. Put only the boxes in the objectList and sort them. Here's the revised class, as found in the DepthTest2.as file:

```
package
{
    import com.friendsofed.isometric.DrawnIsoBox;
    import com.friendsofed.isometric.DrawnIsoTile;
    import com.friendsofed.isometric.IsoUtils;
    import com.friendsofed.isometric.Point3D;

    import flash.display.Sprite;
    import flash.display.StageAlign;
    import flash.display.StageScaleMode;
    import flash.events.MouseEvent;
    import flash.geom.Point;
```

```
[SWF(backgroundColor=0xffffff)]
public class DepthTest2 extends Sprite
{
    private var floor:Sprite;
    private var world:Sprite;
    private var objectList:Array;

    public function DepthTest2()
    {
        stage.align = StageAlign.TOP_LEFT;
        stage.scaleMode = StageScaleMode.NO_SCALE;

        floor = new Sprite();
        floor.x = stage.stageWidth / 2;
        floor.y = 100;
        addChild(floor);

        world = new Sprite();
        world.x = stage.stageWidth / 2;
        world.y = 100;
        addChild(world);

        objectList = new Array();

        for(var i:int = 0; i < 20; i++)
        {
            for(var j:int = 0; j < 20; j++)
            {
                var tile:DrawnIsoTile =
                            new DrawnIsoTile(20, 0xcccccc);
                tile.position = new Point3D(i * 20, 0, j * 20);
                floor.addChild(tile);
            }
        }
        stage.addEventListener(MouseEvent.CLICK, onWorldClick);
    }

    private function onWorldClick(event:MouseEvent):void
    {
        var box:DrawnIsoBox = new DrawnIsoBox(20, Math.random() *
                                        0xffffff, 20);
        var pos:Point3D =
                    IsoUtils.screenToIso(new Point(world.mouseX,
                                            world.mouseY));
        pos.x = Math.round(pos.x / 20) * 20;
        pos.y = Math.round(pos.y / 20) * 20;
        pos.z = Math.round(pos.z / 20) * 20;
```

```
            box.position = pos;
            world.addChild(box);
            objectList.push(box);
            sortList();
        }

        private function sortList():void
        {
            objectList.sortOn("depth", Array.NUMERIC);
            for(var i:int = 0; i < objectList.length; i++)
            {
                world.setChildIndex(objectList[i], i);
            }
        }
    }
}
```

Here, a floor sprite is created and placed in the same position as the world sprite. Because it is added to the display list first, it will be under the world sprite. All the tiles are added to the floor. They are not pushed onto the objectList because they don't need to be sorted.

I changed the mouse click handler to listen for clicks on the stage because the world sprite will at first be empty and won't receive any mouse clicks. Other than that, all the code is the same.

The next step will consolidate a lot of what we just did into a reusable world class.

Isometric World Class

Because most of what we have been doing in terms of creating a floor sprite, a world sprite, and object list and sorting algorithm will be something you'll probably want to do in most projects you do, it makes sense to create a class that handles it all in a generic way that can be used on each project. This is the IsoWorld class, downloadable as the IsoWorld.as file:

```
package com.friendsofed.isometric
{
    import flash.display.Sprite;
    import flash.geom.Rectangle;

    public class IsoWorld extends Sprite
    {
        private var _floor:Sprite;
        private var _objects:Array;
        private var _world:Sprite;

        public function IsoWorld()
        {
            _floor = new Sprite();
            addChild(_floor);
```

```
            _world = new Sprite();
            addChild(_world);

            _objects = new Array();
        }

        public function addChildToWorld(child:IsoObject):void
        {
            _world.addChild(child);
            _objects.push(child);
            sort();
        }

        public function addChildToFloor(child:IsoObject):void
        {
            _floor.addChild(child);
        }

        public function sort():void
        {
            _objects.sortOn("depth", Array.NUMERIC);
            for(var i:int = 0; i < _objects.length; i++)
            {
                _world.setChildIndex(_objects[i], i);
            }
        }
    }
}
```

Most of this is exactly what we did in the last example: it creates a floor sprite, a world sprite, and an object list; and handles sorting. It provides two methods for adding objects. The addChildToFloor method puts an object in the floor sprite, not the object list, and does not sort. Floors are assumed to be flat tiles created in nonoverlapping grids, so sorting should not be necessary. The addChildToWorld method adds the object to the world sprite and the object list, sorts the list, and rearranges the display list. We'll be adding some additional functionality to this class later to assist in collision detection.

Using the IsoWorld class is pretty easy, as seen in the example found in the WorldTest.as file:

```
package
{
    import com.friendsofed.isometric.DrawnIsoBox;
    import com.friendsofed.isometric.DrawnIsoTile;
    import com.friendsofed.isometric.IsoUtils;
    import com.friendsofed.isometric.IsoWorld;
    import com.friendsofed.isometric.Point3D;

    import flash.display.Sprite;
    import flash.display.StageAlign;
```

```
import flash.display.StageScaleMode;
import flash.events.MouseEvent;
import flash.geom.Point;

[SWF(backgroundColor=0xffffff)]
public class WorldTest extends Sprite
{
    private var world:IsoWorld;

    public function WorldTest()
    {
        stage.align = StageAlign.TOP_LEFT;
        stage.scaleMode = StageScaleMode.NO_SCALE;

        world = new IsoWorld();
        world.x = stage.stageWidth / 2;
        world.y = 100;
        addChild(world);

        for(var i:int = 0; i < 20; i++)
        {
            for(var j:int = 0; j < 20; j++)
            {
                var tile:DrawnIsoTile =
                            new DrawnIsoTile(20, 0xcccccc);
                tile.position = new Point3D(i * 20, 0, j * 20);
                world.addChildToFloor(tile);
            }
        }
        stage.addEventListener(MouseEvent.CLICK, onWorldClick);
    }

    private function onWorldClick(event:MouseEvent):void
    {
        var box:DrawnIsoBox = new DrawnIsoBox(20, Math.random() *
                                        0xffffff, 20);
        var pos:Point3D =
                    IsoUtils.screenToIso(new Point(world.mouseX,
                                            world.mouseY));
        pos.x = Math.round(pos.x / 20) * 20;
        pos.y = Math.round(pos.y / 20) * 20;
        pos.z = Math.round(pos.z / 20) * 20;
        box.position = pos;
        world.addChildToWorld(box);
    }
}
```

In fact, this file is almost identical to the original BoxTest class, with world being an IsoWorld instead of a Sprite, and addChildToFloor and addChildToWorld being used instead of addChild. But IsoWorld takes care of creating separate sprites and doing all the sorting.

Moving in 3D

Motion itself is not much of a big deal in isometric 3D, especially when you have a class such as IsoObject that automatically takes care of converting 3D coordinates to screen positions. You just change any property (x, y, or z), and the object then moves to the correct screen position. The only thing to remember is that each time you move an object, you need to call the sort method of the IsoWorld (or otherwise update your depth-sorting routine if you are not using IsoWorld) to account for the fact that the object might be at a different depth.

From there, it's pretty easy to implement just about any kind of motion: basic velocity, acceleration, gravity, friction, bouncing, easing, springs, and so on (as described in *Making Things Move*). In fact, just to make things tidy, I'm going to add three new properties to IsoObject to handle velocity:

```
protected var _vx:Number = 0;
protected var _vy:Number = 0;
protected var _vz:Number = 0;
```

And I'll add some getters and setters for them:

```
/**
 * Sets / gets the velocity on the x axis.
 */
public function set vx(value:Number):void
{
    _vx = value;
}
public function get vx():Number
{
    return _vx;
}

/**
 * Sets / gets the velocity on the y axis.
 */
public function set vy(value:Number):void
{
    _vy = value;
}
public function get vy():Number
{
    return _vy;
}
```

```
/**
 * Sets / gets the velocity on the z axis.
 */
public function set vz(value:Number):void
{
    _vz = value;
}
public function get vz():Number
{
    return _vz;
}
```

The most obvious thing is to set up some keyboard event listeners and move an object based on what key is being pressed. The following demo, found in the `MotionTest.as` downloadable file, does just that:

```
package
{
    import com.friendsofed.isometric.DrawnIsoBox;
    import com.friendsofed.isometric.DrawnIsoTile;
    import com.friendsofed.isometric.IsoWorld;
    import com.friendsofed.isometric.Point3D;

    import flash.display.Sprite;
    import flash.display.StageAlign;
    import flash.display.StageScaleMode;
    import flash.events.Event;
    import flash.events.KeyboardEvent;
    import flash.ui.Keyboard;

    [SWF(backgroundColor=0xffffff)]
    public class MotionTest extends Sprite
    {
        private var world:IsoWorld;
        private var box:DrawnIsoBox;
        private var speed:Number = 20;

        public function MotionTest()
        {
            stage.align = StageAlign.TOP_LEFT;
            stage.scaleMode = StageScaleMode.NO_SCALE;

            world = new IsoWorld();
            world.x = stage.stageWidth / 2;
            world.y = 100;
            addChild(world);
```

```
            for(var i:int = 0; i < 20; i++)
            {
                for(var j:int = 0; j < 20; j++)
                {
                    var tile:DrawnIsoTile =
                                new DrawnIsoTile(20, 0xcccccc);
                    tile.position = new Point3D(i * 20, 0, j * 20);
                    world.addChildToFloor(tile);
                }
            }

            box = new DrawnIsoBox(20, 0xff0000, 20);
            box.x = 200;
            box.z = 200;
            world.addChildToWorld(box);

            stage.addEventListener(KeyboardEvent.KEY_DOWN, onKeyDown);
            stage.addEventListener(KeyboardEvent.KEY_UP, onKeyUp);
        }

        private function onKeyDown(event:KeyboardEvent):void
        {
            switch(event.keyCode)
            {
                case Keyboard.UP :
                box.vx = -speed;
                break;

                case Keyboard.DOWN :
                box.vx = speed;
                break;

                case Keyboard.LEFT :
                box.vz = speed;
                break;

                case Keyboard.RIGHT :
                box.vz = -speed;
                break;

                default :
                break;

            }
            addEventListener(Event.ENTER_FRAME, onEnterFrame);
        }
```

```
        private function onKeyUp(event:KeyboardEvent):void
        {
            box.vx = 0;
            box.vz = 0;
            removeEventListener(Event.ENTER_FRAME, onEnterFrame);
        }

        private function onEnterFrame(event:Event):void
        {
            box.x += box.vx;
            box.y += box.vy;
            box.z += box.vz;
            world.sort();
        }
    }
}
```

This is pretty straightforward. A tile floor is put in place, and a box is on top of it. Listeners are set up for key up and key down events. If any of the cursor keys is pressed, the box's vx or vz is set accordingly. In the onEnterFrame method, the box's velocity values are added to its position. Simple enough. Don't forget to sort the world after each move, as you can see in the last line of onEnterFrame. Actually, in this case (with only a single object in the world) it is not so important, but it's a good habit to get into.

The speed is initially set to 20, so the box moves a full tile space on each move. Try changing that to a lower value to have it move at a slower rate.

Just to show you can do just about any other type of motion of physics, here's a more advanced demo, which you can get it as the MotionTest2.as file:

```
package
{
    import com.friendsofed.isometric.DrawnIsoBox;
    import com.friendsofed.isometric.DrawnIsoTile;
    import com.friendsofed.isometric.IsoWorld;
    import com.friendsofed.isometric.Point3D;

    import flash.display.Sprite;
    import flash.display.StageAlign;
    import flash.display.StageScaleMode;
    import flash.events.Event;
    import flash.events.MouseEvent;
    import flash.filters.BlurFilter;

    [SWF(backgroundColor=0xffffff)]
    public class MotionTest2 extends Sprite
    {
        private var world:IsoWorld;
        private var box:DrawnIsoBox;
```

```
private var shadow:DrawnIsoTile;
private var gravity:Number = 2;
private var friction:Number = 0.95;
private var bounce:Number = -0.9;
private var filter:BlurFilter;

public function MotionTest2()
{
    stage.align = StageAlign.TOP_LEFT;
    stage.scaleMode = StageScaleMode.NO_SCALE;

    world = new IsoWorld();
    world.x = stage.stageWidth / 2;
    world.y = 100;
    addChild(world);

    for(var i:int = 0; i < 20; i++)
    {
        for(var j:int = 0; j < 20; j++)
        {
            var tile:DrawnIsoTile =
                        new DrawnIsoTile(20, 0xcccccc);
            tile.position = new Point3D(i * 20, 0, j * 20);
            world.addChildToFloor(tile);
        }
    }

    box = new DrawnIsoBox(20, 0xff0000, 20);
    box.x = 200;
    box.z = 200;
    world.addChildToWorld(box);

    shadow = new DrawnIsoTile(20, 0);
    shadow.alpha = .5;
    world.addChildToFloor(shadow);

    filter = new BlurFilter();

    addEventListener(Event.ENTER_FRAME, onEnterFrame);
    stage.addEventListener(MouseEvent.CLICK, onClick);
}

private function onClick(event:MouseEvent):void
{
    box.vx = Math.random() * 20 - 10;
    box.vy = -Math.random() * 40;
    box.vz = Math.random() * 20 - 10;
}
```

```
private function onEnterFrame(event:Event):void
{
    box.vy += 2;
    box.x += box.vx;
    box.y += box.vy;
    box.z += box.vz;
    if(box.x > 380)
    {
        box.x = 380;
        box.vx *= -.8;
    }
    else if(box.x < 0)
    {
        box.x = 0;
        box.vx *= bounce;
    }
    if(box.z > 380)
    {
        box.z = 380;
        box.vz *= bounce;
    }
    else if(box.z < 0)
    {
        box.z = 0;
        box.vz *= bounce;
    }
    if(box.y > 0)
    {
        box.y = 0;
        box.vy *= bounce;
    }
    box.vx *= friction;
    box.vy *= friction;
    box.vz *= friction;

    shadow.x = box.x;
    shadow.z = box.z;
    filter.blurX = filter.blurY = -box.y * .25;
    shadow.filters = [filter];
    world.sort();
}
}
}
```

This demo makes use of gravity, bouncing, and friction, as well as motion on the y-axis. When the mouse is clicked, the box gets a random velocity on each axis. When the box goes past zero on the y-axis or beyond any edge of the plane on the x-axis or z-axis, it bounces back. Some friction is also applied.

I also threw in a shadow in the form of a DrawnIsoTile at 50% alpha. This is put on the floor layer, but moved to the same x and z position as the block on each frame. It's also blurred based on the box's height, so it gets fuzzier as the box is higher. Not too complex and it makes a nice illusion.

So far, so good in this nice isolated world with only a single object. What happens when we throw some more objects into the mix? That's what we'll look at next.

Collision Detection

To see why collision detection is important, take the first MotionTest class and another box or two like so:

```
var newBox:DrawnIsoBox = new DrawnIsoBox(20, 0xcccccc, 20);
newBox.x = 300;
newBox.z = 300;
world.addChildToWorld(newBox);
```

They don't have to move or anything; they can just sit there on the grid. Now move the movable box around until it hits one of the new boxes. Not pretty, is it? The boxes will go right through each other and will look fairly horrible in the process. In many cases it will look more like the moving box is going under the stationary box. It appears as if the depth sorting has suddenly broken. But what's really happening is that two objects are trying to occupy the same space. When this happens in the real world, we get a bent fender or a stubbed toe. In an isometric simulation, we get a busted depth sort.

To handle this situation, we need some way of knowing where an object can move and where it can't. Because the IsoWorld class holds a list of all objects in the world, that's a good place to put that functionality. We'll call this method canMove. Here it is:

```
public function canMove(obj:IsoObject):Boolean
{
    var rect:Rectangle = obj.rect;
    rect.offset(obj.vx, obj.vz);

    for(var i:int = 0; i < _objects.length; i++)
    {
        var objB:IsoObject = _objects[i] as IsoObject;
        if(obj != objB && objB.walkable && rect.intersects(objB.rect))
        {
            return false;
        }
    }
    return true;
}
```

The method takes an IsoObject instance and returns whether or not it is safe for that object to move to the position it would be in if its x and z velocity were added to its position.

If you look back to the IsoObject class, you'll remember that it has a rect property that is an instance of flash.geom.Rectangle. It represents the footprint of the object on the x-z plane. We take the rect from the object that has been passed in and offset it by the amount of the x, z velocities of the object. This rect will now represent the object's footprint if it makes its next move.

We then loop through the list of objects in the world. We want to check for three conditions:

- First, that the object being checked is not the object being passed in. You don't want to hit test an object against itself.

- Second, that the object being checked is marked as not walkable (**walkable** means that another object can occupy the same space as that tile). There may be times when an object in the world is just a flat tile that can be walked on, just like a floor tile. Or perhaps a tile is up on the y-axis and it's possible for another object to "walk" underneath it.

- Third, that the offset rectangle we just computed does not intersect with the rect of the object being checked, which is easy to do with the built-in intersects method of the Rectangle class.

If all three of these conditions are true for any object in the list, the object cannot move to a new position based on its x and z velocity. We return false immediately. However, if we make it through the whole list without getting a hit, it is safe to move, and we return true.

The way this is used is to check canMove before adding the velocity to the position. Here's the full example, as seen in the CollisionTest.as file on the book's download page:

```
package
{
    import com.friendsofed.isometric.DrawnIsoBox;
    import com.friendsofed.isometric.DrawnIsoTile;
    import com.friendsofed.isometric.IsoWorld;
    import com.friendsofed.isometric.Point3D;

    import flash.display.Sprite;
    import flash.display.StageAlign;
    import flash.display.StageScaleMode;
    import flash.events.Event;
    import flash.events.KeyboardEvent;
    import flash.ui.Keyboard;

    [SWF(backgroundColor=0xffffff)]
    public class CollisionTest extends Sprite
    {
        private var world:IsoWorld;
        private var box:DrawnIsoBox;
        private var speed:Number = 4;

        public function CollisionTest()
        {
            stage.align = StageAlign.TOP_LEFT;
            stage.scaleMode = StageScaleMode.NO_SCALE;
```

```
        world = new IsoWorld();
        world.x = stage.stageWidth / 2;
        world.y = 100;
        addChild(world);

        for(var i:int = 0; i < 20; i++)
        {
            for(var j:int = 0; j < 20; j++)
            {
                var tile:DrawnIsoTile =
                            new DrawnIsoTile(20, 0xcccccc);
                tile.position = new Point3D(i * 20, 0, j * 20);
                world.addChildToFloor(tile);
            }
        }

        box = new DrawnIsoBox(20, 0xff0000, 20);
        box.x = 200;
        box.z = 200;
        world.addChildToWorld(box);

        var newBox:DrawnIsoBox = new DrawnIsoBox(20, 0xcccccc, 20);
        newBox.x = 300;
        newBox.z = 300;
        world.addChildToWorld(newBox);

        stage.addEventListener(KeyboardEvent.KEY_DOWN, onKeyDown);
        stage.addEventListener(KeyboardEvent.KEY_UP, onKeyUp);
    }

    private function onKeyDown(event:KeyboardEvent):void
    {
        switch(event.keyCode)
        {
            case Keyboard.UP :
            box.vx = -speed;
            break;

            case Keyboard.DOWN :
            box.vx = speed;
            break;

            case Keyboard.LEFT :
            box.vz = speed;
            break;

            case Keyboard.RIGHT :
            box.vz = -speed;
            break;
```

```
                default :
                break;

        }
        addEventListener(Event.ENTER_FRAME, onEnterFrame);
    }

    private function onKeyUp(event:KeyboardEvent):void
    {
        box.vx = 0;
        box.vz = 0;
        removeEventListener(Event.ENTER_FRAME, onEnterFrame);
    }

    private function onEnterFrame(event:Event):void
    {
        if(world.canMove(box))
        {
            box.x += box.vx;
            box.y += box.vy;
            box.z += box.vz;
        }
        world.sort();
    }
  }
}
```

As you can see, the only change here is wrapping the motion code in an if statement to see whether it is safe to move. I also cut the speed down to a low number so you can see that the collision detection is nice and accurate.

And that about covers the basic physics of our isometric engine. The final two sections cover integrating external graphics and designing the layouts of your isometric worlds.

Using External Graphics

The DrawnIsoTile and DrawnIsoBox classes are great for testing and development, but would get old pretty quickly in a real game. More likely, you or your graphic designer will make some more detailed isometric objects in some graphics program such as PhotoShop, Fireworks, or even Flash. You'll need some way to get those graphics into an IsoObject. For this, we now have the GraphicTile class, which you can download as the GraphicTile.as file:

```
package com.friendsofed.isometric
{
    import flash.display.DisplayObject;

    public class GraphicTile extends IsoObject
    {
```

```
        public function GraphicTile(size:Number,
                                    classRef:Class,
                                    xoffset:Number,
                                    yoffset:Number):void
    {
        super(size);
        var gfx:DisplayObject = new classRef() as DisplayObject;
        gfx.x = -xoffset;
        gfx.y = -yoffset;
        addChild(gfx);
    }
  }
}
```

As you can see, this class extends IsoObject and in addition to size, it takes a class reference and an x and y offset. The class reference is a class that is linked to some graphic. Usually this would be done via an embed metadata statement, as covered in *Making Things Move*. But it could also be some other class that extends a visible display object—such as Sprite, Shape, MovieClip, or Bitmap—with code to draw some type of graphic in itself. In any case, the constructor of GraphicTile creates an instance of this class and adds it to its own display list. It then moves it according to the two offset values passed in.

To see how this all works and why the offsets are there, let's first look at some external graphics. I'm no great isometric artist, but I fired up Fireworks and threw together a couple of tiles. The first one is a simple tile, canvas size 40×20, the familiar diamond shape filled with a wood grain texture (see Figure 3-14). I have no doubt you can do *much* better! This tile is saved as tile_01.png in the same directory as the main class.

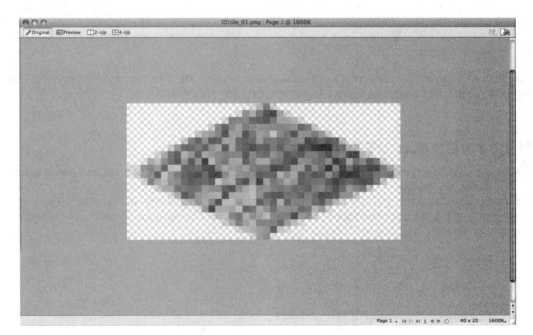

Figure 3-14. A simple isometric tile in Fireworks

The second graphic is a bit larger and more detailed. It is 40×40 with a simple cube, but I added a door and window to make it a house. If you haven't guessed, I spent a lot more time on writing and coding than I did on creating graphics for this section. Anyway, this was saved as tile_02.png (see Figure 3-15).

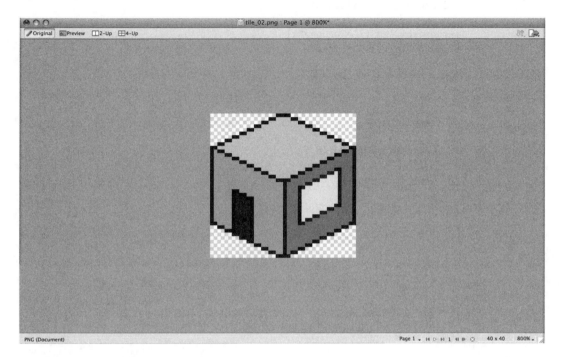

Figure 3-15. Another Fireworks isometric object

For the example (GraphicTest.as file), I reused the WorldTest class, changing the tile types to GraphicTile. I embedded the two graphics I just saved and passed in those classes to the GraphicTile constructor:

```
package
{
    import com.friendsofed.isometric.GraphicTile;
    import com.friendsofed.isometric.IsoUtils;
    import com.friendsofed.isometric.IsoWorld;
    import com.friendsofed.isometric.Point3D;

    import flash.display.Sprite;
    import flash.display.StageAlign;
    import flash.display.StageScaleMode;
    import flash.events.MouseEvent;
    import flash.geom.Point;

    [SWF(backgroundColor=0xffffff)]
    public class GraphicTest extends Sprite
```

```
{
    private var world:IsoWorld;

    [Embed(source="tile_01.png")]
    private var Tile01:Class;

    [Embed(source="tile_02.png")]
    private var Tile02:Class;

    public function GraphicTest()
    {
        stage.align = StageAlign.TOP_LEFT;
        stage.scaleMode = StageScaleMode.NO_SCALE;

        world = new IsoWorld();
        world.x = stage.stageWidth / 2;
        world.y = 100;
        addChild(world);

        for(var i:int = 0; i < 20; i++)
        {
            for(var j:int = 0; j < 20; j++)
            {
                var tile:GraphicTile = new GraphicTile(20, Tile01,
                                                    20, 10);
                tile.position = new Point3D(i * 20, 0, j * 20);
                world.addChildToFloor(tile);
            }
        }
        stage.addEventListener(MouseEvent.CLICK, onWorldClick);
    }

    private function onWorldClick(event:MouseEvent):void
    {
        var box:GraphicTile = new GraphicTile(20, Tile02, 20, 30);
        var pos:Point3D =
                    IsoUtils.screenToIso(new Point(world.mouseX,
                                                world.mouseY));
        pos.x = Math.round(pos.x / 20) * 20;
        pos.y = Math.round(pos.y / 20) * 20;
        pos.z = Math.round(pos.z / 20) * 20;
        box.position = pos;
        world.addChildToWorld(box);
    }
}
}
```

So, back to the question: what are those two offsets all about? Well, the way we've been creating all our graphics thus far is with the center point of the tile as the registration point. In other words, when we place a tile at a certain screen x, y position, the tile is centered around that point. If the tile has height, it extends upward from that point.

But when graphics are embedded, instantiated, and added to a display list, their registration point is the top left and they will extend down and to the right. So we need to move the tile up and to the left so that it is centered on that registration point. The first tile, tile_01.png, is 40×20 and is a simple flat tile, so we need to move it 20 pixels to the left and 10 pixels up in order to center it. The other one, tile_02.png, is a bit more complex. The x offset is again 20 pixels to center the tile horizontally, but we actually need to move it up 30 pixels to center the bottom face of the cube on the registration point. So its offsets are 20, 30.

When you run this demo, you'll see the luxurious wood grain floor (okay, it looks more like a badly rendered sand). Clicking on that, you will start building a small village of identical houses, giving you something like the one in Figure 3-16.

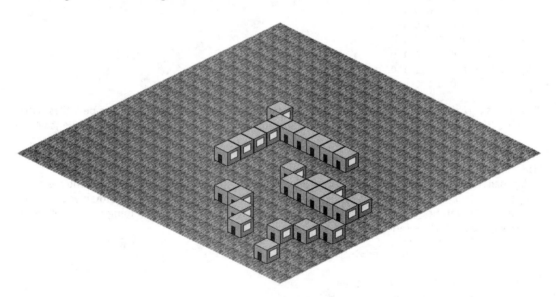

Figure 3-16. GraphicTile in action

Now that we have a way of getting just about any type of graphics into our tiles, we just need a way to specify the layouts of all these tiles.

Isometric Tile Maps

Well we have a nice little isometric engine going. We can position tiles, move them with all kinds of physics, pick up 3D mouse clicks, sort on depths, do collision detection, import any kind of graphics, and so on. Pretty much all the basics we need to start putting together a decent game. The one thing that would be really helpful at this stage is some way to specify and build a world without hard-coding all the positions and types of objects, and then later being able to edit and change the world without recompiling the whole project.

This can all be accomplished with **tile maps**, which are simple text files that map out what types of tiles we want to go where. Here's a simple tile map:

```
0 0 0 0 0 0 0 0 0 0
0 1 1 1 1 1 1 1 1 0
0 1 0 0 0 0 0 0 1 0
0 1 0 0 0 0 0 0 1 0
0 1 0 0 0 0 0 0 1 0
0 1 0 0 0 0 0 0 1 0
0 1 0 0 0 0 0 0 1 0
0 1 0 0 0 0 0 0 1 0
0 1 1 1 1 1 1 1 0
0 0 0 0 0 0 0 0 0 0
```

This shows a 10×10 grid of tiles, mostly of type 0, with an inner square made up of type 1 tiles. What are type 0 and type 1 tiles? That's up to you. Basically, you edit this map text file and save it where your game or application can get to it. The application loads and parses it, and then loops through it, creating tiles and adding them to the world. It's up to you to tell it that type 0 means a DrawnIsoTile, size 20, color 0xcccccc, and walkable (for example). To make this process even simpler, I created a MapLoader class that loads in a specified map file and allows you to register different tile types with different characters. It fires an event when the map is loaded and parsed, and then you can pull a ready-made world out of it. Nothing could be easier. Well, I suppose something could, but this is a pretty good start. Here's the class, as seen in the MapLoader.as file:

```
package com.friendsofed.isometric
{
    import flash.events.Event;
    import flash.events.EventDispatcher;
    import flash.net.URLLoader;
    import flash.net.URLRequest;
    import flash.utils.getDefinitionByName;

    public class MapLoader extends EventDispatcher
    {
        private var _grid:Array;
        private var _loader:URLLoader;
        private var _tileTypes:Object;
```

```
public function MapLoader()
{
    _tileTypes = new Object();
}

/**
 * Loads a text file from the specified url.
 * @param url The location of the text file to load.
 */
public function loadMap(url:String):void
{
    _loader = new URLLoader();
    _loader.addEventListener(Event.COMPLETE, onLoad);
    _loader.load(new URLRequest(url));
}

/**
 * Parses text file into tile definitions and map.
 */
private function onLoad(event:Event):void
{
    _grid = new Array();
    var data:String = _loader.data;

    // first get each line of the file.
    var lines:Array = data.split("\n");
    for(var i:int = 0; i < lines.length; i++)
    {
        var line:String = lines[i];

        // if line is a tile type definition.
        if(isDefinition(line))
        {
            parseDefinition(line);
        }
        // otherwise, if line is not empty and not a comment,
        // it's a list of tile types. add them to grid.
        else if(!lineIsEmpty(line) && !isComment(line))
        {
            var cells:Array = line.split(" ");
            _grid.push(cells);
        }
    }
    dispatchEvent(new Event(Event.COMPLETE));
}
```

```
private function parseDefinition(line:String):void
{
    // break apart the line into tokens
    var tokens:Array = line.split(" ");

    // get rid of #
    tokens.shift();

    // first token is the symbol
    var symbol:String = tokens.shift() as String;

    // loop through the rest of the tokens,
    // which are key/value pairs separated by :
    var definition:Object = new Object();
    for(var i:int = 0; i < tokens.length; i++)
    {
        var key:String = tokens[i].split(":")[0];
        var val:String = tokens[i].split(":")[1];
        definition[key] = val;
    }

    // register the type and definition
    setTileType(symbol, definition);
}

/**
 * Links a symbol with a definition object.
 * @param symbol The character to use for the definition.
 * @param definition An object with definition properties
 */
public function setTileType(symbol:String,
                            definition:Object):void
{
    _tileTypes[symbol] = definition;
}

/**
 * Creates an IsoWorld, iterates through loaded map,
 * adding tiles to it based on map and definitions.
 * @size The tile size to use when making the world.
 * @return A fully populated IsoWorld instance.
 */
public function makeWorld(size:Number):IsoWorld
{
    var world:IsoWorld = new IsoWorld();
    for(var i:int = 0; i < _grid.length; i++)
    {
        for(var j:int = 0; j < _grid[i].length; j++)
        {
```

```
                    var cellType:String = _grid[i][j];
                    var cell:Object = _tileTypes[cellType];
                    var tile:IsoObject;
                    switch(cell.type)
                    {
                        case  "DrawnIsoTile" :
                        tile = new DrawnIsoTile(size,
                                            parseInt(cell.color),
                                            parseInt(cell.height));
                        break;

                        case  "DrawnIsoBox" :
                        tile = new DrawnIsoBox(size,
                                            parseInt(cell.color),
                                            parseInt(cell.height));
                        break;

                        case  "GraphicTile" :
                        var graphicClass:Class = getDefinitionByName(
                                            cell.graphicClass
                                          ) as Class;
                        tile = new GraphicTile(size,
                                            graphicClass,
                                            parseInt(cell.xoffset),
                                            parseInt(cell.yoffset));
                        break;

                        default :
                        tile = new IsoObject(size);
                        break;
                    }
                    tile.walkable = cell.walkable == "true";
                    tile.x = j * size;
                    tile.z = i * size;
                    world.addChild(tile);
                }
            }
        return world;
}

/**
 * Returns true if line contains only spaces.
 * @param line The string to test.
 */
private function lineIsEmpty(line:String):Boolean
{
    for(var i:int = 0; i < line.length; i++)
```

```
            {
                if(line.charAt(i) != " ") return false;
            }
            return true;
        }

        /**
         * Returns true if line is a comment (starts with //).
         * @param line The string to test.
         */
        private function isComment(line:String):Boolean
        {
            return line.indexOf("//") == 0;
        }

        /**
         * Returns true if line is a definition (starts with #).
         * @param line The string to test.
         */
        private function isDefinition(line:String):Boolean
        {
            return line.indexOf("#") == 0;
        }
    }
}
```

This is a fairly complex class, but it makes building a world so much easier. It starts by loading the text file specified in the argument of the loadMap method. Let's look at a sample map file:

```
// this is a comment.

# 0 type:GraphicTile graphicClass:MapTest_Tile01 xoffset:20 yoffset:10➥
walkable:true
# 1 type:GraphicTile graphicClass:MapTest_Tile02 xoffset:20 yoffset:30➥
walkable:false
# 2 type:DrawnIsoBox color:0xff6666 walkable:false height:20
# 3 type:DrawnIsoTile color:0x6666ff walkable:false


0 0 0 0 0 0 0 0 0 0
0 1 1 1 1 1 1 1 1 0
0 1 0 0 0 0 0 0 0 0
0 1 0 3 3 3 3 0 0 0
0 1 0 3 2 2 3 0 0 0
0 1 0 3 2 2 3 0 0 0
0 1 0 3 3 3 3 0 0 0
0 1 0 0 0 0 0 0 0 0
0 1 1 1 1 1 1 1 1 0
0 0 0 0 0 0 0 0 0 0
```

Lines that begin with // are comments and ignored. Lines that begin with # are tile definitions. Tile definitions consist of a symbol (0, 1, 2, 3, in this case) and a list of key/value pairs. All other non-empty lines are rows of tiles.

When the map file loads, the onLoad method will run, which parses the text and does the following:

1. It splits the text file into an array of lines.

2. For each line, it determines whether it is a tile definition, a comment, an empty line, or a row of tiles.

3. If the line is a definition, it is parsed by the parseDefinition method. This method takes each key/value pair and assigns it as a property on a generic object, which is then stored in the _tileTypes object.

4. Lines that are rows of tiles are split into an array of symbols and stored in the _grid array.

5. When all that is done, it broadcasts a complete event, letting you know the file has been loaded and processed. You can then call the makeWorld method, which returns a fully populated world by creating an IsoWorld, looping through the _grid array, and each cell in it. It checks _tileTypes to see what kind of tile to make and uses the other definitions as parameters to create that type of tile, adding it to the world. When it's done, it hands you back the world.

Using this class is very easy. Here's an example, which you can download as the MapTest.as file:

```
package
{
    import com.friendsofed.isometric.IsoWorld;
    import com.friendsofed.isometric.MapLoader;

    import flash.display.Sprite;
    import flash.display.StageAlign;
    import flash.display.StageScaleMode;
    import flash.events.Event;

    [SWF(backgroundColor=0xffffff)]
    public class MapTest extends Sprite
    {
        private var _world:IsoWorld;
        private var _floor:IsoWorld;
        private var mapLoader:MapLoader;

        [Embed(source="tile_01.png")]
        private var Tile01:Class;

        [Embed(source="tile_02.png")]
        private var Tile02:Class;

        public function MapTest()
        {
            stage.align = StageAlign.TOP_LEFT;
            stage.scaleMode = StageScaleMode.NO_SCALE;
```

```
            mapLoader = new MapLoader();
            mapLoader.addEventListener(Event.COMPLETE, onMapComplete);
            mapLoader.loadMap("map.txt");
        }

        private function onMapComplete(event:Event):void
        {
            _world = mapLoader.makeWorld(20);
            _world.x = stage.stageWidth / 2;
            _world.y = 100;
            addChild(_world);
        }
    }
}
```

You create the MapLoader, listen for its complete event, and load a map. When it's done, you call makeWorld and add that to the display list. Figure 3-17 shows the result of this class along with the map file just shown.

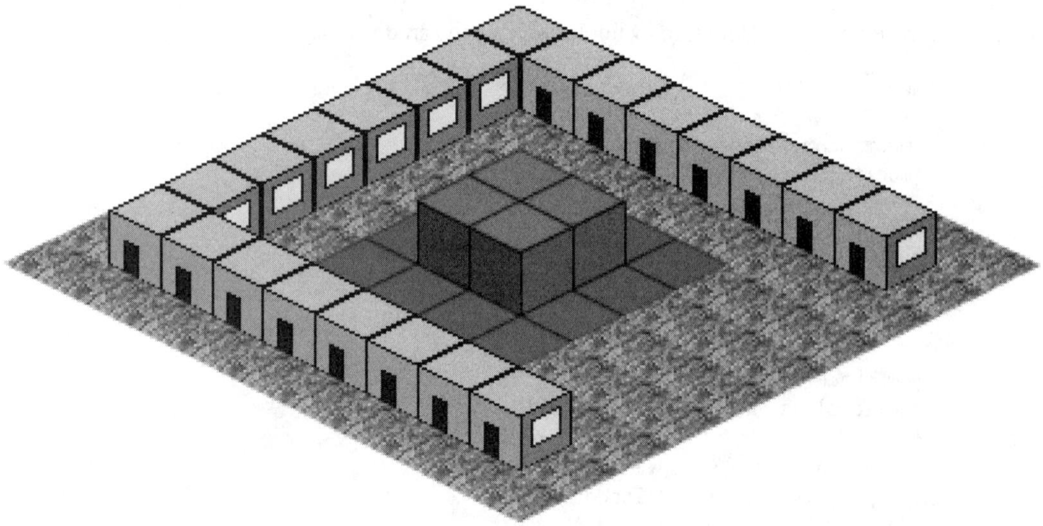

Figure 3-17. The MapLoader class, doing its thing

One thing to mention here is the graphicSymbol property in the tile definition:

```
# 0 type:GraphicTile graphicClass:MapTest_Tile01 xoffset:20 yoffset:10➥
 walkable:true
```

Here it is set to MapTest_Tile01, but in the MapTest class, we have embedded the symbol like so:

```
[Embed(source="tile_01.png")]
private var Tile01:Class;
```

So you might think that you should say graphicClass:Tile01. But Tile01 is actually a private property of the MapTest class. We won't be able to see that private property in the MapLoader class. But it turns out that the real name of the class for an embedded asset is ClassName_PropertyName, where ClassName is the class that does the embedding, and PropertyName is the property the embedded asset is linked to. Because Tile01 is the property and MapTest is the class that embeds the asset, the class itself is MapTest_Tile01.

You can now edit the map file to create all kinds of different layouts with different types of tiles, colors, heights, external graphics, and so on—all without recompiling the SWF. (Of course, if you want to embed new graphics, you'll need to recompile to get them into the SWF.)

There's a lot more that could be done with this class, and I assume that if you do use it, you will tweak it for your personal needs. You might not like the idea of generic objects for definitions and want to replace them with something better. Or you might want to add a way to specify that some tiles should be added to the floor and others to the world. But I think this is a good start and should provide you with a framework to build a pretty cool isometric world without doing it all from scratch.

Summary

Well, I think I've covered all the basics of Isometric 3D here, but I haven't taken all your fun away. I left you plenty of details to sort out and lots of stuff to optimize. But I'm thinking that you are well on your way to making something cool.

Next up, we'll be looking at pathfinding, which covers advanced ways of moving about in a tiled world, completely applicable to the tile-based isometric worlds.

Chapter 4

PATHFINDING

The term **pathfinding** means pretty much what it sounds like—finding a path. You are at point A. You want to go to point B. How do you get there? This subject has been extensively researched by game developers, and none of what I'll present here is new material, but it should cover the basics of the subject and give some decent implementations of the standard solutions in ActionScript 3.0.

Pathfinding Basics

Pathfinding is often applied to a tiled world. Even when applied to a game or world that is not tile based, the world is still usually viewed as some sort of grid from the viewpoint of pathfinding. Thus, the result of pathfinding is a series of tiles that make an unbroken path from a starting tile to an end tile. If it were just a matter of drawing a line between the two, this would be a trivial problem even for a tile-based world— hardly worth a whole chapter, much less the endless pages you will find with a simple Internet search for the term "pathfinding". The complexity increases when you make some of these tiles **unwalkable**, which also means pretty much what it sounds like. A character in the game cannot move on to or across any of these unwalkable tiles and must go around them. If these unwalkable tiles form a barrier between the start and end points, pathfinding now becomes the subject of how to get around this barrier and still get to the goal. Figure 4-1 shows an example.

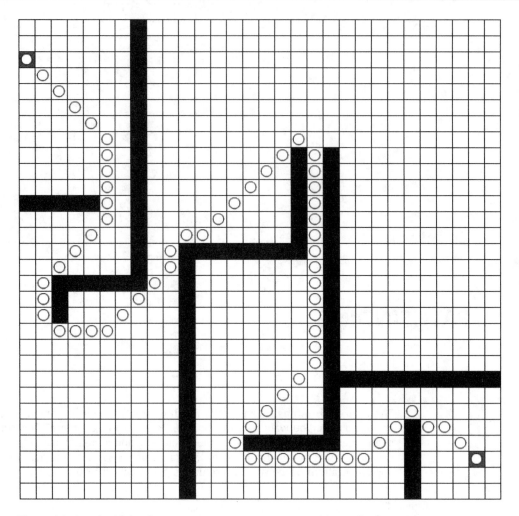

Figure 4-1. A path with barriers

Pathfinding also usually carries with it the idea that you are looking for the best path. In many implementations, the *best* path simply means the *shortest* path—the path made up of the fewest number of tiles. But in pathfinding, we use the concept of the path with the least *cost*. Traveling from any tile to any other tile costs a certain amount of effort. Distance, of course, is a big part of cost—it "costs more" to move across two tiles than it does to just move across one—but there could be other costs as well. In some games, for example, the path that leads through a swamp or over some mountains might be the shortest, but it's harder to climb mountains and move through swamps, so this path might have a higher cost than the path that follows the main road, even though that path might be longer. For a more familiar example, the shortest path from your office to your home might go through the center of town, but if you are going home at rush hour, you probably prefer a somewhat longer path that avoids the worst of the traffic.

A* (A-Star)

If you've done even the most cursory research on pathfinding, you have no doubt come across the term A* (pronounced as "a star"). A* is a general algorithm for finding the best path from a starting point to an ending point. It is pretty much the industry standard for pathfinding, used in almost every game that uses pathfinding. Implemented correctly, A* is guaranteed to find the best path between two points and is relatively efficient in terms of how it searches. For these reasons, many consider the subject of pathfinding a closed case, with A* being the solution. For the kinds of scenarios that A* covers, you are much better off spending some time learning A*, as we'll do in this chapter, than in trying to come up with your own pathfinding algorithm.

One of the powerful aspects of A* is that it is a very general algorithm, more of an outline of how to go about pathfinding than an exact formula. In fact, one of the pieces of the A* algorithm is the *heuristic*, which itself is a subalgorithm used within one of the parts of the overall process. This heuristic is not defined by A*, and there are several common heuristics in use, which give different results in terms of speed and efficiency. In fact just about all aspects of A* can be tweaked and customized based on specific-language feature strengths and application requirements.

In this chapter, we'll go about building an ActionScript 3.0 implementation of A*. I don't claim that it will be the best possible implementation, but I do hope that it will be clear enough for you to learn and understand the basic concepts of the subject. At any rate, it will be perfectly usable for most common applications and ready for you to tweak to your heart's delight to achieve ultimate optimization.

A* basics

In as concise terms as possible, A* consists of choosing a starting tile, visiting each surrounding tile, and assigning a cost to each one. We'll cover cost a lot more soon, but it has to do with the suitability of a particular tile in terms of a path from start to end. The process is then repeated with the lowest-cost tile as the new starting tile. If you continue this way, you'll eventually reach the end tile and be able to track back to the starting tile for the best path between the two.

A* algorithm

Most explanations of A* start out with a pseudocode representation of the A* algorithm and proceed to show some simple diagrams illustrating the progression of the search using the algorithm. That seems to work pretty well, so I will follow suit. First though, let's define some terms:

- *node*: This is essentially a tile in a tile-based world. But instead of using the term **tile**, **cell**, or **point**, A* uses the term **node** to specify the segment of path being examined. So a path will consist of the starting node, the end or goal node, and the list of nodes that form the best path between them.

- *cost*: This is the ranking for each node based on how fitting it is for the path. Nodes with a lower cost are preferable to nodes with a higher cost. **Cost** is made up of two parts: the cost to get to a particular node from the starting node and the estimated cost to get from that node to the goal node. Cost elements are usually signified with the variables f, g, and h, as described next.

- *f*: The total cost of a specific node, defined as g + h.

- *g*: The cost to get from the starting node to a specific node. It can be calculated exactly because you always know the exact path you took to get to that node from the starting node.

- *h*: The *estimated* cost to get from a specific node to the end node. The estimate is done via a heuristic function. It's only an estimate because you don't know the exact path you are going to take. That's what you're trying to figure out!

- *heuristic*: A function that estimates the cost to get from a specific node to the end node. There are various heuristics in general use that give different results in terms of speed, efficiency, and so on.

- *open list*: The list of nodes that have been visited and assigned a cost. The lowest-cost node in this list will be used in the next iteration of the search.

- *closed list*: The list of nodes whose neighbors have all been visited.

- *parent node*: When a node is iterated over, each of its neighbors is examined and assigned that node as a parent. So when you reach the goal node, you can follow the chain of parent nodes back to the start node. Because parent nodes were always the lowest-cost node on the open list, you are guaranteed to have the best path.

Now let's look at the algorithm description:

1. Add the starting node to the open list.

2. Main search loop:

   a. Find the node on the open list that has the least cost. This is the current node.

   b. If the current node is the end node, you're done. Go to step 4.

   c. Examine each surrounding node (in a rectangular grid, there will be eight nodes). For each surrounding node:

      i. If it is not walkable or is already on the open or closed lists, skip it and continue with the next surrounding node; otherwise continue.

      ii. Calculate its cost.

      iii. Set the current node as its parent.

      iv. Add it to the open list.

   d. Add the current node to the closed list.

3. Repeat step 2 with the updated open list.

4. You've found the end node. Create a path list and add the end node to it.

5. Add the parent of the end node to the path list.

6. Add the parent of that node to the path list. Repeat until you reach the starting node. The path list now holds the list of nodes that make up the best path from start to end.

We'll go through this algorithm graphically very soon, but first you need to know how to calculate the cost for a tile.

Calculating cost

As described in the definitions, the cost for a particular node is calculated with the formula $f = g + h$, where g is the cost to get to that node, and h is the *estimated* cost to get from that node to the goal.

The first part of the cost formula is relatively straightforward: how many nodes have to be walked on to get from the start node to that node. For now, we'll say that walking from any node to any surrounding node has a cost of 1.

So, beginning at the starting node and examining each of the surrounding nodes, you would assign each one g=1 (see Figure 4-2).

In the next iteration, you can calculate g as the g of the current node, plus the cost to travel from the current node to the node you are examining. In other words, suppose that the current node is one of the nodes surrounding the starting node. So it has a g of 1. When you look at each node surrounding it, you would assign each one g=2 because it cost you 1 point to travel to the current node and another 1 point to travel to the next node. This is shown in Figure 4-3.

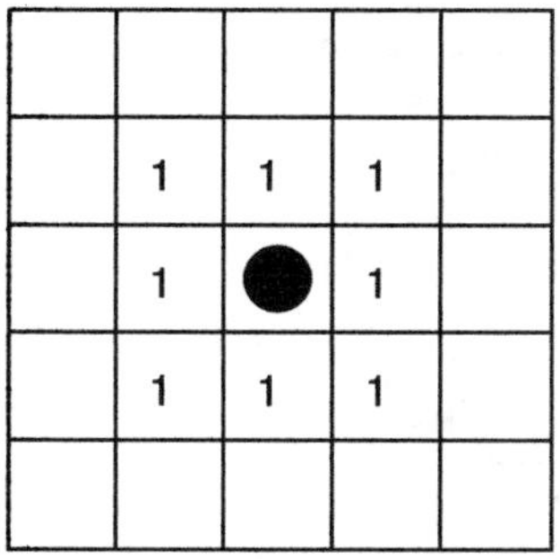

Figure 4-2. Assigning g from the start node

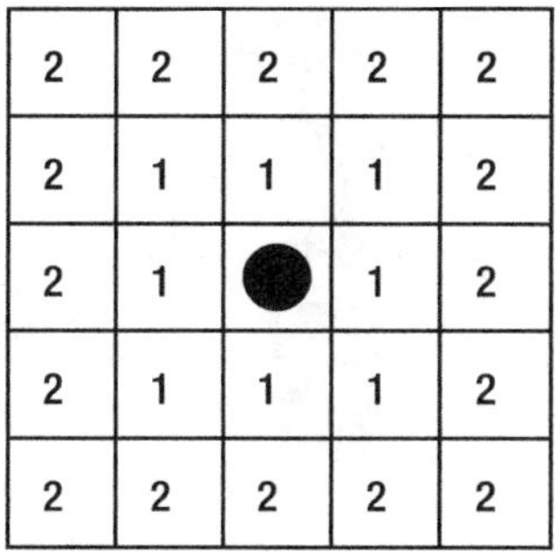

Figure 4-3. Assigning g to a subsequent node

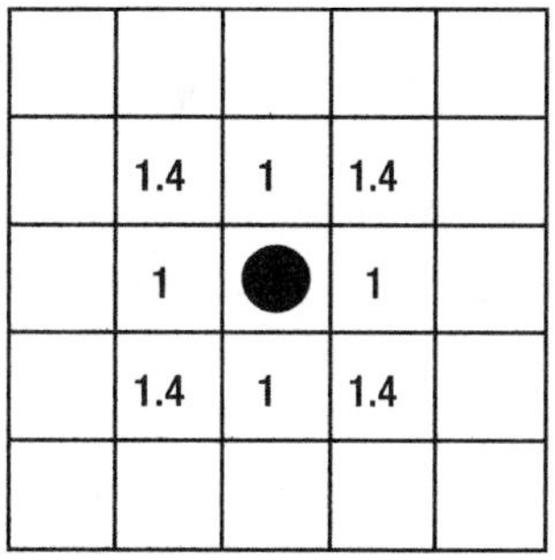

Figure 4-4. The cost for diagonal nodes is more than horizontal or vertical.

In most implementations, however, all surrounding nodes are not equal. If you look at the distance between two nodes in the same row or column, compared with two nodes diagonally next to each other, you'll see that the diagonal ones are actually farther apart. If you do the trig, you'll see that the distance is not simply 1, but 1.414, or the square root of 2. So, you can factor that into your cost. (Don't worry about it too much for now; we'll be going into it soon.) Figure 4-4 shows this step.

The next part of the cost is the estimated cost to move from the specified node to the goal node. Determining this is done with a heuristic, which is just another algorithm or formula. One of the simplest heuristics is to take the distance between the two, using the good old Pythagorean Theorem. How many rows between them? How many columns? Square each figure, add them, and take the square root. Here's the pseudocode:

```
dx = distance between columns
dy = distance between rows
dist = sqrt(dx * dx + dy * dy)
```

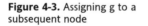

159

That's your h. The cost for the node in question is now f, or g + h.

Again, we'll be looking into this in more detail later, so as long as you have a general idea of what's going on here, that's fine for now.

Visualizing the algorithm

We'll start with a grid, a starting node, an end node, and some unwalkable tiles (see Figure 4-5).

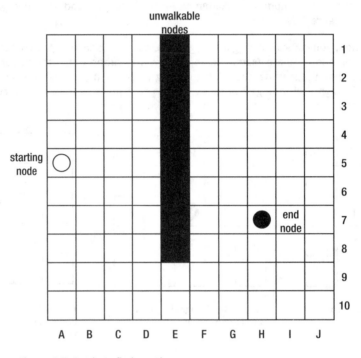

Figure 4-5. Ready to find a path

Proceeding with the algorithm, we add the starting node to the open list. We then look at the starting list for the node with the least cost. There's only one node in the list, the starting node, so that's it.

We then examine each of the nodes surrounding the starting node and assign each a cost. We start by calculating the g for each one. This is 1 for the nodes in the same row or column, and 1.4 for the ones on a diagonal with it. For this exercise, we don't have to be super accurate with the cost—1.4 is close enough. See Figure 4-6.

Next we assign the h's. Using the straight-line heuristic, it's just the distance from each node to the goal node. It's not the pixel distance; it's a unitized distance of the number of nodes between the two using the Pythagorean formula (as shown earlier).

With both parts of the cost figured, we can add them together to get the total cost. Figure 4-7 shows the result.

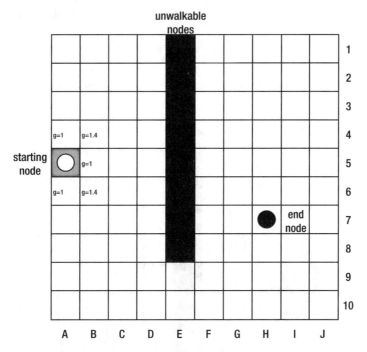

Figure 4-6. The g's have been assigned.

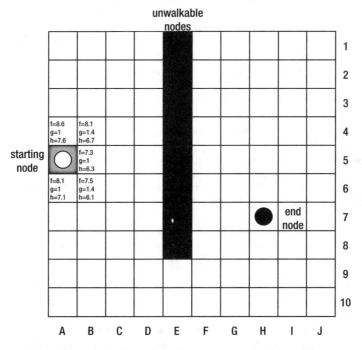

Figure 4-7. Total cost for each node

The current node can now be added to the closed list, and each of these visited nodes can be added to the open list.

We then look at the open list again and find the node with the least cost in it, which is node B5 on the grid, and repeat the process. This time, however, some of the nodes surrounding it are already on the open list or closed list, so we can ignore those. We calculate the cost for the remaining nodes (see Figure 4-8).

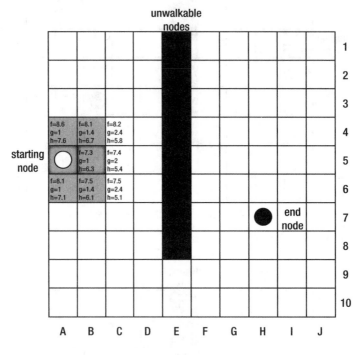

Figure 4-8. Round 2 of pathfinding

Now B5 is added to the closed list and the just-examined nodes are added to the open list. Again we choose the one from the open list with the lowest cost. This time it's C5. We calculate the cost of its surrounding nodes (the results are shown in Figure 4-9).

Now, notice that D5 and D6 have the same cost. Actually, because I'm rounding off the values here for simplicity's sake, they might or might not actually have the same exact cost, but this can happen, so let's say they do. Which one do you choose? Well, it really doesn't matter. In fact, it's not really up to you, but usually up to some sorting algorithm. Now it might be pretty obvious to you that D6 is the way to go because you can see the wall there. The heuristic can't see the wall, though. It's just calculating distance. So, from its viewpoint, either node is valid.

Anyway, suppose that we tossed a coin or ran a sort on the open list, and D5 came up. We then look at the surrounding nodes, but there are none. They are all unwalkable, or on the open or closed list. No problem. This is step 2c of the algorithm. If there are no valid surrounding nodes, we move on to step 3, add node D5 to the closed list, and check the open list again for the node with the lowest cost. This time, D6 is undisputed. We continue the algorithm by checking its neighbors. This brings us to Figure 4-10.

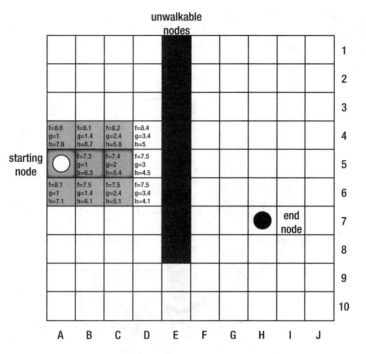

Figure 4-9. Round 3 of pathfinding

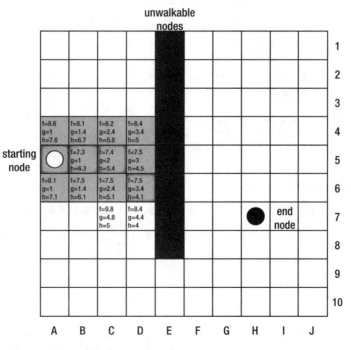

Figure 4-10. Pathfinding continued

We continue this process, finding the lowest-cost node on the open list, calculating the cost for each neighbor and adding them to the open list, putting the current node on the closed list, finding the lowest-cost node on the open list, and so on. Eventually, we'll get to Figure 4-11.

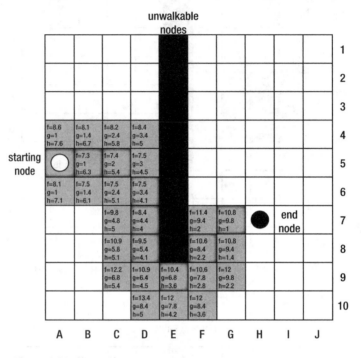

Figure 4-11. Almost there

The current node is G7. When we start to look at the surrounding nodes, we soon see that one of them is the end node. We made it!

At each phase, when checking out new nodes, we set a parent property on each node to be equal to the current node. Thus, we can now walk backward from the end node, all the way back to the starting node. Reversing this path, we have the best path from start to end.

Getting it into code

To start coding A*, we first need some structures to represent a grid and a single node.

First, the Grid class. As with all other code here, you can download it from the book's site at www.friendsofed.com (the file is Grid.as).

```
package
{
    /**
     * Holds a two-dimensional array of Nodes,
     * methods to manipulate them, a start node and an end node.
     */
```

```
public class Grid
{
    private var _startNode:Node;
    private var _endNode:Node;
    private var _nodes:Array;
    private var _numCols:int;
    private var _numRows:int;

    /**
     * Constructor.
     */
    public function Grid(numCols:int, numRows:int)
    {
        _numCols = numCols;
        _numRows = numRows;
        _nodes = new Array();

        for(var i:int = 0; i < _numCols; i++)
        {
            _nodes[i] = new Array();
            for(var j:int = 0; j < _numRows; j++)
            {
                _nodes[i][j] = new Node(i, j);
            }
        }
    }


    /////////////////////////////////////////
    // public methods
    /////////////////////////////////////////

    /**
     * Returns the node at the given coords.
     * @param x The x coord.
     * @param y The y coord.
     */
    public function getNode(x:int, y:int):Node
    {
        return _nodes[x][y] as Node;
    }

    /**
     * Sets the node at the given coords as the end node.
     * @param x The x coord.
     * @param y The y coord.
     */
```

```
public function setEndNode(x:int, y:int):void
{
    _endNode = _nodes[x][y] as Node;
}


/**
 * Sets the node at the given coords as the start node.
 * @param x The x coord.
 * @param y The y coord.
 */
public function setStartNode(x:int, y:int):void
{
    _startNode = _nodes[x][y] as Node;
}


/**
 * Sets the node at the given coords as walkable or not.
 * @param x The x coord.
 * @param y The y coord.
 */
public function setWalkable(x:int, y:int, value:Boolean):void
{
    _nodes[x][y].walkable = value;
}




//////////////////////////////////////
// getters / setters
//////////////////////////////////////

/**
 * Returns the end node.
 */
public function get endNode():Node
{
    return _endNode;
}

/**
 * Returns the number of columns in the grid.
 */
public function get numCols():int
{
    return _numCols;
}

/**
 * Returns the number of rows in the grid.
 */
```

```
        public function get numRows():int
        {
            return _numRows;
        }

        /**
         * Returns the start node.
         */
        public function get startNode():Node
        {
            return _startNode;
        }


    }
}
```

In the constructor, you pass in the number of rows and columns you want in the grid, which creates an array of nodes. We'll look at the Node class next. You can set the start node or end node by specifying the x, y coordinates you want for each. Similarly, you can set any specific node as walkable or not. Finally, you can get a reference to the start node, end node, or any specific node, as well as reading the number of rows and columns in the grid.

Note that the Grid class is merely an object to hold information about the grid—it has no visual representation. We'll create another class for that, but first let's look at the Node class (available in the Node.as file):

```
package
{
    /**
     * Represents a specific node evaluated
     * as part of a pathfinding algorithm.
     */
    public class Node
    {
        public var x:int;
        public var y:int;
        public var f:Number;
        public var g:Number;
        public var h:Number;
        public var walkable:Boolean = true;
        public var parent:Node;

        public function Node(x:int, y:int)
        {
            this.x = x;
            this.y = y;
        }
    }
}
```

The Node class is a simple data object used to hold the properties of a node. It has no behavior itself, so we'll give it only public properties. Note that at this point, all nodes are equal, so the only cost involved is in the length of the path. Later, you'll see how you can have different intrinsic costs for different types of nodes.

The next thing we need is a class that does the work of pathfinding itself. This is the AStar class, available for download as the AStar.as file. I'll just dump it all on you at once; then we'll go through it in more detail:

```
package
{
    public class AStar
    {
        private var _open:Array;
        private var _closed:Array;
        private var _grid:Grid;
        private var _endNode:Node;
        private var _startNode:Node;
        private var _path:Array;
//      private var _heuristic:Function = manhattan;
//      private var _heuristic:Function = euclidian;
        private var _heuristic:Function = diagonal;
        private var _straightCost:Number = 1.0;
        private var _diagCost:Number = Math.SQRT2;


        public function AStar()
        {
        }

        public function findPath(grid:Grid):Boolean
        {
            _grid = grid;
            _open = new Array();
            _closed = new Array();

            _startNode = _grid.startNode;
            _endNode = _grid.endNode;

            _startNode.g = 0;
            _startNode.h = _heuristic(_startNode);
            _startNode.f = _startNode.g + _startNode.h;

            return search();
        }

        public function search():Boolean
        {
            var node:Node = _startNode;
            while(node != _endNode)
```

```
{
    var startX:int = Math.max(0, node.x - 1);
    var endX:int = Math.min(_grid.numCols - 1, node.x + 1);
    var startY:int = Math.max(0, node.y - 1);
    var endY:int = Math.min(_grid.numRows - 1, node.y + 1);

    for(var i:int = startX; i <= endX; i++)
    {
        for(var j:int = startY; j <= endY; j++)
        {
            var test:Node = _grid.getNode(i, j);
            if(test == node || !test.walkable) continue;

            var cost:Number = _straightCost;
            if(!((node.x == test.x) || (node.y == test.y)))
            {
                cost = _diagCost;
            }
            var g:Number = node.g + cost;
            var h:Number = _heuristic(test);
            var f:Number = g + h;
            if(isOpen(test) || isClosed(test))
            {
                if(test.f > f)
                {
                    test.f = f;
                    test.g = g;
                    test.h = h;
                    test.parent = node;
                }
            }
            else
            {
                test.f = f;
                test.g = g;
                test.h = h;
                test.parent = node;
                _open.push(test);
            }
        }
    }
    _closed.push(node);
    if(_open.length == 0)
    {
        trace("no path found");
        return false
    }
    _open.sortOn("f", Array.NUMERIC);
    node = _open.shift() as Node;
}
```

```
        buildPath();
        return true;
    }

    private function buildPath():void
    {
        _path = new Array();
        var node:Node = _endNode;
        _path.push(node);
        while(node != _startNode)
        {
            node = node.parent;
            _path.unshift(node);
        }
    }

    public function get path():Array
    {
        return _path;
    }

    private function isOpen(node:Node):Boolean
    {
        for(var i:int = 0; i < _open.length; i++)
        {
            if(_open[i] == node)
            {
                return true;
            }
        }
        return false;
    }

    private function isClosed(node:Node):Boolean
    {
        for(var i:int = 0; i < _closed.length; i++)
        {
            if(_closed[i] == node)
            {
                return true;
            }
        }
        return false;
    }
```

```
            private function manhattan(node:Node):Number
            {
                return Math.abs(node.x - _endNode.x) * _straightCost +
                        Math.abs(node.y + _endNode.y) * _straightCost;
            }

            private function euclidian(node:Node):Number
            {
                var dx:Number = node.x - _endNode.x;
                var dy:Number = node.y - _endNode.y;
                return Math.sqrt(dx * dx + dy * dy) * _straightCost;
            }

            private function diagonal(node:Node):Number
            {
                var dx:Number = Math.abs(node.x - _endNode.x);
                var dy:Number = Math.abs(node.y - _endNode.y);
                var diag:Number = Math.min(dx, dy);
                var straight:Number = dx + dy;
                return _diagCost * diag +
                        _straightCost * (straight - 2 * diag);
            }

            public function get visited():Array
            {
                return _closed.concat(_open);
            }
        }
    }
```

To begin with, we have some properties, followed by a default constructor:

```
    private var _open:Array;
    private var _closed:Array;
    private var _grid:Grid;
    private var _endNode:Node;
    private var _startNode:Node;
    private var _path:Array;
    //      private var _heuristic:Function = manhattan;
    //      private var _heuristic:Function = euclidian;
    private var _heuristic:Function = diagonal;
    private var _straightCost:Number = 1.0;
    private var _diagCost:Number = Math.SQRT2;

    public function AStar()
    {
    }
```

Here are arrays for the open and closed lists; a grid; a start and end node; an array to hold the final path, which will be a list of nodes; and a heuristic property. I provided a few common heuristics in the class, which are explained in more depth a bit later. You can choose among them by uncommenting the one you want to use and commenting the rest. You might want to devise a more robust way of switching between them, such as using a setHeuristic method, but I'll leave that up to you. Finally there are properties for the cost to travel to a node on a straight line and a diagonal line.

Next is the findPath method:

```
public function findPath(grid:Grid):Boolean
{
    _grid = grid;
    _open = new Array();
    _closed = new Array();

    _startNode = _grid.startNode;
    _endNode = _grid.endNode;

    _startNode.g = 0;
    _startNode.h = _heuristic(_startNode);
    _startNode.f = _startNode.g + _startNode.h;

    return search();
}
```

This method initializes things by creating an empty open and closed list and then grabbing the start and end nodes from the grid that was passed in. It calculates the cost for the start node and then runs the search method, which will iterate through to the end node and return the path.

Let's take a look at how the method calculates the cost for the start node. It first sets the start node's g to zero because g is defined as the cost to get from the start node to the current node. Because they are one and the same, there is no cost. We then call whatever heuristic method we have chosen, passing in the start node, which will return the estimated cost to get from there to the end node. This is h. Finally, we add g and h to get f, the total cost for the node.

Next up is the real meat of the class, the search method. This is what goes through from the start node and eventually ends up at the end node, calculating the best path as it goes:

```
public function search():Boolean
{
    var node:Node = _startNode;
    while(node != _endNode)
    {
        var startX:int = Math.max(0, node.x - 1);
        var endX:int = Math.min(_grid.numCols - 1, node.x + 1);
        var startY:int = Math.max(0, node.y - 1);
        var endY:int = Math.min(_grid.numRows - 1, node.y + 1);
```

```
        for(var i:int = startX; i <= endX; i++)
        {
            for(var j:int = startY; j <= endY; j++)
            {
                var test:Node = _grid.getNode(i, j);
                if(test == node || !test.walkable) continue;
                var cost:Number = _straightCost;
                if(!((node.x == test.x) || (node.y == test.y)))
                {
                    cost = _diagCost;
                }
                var g:Number = node.g + cost;
                var h:Number = _heuristic(test);
                var f:Number = g + h;
                if(isOpen(test) || isClosed(test))
                {
                    if(test.f > f)
                    {
                        test.f = f;
                        test.g = g;
                        test.h = h;
                        test.parent = node;
                    }
                }
                else
                {
                    test.f = f;
                    test.g = g;
                    test.h = h;
                    test.parent = node;
                    _open.push(test);
                }
            }
        }
        _closed.push(node);
        if(_open.length == 0)
        {
            trace("no path found");
            return false
        }
        _open.sortOn("f", Array.NUMERIC);
        node = _open.shift() as Node;
    }
    buildPath();
    return true;
}
```

We start by making a node variable, which keeps track of the current node that begins as the start node. It then runs a while loop, exiting only when the current node is equal to the end node. At this point, we're done.

The first thing we do inside this while loop is to run a double for loop to examine all the nodes surrounding the current node, as shown in Figure 4-12.

First we get the x and y values of the current node and loop from x–1 to x+1 and y–1 to y+1 (remember that the x and y values are integer values representing rows and columns here, not pixel screen positions; nothing is onscreen yet):

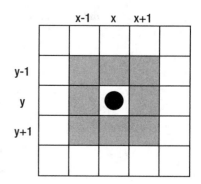

Figure 4-12. The x, y index values of the nodes surrounding the current node

```
var startX:int = Math.max(0, node.x - 1);
var endX:int = Math.min(_grid.numCols - 1, node.x + 1);
var startY:int = Math.max(0, node.y - 1);
var endY:int = Math.min(_grid.numRows - 1, node.y + 1);
for(var i:int = startX; i <= endX; i++)
{
    for(var j:int = startY; j <= endY; j++)
    {
```

We also have to make sure that we don't try to access tiles off the sides or top or bottom of the grid, as you can see in Figure 4-7. We do that by running the indexes through Math.min and Math.max so they are never less than zero or greater than the last row or column of the grid.

For each node, we get the node itself from the grid. If the test node is the current node, or the test node is not walkable, we can just ignore it and move on to the next one:

```
var test:Node = _grid.getNode(i, j);
if(test == node || !test.walkable) continue;
```

If we make it this far, we have a valid test node and need to determine its cost. First we calculate the cost from the start node to this test node (the g cost). We can do this by taking the g of the current node and adding the cost to get from the current node to the test node. A simple way is to assign _straightCost if the node is on a horizontal or vertical line with the current node, or _diagCost if the node is on a diagonal. Then add the current node's g to this to get the total g. We find h by running the heuristic function on the test node, and f by adding g and h together:

```
var cost:Number = _straightCost;
if(!((node.x == test.x) || (node.y == test.y)))
{
    cost = _diagCost;
}
var g:Number = node.g + cost;
var h:Number = _heuristic(test);
var f:Number = g + h;
```

The next part gets a bit tricky, and is something we haven't talked about yet. Earlier, I implied that if a node was on the open or closed list, you wouldn't need to examine it because it was already covered. However, the route you took to get to a node this time might result in a cost that is less than the cost you calculated for it the first time around (for example, if you were calculating the cost based on a diagonal but now you are directly next to a node on the horizontal or vertical, so the cost is lower). So, even if a node is on the open or closed list, it's good to compare the current cost with the previous one. We do that by comparing the test node's f with the f just calculated. If the previous f is greater, we've found a better path this time, and we replace the f, g, and h on the test node. We also set the parent of the test node to the current node. This will let us walk backward to the start point once we reach the goal:

```
if(isOpen(test) || isClosed(test))
{
    if(test.f > f)
    {
        test.f = f;
        test.g = g;
        test.h = h;
        test.parent = node;
    }
}
```

If the test node is not on the open or closed lists, we just assign the f, g, h, and parent straight away. We also push the test node onto the open list because it has a fully calculated cost now and needs to be considered in the next test for best node:

```
else
{
    test.f = f;
    test.g = g;
    test.h = h;
    test.parent = node;
    _open.push(test);
}
```

At this point, we have examined all valid nodes around the current node. There's nothing more that needs to be done with it, so we push it onto the closed list:

```
_closed.push(node);
```

And then we need to find the next current node to repeat the process. We do this by examining the open list and finding the lowest-cost node in it. But first we should check whether there are any nodes on the open list at all. It can happen that the open list empties out. This means that there is no possible path between the start and end nodes:

```
if(_open.length == 0)
{
    trace("no path found");
    return false
}
```

In this implementation, `true` returns if a path is found and `false` returns if no path is possible. This can be checked by the code searching for the path to determine the outcome.

If there are more nodes on the open list, we need to find the lowest-cost one (that is, the one with the lowest f). We can do this by sorting the list by the f property of each element and taking the bottom element off the list:

```
_open.sortOn("f", Array.NUMERIC);
node = _open.shift() as Node;
```

That is the end of this iteration, and we are left with a new current node. The while loop now checks again to see whether the current node is the end node. If not, it will go through the process again and again until either it determines a path cannot be found or the end node is reached.

When we do find the end node, we call the `buildPath` method and return `true`. Let's look at buildPath:

```
private function buildPath():void
{
    _path = new Array();
    var node:Node = _endNode;
    _path.push(node);
    while(node != _startNode)
    {
        node = node.parent;
        _path.unshift(node);
    }
}
```

This code creates a new array for the path and pushes the end node onto it. It then unshifts the end node's parent on to the list. By using unshift instead of push, we add each new node to the start of the array, so it runs from start node to end node when it's done. We repeat this process, adding each parent's parent until we reach the start node. At this point, the path array holds the best path from start to finish. We are done! The code using the AStar class can now check the return value of findPath to see whether it was successful; if so, it grabs the path array with the get path accessor.

If you've had enough of the internals of the AStar class, you can jump ahead to the implementation section. But if you are up for it, let's take a look at the different heuristics included.

Common A* heuristics

The funny thing about A* is that it should give you an optimum path no matter which heuristic you use. Note that I say *an* optimum path here, not *the* optimum path. In just about every case, there will be multiple paths with the same cost. For example, Figure 4-13 shows three paths between the same two nodes. Each path would have a full cost of 4.8 (two diagonal moves at 1.4 each, plus two horizontal moves at 1.0 each).

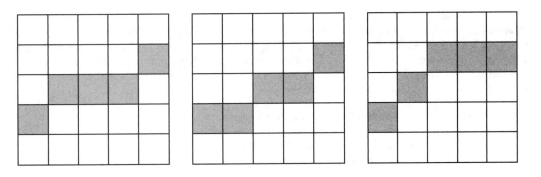

Figure 4-13. Three paths, one cost

As long as the solution comes up with one of these paths (or another path with a cost of 4.8), it is a valid best path.

Thus, using a "better" heuristic doesn't mean that you'll get a shorter path. But some heuristics are quicker than others. The biggest factor is that some heuristics result in more nodes being examined; some result in fewer. The fewer nodes that need to be examined, the quicker you'll get to the end node, the fewer (and smaller) arrays you'll have to sort, and so on.

Also, some heuristics tend to create paths that appear "straighter" to our eyes than others. For example, most people would say that the first or second path in Figure 4-13 is shorter or more direct, even though all three have the same cost. Most would say the third path just looks wrong. So, if a heuristic tends to intersperse diagonal moves with straight moves, it will wind up creating a path that looks more natural instead of grouping them all together.

You could write a whole chapter, possibly a whole book, just on different heuristics and the differences between them. I'll just cover three commonly used heuristics (the ones included in the AStar class), with a brief explanation of each. But if you want to get into it more, do a web search for A* heuristics and you'll get enough reading material to last weeks. See Figure 4-14 to see how each heuristic works as you read about it.

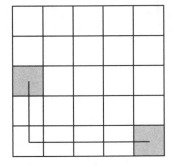

Manhattan Heuristic

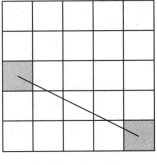

Euclidean Heuristic

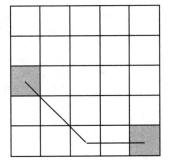

Diagonal Heuristic

Figure 4-14. Three common heuristics

177

First is the so-called **Manhattan heuristic**, which ignores any diagonal movement and just adds the total number of columns and rows between a test node and the end node. The idea is that if you were on a grid like the streets of Manhattan, for example, and you needed to get from 5th and 40th to 8th and 43rd, you'd have to go three blocks in one direction, and three in another. It wouldn't matter if you did all the streets first and then all the avenues, or vice versa; or street, avenue, street, avenue, street, avenue. You'd still be doing three of each.

```
private function manhattan(node:Node):Number
{
    return Math.abs(node.x - _endNode.x) * _straightCost +
           Math.abs(node.y + _endNode.y) * _straightCost;
}
```

So this heuristic just gets the difference between the two nodes in terms of columns and in terms of rows, and then adds them together. Simple enough.

The next common method is sometimes known as the **Euclidian heuristic**. It just calculates a straight line from the test node to the end node and returns the length. This is the good old Pythagorean theorem: $A^2 + B^2 = C^2$.

```
private function euclidian(node:Node):Number
{
    var dx:Number = node.x - _endNode.x;
    var dy:Number = node.y - _endNode.y;
    return Math.sqrt(dx * dx + dy * dy) * _straightCost;
}
```

We take the distance in rows, square it, add the distance in columns (also squared), and take the square root of the sum. Also pretty simple.

The last method, the **Diagonal heuristic**, looks pretty convoluted, but essentially winds up calculating a path as shown in Figure 4-13.

```
private function diagonal(node:Node):Number
{
    var dx:Number = Math.abs(node.x - _endNode.x);
    var dy:Number = Math.abs(node.y - _endNode.y);
    var diag:Number = Math.min(dx, dy);
    var straight:Number = dx + dy;
    return _diagCost * diag +
           _straightCost * (straight - 2 * diag);
}
```

This heuristic, which is the most accurate of the three, will return the actual cost between the two nodes if there are no barriers between the two. In fact, if you run through the heuristic with the figures shown in Figure 4-13, you'll see that it returns a cost of 4.8, spot on.

The next three figures show the results of these three algorithms. Notice that all three have a path including 23 horizontal moves and 25 diagonal moves, resulting in a total cost of 58. The different heuristics had no affect on the length of the path. However, the character of the path and the number of visited nodes (shown in gray on the grid) vary greatly between the different methods. You can see that the Manhattan heuristic (Figure 4-15) wound up visiting almost every node in the grid before finding the end node. Its path is also very unnatural, taking all its horizontal moves at once and then all the diagonals.

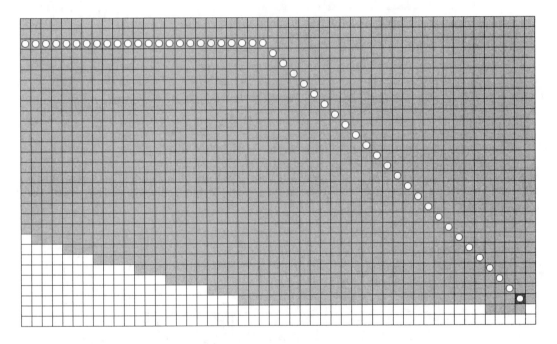

Figure 4-15. Result of the Manhattan heuristic

The next one, the Euclidian heuristic (see Figure 4-16), has a somewhat more natural-looking path, visiting far fewer nodes.

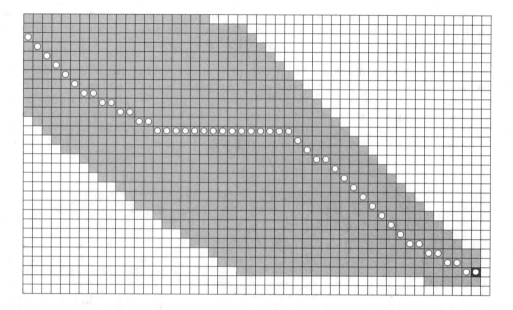

Figure 4-16. Result of the Euclidian heuristic

The Diagonal heuristic (see Figure 4-17) was the most efficient of all, visiting very few unnecessary nodes. Although its path is not quite as natural looking as the Euclidian's path, it's better than Manhattan's path.

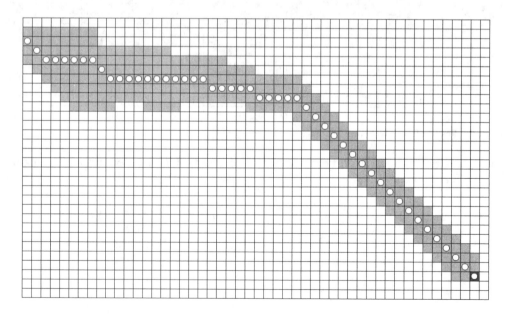

Figure 4-17. Result of the Diagonal heuristic

Of course, there are trade-offs (as with everything). The Manhattan heuristic is the simplest and quickest to execute per node, although it winds up visiting more nodes. The Diagonal heuristic is more complex but winds up being run less often. So, you see there is no "right" or "wrong" heuristic. Each has its strengths, and there are other heuristics out there, as well as variations on the ones I've given. It's a matter of trial and error to find the one that gives the best results for your specific application. And the preceding examples don't show any barriers; once you start adding those in, things get even more complex.

Now that we've covered all the basics, let's see it in action.

Implementing the AStar Class

When you go to implement A* in a real game or application, you'll probably create a tile-based world with tiles that are obviously walkable or not. The starting point would probably be the tile a character is on, and the ending tile might or might not be indicated. It could be a point where the user clicked or the tile where a pot of gold, an enemy, or some other object is located. The path itself would probably not be visualized, but simply used to move the character as it makes its way to the goal. For demonstration purposes, I'll create a GridView class to show this visually (you can download this as the Gridview.as file):

```
package
{
    import flash.display.Sprite;
    import flash.events.MouseEvent;

    /**
     * Serves as a visual representation of a grid of nodes
     * used in a pathfinding solution.
     */
    public class GridView extends Sprite
    {
        private var _cellSize:int = 20;
        private var _grid:Grid;

        /**
         * Constructor.
         */
        public function GridView(grid:Grid)
        {
            _grid = grid;
            drawGrid();
            findPath();
            addEventListener(MouseEvent.CLICK, onGridClick);
        }

        /**
         * Draws the given grid, coloring each cell based on its state.
         */
```

```
public function drawGrid():void
{
    graphics.clear();
    for(var i:int = 0; i < _grid.numCols; i++)
    {
        for(var j:int = 0; j < _grid.numRows; j++)
        {
            var node:Node = _grid.getNode(i, j);
            graphics.lineStyle(0);
            graphics.beginFill(getColor(node));
            graphics.drawRect(i * _cellSize,
                              j * _cellSize,
                              _cellSize,
                              _cellSize);
        }
    }
}

/**
 * Determines the color of a given node based on its state.
 */
private function getColor(node:Node):uint
{
    if(!node.walkable) return 0x000000;
    if(node == _grid.startNode) return 0x666666;
    if(node == _grid.endNode) return 0x666666;
    return 0xffffff;
}

/**
 * Handles the click event on the GridView.
 * Finds the clicked on cell and toggles its walkable state.
 */
private function onGridClick(event:MouseEvent):void
{
    // Convert the mouse coordinates into a grid position
    var xpos:int = Math.floor(event.localX / _cellSize);
    var ypos:int = Math.floor(event.localY / _cellSize);

    //and toggle its walkability
    _grid.setWalkable(xpos, ypos,
                      !_grid.getNode(xpos, ypos).walkable);
    drawGrid();
    findPath();
}

/**
 * Creates an instance of AStar and uses it to find a path.
 */
```

```
private function findPath():void
{
    var astar:AStar = new AStar();
    if(astar.findPath(_grid))
    {
        showVisited(astar);
        showPath(astar);
    }

}

/**
 * Highlights all nodes that have been visited.
 */
private function showVisited(astar:AStar):void
{
    var visited:Array = astar.visited;
    for(var i:int = 0; i < visited.length; i++)
    {
        graphics.beginFill(0xcccccc);
        graphics.drawRect(visited[i].x * _cellSize,
                          visited[i].y * _cellSize,
                          _cellSize, _cellSize);
        graphics.endFill();
    }
}

/**
 * Highlights the found path.
 */
private function showPath(astar:AStar):void
{
    var path:Array = astar.path;
    for(var i:int = 0; i < path.length; i++)
    {
        graphics.lineStyle(0);
        graphics.beginFill(0xffffff);

        // draw a circle with its center in the middle of the
        // cell with a radius that's a third of the cell width

        graphics.drawCircle(path[i].x * _cellSize +
                            _cellSize / 2,
                            path[i].y * _cellSize +
                            _cellSize / 2,
                            _cellSize / 3);
    }
  }
 }
}
```

The constructor of the GridView class takes a Grid instance, which contains the list of all nodes, as well as separate references to the start and end nodes. The drawGrid method loops through all the nodes, drawing a small square for each node. The size of the square is determined by the _cellSize property. The color of the square is determined by the getColor method, which returns black for a nonwalkable node, gray for the start and end nodes, and white otherwise.

Then the findPath method is called, which creates an instance of the AStar class and calls its findPath method, passing in the grid. If a path is found, it shows all the nodes that have been visited by coloring them a light gray and shows all the nodes on the path by drawing a small circle on them. The results are what you saw in Figures 4-15, 4-16, and 4-17.

Of course, finding a path with no obstacles isn't too exciting, so we add an event listener for the mouse click event that calls onGridClick. This finds the node associated with the point where the mouse was clicked and then toggles its walkability on or off. It then clears the grid view and finds the path again, which will redisplay the grid and its found path.

All we need now is something to tie this all together, our main document class, which you can find in the Pathfinding.as file:

```
package {
    import flash.display.Sprite;
    import flash.display.StageAlign;
    import flash.display.StageScaleMode;
    import flash.events.MouseEvent;

    [SWF(backgroundColor=0xffffff)]
    public class Pathfinding extends Sprite
    {
        private var _grid:Grid;
        private var _gridView:GridView;


        public function Pathfinding()
        {
            stage.align = StageAlign.TOP_LEFT;
            stage.scaleMode = StageScaleMode.NO_SCALE;

            _grid = new Grid(50, 30);
            _grid.setStartNode(0, 2);
            _grid.setEndNode(48, 27);

            _gridView = new GridView(_grid);
            _gridView.x = 20;
            _gridView.y = 20;
            addChild(_gridView);
        }

    }
}
```

All this code does is to create a Grid and a GridView and tie them together. You can set different start and end nodes; once the movie is up and running, you can click on various squares to create barriers that cut across the existing path. Notice that as long as you allow some space for a path to get through, A* will always find a path to the goal, and it will always be an optimal path, as you can see in Figure 4-18.

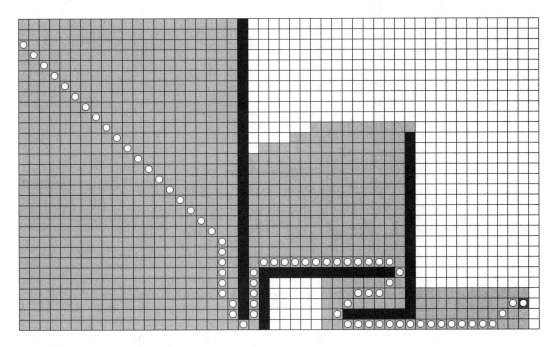

Figure 4-18. Pathfinding is complete

Refining the path: Corners

There's one potential problem so far, which isn't entirely noticeable in the examples, but can be seen in Figure 4-18. When the path goes around the edge of a barrier, it kind of cuts the corner a bit, going on a diagonal path from one side of the barrier to another. It doesn't look too bad so far, but when we get something like the path shown in Figure 4-19, we start to see a problem.

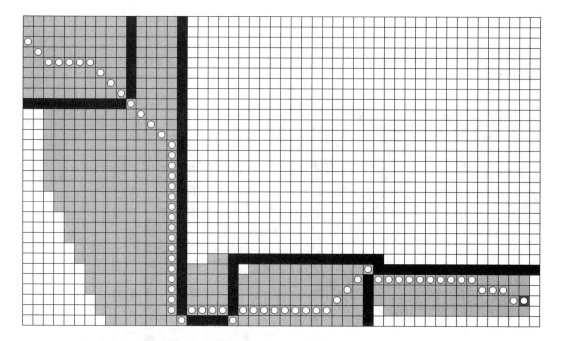

Figure 4-19. Slipping through cracks

Here, the path is finding its way through cracks between unwalkable paths. You might think you closed off the path, but because walking diagonally is a perfectly valid move, that's what the path does. It just doesn't look right. What we should really do is never cut corners around unwalkable tiles. This forces us to go fully around these tiles, and in the case where two corners join together diagonally (as in Figure 4-19), there will be no valid path found across them.

Taking a look at Figure 4-20, we can see the situation close up.

The black circle represents the current node we are examining, and the gray square is the node we are currently testing to determine its cost. We are at this point in the search method of the AStar class:

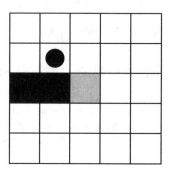

Figure 4-20. Close-up of a corner

```
for(var i:int = startX; i <= endX; i++)
{
    for(var j:int = startY; j <= endY; j++)
    {
        var test:Node = _grid.getNode(i, j);
        if(test == node || !test.walkable) continue;
```

We make sure that the test node is not the current node and that the test node is walkable. If either one of those cases is false, we skip it and move on to the next surrounding node. We want to throw in one more condition: we want to skip this node if it is cutting the corner of an unwalkable node. When node and test are on a diagonal like that, two other nodes have to be tested. These nodes are at the following coordinates:

```
node.x, test.y
```

and

```
test.x, node.y
```

In other words, the node that's at the same row as node and the same column as test (and vice versa), as you can see in Figure 4-21. You might have to work that out a bit more on paper, but you'll see that it makes sense.

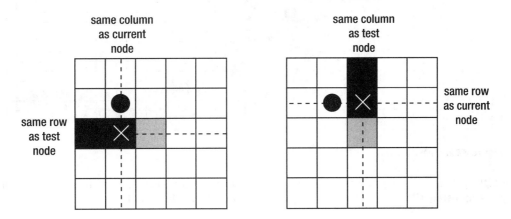

Figure 4-21. Finding a corner

So all we have to do is check to see whether either of those nodes is unwalkable. If so, we skip test and move on to the next surrounding node. Here's the revised code:

```
for(var i:int = startX; i <= endX; i++)
{
    for(var j:int = startY; j <= endY; j++)
    {
        var test:Node = _grid.getNode(i, j);
        if(test == node ||
            !test.walkable ||
            !_grid.getNode(node.x, test.y).walkable ||
            !_grid.getNode(test.x, node.y).walkable)
        {
            continue;
        }
    }
}
```

With this simple addition, we now get paths as shown in Figure 4-22.

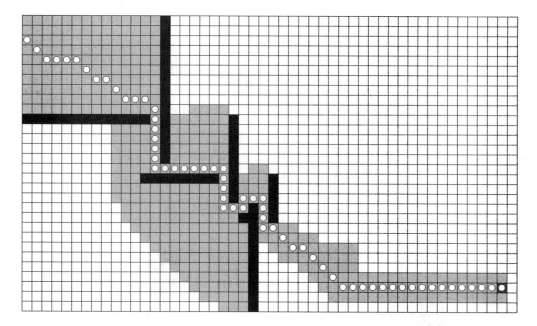

Figure 4-22. Better corners

Here, the path is now going fully around unwalkable nodes instead of cutting across them. Furthermore, if you completely close off an area, as in Figure 4-23, no path will be found.

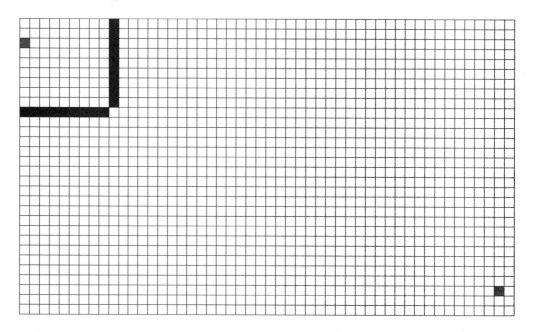

Figure 4-23. There is no path.

The corner-cutting fix is something that you might or might not want to implement. In some implementations or games it makes sense; in others it doesn't. You have to decide which kind of behavior you want for your specific game or application. You might even want to design it to be a configurable option on the class. Also, the way it is implemented here could be a target for optimization. Right now, it's always checking for corners even if the test node is not diagonal, which is a bit of a waste. I'll leave it that way for clarity, but you might want to fine-tune it later.

Using AStar in a Game

The previous example with the `GridView` class is mostly for demonstration purposes—to see how the path is made, to see which nodes get visited, and to experiment with what happens when different nodes are made unwalkable to see how the path is affected.

In a real-life situation, things are almost exactly the opposite—the walkable states of various nodes are set at the start and generally don't change, but the start and end nodes are fairly dynamic. The start node is wherever a particular character happens to be, and the end node is often where the user wants the character to go, usually indicated by clicking somewhere on the grid. So let's do a very simple implementation of that kind of behavior. This is all jammed into the Game class, which you can download from the book's site on www.friendsofed.com as the `Game.as` file:

```
package
{
    import flash.display.Sprite;
    import flash.display.StageAlign;
    import flash.display.StageScaleMode;
    import flash.events.Event;
    import flash.events.MouseEvent;

    public class Game extends Sprite
    {
        private var _cellSize:int = 20;
        private var _grid:Grid;
        private var _player:Sprite;
        private var _index:int;
        private var _path:Array;

        public function Game()
        {
            stage.align = StageAlign.TOP_LEFT;
            stage.scaleMode = StageScaleMode.NO_SCALE;

            makePlayer();
            makeGrid();
            stage.addEventListener(MouseEvent.CLICK, onGridClick);
        }
```

```
/**
 * Creates the player sprite. Just a circle here.
 */
private function makePlayer():void
{
    _player = new Sprite();
    _player.graphics.beginFill(0xff0000);
    _player.graphics.drawCircle(0, 0, 5);
    _player.graphics.endFill();
    _player.x = Math.random() * 600;
    _player.y = Math.random() * 600;
    addChild(_player);
}

/**
 * Creates a grid with a bunch of random unwalkable nodes.
 */
private function makeGrid():void
{
    _grid = new Grid(30, 30);
    for(var i:int = 0; i < 200; i++)
    {
        _grid.setWalkable(Math.floor(Math.random() * 30),
                          Math.floor(Math.random() * 30),
                          false);
    }
    drawGrid();
}

/**
 * Draws the given grid, coloring each cell based on its state.
 */
private function drawGrid():void
{
    graphics.clear();
    for(var i:int = 0; i < _grid.numCols; i++)
    {
        for(var j:int = 0; j < _grid.numRows; j++)
        {
            var node:Node = _grid.getNode(i, j);
            graphics.lineStyle(0);
            graphics.beginFill(getColor(node));
            graphics.drawRect(i * _cellSize,
                              j * _cellSize, _cellSize,
                              _cellSize);
        }
    }
}
```

```
/**
 * Determines the color of a given node based on its state.
 */
private function getColor(node:Node):uint
{
    if(!node.walkable) return 0;
    if(node == _grid.startNode) return 0xcccccc;
    if(node == _grid.endNode) return 0xcccccc;
    return 0xffffff;
}

/**
 * Handles the click event on the GridView.
 * Sets the start and end node of the grid and finds path.
 */
private function onGridClick(event:MouseEvent):void
{
    var xpos:int = Math.floor(mouseX / _cellSize);
    var ypos:int = Math.floor(mouseY / _cellSize);
    _grid.setEndNode(xpos, ypos);

    xpos = Math.floor(_player.x / _cellSize);
    ypos = Math.floor(_player.y / _cellSize);
    _grid.setStartNode(xpos, ypos);

    drawGrid();
    findPath();
}

/**
 * Creates an instance of AStar and uses it to find a path.
 */
private function findPath():void
{
    var astar:AStar = new AStar();
    if(astar.findPath(_grid))
    {
        _path = astar.path;
        _index = 0;
        addEventListener(Event.ENTER_FRAME, onEnterFrame);
    }
}

/**
 * Finds the next node on the path and eases to it.
 */
```

```
        private function onEnterFrame(event:Event):void
        {
            var targetX:Number = _path[_index].x * _cellSize
                                 + _cellSize / 2;
            var targetY:Number = _path[_index].y * _cellSize
                                 + _cellSize / 2;
            var dx:Number = targetX - _player.x;
            var dy:Number = targetY - _player.y;
            var dist:Number = Math.sqrt(dx * dx + dy * dy);
            if(dist < 1)
            {
                _index++;
                if(_index >= _path.length)
                {
                    removeEventListener(Event.ENTER_FRAME,
                                        onEnterFrame);
                }
            }
            else
            {
                // perform an ease by moving half way to the target
                _player.x += dx * .5;
                _player.y += dy * .5;
            }
        }
    }
}
```

This class has a lot of similarities to the GridView example, but there are also some important differences. In the constructor, we create a player, which is just a sprite with a circle drawn in it that's placed randomly on the stage. We also create a Grid and mark a whole bunch of nodes in it as unwalkable.

The drawGrid and getColor methods are essentially the same as in the previous example.

Then we listen for a click event. When the grid is clicked on, we set the start node to whatever node the player happens to be on and the end node to whatever node was clicked on. We then redraw the grid to reflect those changes and try to find a path with the findPath method.

The findPath method simply creates an instance of AStar and tries to find a path on the grid. If one is found, it grabs the path and sets an index property to zero so we are starting on the first node of the path. Then it listens for the enterFrame event, calling onEnterFrame.

The onEnterFrame handler grabs the next node on the path, as defined by the index property, gets the distance from the player to that node, and performs a simple ease to it. If the player gets close enough, it moves onto the next node on the path. When it reaches the last node on the path (the end node), it removes the enterFrame event listener.

Advanced Terrain

There's one concept that was mentioned at the start of the chapter that we haven't touched on yet. It's the idea of having different costs for tiles beyond simply straight and diagonal movement—having some tiles that are harder to traverse and others that are easier. We won't go too deeply into this, but I did want to cover it for completeness.

As an example, a dirt road node would have an inherently higher cost than a paved road node, and a swamp or mountain node would be costlier. Different costs for terrain can be implemented by adding an additional cost factor property to the Node class, which would probably be a multiplier. An ideal walkable node would have a cost multiplier of 1.0, so to travel to it horizontally or vertically would still be a cost of 1 and diagonally 1.414. However, nodes with a more difficult terrain might have a cost multiplier of 2.0, for example, so their end cost would be 2 or 2.828.

This makes AStar tend to avoid tougher terrain nodes in favor of easier nodes, even if the easier path was longer. But at a certain point, the cost of "going through the swamp" might still wind up shorter than traveling all the way around it. This is different from having an unwalkable node because even a difficult node will still be walkable, but AStar will look for an easier way around it first.

To implement this, first we'll add a single new property to the Node class, costMultiplier:

```
package
{
    /**
     * Represents a specific node evaluated as part of a
     * pathfinding algorithm.
     */
    public class Node
    {
        public var x:int;
        public var y:int;
        public var f:Number;
        public var g:Number;
        public var h:Number;
        public var walkable:Boolean = true;
        public var parent:Node;
        public var costMultiplier:Number = 1.0;

        public function Node(x:int, y:int)
        {
            this.x = x;
            this.y = y;
        }
    }
}
```

Then it takes one small change to implement in the search method of the AStar class. Go down to the line where the g part of the cost is calculated:

```
var g:Number = node.g + cost;
```

Change it to this:

```
var g:Number = node.g + (cost * test.costMultiplier);
```

Now the cost for this one node will be adjusted based on its multiplier. In Figure 4-24, I altered the GridView class to assign each node a different costMultiplier based on some random sine and cosine calculations. In addition, I drew each node lighter or darker depending on its cost multiplier. White nodes are easier to traverse than darker ones. You can find the changes in the GridView2.as file, available on the book's web site. Notice that the path follows the easier route where at all possible.

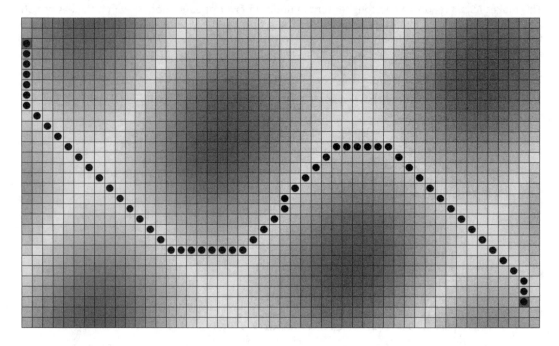

Figure 4-24. The path of least resistance

However, if you force the issue by making unwalkable nodes, AStar will begrudgingly go through the tough areas, as you can see in Figure 4-25.

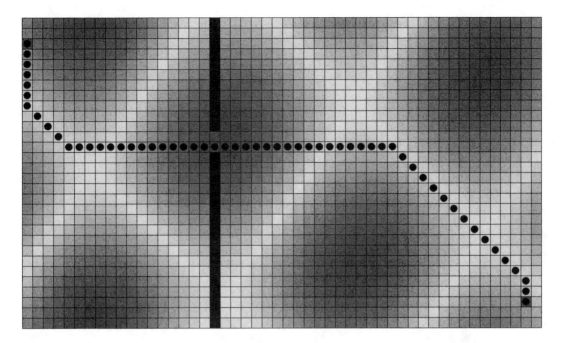

Figure 4-25. Forcing the path into difficult terrain

Summary

This final game example is pretty simple and leaves a lot for you to improve upon, but it shows you the basic setup for using A* pathfinding in a real game. Play around with it and see how the player navigates around the obstacles to get to where you clicked, if at all possible. Now you can imagine making a more animated player that looks more like a little person on a quest, who turns to walk in the direction he's going, and so on. And you might want to redo the walking motion so he's just walking in a smooth motion instead of easing from node to node. And, of course, some nice graphically designed tiles to represent grass or roads (walkable nodes) and maybe rivers and mountains (unwalkable nodes).

You can also relatively easily apply pathfinding to an isometric world, particularly if you've read and understood the previous chapter on isometric worlds. I'll leave that as an exercise to you.

Next up, we'll go in a completely different direction, looking at ways to use the microphone and camera not just to capture sound and images, but also to function as a way for a user to control an application with motion and noise.

Chapter 5

ALTERNATE INPUT: THE CAMERA AND MICROPHONE

If you've ever taken any kind of introductory computer science course, it's a sure bet that you ran across a diagram on your first day or in the first chapter of your text that was some variation of the one shown in Figure 5-1.

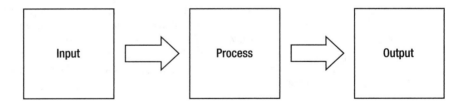

Figure 5-1. Input, process, output

If you were in the advanced course, there might have been another box hanging off somewhere labeled Storage.

And that's pretty much just what a computer does. It reads in some kind of data as input, does something with it, possibly stores it, possibly later retrieves it, and then spits it out in some form.

The vast majority of what has been written about computers and software focuses on the middle box—processing some data to create something worthy of output.

Input is generally assumed to be via the keyboard or mouse, and output almost always consists of writing something to the screen or making a sound come out of the speaker(s). Of course, there are lots of alternatives and infinite variations, but most daily operations for average programmers and end users deal with the mouse, keyboard, screen, and audio device.

To be fair, there's a whole lot you can do with a keyboard and mouse in terms of input. It's certainly a far cry from the earliest "personal computers," for which input meant flipping a series of switches, and output meant interpreting the on/off state of a row of LEDs. But I feel there's a bit of a disconnect in the fact that most of our input is mechanical or tactile, and most of our output is audible and visual.

Now, if you are into science fiction, you know that eventually we'll all be controlling our computers visually à la *Minority Report* and have conversations with them as in *2001: A Space Odyssey* (hopefully things work out better than the end of that movie). And although progress has been made in both areas, current touch screens tend to just mimic existing keyboards and existing physical input devices, and voice recognition technology, although improving, hasn't shown itself to be ready for prime time.

So, although I don't recommend that you write your next novel (or even your next program) via your microphone, exploring alternate input methods can be great fun and is what we'll explore in this chapter, specifically via the microphone and camera.

Cameras and Microphones

One of the barriers to using alternate input methods is that any input requires an input device. Alternate input requires an alternate device. Although you'd be hard-pressed to find a computer these days without a keyboard and mouse/trackball/trackpad, some forms of input require specialized, hard to get, and often expensive hardware. You also need to install special drivers, software, or even local servers to interact with that hardware and make its input available for your program.

Fortunately, almost every consumer laptop produced in the last couple of years seems to have a built-in camera and microphone, and even if your computer doesn't have them, you can pick them both up at almost any corner store for less than what you paid for this book. If you do need to buy them, microphones are usually plug-and-play, and webcams always come with an easy installation program that takes about three minutes to set up. And as a Flash developer, you have direct access to the camera and microphone to use as input devices.

People often think of the camera and microphone only in terms of making a chat or video conferencing type of application (in other words, taking the voice or camera stream, sending it to another computer, and playing it back pretty much as it came in). But a few people have experimented with the idea of using sound and video as a more direct input device—capturing the audio or video input, analyzing it, and using it to affect something that's going on in a program.

This chapter gives you some ideas of how to use a camera and/or microphone as an input device. Of course, there's no way I could even come close to describing every possible way, but I'll discuss the basic techniques of how to capture video and sound, and show some ways to manipulate them. From there, it's all a matter of your own creativity for what you do with them. We'll start out with the relatively simple case of handling the microphone.

Sound as Input

Microphone input in Flash is done via (no surprise) the Microphone class. This class is quite easy to work with, but unfortunately that's because it is also rather limited in what you can do with it. Many people who are familiar with ActionScript's Sound class learn about the Microphone class and immediately try to compute real-time sound spectrums. If this is what you are expecting, let me dash your hopes right here and now. Don't think you can record the sound coming in through the microphone, either. Neither is supported by the Microphone class.

The Microphone class's main functionality is returning the current **activity level** of a particular microphone. This activity level is a number from 0 to 100, indicating how much sound is being received by the microphone—0 is no sound, and 100 is the maximum amount of sound it can register. With a little creativity, you can do some cool things with this value. First let's look at how to get access to the microphone via ActionScript.

The Microphone class has a static method called getMicrophone, which returns an instance of the Microphone class that represents a single physical microphone attached to the computer. If you call the method with no parameters, it will return the first microphone it finds on the system. If you pass a value of –1 to getMicrophone, it will return the default microphone on the system. In most cases, they are the same thing, and that is the microphone you are looking for. You can get fancy and retrieve a list of all microphones on the system and use an index of that list to select a specific microphone to use in Flash, but this is usually overkill.

You can try the following MicrophoneTest class to play around with the getMicrophone method. Like the rest of the code in this book, it's available for download from the book's download page at www.friendsofed.com (the file is MicrophoneTest.as):

```
package {
    import flash.display.Sprite;
    import flash.media.Microphone;

    public class MicrophoneTest extends Sprite
    {
        private var _mic:Microphone;

        public function MicrophoneTest()
        {
            _mic = Microphone.getMicrophone();
            trace(_mic.name);
        }
    }
}
```

Try passing in different values to getMicrophone and see what it traces out. Eventually, you'll try to index a microphone that doesn't exist. This will return null and you'll get an error saying you can't access a property or method of a null object, which is exactly what should happen.

If you want to prompt your users to choose a microphone, you do so by calling up the Microphone settings panel via the Security.showSettings method, like so:

```
package {
    import flash.display.Sprite;
    import flash.media.Microphone;
    import flash.system.Security;
    import flash.system.SecurityPanel;

    public class MicrophoneTest extends Sprite
    {
        private var _mic:Microphone;

        public function MicrophoneTest()
        {
            _mic = Microphone.getMicrophone();
            Security.showSettings(SecurityPanel.MICROPHONE);
        }
    }
}
```

This will present the user with the Microphone dialog box shown in Figure 5-2, which prompts a microphone selection.

After you choose a microphone and press the Close button, the Camera and Microphone Access dialog box displays, as you can see in Figure 5-3.

Figure 5-2. Microphone dialog box

Figure 5-3. Camera and Microphone Access dialog box

You've probably seen this dialog box before—it simply confirms that it is okay for the Flash movie to use the microphone and/or camera on the computer. As you can imagine, it would be a problem if a Flash movie could access your camera and microphone and start broadcasting your personal life without your knowledge!

You might wonder why you didn't get the access dialog box in the first example. Although you did grab a reference to the microphone, you didn't actually start using it, so there was no risk at that point. Flash will know when the microphone's data itself is accessed for the first time and will display the access dialog box at that point.

Now let's start accessing this microphone and reading the activity level. The activity level will change constantly, so we'd better keep checking it. Sounds like a job for an enterFrame handler. Our first attempt as follows:

```
package {
    import flash.display.Sprite;
    import flash.events.Event;
    import flash.media.Microphone;
    import flash.system.Security;
    import flash.system.SecurityPanel;

    public class MicrophoneTest extends Sprite
    {
        private var _mic:Microphone;

        public function MicrophoneTest()
        {
            _mic = Microphone.getMicrophone();
            addEventListener(Event.ENTER_FRAME, onEnterFrame);
        }

        private function onEnterFrame(event:Event):void
        {
            trace(_mic.activityLevel);
        }
    }
}
```

Simple enough. In the onEnterFrame handler, you just trace out _mic.activityLevel. However, when you try this, you'll just get a long column of –1s tracing out. Doesn't matter how loud you talk, which microphone you select, or whether you grant access to the Flash movie to use your microphone, there just isn't any activity registering. Again, this is because the Flash movie is not yet doing anything with the microphone data.

There are two ways to get the Flash movie to start using the data. One is to attach the microphone to a NetStream, which usually happens in some kind of chat application or voice recording system, by using a streaming server such as Flash Media Server or Red5. The other way is to set the microphone's input to loop back through the speakers via the setLoopback method. Passing in true to this method causes Flash to start accessing the microphone's input, and you should see an activity level when you make some noise. As you might expect, passing in false stops the activity. If you don't want to hear your own voice coming back at you, simply turn down the volume of the output on your specific computer.

```
package {
    import flash.display.Sprite;
    import flash.events.Event;
    import flash.media.Microphone;

    public class MicrophoneTest extends Sprite
    {
        private var _mic:Microphone;
```

```
            public function MicrophoneTest()
            {
                _mic = Microphone.getMicrophone();
                _mic.setLoopBack(true);
                addEventListener(Event.ENTER_FRAME, onEnterFrame);
            }

            private function onEnterFrame(event:Event):void
            {
                trace(_mic.activityLevel);
            }
        }
    }
```

Run this example, talk into your microphone, and see what numbers trace out. If these numbers are very low, despite making a lot of noise, you might need to adjust the gain. **Gain** is essentially a level of amplification that is applied to the microphone before its data is accessed in Flash. Gain can be set in two ways: visually and by code. In the Microphone dialog box shown in Figure 5-2, there is a slider labeled Record Volume. Changing this slider changes the gain. To change this value via code, just set the microphone's gain property to a value between 0 and 100, with 100 as the maximum amplification.

Assuming that you now have some interesting numbers tracing out, let's do something with those numbers besides just tracing them out. The next example creates a bitmap and uses the activity level to set a pixel in it on each frame. The bitmap is scrolled to the left, so you get a running recording of the sound volume reaching the microphone:

```
    package {
        import flash.display.Bitmap;
        import flash.display.BitmapData;
        import flash.display.Sprite;
        import flash.display.StageAlign;
        import flash.display.StageScaleMode;
        import flash.events.Event;
        import flash.media.Microphone;

        public class MicrophoneTest extends Sprite
        {
            private var _mic:Microphone;
            private var _bmpd:BitmapData;

            public function MicrophoneTest()
            {
                stage.align = StageAlign.TOP_LEFT;
                stage.scaleMode = StageScaleMode.NO_SCALE;

                _bmpd = new BitmapData(400, 50, false, 0xffffff);
                addChild(new Bitmap(_bmpd));
```

```
            _mic = Microphone.getMicrophone();
            _mic.setLoopBack(true);
            addEventListener(Event.ENTER_FRAME, onEnterFrame);
        }

        private function onEnterFrame(event:Event):void
        {
            // draw a pixel at coordinates:
            // x = 298
            // y = 50 minus half of the mic level
            _bmpd.setPixel(298, 50 - _mic.activityLevel / 2, 0);
            // scroll the bitmap to the left
            _bmpd.scroll(-1, 0);
        }
    }
}
```

This gives you the result shown in Figure 5-4.

Figure 5-4. Visually graphing the activity level

Now that's fine for visualization purposes, but it's not really using the microphone as an alternate input method. How about a simple game using sound to control a character's movement? The next example does just that.

A sound-controlled game

The next example is a class called SoundFlier (you can find it as SoundFlier.as in the book's downloadable files). We create an airplane-like vehicle that flies through a roughly drawn cave full of rather rectangular stalactites and stalagmites, using the microphone activity level to control its lift:

```
package {
    import flash.display.Bitmap;
    import flash.display.BitmapData;
    import flash.display.Sprite;
    import flash.display.StageAlign;
    import flash.display.StageScaleMode;
    import flash.events.Event;
    import flash.geom.Rectangle;
    import flash.media.Microphone;
```

```
[SWF(backgroundColor=0xffffff)]
public class SoundFlier extends Sprite
{
    private var _mic:Microphone;
    private var _flier:Sprite;
    private var _bg:Bitmap;
    private var _yVelocity:Number = 0;

    public function SoundFlier()
    {
        stage.align = StageAlign.TOP_LEFT;
        stage.scaleMode = StageScaleMode.NO_SCALE;

        makeBackground();
        makeFlier();

        _mic = Microphone.getMicrophone();
        _mic.setLoopBack(true);
        addEventListener(Event.ENTER_FRAME, onEnterFrame);
    }

    private function makeBackground():void
    {
        var bmpd:BitmapData = new BitmapData(stage.stageWidth,
                                             stage.stageHeight,
                                             false);
        _bg = new Bitmap(bmpd);
        addChild(_bg);
    }

    private function makeFlier():void
    {
        _flier = new Sprite();
        _flier.graphics.lineStyle(0);
        _flier.graphics.moveTo(-10, 0);
        _flier.graphics.lineTo(-10, -8);
        _flier.graphics.lineTo(-7, -4);
        _flier.graphics.lineTo(10, 0);
        _flier.graphics.lineTo(-10, 0);
        _flier.x = 100;
        _flier.y = stage.stageHeight - 50;
        addChild(_flier);
    }
```

```
private function onEnterFrame(event:Event):void
{
    _yVelocity += .4;
    _yVelocity -= _mic.activityLevel * .02;
    _flier.y += _yVelocity;
    _yVelocity *= .9;
    _flier.y = Math.min(_flier.y, stage.stageHeight - 20);
    _flier.y = Math.max(_flier.y, 20);

    var h:Number = Math.random() * 120;
    _bg.bitmapData.fillRect(new Rectangle(
                            stage.stageWidth - 20,
                            0, 5, h),
                            0xcccccc);

    h = Math.random() * 120;
    _bg.bitmapData.fillRect(new Rectangle(
                            stage.stageWidth - 20,
                            stage.stageHeight - h,
                            5, h),
                            0xcccccc);

    _bg.bitmapData.scroll(-5, 0);
    }
  }
}
```

The flier is a sprite, and the background is a scrolling bitmap with random rectangles drawn over to the right. The important part is right here in the onEnterFrame method:

```
_yVelocity += .4;
_yVelocity -= _mic.activityLevel * .02;
_flier.y += _yVelocity;
_yVelocity *= .9;
_flier.y = Math.min(_flier.y, stage.stageHeight - 20);
_flier.y = Math.max(_flier.y, 20);
```

We keep track of a vertical velocity in the _yVelocity property. We add .4 to it each frame for gravity and then subtract the activity level * .02 for some lift. These numbers were arrived at through lots of trial and error. (Thanks to my six-year-old daughter Kristine for all the help in testing!) The velocity is then added to the flier's y position, some pseudo friction is applied through multiplying by .9, and finally the flier's position is bracketed within a minimum and maximum area to keep it visible. The result is shown in Figure 5-5.

Figure 5-5. Sound flier!

As you talk or otherwise make noise into the microphone, the flier will fly. Shut up, and it falls to earth. The stalagmites and friends scroll to the left, giving the illusion of the flier flying to the right. There's no collision detection implemented (I don't want to do all your work for you!), but you get the idea. Make just enough noise to keep the flier in the middle area. One thing you can say about a game like this is that it's not the kind of game you stealthily play in your cubicle when the boss isn't looking.

Although really just the beginning of a game, this example should hopefully spark a few ideas on how you can use a microphone to control some portion of a game or application. Next we'll take a look at an alternate way of handling microphone activity.

Activity events

In the SoundFlier game, we check the activity level on every frame. For that type of game, which requires quick reflexes by the user and instantaneous reactions by the game itself, constant checking and updating is vital. But you might envision an application that needs to do something only if the sound reaches a certain threshold. You might try running an enterFrame handler and checking the activity level on each frame to see whether it is above a certain value. But this process would be very inefficient, using up CPU cycles constantly when it should just be sitting and waiting for something to happen.

Fortunately, the Microphone class provides an exact solution for this situation: the ActivityEvent, which is an event class that the Microphone class dispatches whenever a specified sound threshold level is crossed. Interestingly, an ActivityEvent is dispatched in two circumstances: when the activity level rises above the threshold and again when it drops below that threshold. To distinguish between the two, the event has a Boolean value named activating. If it is true, the activity level has gone from a quieter state, crossing the threshold on the way up. If it is false, the threshold has been crossed as things are quieting down.

By listening for this event, you can have your application stand by in an idle state and react only when the noise reaches a certain volume and again when it quiets down.

You can use this as a sort of "noise-activated switch" to control just about any aspect of any application or game. You might want to think beyond browser-based applications here and consider how it might be used in an AIR-based desktop application. You could even create a crude security system. Imagine that when an application "heard a noise" at your house, it activated your webcam and notified you at work, allowing you to see what's happening there.

Or going the other way, you could set the microphone next to some machinery. If and when the machinery stopped running, the application would sense the drop in activity below the threshold and take action.

Let's just run through a really quick example to see it in action. There's not too much to wrap your head around, so once you see how this works, you'll be able to use this mechanism to control anything. This will be a re-creation of an old device that you attach to the lamps in your house to turn them on or off by clapping. So we'll call the class Clapper (it is in the Clapper.as downloadable file):

```
package {
    import flash.display.Sprite;
    import flash.display.StageAlign;
    import flash.display.StageScaleMode;
    import flash.events.ActivityEvent;
    import flash.media.Microphone;

    public class Clapper extends Sprite
    {
        private var _mic:Microphone;
        private var _on:Boolean = false;

        public function Clapper()
        {
            stage.align = StageAlign.TOP_LEFT;
            stage.scaleMode = StageScaleMode.NO_SCALE;

            _mic = Microphone.getMicrophone();
            _mic.setLoopBack();
            _mic.setSilenceLevel(25, 500);
            _mic.addEventListener(ActivityEvent.ACTIVITY, onActivity);

            update();
        }

        private function onActivity(event:ActivityEvent):void
        {
            if(event.activating)
```

```
        {
            _on = !_on;
            update();
        }
    }

    private function update():void
    {
        graphics.clear();
        if(_on)
        {
            graphics.beginFill(0xffffff);
        }
        else
        {
            graphics.beginFill(0);
        }
        graphics.drawRect(0, 0,
                          stage.stageWidth, stage.stageHeight);
    }
  }
}
```

Pretty basic stuff here. We get a microphone, set it to loopback so Flash will start listening to its input, and add a listener for ActivityEvent.ACTIVITY. Note that we also call a method named setSilenceLevel. Remember when I mentioned the concept of a threshold a few times in the preceding discussion? This is how you define that threshold: it is the value below which Flash will consider silence and above which Flash considers activity. When the activityLevel of the microphone crosses this level—going in either direction—an ActivityEvent will fire. I set it to 25 so it takes a bit of noise to get it to trigger, but you don't have make a huge racket. If you don't call setSilenceLevel, the default threshold the microphone uses is 10.

The second parameter of setSilenceLevel is a timeout value measured in milliseconds. When an ActivityEvent is dispatched, the microphone will ignore any other potential activity events for this amount of time. Suppose that you want to pay attention to a sound that is not constant, such as a bang, bang, bang. With each bang, the activity level goes up and then down, so you'll get two events for each bang. Instead, you just want to know when the banging starts and when it stops. By tweaking this timeout, you can ignore the spaces in between the bangs. The default is 2000, or a 2-second delay, which is probably optimal for a chat application in which a person might pause for a second or so while speaking, but you don't want to take it as silence. I set this a bit lower, down to 500 for this application, so you can clap pretty quickly to toggle the "lamp" on and off.

The onActivity method checks the value of event.activating. Again, this will be true if the activity has gone from silence to noise, and will be false if it has gone from noise to silence. We'll ignore the second case and just focus on new loud noises coming in: a clap. In here, we toggle the _on variable and call update. The update method just draws a black or white rectangle, depending on the state of _on.

Try it out. Clap on, clap off! I recommend experimenting with the parameters of setSilenceLevel to see how they affect things. It's also worth mentioning that there are read-only properties on the Microphone class for silenceLevel and silenceTimeout if you want to see their current settings.

Okay, those are the basics of using the microphone. As I said, there isn't much complex functionality there, but then again there isn't much complex functionality with a keyboard or mouse, either, and look what we do with them. Now let's take a look at alternate input using video.

Video as Input

Although sound input is handled through the Microphone class, video input is handled through the Camera class. Although they handle different things, these two classes are quite similar. You get a reference to a camera attached to the computer by calling Camera.getCamera. The Camera class has an activityLevel property, dispatches ActivityEvents, and has a setMotionLevel analogous to the Microphone class's setSilenceLevel. Both are designed to be used either locally or in conjunction with a streaming server such as Red5 or Flash Media Server. Again, we'll be using Camera just for local input in this chapter.

But despite the similarities, there is a lot more you can do with a camera. First, in addition to simply reading the activity level or responding to activity events, you can view the input of the camera via a Video object, which is a display object that you add to the display list and can do anything you do to a display object: filters, transformations, blend modes, and so on. And perhaps the most powerful use of the camera is to draw the video to a BitmapData. When you do that, you can start analyzing the image pixel by pixel or frame by frame, comparing areas of the image with each other or comparing one frame to the next. Once you start doing that, the possibilities really are endless. I'll try to spark your imagination with a few examples in this chapter, but even if I spent an entire book writing about what you could do here, I'm sure you'd wind up with something a week later that I'd never imagined.

But all things start at the beginning, so let's look at how to get a hold of the camera and see its input. The first steps are almost identical to getting a microphone. The next class is available for download as CameraTest.as:

```
package {
    import flash.display.Sprite;
    import flash.media.Camera;
    import flash.system.Security;
    import flash.system.SecurityPanel;

    public class CameraTest extends Sprite
    {
        private var _cam:Camera;

        public function CameraTest()
        {
            _cam = Camera.getCamera();
            trace(_cam.name);

            Security.showSettings(SecurityPanel.CAMERA);
        }
    }
}
```

You call Camera.getCamera to—well, to get a camera. You can pass a string referring to the name of a camera on the system, but in general you won't have any idea of what the cameras are, so it's best to pass nothing and get the default camera. However, it's often a good idea to call up the Camera settings dialog box to prompt the user to choose a specific camera. This is shown in the last line in the example, and will result in the dialog box shown in Figure 5-6. Although I won't show it in future examples in this chapter, you should remember that it's there and consider using it in your applications to make sure that the user knows how to select the camera.

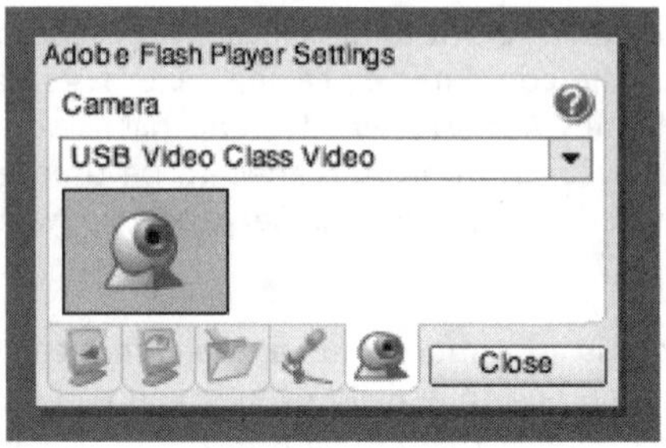

Figure 5-6. Camera dialog box

Now that we have a camera reference, let's make it visible. You do this by attaching it to a Video instance. The Video class is, as I just mentioned, a display object. So you create one, attach the camera to it, and add it to the display list:

```
package {
    import flash.display.Sprite;
    import flash.display.StageAlign;
    import flash.display.StageScaleMode;
    import flash.media.Camera;
    import flash.media.Video;

    public class CameraTest extends Sprite
    {
        private var _cam:Camera;
        private var _vid:Video;

        public function CameraTest()
        {
            stage.align = StageAlign.TOP_LEFT;
            stage.scaleMode = StageScaleMode.NO_SCALE;

            _cam = Camera.getCamera();
            _vid = new Video();
            _vid.attachCamera(_cam);
            addChild(_vid);
        }
    }
}
```

If all goes well, and if unlike me, you are in a decently lit room, you should see your beautiful face staring back at you (I just see a grainy gray blob on a grainy gray rectangle, but I'm pretty sure it's me). After you run this file, you'll see the Camera and Microphone Access dialog box shown in Figure 5-3 again because you are now accessing the camera's input.

Video size and quality

You now have a camera capturing video and displaying it to the screen. All very good, but it's not very big and probably doesn't look as detailed as other applications you use on the same computer with the same camera. That's not because Flash is bad, but simply because you're using default settings and sizes for both the camera and video.

You can specify the size of the video right when you create it. It defaults to 320×240, but you can pass in a larger size:

```
_vid = new Video(640, 480);
```

Alternately, you can set the video's width and height after it has been created.

You now have a bigger video, but it's not necessarily a better picture. To improve it, we have to go back to the Camera class and its setMode method. It takes four arguments, but we'll discuss only the first three here: width, height, and frames per second (fps). (The fourth argument determines how Flash will handle a mode that can't be matched by your camera. Feel free to read up on it.) By default, these arguments are set to 160×120 at 15 fps. Aha! That's why the video looked so bad. Bump this up to 320×240 or even 640×480 to see the difference. The 15 fps setting is probably fine for now:

```
package {
    import flash.display.Sprite;
    import flash.display.StageAlign;
    import flash.display.StageScaleMode;
    import flash.media.Camera;
    import flash.media.Video;

    public class CameraTest extends Sprite
    {
        private var _cam:Camera;
        private var _vid:Video;

        public function CameraTest()
        {
            stage.align = StageAlign.TOP_LEFT;
            stage.scaleMode = StageScaleMode.NO_SCALE;

            _cam = Camera.getCamera();
            _cam.setMode(640, 480, 15);
            _vid = new Video(640, 480);
            _vid.attachCamera(_cam);
            addChild(_vid);
        }
    }
}
```

Realize that the higher the fps and resolution for your camera, the more work your computer will have to do to process all that incoming video data. As you'll soon see, when using a camera for input, the quality and size of the video might have less importance than when using it for something like video conferencing. So don't go overboard if you don't need to. And if you're digging around, you might come across a setQuality method. It has to do with bandwidth and compression for sending the video stream to a streaming server, and is not really applicable for what we'll be doing in this chapter, so don't worry about it for now.

If this is the first time you've programmed with the camera in Flash, take some time to play. Throw some filters or blend modes on the video, rotate, scale, move around, and have fun. When you're done, we'll start digging in to dissect that video stream.

Videos and bitmaps

As mentioned earlier, some of the real power of using a camera as input is discovered when you start combining it with the BitmapData class. To do this, simply draw the video onto a BitmapData object using the BitmapData draw method. Now you have pixel-level access to and control of the whole thing. Of course, for a moving image, you'll want to do this repeatedly, via either a timer or frames. Here's the basic setup, available in the CameraBitmap.as downloadable file:

```
package {
    import flash.display.Bitmap;
    import flash.display.BitmapData;
    import flash.display.Sprite;
    import flash.display.StageAlign;
    import flash.display.StageScaleMode;
    import flash.events.Event;
    import flash.media.Camera;
    import flash.media.Video;

    public class CameraBitmap extends Sprite
    {
        private var _cam:Camera;
        private var _vid:Video;
        private var _bmpd:BitmapData;

        public function CameraBitmap()
        {
            stage.align = StageAlign.TOP_LEFT;
            stage.scaleMode = StageScaleMode.NO_SCALE;

            _cam = Camera.getCamera();
            _cam.setMode(320, 240, 15);
            _vid = new Video(320, 240);
            _vid.attachCamera(_cam);

            _bmpd = new BitmapData(320, 240, false);
            addChild(new Bitmap(_bmpd));
```

```
        addEventListener(Event.ENTER_FRAME, onEnterFrame);
    }

    private function onEnterFrame(event:Event):void
    {
        _bmpd.draw(_vid);
    }
}
}
```

Here we create a `BitmapData`, wrap it in a `Bitmap`, and add it to the display list instead of the video. On each frame, we draw the video onto the `BitmapData`. I bumped the size back down to 320×240 to give the CPU a break. Other than that, you shouldn't really be able to tell that you're watching a bitmap instead of a video. But you now have the full power of `BitmapData` and the ability to read and tweak every pixel of that video in every frame.

Flipping the Image

One thing to keep in mind is that the user will be facing the camera and making various physical gestures in an attempt to control things. If he moves left, he expects that motion to move something to the left. If he moves right, he expects something to move to the right. But the camera displays the user's image exactly if someone were looking directly at him instead of looking in a mirror. This will feel backward and confuse the user. But we can flip the image as we draw it to take care of this confusion.

Just change the line that draws the video to the bitmap to read as follows:

```
var matrix:Matrix = new Matrix(-1, 0, 0, 1, _bmpd.width, 0);
_bmpd.draw(_vid, matrix);
```

Make sure that you import the `flash.geom.Matrix` class. Passing in a matrix transforms the object as it is drawn. You can do a lot with a matrix, but (very simply put) the first four parameters control scaling, rotation, and skew. Here −1 scales the image on the x-axis, flipping it. The zeros mean that the image will not rotate or skew, and the next 1 means it will be scaled to 100% on the y-axis. But now it will extend off the left of the bitmap, so you won't see anything. The last two parameters move the image on the x- and y-axis. So we move it on the x-axis by its own width, moving it back into viewing range, and zero on the y-axis. Try this out with the previous example. Now it seems like you are looking in a mirror and will allow controls to be much more natural.

Analyzing pixels

Now that you have your pixels, what do you do with them? Remember when I said that high-quality and high-resolution video is not always necessary in video input? I'll take that a step further and say that it's probably even better to go as low-res and low-quality as you can. If you take even a 320×240 video image, that's 76,800 pixels to analyze per frame. Chances are you won't need all that data. Furthermore, trying to process it all will make your CPU work hard, which will make your computer run hot, burn your legs, waste your battery, and make everything else on your computer run slow. So give it all a break and don't go crazy on the video size.

As a matter of fact, you'll see that the first few things we do are designed to get rid of a vast majority of the information in all those pixels, anyway. All we are generally interested in are specific areas of the video where a certain color appears, or there is a certain contrast, or something is changing.

Analyzing colors

For our first attempt, let's try to track a particular color. We can then have the user hold something up in front of the camera with a distinct color, say bright red, and track the location of that color as he or she moves the object around, so it acts almost like a virtual joystick.

We can use a built-in method of BitmapData to track certain color pixels: getColorBoundsRect. Essentially, we pass in a color to look for and it gives us back a rectangle describing a bounding box that surrounds any and all pixels containing that color. The method looks like this:

```
bitmapData.getColorBoundsRect(mask:uint,
                              color:uint,
                              findColor:Boolean);
```

The mask allows you to look for particular color channels. For example, if you pass in 0xFF0000 as a mask, the method will look only at the red component of pixels to determine a match. This is because the red channel of the mask is FF, and the green and blue channels are 00, so it ignores those and looks only at red. The color is obviously the color you are trying to find. The findColor parameter, if true, finds the rectangle surrounding all the pixels of the color you passed in; if false, it returns the rectangle that surrounds all the pixels that are *not* that color.

Because we don't know what color users will try to track, we'll let them click the bitmap to choose a color. We'll find the rectangle surrounding that color and draw a rectangle in a sprite on top of the bitmap. Here's what it looks like so far (in the ColorTracking.as file):

```
package {
    import flash.display.Bitmap;
    import flash.display.BitmapData;
    import flash.display.Sprite;
    import flash.display.StageAlign;
    import flash.display.StageScaleMode;
    import flash.events.Event;
    import flash.events.MouseEvent;
    import flash.geom.Matrix;
    import flash.geom.Rectangle;
    import flash.media.Camera;
    import flash.media.Video;

    public class ColorTracking extends Sprite
    {
        private var _cam:Camera;
        private var _vid:Video;
        private var _bmpd:BitmapData;
        private var _cbRect:Sprite;
        private var _color:uint = 0xffffff;
```

```
public function ColorTracking()
{
    stage.align = StageAlign.TOP_LEFT;
    stage.scaleMode = StageScaleMode.NO_SCALE;

    _cam = Camera.getCamera();
    _cam.setMode(320, 240, 15);
    _vid = new Video(320, 240);
    _vid.attachCamera(_cam);

    _bmpd = new BitmapData(320, 240, false);
    addChild(new Bitmap(_bmpd));

    _cbRect = new Sprite();
    addChild(_cbRect);

    addEventListener(Event.ENTER_FRAME, onEnterFrame);
    stage.addEventListener(MouseEvent.CLICK, onClick);
}

private function onClick(event:MouseEvent):void
{
    _color = _bmpd.getPixel(mouseX, mouseY);
}

private function onEnterFrame(event:Event):void
{
    _bmpd.draw(_vid, new Matrix(-1, 0, 0, 1, _bmpd.width, 0));
    var rect:Rectangle = _bmpd.getColorBoundsRect(0xffffff,
                                                  _color,
                                                  true);

    _cbRect.graphics.clear();
    _cbRect.graphics.lineStyle(1, 0xff0000);
    _cbRect.graphics.drawRect(rect.x, rect.y,
                              rect.width, rect.height);
}
    }
}
```

There's no real rocket science going on here (yet). We create a sprite called _cbRect into which we'll draw the color bounds rectangle. When users click the bitmap, we use getPixel to find out what color pixel they clicked. This is passed to getColorBoundsRect on each frame. Notice that we use a mask of 0xFFFFFF, so we're looking at all channels of the color. When we get the rectangle, we draw that rectangle with a red line in _cbRect. Simple enough.

Now, try this by holding some brightly colored object up in front of the camera, clicking it in the bitmap, and then moving it around. You might see a rectangle appear on some frames, but it is probably very tiny. It might disappear for awhile and then come back, get really big suddenly, and then go again. It might work pretty well, tracking the object for awhile, but it's certainly not stable enough.

The problem is that there is just too much pixel information there—76,800 pixels, and each one can be any one of more than 16 million possible color values. You've chosen one of those values. Even if you have a solid colored object, the lighting, shadows, texture, shape, and so on cause all kinds of variations in color across its surface. The lighting and angle change when you start moving things around. At any given point there might be no pixels with that exact color value, or there might be a few that are far apart.

Basically, we need to simplify things and make less variation in color. There are a number of ways to do this. We can start off with a simple blur. Right after creating the Video object, add a blur filter to it:

```
_vid = new Video(320, 240);
_vid.attachCamera(_cam);
_vid.filters = [new BlurFilter(10, 10, 1)];
```
This might or might not help immediately. This causes the variation between adjacent pixels to be less, but they still aren't exactly the same.

There are a several options here. If you haven't played with the BitmapData class or the bitmap filters, look them over. There are all kinds of manipulations you can do. Color transformations with the ColorTransform class are helpful, manipulating color channels with copyChannel can be useful, and the threshold function is great at breaking down an image into simpler parts. But one I've found really useful in this case is the paletteMap method.

The paletteMap method takes each of the red, green, and blue (and even alpha if you want) channels of a bitmap and maps their values to another array. For each pixel in an image, each channel contains a value from 0 to 255 (or 0x00 to 0xFF if you are into hexadecimal). Each of these channels can be mapped to an array. The array would contain 256 values. So if the original value were 127, paletteMap would look at element 127 of the array to decide what value to give that pixel for that channel. What gets a little confusing, however, is that the arrays themselves contain 32-bit numbers, not 0–255. So your red channel mapping array would contain values from 0x000000 to 0xFF0000. The green channel mapping array would contain values from 0x000000 to 0x00FF00, and blue would contain 0x000000 to 0x0000FF. Thus if you reversed each of these arrays, so that blue contained 0x0000FF through 0x000000, for example, it would totally invert the colors in your image. You can also mix and match the channels, putting elements of red into the green channel, and so on.

All we are interested in doing here is reducing the number of colors per channel. We can do that by saying that for a certain range of indexes in each array, all elements will have the same value—basically rounding them off. For example, in the red array we say that from 0 to 15, all elements will contain 0x000000 (0x00 in the red channel). From 16 to 31, they will contain 0x100000 (0x10 in the red channel); from 32 to 63, they will contain 0x200000 (0x20 in red), and so on. If we do that on each channel, each channel will contain just 16 different values instead of 256 individual values, for a possible total of only 4,086 colors in the image.

We'll call the method to do this makePaletteArrays, and here it is:

```
private function makePaletteArrays():void
{
    _red = new Array();
    _green = new Array();
    _blue = new Array();
    var levels:int = 8;
```

```
        var div:int = 256 / levels;
        for(var i:int = 0; i < 256; i++)
        {
            var value:Number = Math.floor(i / div ) * div;
            _red[i] = value << 16;
            _green[i] = value << 8;
            _blue[i] = value
        }
    }
}
```

Here, we are actually breaking each channel down into 8 individual values, for a total of only 256 colors in the image. Doing this will make it quite easy to track an individual color. You can also change it by changing the levels variable. Here's the class with all this implemented:

```
package {
    import flash.display.Bitmap;
    import flash.display.BitmapData;
    import flash.display.Sprite;
    import flash.display.StageAlign;
    import flash.display.StageScaleMode;
    import flash.events.Event;
    import flash.events.MouseEvent;
    import flash.filters.BlurFilter;
    import flash.geom.Matrix;
    import flash.geom.Point;
    import flash.geom.Rectangle;
    import flash.media.Camera;
    import flash.media.Video;

    public class ColorTracking extends Sprite
    {
        private var _cam:Camera;
        private var _vid:Video;
        private var _bmpd:BitmapData;
        private var _cbRect:Sprite;
        private var _color:uint = 0xffffff;
        private var _red:Array;
        private var _green:Array;
        private var _blue:Array;
        public function ColorTracking()
        {
            stage.align = StageAlign.TOP_LEFT;
            stage.scaleMode = StageScaleMode.NO_SCALE;

            _cam = Camera.getCamera();
            _cam.setMode(320, 240, 15);
            _vid = new Video(320, 240);
            _vid.attachCamera(_cam);
            _vid.filters = [new BlurFilter(10, 10, 1)];
```

```
        _bmpd = new BitmapData(320, 240, false);
        addChild(new Bitmap(_bmpd));

        _cbRect = new Sprite();
        addChild(_cbRect);

        makePaletteArrays();

        addEventListener(Event.ENTER_FRAME, onEnterFrame);
        stage.addEventListener(MouseEvent.CLICK, onClick);

    }

    private function makePaletteArrays():void
    {
        _red = new Array();
        _green = new Array();
        _blue = new Array();
        var levels:int = 8;
        var div:int = 256 / levels;
        for(var i:int = 0; i < 256; i++)
        {
            var value:Number = Math.floor(i / div ) * div;
            _red[i] = value << 16;
            _green[i] = value << 8;
            _blue[i] = value
        }
    }

    private function onClick(event:MouseEvent):void
    {
        _color = _bmpd.getPixel(mouseX, mouseY);
    }

    private function onEnterFrame(event:Event):void
    {
        _bmpd.draw(_vid, new Matrix(-1, 0, 0, 1, _bmpd.width, 0));
        _bmpd.paletteMap(_bmpd, _bmpd.rect, new Point(),
                        _red, _green, _blue);

        var rect:Rectangle = _bmpd.getColorBoundsRect(0xffffff,
                                                    _color,
                                                    true);
        _cbRect.graphics.clear();
        _cbRect.graphics.lineStyle(1, 0xff0000);
        _cbRect.graphics.drawRect(rect.x, rect.y,
                                rect.width, rect.height);
    }
    }
}
```

This doesn't always work perfectly and it generally requires a bit of tweaking with lighting and background. But if you have a distinctly colored object and have it well lit with a darker background, it can work pretty well. You can also adjust the levels variable to get just the right amount of color variation to keep it stable. In fact, you might want to make a sensitivity control in your application to allow the user to adjust that value on the fly. Just make sure you recalculate the channel palette map every time it changes.

Using tracked colors as input

Okay, now that we're tracking this rectangle, what do we do with it? Well, let's use its position to move something around. The next example creates a ball that will follow the motion of your object. You can have it follow the object right on the image, but you can also have it move in a whole separate area to perhaps control the character in a *Space Invaders*–type game.

The final code listing for this example throws in a sprite with a circle drawn in it and moves it around the stage with the same motion you are moving your tracked object:

```
package {
    import flash.display.Bitmap;
    import flash.display.BitmapData;
    import flash.display.Sprite;
    import flash.display.StageAlign;
    import flash.display.StageScaleMode;
    import flash.events.Event;
    import flash.events.MouseEvent;
    import flash.filters.BlurFilter;
    import flash.geom.Matrix;
    import flash.geom.Point;
    import flash.geom.Rectangle;
    import flash.media.Camera;
    import flash.media.Video;

    public class ColorTracking extends Sprite
    {
        private var _cam:Camera;
        private var _vid:Video;
        private var _bmpd:BitmapData;
        private var _cbRect:Sprite;
        private var _color:uint = 0xffffff;
        private var _red:Array;
        private var _green:Array;
        private var _blue:Array;
        private var _ball:Sprite;

        public function ColorTracking()
        {
            stage.align = StageAlign.TOP_LEFT;
            stage.scaleMode = StageScaleMode.NO_SCALE;

            _cam = Camera.getCamera();
            _cam.setMode(320, 240, 15);
```

219

```
        _vid = new Video(320, 240);
        _vid.attachCamera(_cam);
        _vid.filters = [new BlurFilter(10, 10, 1)];

        _bmpd = new BitmapData(320, 240, false);
        addChild(new Bitmap(_bmpd));

        _cbRect = new Sprite();
        addChild(_cbRect);

        _ball = new Sprite();
        _ball.graphics.beginFill(0x0000ff);
        _ball.graphics.drawCircle(0, 0, 40);
        _ball.graphics.endFill();
        addChild(_ball);

        makePaletteArrays();

        addEventListener(Event.ENTER_FRAME, onEnterFrame);
        stage.addEventListener(MouseEvent.CLICK, onClick);
    }

    private function makePaletteArrays():void
    {
        _red = new Array();
        _green = new Array();
        _blue = new Array();
        var levels:int = 4;
        var div:int = 256 / levels;
        for(var i:int = 0; i < 256; i++)
        {
            var value:Number = Math.floor(i / div ) * div;
            _red[i] = value << 16;
            _green[i] = value << 8;
            _blue[i] = value
        }
    }

    private function onClick(event:MouseEvent):void
    {
        _color = _bmpd.getPixel(mouseX, mouseY);
    }

    private function onEnterFrame(event:Event):void
    {
        _bmpd.draw(_vid, new Matrix(-1, 0, 0, 1, _bmpd.width, 0));
        _bmpd.paletteMap(_bmpd, _bmpd.rect, new Point(),
                        _red, _green, _blue);
```

```
          var rect:Rectangle = _bmpd.getColorBoundsRect(0xffffff,
                                                        _color,
                                                        true);
    _cbRect.graphics.clear();
    _cbRect.graphics.lineStyle(1, 0xff0000);
    _cbRect.graphics.drawRect(rect.x, rect.y,
                              rect.width, rect.height);

    if(!rect.isEmpty())
    {
        var xCenter:Number = rect.x + rect.width / 2;
        var yCenter:Number = rect.y + rect.height / 2;
        _ball.x = xCenter / _bmpd.width * stage.stageWidth;
        _ball.y = yCenter / _bmpd.height * stage.stageHeight;
    }
}
}
}
```

In the constructor, the ball is created and added to the display list. In the enterFrame handler, we first see whether the color bounds rectangle is empty, meaning that no pixels of our color were found. If so, we won't move the ball at all. Without this check, the ball would suddenly jump to the top-left corner any time no pixels were found. If we do have a rectangle, we find its center and the ratio of the center to the dimensions of the bitmap. Then we move the ball to the same relative position on the stage.

Again, this is just one way to track color. I highly encourage you to play around with some of the other methods of manipulating bitmaps, particularly the threshold method, color channels, color transforms, and other filters and blend modes. Instead of tracking specific colors, another strategy is to just track areas of dark and light.

Next up, we'll look at a more general way of tracking motion.

Analyzing areas of motion

In the last example, we attempted to track a specific object based on its color or (if you took up the challenge) based on dark and light. In this section, we aren't so much trying to keep track of the motion of a particular object, but picking up any motion whatsoever.

Here's the basic concept: if there is no motion, the bitmap will be pretty much the same from frame to frame. So, if we compare two consecutive frames, the areas where pixels are different indicate areas in which something has moved.

This implies two things. First, we'll need two bitmaps: a before and after. Second, we need some method of comparing the two to see what's different. True enough. But, if you're thinking that we need to loop through all the pixels of each bitmap to compare them, there's another trick that makes things much easier: using blend modes.

When you draw an object onto a BitmapData using its draw method, you have a few options. You've already seen the use of a matrix to transform the object's shape and position while drawing. There are a few more optional parameters after matrix: the next is a `ColorTransform`, and the next after that is a blend mode.

Drawing with a blend mode changes how the newly drawn pixels affect existing pixels. If you don't specify a blend mode, the new pixel values will simply overwrite the existing values. That's what we've been doing so far. The old image is completely wiped out, leaving only the new one. But using blend modes allows you to blend the two images together in a variety of ways. For our purposes, there is a blend mode called **difference**, which basically compares the red, green, and blue channels of each pixel in the two images and then gives you the difference between them. Comparing the same pixel in both images, if they are exactly the same, the difference will be zero for each channel, and the resulting pixel will be colored black. For any pixel that is not exactly the same in both images, the resulting pixel will have some other value. We have then simplified the problem down to looking for nonblack pixels to find areas of motion.

Although we could probably get away with two bitmaps for this, let's use three for clarity: one for the old frame, one for the new frame, and one for the blend. Figure 5-7 shows roughly what we'll be doing.

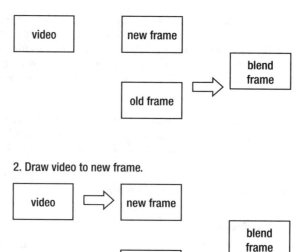

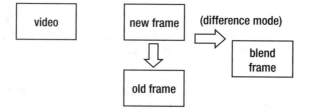

Figure 5-7. Combining old and new frames with the difference blend mode

The new frame, old frame, and blend frame refer to the BitmapData instances. First we draw the old frame to the blend frame with no blend mode so it wipes out what was there. Then we draw the video to the new frame, again with no blend mode.

Next, we draw the new frame to the old frame again with no blend mode, so it represents the previous frame next time around. Finally we draw the new frame to the blend frame with the difference blend mode.

Here's what it all looks like in code, which you can see in the MotionTracking.as file:

```
package {
    import flash.display.Bitmap;
    import flash.display.BitmapData;
    import flash.display.BlendMode;
    import flash.display.Sprite;
    import flash.display.StageAlign;
    import flash.display.StageScaleMode;
    import flash.events.Event;
    import flash.filters.BlurFilter;
    import flash.geom.Matrix;
    import flash.media.Camera;
    import flash.media.Video;

    public class MotionTracking extends Sprite
    {
        private var _cam:Camera;
        private var _vid:Video;
        private var _newFrame:BitmapData;
        private var _oldFrame:BitmapData;
        private var _blendFrame:BitmapData;


        public function MotionTracking()
        {
            stage.align = StageAlign.TOP_LEFT;
            stage.scaleMode = StageScaleMode.NO_SCALE;

            _cam = Camera.getCamera();
            _cam.setMode(320, 240, 15);
            _vid = new Video(320, 240);
            _vid.attachCamera(_cam);
            _vid.filters = [new BlurFilter(10, 10, 1)];

            _newFrame = new BitmapData(320, 240, false);
            _oldFrame = _newFrame.clone();
            _blendFrame = _newFrame.clone();
            addChild(new Bitmap(_blendFrame));

            addEventListener(Event.ENTER_FRAME, onEnterFrame);
        }
```

```
private function onEnterFrame(event:Event):void
{
    _blendFrame.draw(_oldFrame);
    _newFrame.draw(_vid, new Matrix(-1, 0, 0, 1,
                                    _newFrame.width, 0));
    _oldFrame.draw(_newFrame);
    _blendFrame.draw(_newFrame, null, null,
                     BlendMode.DIFFERENCE);
        }
    }
}
```

Hopefully you should be able to understand most of this now. We create the new frame bitmap and then create the rest by cloning it. We add only the last one to the display list. In the enterFrame handler we do the drawing in the same order specified in Figure 5-7.

When you first run this, you might see nothing but a black rectangle. But then move a bit and you'll see some ghostly white outlines (see Figure 5-8). These outlines are the areas that are different between frames.

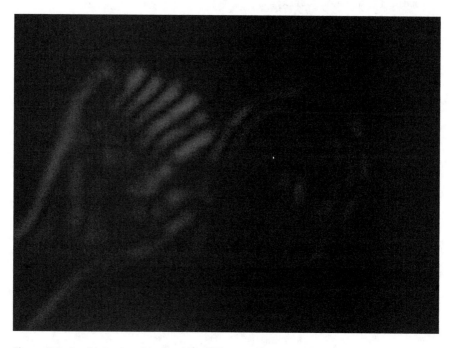

Figure 5-8. Combining two frames with a difference blend mode

Now let's see if we can use a color bounds rectangle to capture the areas of change. Create the _cbRect sprite the same way you did in the previous example. In the enterFrame handler, we do it a bit differently:

```
private function onEnterFrame(event:Event):void
{
    _blendFrame.draw(_oldFrame);
    _newFrame.draw(_vid, new Matrix(-1, 0, 0, 1, _newFrame.width, 0));
    _oldFrame.draw(_newFrame);
    _blendFrame.draw(_newFrame, null, null, BlendMode.DIFFERENCE);

    var rect:Rectangle = _blendFrame.getColorBoundsRect(0xffffff,
                                                        0x000000,
                                                        false);

    _cbRect.graphics.clear();
    _cbRect.graphics.lineStyle(1, 0xff0000);
    _cbRect.graphics.drawRect(rect.x, rect.y, rect.width, rect.height);
}
```

Note that this time we are looking for the color 0x000000 (black), but we are specifying false for the last argument, meaning that we'll get the rectangle that surrounds all nonblack pixels. But when you go ahead and try it, you'll find that the rectangle surrounds the entire bitmap (for the most part). Hmmm. It looks like all those pixels that appear black are not actually completely black. So, pixel per pixel, the two images weren't exactly the same—just very close. Close enough to make the difference look black to our eyes, but it's just not equal to 0x000000.

Let's pull another bitmap tool out of our bitmap toolbox—threshold—which is one of the more complex methods, but also one of the most powerful. I always struggle with it for awhile before I figure out how to make it do what I want, so if you have a hard time grasping it, don't feel alone.

The threshold method works by examining a bitmap and comparing each pixel with a value. The comparisons are almost all the numerical comparison operators: <, <=, ==, >=, >, and !=. If the comparison for a particular pixel evaluates to true, it colors that pixel a color of your choice. You can also specify a mask so that you are just looking at an individual color channel.

The mask is useful because you can't really directly compare two full-color values. For example, 0x010000 is almost pure black, with just the tiniest bit of red in it; and 0x0000FF is 100% blue, much brighter than 0x010000. Yet the blue would be evaluated as "less than" the almost black because numerically it is a smaller value. Here's what the threshold method looks like:

```
bitmapData.threshold(sourceBitmapData,
                sourceRect, destPoint, operation,
                threshold, color, mask, copySource)
```

The first parameter, sourceBitmapData, is the BitmapData whose pixels are being examined. The results will be drawn to the BitmapData on which we are calling the threshold method. Quite often this is the same BitmapData (as it is in our case), but you can examine one bitmap and draw the threshold results to another.

The sourceRect and destPoint determined the area of the bitmap to examine and where to place the results. Using the rect property of BitmapData and a new Point means it will examine the entire bitmap and place the results at 0, 0. The operation is a string containing >, >=, ==, <=, <, or !=. The threshold is the value you are comparing each pixel to, color is the value to set the pixel if the comparison is true, and mask is used to specify a particular color channel. The copySource parameter is used if you are examining one bitmap and drawing it to another. If so, you can choose to draw the source bitmap's pixels to the destination bitmap if the comparison is false. In our case, it doesn't matter because we're using only a single bitmap.

In this case, everything is so close to black that it doesn't really matter which channel we choose to do our comparison on. Red is as good as any. Here's the revised enterFrame handler:

```
private function onEnterFrame(event:Event):void
{
    _blendFrame.draw(_oldFrame);
    _newFrame.draw(_vid, new Matrix(-1, 0, 0, 1, _newFrame.width, 0));
    _oldFrame.draw(_newFrame);
    _blendFrame.draw(_newFrame, null, null, BlendMode.DIFFERENCE);
    _blendFrame.threshold(_blendFrame, _blendFrame.rect, new Point(),
                    "<", 0x00330000, 0xff000000, 0x00ff0000,
                    true);

    var rect:Rectangle = _blendFrame.getColorBoundsRect(0xffffff,
                                                        0x000000,
                                                        false);
    _cbRect.graphics.clear();
    _cbRect.graphics.lineStyle(1, 0xff0000);
    _cbRect.graphics.drawRect(rect.x, rect.y, rect.width, rect.height);
}
```

So, if the pixel's red channel (see how we masked red with 0x00ff0000) is less than (<) 0x00330000, color it black (0xff000000). Otherwise, copy the source (which doesn't matter because source and destination are the same). To put it in even simpler terms, if the pixel is *almost* black, make it *completely* black.

Note that I'm using 32-bit values for everything here. The threshold method is funny that way. Even if you are using opaque bitmaps, if you don't specify the alpha channel it will draw a transparent pixel. So we use 0xff000000 instead of just 0x000000 for black.

If you try this, it should work quite well, drawing the rectangle exactly where you would expect based on your movement.

So just what the heck should you use this moving rectangle for? Again, your imagination is the limit. The first thing I thought of was a sort of breakout game in which you move the paddle across the bottom of the screen to bounce a ball. But you could move the paddle by creating motion on either the left or right side of the screen. Here's a very rough example of how to begin:

```
package {
    import flash.display.Bitmap;
    import flash.display.BitmapData;
    import flash.display.BlendMode;
    import flash.display.Sprite;
    import flash.display.StageAlign;
    import flash.display.StageScaleMode;
```

```actionscript
import flash.events.Event;
import flash.filters.BlurFilter;
import flash.geom.Matrix;
import flash.geom.Point;
import flash.geom.Rectangle;
import flash.media.Camera;
import flash.media.Video;

public class MotionTracking extends Sprite
{
    private var _cam:Camera;
    private var _vid:Video;
    private var _newFrame:BitmapData;
    private var _oldFrame:BitmapData;
    private var _blendFrame:BitmapData;
    private var _cbRect:Sprite;
    private var _paddle:Sprite;


    public function MotionTracking()
    {
        stage.align = StageAlign.TOP_LEFT;
        stage.scaleMode = StageScaleMode.NO_SCALE;

        _cam = Camera.getCamera();
        _cam.setMode(320, 240, 15);
        _vid = new Video(320, 240);
        _vid.attachCamera(_cam);
        _vid.filters = [new BlurFilter(10, 10, 1)];

        _newFrame = new BitmapData(320, 240, false);
        addChild(new Bitmap(_newFrame));
        _oldFrame = _newFrame.clone();
        _blendFrame = _newFrame.clone();

        _cbRect = new Sprite();
        addChild(_cbRect);

        _paddle = new Sprite();
        _paddle.graphics.beginFill(0xffffff);
        _paddle.graphics.drawRect(-100, -20, 200, 40);
        _paddle.graphics.endFill();
        _paddle.x = stage.stageWidth / 2;
        _paddle.y = stage.stageHeight - 50;
        addChild(_paddle);

        addEventListener(Event.ENTER_FRAME, onEnterFrame);
    }
```

227

```
private function onEnterFrame(event:Event):void
{
    _blendFrame.draw(_oldFrame);
    _newFrame.draw(_vid, new Matrix(-1, 0, 0, 1,
                                    _newFrame.width, 0));
    _oldFrame.draw(_newFrame);
    _blendFrame.draw(_newFrame, null, null,
                    BlendMode.DIFFERENCE);
    _blendFrame.threshold(_blendFrame, _blendFrame.rect,
                        new Point(), "<", 0x00330000,
                        0xff000000, 0x00ff0000, true);

    var rect:Rectangle =
            _blendFrame.getColorBoundsRect(0xffffff, 0, false);
    _cbRect.graphics.clear();
    _cbRect.graphics.lineStyle(1, 0xff0000);
    _cbRect.graphics.drawRect(rect.x, rect.y,
                            rect.width, rect.height);

    if(!rect.isEmpty())
    {
        if(rect.x < _blendFrame.width / 2)
        {
            _paddle.x -= 20;
        }
        else
        {
            _paddle.x += 20;
        }
    }
}
}
}
```

Actually pretty simple. Create a paddle sprite and draw a shape in it. If the color bounds rectangle is to the right of center, move the paddle to the right. If it's to the left, move the paddle to the left. Brilliant, aren't I? Again, this is a mere sketch of how to get started. I'll leave it to you to make it pretty and smooth. Notice that I also decided not to add the blend bitmap to the display list, adding the new frame bitmap instead. This gives users an idea of where they are in the frame. Of course, the threshold and color bounds and all the rest work whether the bitmap is visible or not. Hide that stuff and make the motion detection seem like magic! Anyway, Figure 5-9 gives you an idea what this looks like.

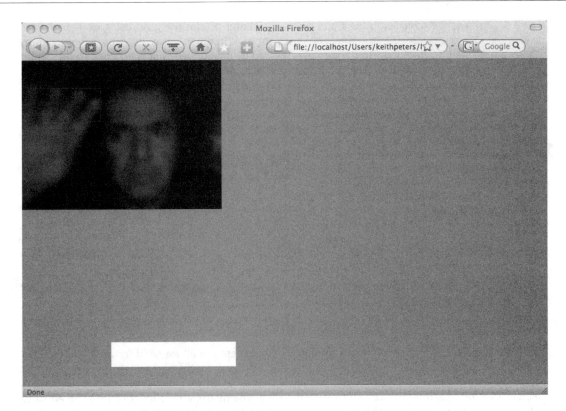

Figure 5-9. Controlling an object with hand motion

Analyzing edges

For our last foray into this subject, let's re-create a popular effect: detecting edges in an image and having things land on them. This makes for popular interactive exhibits often seen at children's museums and such, with the child's image onscreen and snow falling on it, butterflies landing on it, and so on. It's also been done in Flash a few times, probably most notably by Grant Skinner (www.gskinner.com), but let's have a go at it.

There are numerous ways to go about this, but what comes to mind immediately is to create a horizontal edge detection filter using the ConvolutionFilter class. A convolution filter goes through a bitmap, taking each pixel and comparing it with a grid or matrix of surrounding pixels. Each pixel's value is weighted and added to a total and then potentially divided by some factor. The result is applied to the original pixel. Convolution matrices are used extensively in image processing for blurring, sharpening, embossing, edge detection and enhancement, and so on.

Figure 5-10 shows the basic setup for a blur filter. The center pixel is the pixel being examined. Each pixel in the 3×3 grid is added to the total with a weight of 1. In other words, its value is multiplied by 1 before it is added to the total. Then the total is divided by 9, and the result is assigned to the center pixel. This has the effect of averaging out all surrounding pixels, giving you a blur. For a larger blur, you can use a larger grid.

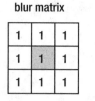

blur matrix

add all pixels, divide by 9
assign result to center pixel

Figure 5-10. Convolution matrix used for a blur

If you're interested in convolution matrices, a web search will turn up plenty of information and examples, most of which can be used right in ActionScript. With a bit of digging around and experimentation, I came up with some decent settings to create a horizontal edge-detecting filter. The ConvolutionFilter constructor looks like this:

```
ConvolutionFilter(matrixX, matrixY, matrix, divisor)
```

There are actually several more optional parameters, but these are all we need for now. The matrixX and matrixY parameters are Numbers that specify the width and height of the matrix, or the grid that will surround the pixel being examined. The matrix is an array of weights, which is what each pixel's value will be multiplied by before adding it to the total. The matrix array's length should be equal to matrixX times matrixY. Finally, the divisor is what the total is divided by before assigning it back to the original pixel. So, if we wanted to create a blur filter using the example shown in Figure 5-10, it would look like this:

```
new ConvolutionFilter(3, 3, [1,1,1,1,1,1,1,1,1], 9);
```

This sets up a 3×3 matrix and fills all the elements with 1. The result is divided by 9. Simple.

Here are the convolution settings I came up with for horizontal edges:

```
new ConvolutionFilter(1, 3, [0, 4, -4], 1);
```

Even simpler. It creates a 1×3 matrix, multiplies the current pixel by 4, and multiplies the lower pixel by −4. The divisor is 1, so the total is applied to the center pixel as is. Again, you can read more about how convolution matrices work if you want. This has the effect of darkening most pixels but lightening those that fall on a visual horizontal edge. Let's see it in action on a video. Here's the class, which you can find in the EdgeTracking.as file:

```
package {
    import flash.display.Bitmap;
    import flash.display.BitmapData;
    import flash.display.Sprite;
```

```
import flash.display.StageAlign;
import flash.display.StageScaleMode;
import flash.events.Event;
import flash.filters.BlurFilter;
import flash.filters.ConvolutionFilter;
import flash.geom.Matrix;
import flash.geom.Point;
import flash.media.Camera;
import flash.media.Video;

public class EdgeTracking extends Sprite
{
    private var _cam:Camera;
    private var _vid:Video;
    private var _bmpd:BitmapData;

    public function EdgeTracking()
    {
        stage.align = StageAlign.TOP_LEFT;
        stage.scaleMode = StageScaleMode.NO_SCALE;

        _cam = Camera.getCamera();
        _cam.setMode(320, 240, 15);
        _vid = new Video(320, 240);
        _vid.attachCamera(_cam);
        _vid.filters = [new ConvolutionFilter(1, 3, [0, 4, -4]),
                        new BlurFilter()];

        _bmpd = new BitmapData(320, 240, false);
        addChild(new Bitmap(_bmpd));

        addEventListener(Event.ENTER_FRAME, onEnterFrame);
    }

    private function onEnterFrame(event:Event):void
    {
        _bmpd.draw(_vid, new Matrix(-1, 0, 0, 1, _bmpd.width, 0));
    }
}
}
```

Almost none of this is new ground, except the ConvolutionFilter. I also threw a blur in there to smooth things out. The result is shown in Figure 5-11.

Figure 5-11. Creating horizontal edge detection

Here you can plainly see that any horizontal edges are nice and bright, and the rest of the image is nearly black. (Hint: The fact that I said "nearly black" should be a clue to you that we might be seeing a threshold in use soon.)

So what do we do with this? Let's make some snow fall on my head. First, let's make a simple class to represent snow (you can find it as the Snow.as file):

```
package
{
    import flash.display.Sprite;

    public class Snow extends Sprite
    {
        public var vx:Number;
        public var vy:Number;

        public function Snow()
        {
            graphics.beginFill(0xffffff, .7);
            graphics.drawCircle(0, 0, 2);
            graphics.endFill();

            vx = 0;
            vy = 1;
        }
```

```
        public function update():void
        {
            vx += Math.random() * .2 - .1;
            vx *= .95;
            x += vx;
            y += vy;
        }
    }
}
```

This class draws a small, round, white circle that has an x and y velocity and a method to update itself. Updating means randomly changing the x velocity and adding the velocity to the position. Good enough.

The plan is to create a new snow instance on each frame, add it to an array, and update each snow in the array. But first, we'll check to see whether the snow happens to be on an edge. In other words, is the pixel at the x, y position of that snow greater than 0? Here's where that threshold comes in—to make those "nearly black" pixels completely black. Here's the revised code:

```
package {
    import flash.display.Bitmap;
    import flash.display.BitmapData;
    import flash.display.Sprite;
    import flash.display.StageAlign;
    import flash.display.StageScaleMode;
    import flash.events.Event;
    import flash.filters.BlurFilter;
    import flash.filters.ConvolutionFilter;
    import flash.geom.Matrix;
    import flash.geom.Point;
    import flash.media.Camera;
    import flash.media.Video;

    public class EdgeTracking extends Sprite
    {
        private var _cam:Camera;
        private var _vid:Video;
        private var _bmpd:BitmapData;
        private var _flakes:Array;

        public function EdgeTracking()
        {
            stage.align = StageAlign.TOP_LEFT;
            stage.scaleMode = StageScaleMode.NO_SCALE;

            _cam = Camera.getCamera();
            _cam.setMode(320, 240, 15);
            _vid = new Video(320, 240);
            _vid.attachCamera(_cam);
            _vid.filters = [new ConvolutionFilter(1, 3, [0, 4, -4]),
                            new BlurFilter()];
```

```
            var vid2:Video = new Video(320, 240);
            vid2.attachCamera(_cam);
            vid2.scaleX = -1;
            vid2.x = 320;
            addChild(vid2);

            _bmpd = new BitmapData(320, 240, false);

            _flakes = new Array();

            addEventListener(Event.ENTER_FRAME, onEnterFrame);
        }

        private function onEnterFrame(event:Event):void
        {
            _bmpd.draw(_vid, new Matrix(-1, 0, 0, 1, _bmpd.width, 0));
            _bmpd.threshold(_bmpd, _bmpd.rect, new Point(), "<",
                        0x00220000, 0xff000000, 0x00ff0000, true);

            var snow:Snow = new Snow();
            snow.x = Math.random() * _bmpd.width;
            addChild(snow);
            _flakes.push(snow);

            for(var i:int = _flakes.length - 1; i >= 0; i--)
            {
                snow = _flakes[i] as Snow;
                if(_bmpd.getPixel(snow.x, snow.y) == 0)
                {
                    snow.update();
                    if(snow.y > _bmpd.height)
                    {
                        removeChild(snow);
                        _flakes.splice(i, 1);
                    }
                }
            }
        }
    }
}
```

First, we create a _flakes array to hold all the Snow instances.

Notice also that we have a second video that is flipped around and added to the display list instead of _bmpd. As in the motion-detection example, it lets users see their own unprocessed image instead of the convoluted, blurred image.

We then apply a threshold, as mentioned, to make all the dark pixels completely black.

On each frame we create a new Snow instance, adding it to the display list and the _flakes array. We then loop through this array, getting a reference to each Snow in it. If the pixel represented by an individual Snow is equal to zero, we update it, causing it to move randomly left or right a bit and one pixel down. If the pixel is not zero (nonblack), the pixel is on a horizontal edge, so we just leave it there.

Finally, if the pixel has moved off the bottom of the image, we remove it from the display list and the _flakes array. The result is shown in Figure 5-12.

Figure 5-12. Video snow!

Granted, this isn't an exactly useful example, but it is fun. Your kids will play with this endlessly (I speak from experience). But, once you understand the workings of something like this, you will surely start to see variations and other ideas will start to come to you. I look forward to seeing what you create.

Summary

In this chapter you saw some rather experimental examples of using both sound and video as input methods. They are but a few samples of the many possible ways to use a camera or microphone to affect elements of your Flash applications or games. I hope at least to have sparked some ideas in you because there is so much that can be done along these lines. Again, I look forward to eventually seeing what readers come up with, taking these examples far beyond what I have presented here.

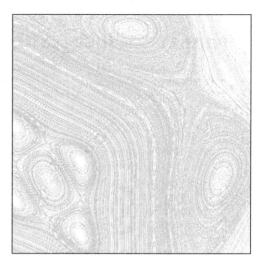

Chapter 6

ADVANCED PHYSICS: NUMERICAL INTEGRATION

In *Making Things Move*, I presented some elementary physics formulas for programming motion in Flash. It mainly came down to this: add acceleration to velocity and add velocity to position in every frame. I knew this wasn't the most accurate physics possible and made lots of disclaimers to that point. Still, I knew it was good enough for games and animations most people would be doing in Flash.

After writing the first version of the book, I discovered that what I was describing is commonly known as **Euler integration**. And it is indeed pretty inaccurate. It's also fairly simple, good enough for most casual applications, and pretty widely used. But if Euler integration is not so great, what are the alternatives? This chapter is at least a partial answer to that question. We'll take a look at what numerical integration is and what's wrong with Euler, along with two alternatives and why you might want to consider using them.

Also, I'll save you some embarrassment at your next dinner party and tell you that Euler (which is pronounced "oiler", not "you-ler") is named after Leonhard Euler, a physicist and mathematician from the 18th century. Then again, if you're talking about Euler integration at a dinner party, embarrassment might be unavoidable.

Numerical Integration and Why Euler Is "Bad"

First of all, when I say "bad," I mean inaccurate. In other words, if you were to simulate an object moving according to various forces using Euler integration, it would not be a perfectly accurate picture of what would happen to that object in the real world. However, it would be close enough for casual games, animations, nonscientific simulations, and so on—and most people would never see anything wrong with it. But in cases where you want or need a higher degree of accuracy, Euler just won't cut it.

Why not? Well, the formulas for motion, velocity, mass, and acceleration have all been worked out for centuries (thank Isaac Newton), and they work really well. If you took high school algebra, you probably remember the word problem that says, "A boy standing on a roof 50 feet off the ground throws a ball up into the air at a velocity of 30 feet per second...." And then you have to calculate when it will hit the ground or how high it is at a certain time. The formula you use is the following, where t is the time in seconds, v0 is the initial velocity, h0 is the initial height, and y is the height at the given time:

$$y = -16t^2 + v0 * t + h0$$

If you follow that formula, you'll have no problem. It's perfectly accurate. So why don't we just use it for all our motion and be done with it? First, it describes a single axis of motion for a single object moving in a single arc, with no other forces than gravity acting on it. Throw in another dimension or two, such as air resistance, bouncing, additional objects and collisions; and any other forces such as wind, and it suddenly becomes incredibly complex.

A far more practical approach is to take a snapshot of the object at discrete intervals, take any forces acting on it at that one instance, calculate its velocity, and update its position. This process is called **integration**. The ideal goal of integration is shown in Figure 6-1.

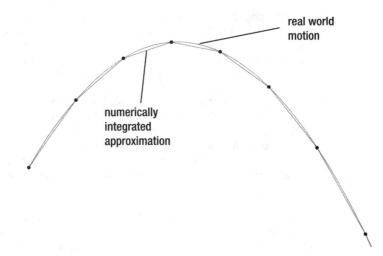

Figure 6-1. Real world motion and integrated approximation (ideal)

The top line is the smooth curve that an object would actually travel through. The lower segmented line represents the velocities and positions you try to achieve with integration. The various methods of integration are attempts to draw a series of straight lines that closely match the curve.

The problem with this is that physical forces act continuously in the real world. The forces on an object are changing its position and velocity continuously, not in discrete jumps like that. For example, gravity would be acting continuously on a falling object, increasing its speed, thus changing its position smoothly over time. If we just apply gravity to an object and update its velocity and position once per frame, we are missing the effects of gravity and velocity for all the points in between. So the more often you update, the more accurate you are, but there's always some discrepancy.

The Euler integration solution to this discrepancy is to ignore it, so it isn't very accurate. I can't put it any simpler than that. Figure 6-2 shows the actual result of Euler integration calculated in one-second intervals to exaggerate the error.

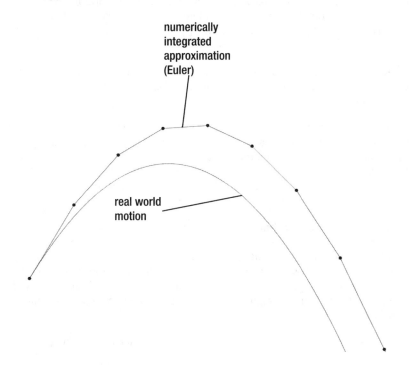

Figure 6-2. Real world motion and Euler integration

Again, if you decrease the interval, you get a better result, but it will be accurate only when increased infinitely. Good luck with that.

Furthermore, Euler can also get into situations in which it becomes unstable. This can happen quite easily with springs. The inaccuracies in the integration can sometimes lead to a point where the velocity keeps increasing and the whole thing blows apart.

But if Euler is that bad, what are the alternatives? The two we'll cover here are called **Runge-Kutta integration** and **Verlet integration**. Like Euler, they are named for the people who came up with them: Carl Runge, Martin Wilhelm Kutta, and Loup Verlet. As you will see, these two other methods have their strengths in different areas: Runge-Kutta is used when a higher degree of accuracy is desired, and Verlet is often used in computer graphics for creating "rag doll physics," a sort of inverse kinematics. If that doesn't make much sense to you now, don't worry. When we get there, you'll see that it's pretty easy to work with and can create some really great effects. First up, let's dive into Runge-Kutta.

Runge-Kutta Integration

As discussed in the previous section, Euler integration fails because it tries to integrate acceleration, velocity, and position in discrete steps. Because those things are changing continuously, this type of integration results only in an approximation, which is not quite accurate. Runge-Kutta integration doesn't actually get around this time-step inaccuracy problem, but it does add in some extra calculations designed to get a better estimation of position and velocity. Just make sure that you're clear on that; just because you're using Runge-Kutta doesn't mean you will have a *perfectly* accurate simulation, just a *more* accurate one.

So how accurate is Runge-Kutta? I'll go out on a limb and say it's probably as accurate as you'll ever need for any kind of simulation you'll ever do in Flash. If your application is *that* critical, you probably shouldn't be using Flash in the first place.

I think the second time I ever heard the term *Runge-Kutta* was at a Flash user group meeting in Boston, at which James Battat presented a series of physics simulations he and a colleague had done using ActionScript 2.0 and Runge-Kutta integration for an introductory physics course in mechanical systems they were teaching at Harvard University under the Presidential Instructional Technology Fellowship Summer Program. That was a pretty good testimonial to its accuracy and made me want to look into it further.

Naturally there is our old friend, the technology trade-off. Runge-Kutta is more accurate, but that accuracy comes at the cost of more calculations, meaning more CPU use, slower execution, and so on. So please *do not* jump on the Runge-Kutta bandwagon just because it's "better," more accurate, or because all the cool kids are doing it. Make sure that extra accuracy is something you absolutely need. Even though I'm writing a half a chapter about it, I'll tell you flat out that in almost every case you'll come across in Flash, you *don't* need that high degree of accuracy and you'll just be heating up your CPU for no good reason.

Okay, warnings out of the way. Let's see how Runge-Kutta works. And let's start calling it **RK** for short.

RK still does the time-step thing, but instead of blindly adding acceleration to velocity and velocity to position for each step and calling it a day, it samples the curve multiple times within a single time step to get an idea of what the curve is actually doing at that point. It then takes a weighted average of these samples to try to get a better approximation of the curve. Not too complex an idea, really. Let's go a bit deeper and see exactly how it's implemented.

There are two main flavors of RK: Runge-Kutta second order integration (**RK2** for short) and Runge-Kutta fourth order integration (**RK4**). The numbers refer to the number of intermediate samplings done. RK2 samples two values per time step, and RK4 samples four. Most often you'll hear about RK4, which is good because talking about "Runge-Kutta fourth order integration" makes you sound really intelligent.

We'll look at RK2 first because it's a bit simpler to understand and is a good lead-in to RK4. You might also see this technique listed under other names: "improved Euler," "midpoint Euler," or just "the midpoint method." It's all the same thing. As its alternate names suggest, RK2 is not too different from the Euler method of integration and indeed does something with a midpoint.

The strategy is to compute the acceleration, velocity, and position as they exist for the current state of the object (basic Euler integration); then calculate what the state of the object would be after applying the acceleration and velocity you just computed, averaging those two, and applying it to the state of the object. In other words, where Euler tries to guess the overall velocity over a span of time based on a single point, RK2 gets the velocity at the beginning and end points of that time span and averages them to get an estimate of the velocity over that period. Again it's not 100% accurate, but it is far more accurate than Euler alone. Figure 6-3 shows the result of Euler versus RK2.

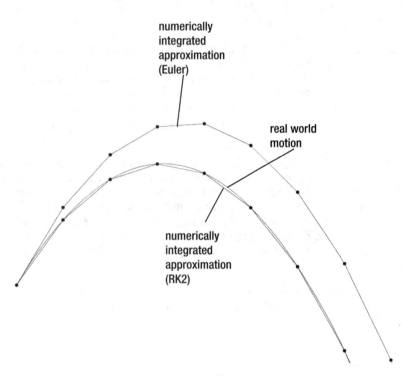

Figure 6-3. Real world motion, Euler integration, and RK2

At this resolution and this time span, you can't really see any discrepancy in the RK2 graph. That's pretty good—probably more than good enough for anything you're going to do in Flash.

Of course, if that's not good enough, there's always RK4, which averages out the slope of the curve based on four samples within the segment. I won't show this because it would be indistinguishable from RK2 at this resolution. But it goes without saying that it is more accurate.

Time-based motion

Okay, okay, enough talking. Show us some code!

All right, all right, I will. But one more explanation first. All the code we use in this section will be using time-based instead of frame-based motion code. This topic is covered in Chapter 19 of *Making Things Move*, but I'll cover it briefly here.

In a lot of simple Flash-based motion code, there are values for velocity and acceleration, and we apply them to our objects on each frame. The number of units we are moving things is considered to be pixels, and the time interval is one frame. So our speed is in terms of "pixels per frame" instead of miles per hour or feet per second. And we tweak the values for gravity, speed, and various forces based on what looks good in the final movie. But if we're going through all this extra work to come up with something that is more accurate, we probably want to use standard measurements, at least for time. So we'll be keeping track of real live milliseconds and updating everything based on how many seconds have passed in real time. The objects will move at the same speed as they would in the real world, and we can measure them pretty accurately.

To do that, we have to use the flash.utils.getTimer method to measure the elapsed time since the last update. This elapsed time feeds right into all the standard equations for motion, even Euler. For example, the Euler equation for velocity is new position = old position + velocity * elapsed time. The only reason you get away without it in frame-based animation is because you are using pixels per frame—updating every frame, the elapsed time is one. Velocity times one equals velocity so you can just say new position = old position + velocity.

We'll also do a few other things that are worth mentioning. One is to store position, velocity, and acceleration in Point objects. The Point class contains x and y properties, so instead of having vx and vy for velocity, we'll have just a single velocity variable. And we'll keep track of position the same way—assigning it back to the display object after all the calculations are done. Finally, instead of adding gravity directly to velocity, we'll create an acceleration method that will return a point containing acceleration values on the x- and y-axis. For now, this will just be 0 on x and the gravity value on y, but when you start adding more complex forces, it can do much more. In those cases, the resulting acceleration could be affected by an object's position and velocity, so we'll pass those in to the acceleration method as parameters.

Just to get used to using all this in a familiar setting, let's do it for Euler. Here's the class, available as the Euler.as file from the book's download page at www.friendsofed.com:

```
package {
    import flash.display.Sprite;
    import flash.display.StageAlign;
    import flash.display.StageScaleMode;
    import flash.events.Event;
    import flash.geom.Point;
    import flash.utils.getTimer;

    public class Euler extends Sprite
    {
        private var _ball:Sprite;
        private var _position:Point;
        private var _velocity:Point;
        private var _gravity:Number = 32;
        private var _bounce:Number = -0.6;
        private var _oldTime:int;
```

```
public function Euler()
{
    stage.align = StageAlign.TOP_LEFT;
    stage.scaleMode = StageScaleMode.NO_SCALE;

    _ball = new Sprite();
    _ball.graphics.beginFill(0xff0000);
    _ball.graphics.drawCircle(0, 0, 20);
    _ball.graphics.endFill();
    _ball.x = 50;
    _ball.y = 50;
    addChild(_ball);

    _velocity = new Point(100, 0);
    _position = new Point(_ball.x, _ball.y);

    _oldTime = getTimer();
    addEventListener(Event.ENTER_FRAME, onEnterFrame);
}

private function onEnterFrame(event:Event):void
{
    var time:int = getTimer();
    var elapsed:Number = (time - _oldTime) / 1000;
    _oldTime = time;

    var accel:Point = acceleration(_position, _velocity);
    _position.x += _velocity.x * elapsed;
    _position.y += _velocity.y * elapsed;
    _velocity.x += accel.x * elapsed;
    _velocity.y += accel.y * elapsed;

    // check if object has gone past any boundaries
    // and bounce off them.
    if(_position.y > stage.stageHeight - 20)
    {
        _position.y = stage.stageHeight - 20;
        _velocity.y *= _bounce;
    }
    if(_position.x > stage.stageWidth - 20)
    {
        _position.x = stage.stageWidth - 20;
        _velocity.x *= _bounce
    }
    else if(_position.x < 20)
    {
        _position.x = 20;
        _velocity.x *= _bounce;
    }
```

```
            _ball.x = _position.x;
            _ball.y = _position.y;
        }

        private function acceleration(p:Point, v:Point):Point
        {
            return new Point(0, _gravity);
        }
    }
}
```

We create a ball, set the position and velocity values, and take note of the current time with the getTimer method, which returns the amount of time that the movie has been running in milliseconds,. We store that in _oldTime. On each frame we call it again. The difference between the old time and the new time is the elapsed time since the last frame. Divide it by 1000 to have seconds instead of milliseconds. Make sure that we reset _oldTime so it's accurate the next time around.

Then we call the acceleration method to get the force(s) that will be applied to the object. Again, it's just gravity in this case.

Now, before we add velocity to the ball's position, we multiply it by the elapsed time. Same with adding the acceleration to the velocity. Thus if more time elapses between frames, the acceleration and velocity are multiplied by a higher number, and the ball moves more. If less time has elapsed between frames, it moves less. You can actually run this movie at a variety of different frame rates and observe the same motion. Of course, on a slower frame rate, it will be choppier and smoother on a higher frame rate, but the ball should move the same distance across the screen in the same amount of time. Go ahead and set stage.frameRate to 10 and then to 100. Although 100 looks a lot smoother, the ball moves in the same path at the same speed.

I also threw a bounce in there just to keep the thing on screen long enough for you to see what's happening. I'll talk about that later.

Now you might be thinking, "Okay, but the ball is falling awfully slowly. That's not very realistic." We set gravity to 32, which is what gravity is in the real world: 32 feet per second, per second. In other words, a falling object will increase its speed by 32 feet per second for each second it is falling. So if the units are feet and seconds, and we're applying that unchanged to the position of a sprite, our scale is one pixel = one foot. So imagine a 40-foot round ball falling from the top of an 800- or 900-feet tall building—maybe it will look a bit more realistic!

You might want to scale things. Suppose that we want 100 pixels to equal 1 foot. We can set that in a variable and apply it whenever we go between foot-based positions and pixel-based positions:

```
package {
    import flash.display.Sprite;
    import flash.display.StageAlign;
    import flash.display.StageScaleMode;
    import flash.events.Event;
    import flash.geom.Point;
    import flash.utils.getTimer;
```

```
public class Euler extends Sprite
{
    private var _ball:Sprite;
    private var _position:Point;
    private var _velocity:Point;
    private var _gravity:Number = 32;
    private var _bounce:Number = -0.6;
    private var _oldTime:int;
    private var _pixelsPerFoot:Number = 100;

    public function Euler()
    {
        stage.align = StageAlign.TOP_LEFT;
        stage.scaleMode = StageScaleMode.NO_SCALE;

        _ball = new Sprite();
        _ball.graphics.beginFill(0xff0000);
        _ball.graphics.drawCircle(0, 0, 20);
        _ball.graphics.endFill();
        _ball.x = 50;
        _ball.y = 50;
        addChild(_ball);

        _velocity = new Point(10, 0);
        _position = new Point(_ball.x / _pixelsPerFoot,
                              _ball.y / _pixelsPerFoot);

        _oldTime = getTimer();
        addEventListener(Event.ENTER_FRAME, onEnterFrame);
    }

    private function onEnterFrame(event:Event):void
    {
        var time:int = getTimer();
        var elapsed:Number = (time - _oldTime) / 1000;
        _oldTime = time;

        var accel:Point = acceleration(_position, _velocity);
        _position.x += _velocity.x * elapsed;
        _position.y += _velocity.y * elapsed;
        _velocity.x += accel.x * elapsed;
        _velocity.y += accel.y * elapsed;

        if(_position.y > (stage.stageHeight - 20) / _pixelsPerFoot)
        {
            _position.y = (stage.stageHeight - 20) /
                            _pixelsPerFoot;
            _velocity.y *= _bounce;
        }
```

```
            if(_position.x > (stage.stageWidth - 20) / _pixelsPerFoot)
            {
                _position.x = (stage.stageWidth - 20) / _pixelsPerFoot;
                _velocity.x *= _bounce
            }
            else if(_position.x < 20 / _pixelsPerFoot)
            {
                _position.x = 20 / _pixelsPerFoot;
                _velocity.x *= _bounce;
            }

            _ball.x = _position.x * _pixelsPerFoot;
            _ball.y = _position.y * _pixelsPerFoot;
        }

        private function acceleration(p:Point, v:Point):Point
        {
            return new Point(0, _gravity);
        }
    }
}
```

Now you have something like a four- or five-inch round ball falling from eight or nine feet up. (Note that I also adjusted the initial velocity to be a bit less.) This might be closer to your expectations.

Okay, that's Euler integration in a time-based environment. Now let's get back to Runge-Kutta.

Coding Runge-Kutta second order integration (RK2)

To recap RK2, the plan is to calculate the acceleration and velocity at the beginning of the time step, again at the end of the time step, and take a sort of average between the two.

Let's go through it in pseudocode.

First, calculate the acceleration at the start of the time step; then calculate position and velocity, exactly as we just did with Euler. But this time we'll store the new position and velocity in separate variables:

```
// position1 is current position of object
// velocity1 is current velocity of object
acceleration1 = acceleration(position1, velocity1)

position2 = position1 + velocity1 * time
velocity2 = velocity1 + acceleration1 * time
```

Now position2 and velocity2 represent where the object will be at the end of this time step. Next we'll need the acceleration at the end of that step:

```
acceleration2 = acceleration(position2, velocity2)
```

Now here's the key part of RK2, in which we average the velocity and acceleration of these two states:

```
position1 += (velocity1 + velocity2) / 2 * time
velocity1 += (acceleration1 + acceleration2) / 2 * time
```

We basically just take the start and end velocity and average them, multiply by the elapsed time, and add that to the object's position. Average the start and end accelerations, times elapsed time, and add that to the velocity.

And that is RK2! Let's see it in code:

```
package {
    import flash.display.Sprite;
    import flash.display.StageAlign;
    import flash.display.StageScaleMode;
    import flash.events.Event;
    import flash.geom.Point;
    import flash.utils.getTimer;

    public class RK2 extends Sprite
    {
        private var _ball:Sprite;
        private var _position:Point;
        private var _velocity:Point;
        private var _gravity:Number = 32;
        private var _bounce:Number = -0.6;
        private var _oldTime:int;
        private var _pixelsPerFoot:Number = 10;


        public function RK2()
        {
            stage.align = StageAlign.TOP_LEFT;
            stage.scaleMode = StageScaleMode.NO_SCALE;

            _ball = new Sprite();
            _ball.graphics.beginFill(0xff0000);
            _ball.graphics.drawCircle(0, 0, 20);
            _ball.graphics.endFill();
            _ball.x = 50;
            _ball.y = 50;
            addChild(_ball);

            _velocity = new Point(10, 0);
            _position = new Point(_ball.x / _pixelsPerFoot,
                                  _ball.y / _pixelsPerFoot);
```

```
        _oldTime = getTimer();
        addEventListener(Event.ENTER_FRAME, onEnterFrame);
    }

    private function onEnterFrame(event:Event):void
    {
        var time:int = getTimer();
        var elapsed:Number = (time - _oldTime) / 1000;
        _oldTime = time;

        var accel1:Point = acceleration(_position, _velocity);

        var position2:Point = new Point();
        position2.x = _position.x + _velocity.x * elapsed;
        position2.y = _position.y + _velocity.y * elapsed;

        var velocity2:Point = new Point();
        velocity2.x = _velocity.x + accel1.x * elapsed;
        velocity2.y = _velocity.y + accel1.x * elapsed;

        var accel2:Point = acceleration(position2, velocity2);

        _position.x += (_velocity.x + velocity2.x) / 2 * elapsed;
        _position.y += (_velocity.y + velocity2.y) / 2 * elapsed;

        _velocity.x += (accel1.x + accel2.x) / 2 * elapsed;
        _velocity.y += (accel1.y + accel2.y) / 2 * elapsed;

        if(_position.y > (stage.stageHeight - 20) / _pixelsPerFoot)
        {
            _position.y = (stage.stageHeight - 20) /
                            _pixelsPerFoot;
            _velocity.y *= _bounce;
        }
        if(_position.x > (stage.stageWidth - 20) / _pixelsPerFoot)
        {
            _position.x = (stage.stageWidth - 20) / _pixelsPerFoot;
            _velocity.x *= _bounce
        }
        else if(_position.x < 20 / _pixelsPerFoot)
        {
            _position.x = 20 / _pixelsPerFoot;
            _velocity.x *= _bounce;
        }

        _ball.x = _position.x * _pixelsPerFoot;
        _ball.y = _position.y * _pixelsPerFoot;
    }
```

```
        private function acceleration(p:Point, v:Point):Point
        {
            return new Point(0, _gravity);
        }
    }
}
```

If you understood the explanations, you should see what's going on in the code just fine. Now run this file and see how much better and more realistic it looks than the Euler version! What? It looks the same to you? Well it looks the same to me, too, but it really is slightly different. This is why I said that Euler is good enough for most of what you'll ever need to do in Flash. And realize that Figure 6-3 was calculated with a one-second time step, so it's exaggerated. If your Flash movie is running at 24 frames per second, that's a much smaller time step, and Euler will be much closer to RK2.

But also realize that this is a very simple simulation. When you start adding additional forces and carry the simulation on longer than a few seconds, you will see more variance. At any rate, if accuracy is what you need, you now know how to squeeze a bit more of it out of your Flash physics.

But wait! There's more! That's only RK2. We still have RK4 to discuss!

Coding Runge-Kutta fourth order integration (RK4)

RK4 is the big daddy of numerical integration. If people refer to "Runge-Kutta," they are most likely talking about RK4. If you have a decent idea about what's going on with RK2, this shouldn't be that big a leap for you. We'll do pretty much the same thing, but instead of just sampling the beginning and end points of the segment, we'll sample and average a total of four points.

In RK4, however, the average is a bit different. Let's see how it looks in pseudocode. It gets pretty long, so I shortened the names here:

```
// pos1 is current position of object
// vel1 is current velocity of object
acc1 = acceleration(pos1, vel1)

pos2 = pos1 + vel1 / 2 * time
vel2 = vel1 + acc1 / 2 * time
acc2 = acceleration(pos2, vel2)

pos3 = pos1 + vel2 / 2 * time
vel3 = vel1 + acc2 / 2 * time
acc3 = acceleration(pos3, vel3)

pos4 = pos1 + vel3 * time
vel4 = vel1 + acc3 * time
acc3 = acceleration(pos4, vel4)

pos1 += (vel1 + vel2 * 2 + vel3 * 2 + vel4) / 6 * time
vel1 += (acc1 + acc2 * 2 + acc3 * 2 + acc4) / 6 * time
```

Note that the first and fourth order values are taken as is, but the second and third order values are divided by two when being calculated, and multiplied by two when averaged. This gives a special weighting to the ends and the middle of the curve. In other words, instead of all four sampled points being equally added up and divided by four, the middle two are doubled, and the total is divided by six. Do I understand exactly what is going on here? No. But it took both Runge *and* Kutta to figure this one out, and they are both much smarter than me. I think it took them a long time, so I'm okay with my vague understanding. The important thing is that I understand it just enough to actually get it working in ActionScript. All right, take a deep breath; here's the code:

```
package {
    import flash.display.Sprite;
    import flash.display.StageAlign;
    import flash.display.StageScaleMode;
    import flash.events.Event;
    import flash.geom.Point;
    import flash.utils.getTimer;

    public class RK4 extends Sprite
    {
        private var _ball:Sprite;
        private var _position:Point;
        private var _velocity:Point;
        private var _gravity:Number = 32;
        private var _bounce:Number = -0.6;
        private var _oldTime:int;
        private var _pixelsPerFoot:Number = 10;


        public function RK4()
        {
            stage.align = StageAlign.TOP_LEFT;
            stage.scaleMode = StageScaleMode.NO_SCALE;

            _ball = new Sprite();
            _ball.graphics.beginFill(0xff0000);
            _ball.graphics.drawCircle(0, 0, 20);
            _ball.graphics.endFill();
            _ball.x = 50;
            _ball.y = 50;
            addChild(_ball);

            _velocity = new Point(10, 0);
            _position = new Point(_ball.x / _pixelsPerFoot,
                                  _ball.y / _pixelsPerFoot);

            _oldTime = getTimer();
            addEventListener(Event.ENTER_FRAME, onEnterFrame);
        }
```

```
private function onEnterFrame(event:Event):void
{
    var time:int = getTimer();
    var elapsed:Number = (time - _oldTime) / 1000;
    _oldTime = time;

    var accel1:Point = acceleration(_position, _velocity);

    var position2:Point = new Point();
    position2.x = _position.x + _velocity.x / 2 * elapsed;
    position2.y = _position.y + _velocity.y / 2 * elapsed;

    var velocity2:Point = new Point();
    velocity2.x = _velocity.x + accel1.x / 2 * elapsed;
    velocity2.y = _velocity.y + accel1.x / 2 * elapsed;

    var accel2:Point = acceleration(position2, velocity2);

    var position3:Point = new Point();
    position3.x = _position.x + velocity2.x / 2 * elapsed;
    position3.y = _position.y + velocity2.y / 2 * elapsed;

    var velocity3:Point = new Point();
    velocity3.x = _velocity.x + accel2.x / 2 * elapsed;
    velocity3.y = _velocity.y + accel2.y / 2 * elapsed;

    var accel3:Point = acceleration(position3, velocity3);

    var position4:Point = new Point();
    position4.x = _position.x + velocity3.x * elapsed;
    position4.y = _position.y + velocity3.y * elapsed;

    var velocity4:Point = new Point();
    velocity4.x = _velocity.x + accel3.x * elapsed;
    velocity4.y = _velocity.y + accel3.y * elapsed;

    var accel4:Point = acceleration(position4, velocity4);

    _position.x += (_velocity.x +
                    2 * velocity2.x +
                    2 * velocity3.x +
                    velocity4.x) / 6 * elapsed;

    _position.y += (_velocity.y +
                    2 * velocity2.y +
                    2 * velocity3.y +
                    velocity4.y) / 6 * elapsed;
```

```
        _velocity.x += (accel1.x +
                            2 * accel2.x +
                            2 * accel3.x +
                            accel4.x) / 6 * elapsed;

        _velocity.y += (accel1.y +
                            2 * accel2.y +
                            2 * accel3.y +
                            accel4.y) / 6 * elapsed;

    if(_position.y > (stage.stageHeight - 20) / _pixelsPerFoot)
    {
        _position.y = (stage.stageHeight - 20) /
                        _pixelsPerFoot;
        _velocity.y *= _bounce;
    }
    if(_position.x > (stage.stageWidth - 20) / _pixelsPerFoot)
    {
        _position.x = (stage.stageWidth - 20) / _pixelsPerFoot;
        _velocity.x *= _bounce
    }
    else if(_position.x < 20 / _pixelsPerFoot)
    {
        _position.x = 20 / _pixelsPerFoot;
        _velocity.x *= _bounce;
    }

    _ball.x = _position.x * _pixelsPerFoot;
    _ball.y = _position.y * _pixelsPerFoot;
}

private function acceleration(p:Point, v:Point):Point
{
    return new Point(0, _gravity);
}
    }
}
```

Wow. I'm thinking that if you had any inclination toward using RK4 just because it is "cool," it just went out the window after seeing this code. Yeah, it's long, but if you have a basic idea of what's going on in the pseudocode, you should be able to follow along.

Again, if you can see any difference between this and RK2, or even Euler for that matter, you have better eyes than I do. I won't show any more in-depth examples for this reason and because implementing RK4 is only the tip of the iceberg in creating a truly accurate simulation, as we'll see in the next section.

Weak links

Right now, the basic code for the ball's motion is about as accurate as you are realistically going to get using numerical integration. However, as an accurate model of motion, the file as it stands now is useless. That's because the bounce mechanism we are using is totally bogus. Even worse than Euler integration, this method of bouncing was purely developed as a quick and easy method that looks good to the eye. It is not at all accurate from a physics standpoint, however. Likewise with most of the other motion code from *Making Things Move*: friction, collision reactions, large body gravity, springs, and so on. Most of them are based on real world physics formulas, but almost all contain some simplification or trick to make them a bit easier to code and a bit kinder to the CPU.

If you go through all the trouble to code RK4 and sacrifice all that extra compilation for the sake of accuracy, don't sabotage yourself by implementing inaccurate solutions to other parts of the simulation. Unfortunately, I can't rewrite all of *Making Things Move* for perfect accuracy *and* fit it into one chapter, so you're on your own from here. But you should find just about everything you need in a decent college physics text book.

Runge-Kutta summary

Although I've given you several warnings about diving into Runge-Kutta integration needlessly, that's not to belittle or demean it; it's a valuable tool for accurate simulations and is pretty much the standard for quality physics code in the programming community. Besides being more accurate than Euler, it is more stable, so if your springs keep blowing apart, you might want to look into RK. I don't imagine that it's something most ActionScript developers will need on a day-to-day basis, but I do hope that this chapter helps a few people when they need it.

Now, in the second part of this chapter, we'll cover yet another form of numerical integration that I think you'll find extremely useful and quite fun to create with: Verlet integration.

Verlet Integration

Verlet (pronounced *ver-lay*) integration was originally developed as a means of simulating molecular interactions. In such a case, you have many particles that interact with each other in fixed relationships. Each particle can have many other particles pushing or pulling it this way or that way, and there are other forces acting on it to change its position and velocity. Existing forms of integration can become too complex and too unstable in such situations, so Verlet integration was devised as a more efficient, more stable solution.

In today's software world, Verlet integration is often used for the creation of "rag doll physics" systems or for programmed character animation. The technique was popularized in a 2003 article titled, "Advanced Character Physics," by Thomas Jakobsen, which is still available on www.gamasutra.com (an excellent resource for gaming, physics, and other programming related knowledge, by the way). The code in this section is largely based on the system described in that article (modified for use in ActionScript 3.0, of course).

Because Verlet integration's strong point is not super accuracy like Runge-Kutta, I'll move back into frame-based animation just to keep things a bit more simple and clear (there's nothing preventing it from being applied in a time-based system).

One of the key features of Verlet integration is that you don't explicitly store an object's velocity. Instead, you store its last position. Then when you need to know its velocity, you subtract the last position from its current position. Thus, every time you move an object, you are also changing its velocity. This simplifies a lot of things. Say an object is at an x coordinate of 100, and I move it to 110. The next time it updates, it will see that it moved 10 pixels to the right since the last update and take on a value of 10 as its x velocity. On each successive update, the old x will continue to be 10 pixels to the left of the current x, so the object will continue moving across the screen to the right. So you can see that you impart velocity just by changing an object's position.

You might be able to see how this process is useful for molecular simulations. If you have a large number of particles all banging around together, each one attracting and repelling several others while trying to maintain specific distances from each other, they can all just change each others' positions and let Verlet integration take care of the acceleration and velocity that those changes imply.

Another common feature of Verlet integration, as it is commonly used in software, is the concept of constraints between objects. Two objects can be paired to each other and told to maintain a specific distance from each other. If they get farther apart or closer together, they will then adjust themselves back to the positions needed to maintain their distance, which of course changes their velocity. Objects can have multiple relationships so that a single object can be tied to more than one other object. Verlet is very efficient at handling all these relationships and maintaining all these individual distance requirements. So it becomes a great tool to use to start building up complex moving structures such as rag dolls.

Although I keep referring to them as *objects*, the things moving around usually don't have any shape or form. They really just points. And I like to refer to the fixed distance between two points as a **stick**. A stick is made up of two points, and structures are made up of one or more sticks. Also, as just mentioned, two or more sticks can share a point, which lets you make hinged parts. Figure 6-4 shows their relationships.

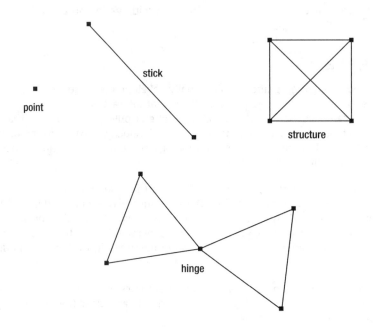

Figure 6-4. Points, sticks, structures, and hinges in Verlet integration

Let's start at the beginning and get a point moving around.

Verlet points

We'll create a VerletPoint class to encapsulate the behavior of a single point acting with Verlet integration. The point will, of course, need x and y properties, properties for the old x and old y, and an update method. The update method tells the point to take the difference of where it was after its last update and where it is now, and use that value as its current velocity. It will then add that velocity to its current position. But just before doing that, it has to store the current position as its "old" position so that on the next update it knows where it was. Here's the basic logic:

```
temp = currentPosition
velocity = currentPosition - oldPosition
currentPosition += velocity
oldPosition = temp
```

You need to store the current position in a temporary variable because you'll be changing it before you get a chance to assign it to the old position. And you can't assign it to the old position earlier because you need to use the "current old position" within the calculation.

Then you can calculate velocity as the current position minus the old position, and add that velocity to the position. Finally you assign what was the current position over to the old position.

Here's the VerletPoint class:

```
package
{
    import flash.display.Graphics;
    import flash.geom.Rectangle;

    public class VerletPoint
    {
        public var x:Number;
        public var y:Number;

        private var _oldX:Number;
        private var _oldY:Number;


        public function VerletPoint(x:Number, y:Number)
        {
            setPosition(x, y);
        }

        // basic verlet formula
        public function update():void
        {
            var tempX:Number = x;
            var tempY:Number = y;
            x += vx;
```

```
            y += vy;
            _oldX = tempX;
            _oldY = tempY;
        }

        // set position without changing velocity
        public function setPosition(x:Number, y:Number):void
        {
            this.x = _oldX = x;
            this.y = _oldY = y;
        }

        // make sure point does not go outside rect
        public function constrain(rect:Rectangle):void
        {
            x = Math.max(rect.left, Math.min(rect.right, x));
            y = Math.max(rect.top, Math.min(rect.bottom, y));
        }

        // velocity is current position - old position
        public function set vx(value:Number):void
        {
            _oldX = x - value;
        }
        public function get vx():Number
        {
            return x - _oldX;
        }

        // velocity is current position - old position
        public function set vy(value:Number):void
        {
            _oldY = y - value;
        }
        public function get vy():Number
        {
            return y - _oldY;
        }

        public function render(g:Graphics):void
        {
            g.beginFill(0);
            g.drawCircle(x, y, 4);
            g.endFill();
        }

    }
}
```

Amazingly simple. You might be wondering why there are getters and setters for x velocity and y velocity (vx and vy) when I said Verlet integration doesn't explicitly store velocity. Those getters and setters aren't storing anything. When you set vx, for example, it subtracts that amount from the current x and assigns that to _oldX. This ensures that when update runs and subtracts _oldX from x, that very same x velocity will be found. As for the getter, it's just subtracting old from current. So no velocity is stored explicitly.

I also threw in a setPosition method, which sets both the old and the new values to the specified position. This is useful if you want to move a point to a certain location but not have that move change the point's velocity. Because the old and new positions are the same, the velocity will be zero.

I'll cover that constrain method in a moment, but first I'll mention the render method here. Because the VerletPoint is not a display object, we can't directly see it on stage. The render method takes an instance of Graphics and draws a small dot there, based on its position. This isn't something you'd probably want to do in your final movie or game, but it's useful for debugging and testing.

Let's see it in action:

```
package {
    import flash.display.Sprite;
    import flash.display.StageAlign;
    import flash.display.StageScaleMode;
    import flash.events.Event;

    public class VerletPointTest extends Sprite
    {
        private var _point:VerletPoint;

        public function VerletPointTest()
        {
            stage.align = StageAlign.TOP_LEFT;
            stage.scaleMode = StageScaleMode.NO_SCALE;

            _point = new VerletPoint(100, 100);
            addEventListener(Event.ENTER_FRAME, onEnterFrame);
        }

        private function onEnterFrame(event:Event):void
        {
            _point.update();
            graphics.clear();
            _point.render(graphics);
        }
    }
}
```

In the constructor, we create a VerletPoint and listen for the enterFrame event. In that handler, we call update on the point and then clear the graphics and call render. Now, if you run it, you should see the dot, but it will just be sitting there. We need to add some velocity. You can do that by setting vx or vy, like so, anywhere in the constructor after the point is created:

```
_point.vx = 5;
```

This would move back the old x so that the update method sees a five-pixel change and takes that as velocity. But you can also just move the point:

```
_point.x += 5;
```

In most systems, this process would just change the point's position and not affect its velocity at all. But in Verlet integration, it also sets the point moving in that direction. It might help to think of it in these terms: instead of picking up the point and placing it five pixels over, it's more like you are *pushing* it five pixels over—giving it a little shove, after which it just keeps on going.

When you apply gravity, you have the same options. You can do it by adding to the y velocity or just by adding to the y position. Putting either of these lines in the onEnterFrame method, just before the update, takes care of gravity:

```
_point.vy += .5;
```

or

```
_point.y += .5;
```

The second line seems to be just changing position linearly, but remember that changing the position will change the velocity, so it does act to constantly increase the velocity, like gravity. Although changing the velocity through the vx and vy accessors probably makes it clearer what is going on, changing the position is much more efficient because you're changing only a single public variable. If there are lots of particles interacting, and you need to make things really efficient, this will help.

Constraining points

You might think that it would be nice to keep these points on stage. Constraining points to an area is another integral part of Verlet integration and is quite simple. All we really have to do is ensure that a point is within the rectangle that is our stage (or another rectangular area if you want to define one). To do this, we make sure that the point's x is no less than the rectangle's left edge and no more than its right edge, and not higher or lower than the rectangle's top and bottom. Here's where that constrain method comes into play. In our main class, we'll create a rectangle describing the area of the stage (or again, any rectangular area you want). We'll pass this in through the constrain method on each frame, just before the update. All this does is make sure that the x value of the point is no less or greater than the bounds of the rectangle. It's kind of a shortcut into a couple of lines, but if you do the logic you'll see that it works. Here's that constrain method from VerletPoint again:

```
public function constrain(rect:Rectangle):void
{
    x = Math.max(rect.left, Math.min(rect.right, x));
    y = Math.max(rect.top, Math.min(rect.bottom, y));
}
```

And here's the test class utilizing it:

```
package {
    import flash.display.Sprite;
    import flash.display.StageAlign;
```

```
import flash.display.StageScaleMode;
import flash.events.Event;
import flash.geom.Rectangle;

public class VerletPointTest extends Sprite
{
    private var _point:VerletPoint;
    private var _stageRect:Rectangle;

    public function VerletPointTest()
    {
        stage.align = StageAlign.TOP_LEFT;
        stage.scaleMode = StageScaleMode.NO_SCALE;
        _stageRect = new Rectangle(0, 0,
                                    stage.stageWidth,
                                    stage.stageHeight);

        _point = new VerletPoint(100, 100);
        _point.x += 5;
        addEventListener(Event.ENTER_FRAME, onEnterFrame);
    }

    private function onEnterFrame(event:Event):void
    {
        _point.y += .5;
        _point.update();
        _point.constrain(_stageRect);

        graphics.clear();
        _point.render(graphics);
    }
}
}
```

Now I know what you're going to say: it doesn't bounce. That's right, it doesn't. Now, you could probably modify constrain to add in a bounce. It would get a bit more complex, but it would have those points looking a lot better when they hit the walls. But remember that in general, points are really used only to define sticks and structures, and generally don't have any real visual representation themselves. So let's keep an eye on this one, see how sticks and structures react when they hit a wall, and not add any additional complexity to the VerletPoint class unless we decide we need it.

Speaking of sticks, let's take a look at them now!

Verlet sticks

Again, a stick binds two points together. It has a length property, which is the distance that it tries to keep between its two points. If the points are not exactly that distance apart, it will move them closer together or farther apart to satisfy the length property.

Here is the VerletStick class:

```
package
{
    import flash.display.Graphics;

    public class VerletStick
    {
        private var _pointA:VerletPoint;
        private var _pointB:VerletPoint;
        private var _length:Number;

        public function VerletStick(pointA:VerletPoint,
                                    pointB:VerletPoint,
                                    length:Number = -1)
        {
            _pointA = pointA;
            _pointB = pointB;
            if(length == -1)
            {
                var dx:Number = _pointA.x - _pointB.x;
                var dy:Number = _pointA.y - _pointB.y;
                _length = Math.sqrt(dx * dx + dy * dy);
            }
            else
            {
                _length = length;
            }
        }

        public function update():void
        {
            var dx:Number = _pointB.x - _pointA.x;
            var dy:Number = _pointB.y - _pointA.y;
            var dist:Number = Math.sqrt(dx * dx + dy * dy);
            var diff:Number = _length - dist;
            var offsetX:Number = (diff * dx / dist) / 2;
            var offsetY:Number = (diff * dy / dist) / 2;
            _pointA.x -= offsetX;
            _pointA.y -= offsetY;
            _pointB.x += offsetX;
            _pointB.y += offsetY;
        }

        public function render(g:Graphics):void
        {
            g.lineStyle(0);
            g.moveTo(_pointA.x, _pointA.y);
            g.lineTo(_pointB.x, _pointB.y);
        }
    }
}
```

The constructor takes two VerletPoint instances and an optional length. If no length is given, it will calculate the initial length between the two points passed in and take that as its length. Like VerletPoint, there is also a render method that draws a line between the two points on a Graphics instance, mostly for debugging and testing purposes. The meat of the class is in its update method, and this will take some explaining.

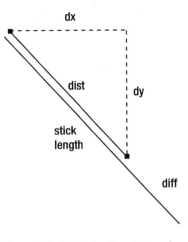

First we get the distance between the two points and subtract it from the length property of the stick. This tells us how much longer or shorter the stick currently is from its ideal length. This is stored in the diff variable (see Figure 6-5).

We then do some tricky trigonometry to get the x and y components of this difference. Realize that because cosine is adjacent/hypotenuse and sine is opposite/hypotenuse, the following

Figure 6-5. Calculating the distance between the two points and the difference between it and its ideal length

```
diff * dx / dist
diff * dy / dist
```

is actually the same as this, where angle is the angle between the two points:

```
diff * cos(angle)
diff * sin(angle)
```

But this lets us avoid three trigonometry operations: Math.atan2 to get the angle, and Math.cos and Math.sin to get the x and y offsets. You can see this in Figure 6-6.

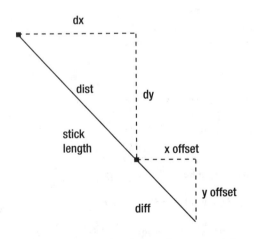

Figure 6-6. Calculating the x and y components of the difference

Note that we divide the result of this by 2 because we'll be moving both points one-half the distance to their ideal spots. Finally, we take this offsetX and offsetY and subtract them from the first point; then add them to the second point. This puts them exactly the distance away from each other to satisfy the length property, as shown in Figure 6-7.

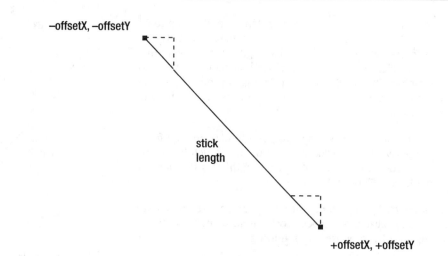

Figure 6-7. Moving each point by half the difference on each axis makes the distance equal to the stick length.

There are other ways to calculate this same thing, and some might be more efficient. But with only a single Math class operation, this one is not bad. And I think it's relatively clear what it's doing (after my explanations and diagrams, anyway), which is good for the purposes of this book.

Let's make a stick and see what it does!

```
package {
    import flash.display.Sprite;
    import flash.display.StageAlign;
    import flash.display.StageScaleMode;
    import flash.events.Event;
    import flash.geom.Rectangle;

    public class VerletStickTest extends Sprite
    {
        private var _pointA:VerletPoint;
        private var _pointB:VerletPoint;
        private var _stick:VerletStick;
        private var _stageRect:Rectangle;

        public function VerletStickTest()
        {
            stage.align = StageAlign.TOP_LEFT;
            stage.scaleMode = StageScaleMode.NO_SCALE;
            _stageRect = new Rectangle(0, 0,
                                    stage.stageWidth,
                                    stage.stageHeight);

            _pointA = new VerletPoint(100, 100);
            _pointB = new VerletPoint(105, 200);
```

```
        _stick = new VerletStick(_pointA, _pointB);

        addEventListener(Event.ENTER_FRAME, onEnterFrame);
    }

    private function onEnterFrame(event:Event):void
    {
        _pointA.y += .5;
        _pointA.update();
        _pointA.constrain(_stageRect);

        _pointB.y += .5;
        _pointB.update();
        _pointB.constrain(_stageRect);

        _stick.update();

        graphics.clear();
        _pointA.render(graphics);
        _pointB.render(graphics);
        _stick.render(graphics);
    }
}
}
```

As you can see, there's not much to do at all to add a single stick. First make the points; then make the stick, passing it two points. Then in the enterFrame handler, update the stick after updating the points. And render it of course.

When you run this one, you should see the stick appear and fall to the bottom of the stage. And magically it actually bounces a bit! How did this happen—because we didn't add any bounce code? This is because the update code for the stick is trying to push the points apart, but when the bottom point hits the edge of the rectangle, the constrain code pushes it back up. These two actions fight against each other briefly, and the result is that both points wind up moving upward a bit trying to satisfy all conditions.

Actually, this bouncing is kind of a side effect. I sort of like it, but because we didn't explicitly code it, it could be seen as a problem. To get rid of the bounce, we need to run through the point constrain calls and the stick update calls a few times to let them settle out before moving on. We can change the onEnterFrame method to do this:

```
    private function onEnterFrame(event:Event):void
    {
        _pointA.y += .5;
        _pointA.update();

        _pointB.y += .5;
        _pointB.update();
```

```
    for(var i:int = 0; i < 5; i++)
    {
        _pointA.constrain(_stageRect);
        _pointB.constrain(_stageRect);
        _stick.update();
    }

    graphics.clear();
    _pointA.render(graphics);
    _pointB.render(graphics);
    _stick.render(graphics);
}
```

Looping through the points' constrain methods and the stick's update method a few times gives them a chance to arrive at a consensus on where the points should end up. Because you are not adding gravity or updating the points during these iterations, the only velocity that gets added is the difference from where each point was to where it ends up at the end of the loop, so you don't get that spring and bounce here. It's more like a steel rod than a springy green branch. Now you can adjust this loop to change the character of your simulation—either kind of bouncy with a lot of elasticity by just doing a single iteration through the loop or very rigid by adding more iterations.

Realize, however, that those iterations are executing quite a bit of code, particularly in the stick's update method. It's not bad here for a single stick, but when you have larger structures, more iterations can start taxing your computer's resources. My advice is to leave it at one iteration and adjust it upward if you feel you absolutely need to.

Verlet structures

A Verlet structure is more than one stick with some common points. The simplest solid structure is a triangle. We just make three points and add three sticks connecting them:

```
package {
    import flash.display.Sprite;
    import flash.display.StageAlign;
    import flash.display.StageScaleMode;
    import flash.events.Event;
    import flash.geom.Rectangle;

    public class Triangle extends Sprite
    {
        private var _pointA:VerletPoint;
        private var _pointB:VerletPoint;
        private var _pointC:VerletPoint;
        private var _stickA:VerletStick;
        private var _stickB:VerletStick;
        private var _stickC:VerletStick;
        private var _stageRect:Rectangle;
```

```
public function Triangle()
{
    stage.align = StageAlign.TOP_LEFT;
    stage.scaleMode = StageScaleMode.NO_SCALE;
    _stageRect = new Rectangle(0, 0,
                                stage.stageWidth,
                                stage.stageHeight);

    _pointA = new VerletPoint(100, 100);
    _pointB = new VerletPoint(200, 100);
    _pointC = new VerletPoint(150, 200);

    _stickA = new VerletStick(_pointA, _pointB);
    _stickB = new VerletStick(_pointB, _pointC);
    _stickC = new VerletStick(_pointC, _pointA);

    addEventListener(Event.ENTER_FRAME, onEnterFrame);
}

private function onEnterFrame(event:Event):void
{
    _pointA.y += .5;
    _pointA.update();

    _pointB.y += .5;
    _pointB.update();

    _pointC.y += .5;
    _pointC.update();

    for(var i:int = 0; i < 1; i++)
    {
        _pointA.constrain(_stageRect);
        _pointB.constrain(_stageRect);
        _pointC.constrain(_stageRect);
        _stickA.update();
        _stickB.update();
        _stickC.update();
    }

    graphics.clear();
    _pointA.render(graphics);
    _pointB.render(graphics);
    _pointC.render(graphics);
    _stickA.render(graphics);
    _stickB.render(graphics);
    _stickC.render(graphics);
}
}
}
```

Here we make three points: A, B, and C; and three sticks: also A, B, and C. Each stick uses two different points so they form a triangle. Run this one, and you should see the triangle fall to the bottom of the stage, bounce up a bit, tip over, and land on its side. Try changing the constrain/update iteration variable to something larger than one and you can really see how this makes the structure more rigid.

Let's try for a square next. Your first attempt might be like this:

```
package {
    import flash.display.Sprite;
    import flash.display.StageAlign;
    import flash.display.StageScaleMode;
    import flash.events.Event;
    import flash.geom.Rectangle;

    public class Square extends Sprite
    {
        private var _pointA:VerletPoint;
        private var _pointB:VerletPoint;
        private var _pointC:VerletPoint;
        private var _pointD:VerletPoint;
        private var _stickA:VerletStick;
        private var _stickB:VerletStick;
        private var _stickC:VerletStick;
        private var _stickD:VerletStick;
        private var _stageRect:Rectangle;

        public function Square()
        {
            stage.align = StageAlign.TOP_LEFT;
            stage.scaleMode = StageScaleMode.NO_SCALE;
            _stageRect = new Rectangle(0, 0,
                                       stage.stageWidth,
                                       stage.stageHeight);

            _pointA = new VerletPoint(100, 100);
            _pointB = new VerletPoint(200, 100);
            _pointC = new VerletPoint(200, 200);
            _pointD = new VerletPoint(100, 200);

            _stickA = new VerletStick(_pointA, _pointB);
            _stickB = new VerletStick(_pointB, _pointC);
            _stickC = new VerletStick(_pointC, _pointD);
            _stickD = new VerletStick(_pointD, _pointA);

            addEventListener(Event.ENTER_FRAME, onEnterFrame);
        }
```

```
private function onEnterFrame(event:Event):void
{
    _pointA.y += .5;
    _pointA.update();

    _pointB.y += .5;
    _pointB.update();

    _pointC.y += .5;
    _pointC.update();

    _pointD.y += .5;
    _pointD.update();

    for(var i:int = 0; i < 1; i++)
    {
        _pointA.constrain(_stageRect);
        _pointB.constrain(_stageRect);
        _pointC.constrain(_stageRect);
        _pointD.constrain(_stageRect);
        _stickA.update();
        _stickB.update();
        _stickC.update();
        _stickD.update();
    }

    graphics.clear();
    _pointA.render(graphics);
    _pointB.render(graphics);
    _pointC.render(graphics);
    _pointD.render(graphics);
    _stickA.render(graphics);
    _stickB.render(graphics);
    _stickC.render(graphics);
    _stickD.render(graphics);
}
}
}
```

Make four points and connect them with four lines, right? That looks all right at first, but after it lands, it kind of falls flat—literally. In this case, it's a problem, but you're seeing your first glimpse of hinges here, which is a very cool feature. But before we go there, let's reinforce this box so it doesn't keep falling apart. We can do that with one more stick. Declare a _stickE variable and make it go diagonally from point A to point C:

```
_stickE = new VerletStick(_pointA, _pointC);
```

Make sure that you update it and render it in the enterFrame handler, too. If you really want to make it strong, you can put another one from point B to point D.

If this falling-straight-down business is too boring, you can give it some spin. Just shove one of the points a bit after you create it:

```
_pointA = new VerletPoint(100, 100);
_pointA.vx = 10;
```

Because only one corner has any initial velocity, the whole thing will start spinning.

Now before we go any further, we should start thinking about cleaning up this code. Even with only four points and five sticks, it's getting a bit messy. Fortunately, after creating the sticks and points, we'll do the same things with each one: adding gravity to the points and updating them, constraining each point and updating each stick (perhaps multiple times), and then rendering all the points and sticks.

We can easily create an array of points and an array of sticks and do all these actions in a loop:

```
package {
    import flash.display.Sprite;
    import flash.display.StageAlign;
    import flash.display.StageScaleMode;
    import flash.events.Event;
    import flash.geom.Rectangle;

    public class Square extends Sprite
    {
        private var _points:Array;
        private var _sticks:Array;
        private var _stageRect:Rectangle;

        public function Square()
        {
            stage.align = StageAlign.TOP_LEFT;
            stage.scaleMode = StageScaleMode.NO_SCALE;
            _stageRect = new Rectangle(0, 0,
                                       stage.stageWidth,
                                       stage.stageHeight);

            _points = new Array();
            _sticks = new Array();

            var pointA:VerletPoint = makePoint(100, 100);
            pointA.vx = 10;
            var pointB:VerletPoint = makePoint(200, 100);
            var pointC:VerletPoint = makePoint(200, 200);
            var pointD:VerletPoint = makePoint(100, 200);
```

```actionscript
        makeStick(pointA, pointB);
        makeStick(pointB, pointC);
        makeStick(pointC, pointD);
        makeStick(pointD, pointA);
        makeStick(pointA, pointC);

        addEventListener(Event.ENTER_FRAME, onEnterFrame);
    }

    private function onEnterFrame(event:Event):void
    {
        updatePoints();

        for(var i:int = 0; i < 1; i++)
        {
            constrainPoints();
            updateSticks();
        }

        graphics.clear();
        renderPoints();
        renderSticks();
    }

    private function makePoint(xpos:Number,
                              ypos:Number):VerletPoint
    {
        var point:VerletPoint = new VerletPoint(xpos, ypos);
        _points.push(point);
        return point;
    }

    private function makeStick(pointA:VerletPoint,
                              pointB:VerletPoint,
                              length:Number = -1):VerletStick
    {
        var stick:VerletStick = new VerletStick(pointA,
                                               pointB,
                                               length);
        _sticks.push(stick);
        return stick;
    }
```

```
private function updatePoints():void
{
    for(var i:int = 0; i < _points.length; i++)
    {
        var point:VerletPoint = _points[i] as VerletPoint;
        point.y += .5;
        point.update();
    }
}

private function constrainPoints():void
{
    for(var i:int = 0; i < _points.length; i++)
    {
        var point:VerletPoint = _points[i] as VerletPoint;
        point.constrain(_stageRect);
    }
}

private function updateSticks():void
{
    for(var i:int = 0; i < _sticks.length; i++)
    {
        var stick:VerletStick = _sticks[i] as VerletStick;
        stick.update();
    }
}

private function renderPoints():void
{
    for(var i:int = 0; i < _points.length; i++)
    {
        var point:VerletPoint = _points[i] as VerletPoint;
        point.render(graphics);
    }
}

private function renderSticks():void
{
    for(var i:int = 0; i < _sticks.length; i++)
    {
        var stick:VerletStick = _sticks[i] as VerletStick;
        stick.render(graphics);
    }
}
    }
}
```

Now we have a lot more small functions, but we're no longer stuck with individual variables for each point and stick. Look how clean the enterFrame handler has become. Furthermore, we can now add as many new points and sticks as we want, and not have to change any other code. They'll automatically go into the arrays and be updated, constrained, and rendered.

Hinges

Now that we have a nice code structure going on, we can go crazy making different kinds of forms. This is a good time to look at **hinges**, which are two structures that share a single point. They can each have freedom of movement, but will pivot around that one common point.

Here's how to do a swinging arm. I included only the constructor this time, which creates the points and sticks. All the other methods are exactly the same as in the last example:

```
public function Hinge()
{
    stage.align = StageAlign.TOP_LEFT;
    stage.scaleMode = StageScaleMode.NO_SCALE;
    _stageRect = new Rectangle(0, 0,
                               stage.stageWidth,
                               stage.stageHeight);

    _points = new Array();
    _sticks = new Array();

    // base
    var pointA:VerletPoint = makePoint(stage.stageWidth / 2,
                                    stage.stageHeight - 500);
    var pointB:VerletPoint = makePoint(0, stage.stageHeight);
    var pointC:VerletPoint = makePoint(stage.stageWidth,
                                    stage.stageHeight);

    // arm
    var pointD:VerletPoint = makePoint(stage.stageWidth / 2 + 350,
                                    stage.stageHeight - 500);

    // weight
    var pointE:VerletPoint = makePoint(stage.stageWidth / 2 + 360,
                                    stage.stageHeight - 510);
    var pointF:VerletPoint = makePoint(stage.stageWidth / 2 + 360,
                                    stage.stageHeight - 490);
    var pointG:VerletPoint = makePoint(stage.stageWidth / 2 + 370,
                                    stage.stageHeight - 500);
```

```
    // base
    makeStick(pointA, pointB);
    makeStick(pointB, pointC);
    makeStick(pointC, pointA);

    // arm
    makeStick(pointA, pointD);

    // weight
    makeStick(pointD, pointE);
    makeStick(pointD, pointF);
    makeStick(pointE, pointF);
    makeStick(pointE, pointG);
    makeStick(pointF, pointG);

    addEventListener(Event.ENTER_FRAME, onEnterFrame);
}
```

This code creates a triangle base with an arm attached to the top point of the triangle and a weight attached to end of the arm. Because the arm and base share only one point, the arm can swing. The weight can also pivot on the end of the arm, although that's not as noticeable because of its size.

Taking it further

There is so much more you can do, such as moving all the update, constrain, and render methods to their own classes—maybe PointManager and StickManager or something. And building a visual editor for it sounds like a lot of fun. Okay, I actually built a couple of visual editors for this kind of thing, and it is a lot of fun!

You might want to create some more interesting graphics for each stick. If you place a graphic so its left edge is centered on the first point of a stick, scale it so it is the same size as the length of the stick and rotate it to match the stick's orientation, you now have a custom graphic for each stick instead of a black line. Customizing entire structures is a bigger challenge, but it can be done.

We are running out of room here, and I don't want to take all the fun away from you, so we'll end here and I'll let you go wild with this stuff. I have a feeling that when more people understand Verlet integration in Flash, there will be some really cool stuff appearing on the Web.

Summary

This chapter covered numerical integration—what it is and the problems that come with it. You now know that you've probably been using Euler integration (and you now know how to pronounce it) and you have a few alternatives available to use. And most importantly, you hopefully have an idea about when to use each one because they all have strengths and weaknesses.

Euler, Runge-Kutta, and Verlet are not the only forms of numerical integration. A quick check on Wikipedia brings up this list of interesting sounding names: Backward Euler, Semi–implicit Euler, Velocity Verlet, Beeman's algorithm, Heun's method, Newmark-beta method, Leapfrog integration, and Monte Carlo integration. I have no idea what they all are, but it might be fun to find out. Over to you!

Next up, we'll dive into some brand new Flash 10 features regarding 3D!

Chapter 7

3D IN FLASH 10

Since I've been involved in Flash, I've seen a new version of the Flash authoring tool, along with a new Flash Player, come out about every 18 months. Shortly after each version is released, the rumors, speculations, and wish lists for what will be in the next version begin. Routinely, one of the longed-for features is native 3D. And just as routinely, hopes are dashed when it doesn't appear. Until Flash 10.

You could always do 3D in Flash by scaling and positioning things to make them look like they are nearer or farther away. With ActionScript came the capability to write real 3D engines. I covered the basics of this in *Making Things Move*, and in the last couple of years, numerous powerful 3D engines have appeared for Flash. PaperVision3D, Away3D, and others have the capability to load full 3D models and textures from professional modeling tools, and render and manipulate them in real time. But all these processes are done in ActionScript via classes that have been written by members of the community. They are compiled and run in the Player instead of being a native part of the Player itself.

In Flash 10, for the first time ever, we have the ability to create a display object—a sprite, movie clip, text field, and so on—and then directly manipulate it in 3D space. You can do this right in the Flash authoring tool itself and also via ActionScript. This chapter will focus on the ActionScript part.

Although this feature doesn't have anywhere near the capabilities of PaperVision3D—such as loading in models and textures, automatic depth sorting, and so on—it is extremely easy to work with and will be more than enough for many basic 3D effects you want to do in Flash. Well, what are we waiting for? Let's do 3D.

Flash 10 3D Basics

This is an advanced book, so I assume that you know at least a little bit about 3D. You have three dimensions: x is horizontal, y is vertical, and z is in and out. In Flash, the origin, or zero point, is the top-left corner of the screen, at least in 2D. The y-axis might seem upside down to you if you are used to working in normal Cartesian coordinates, but you'll get used to it. In Flash 10 3D, z-axis values get higher as an object moves "into the screen" or away from the viewer. In other words, an object with a lower z position will appear in front of an object with a higher z position. See Figure 7-1.

It's also worth mentioning how rotation works on various axes in Flash 10 3D. Rotation around the z-axis goes clockwise as the angle increases, as viewed from in front. Again, this is opposite of what you might be used to. Rotation on the y-axis also goes clockwise (as viewed from above). On the x-axis, rotation goes clockwise when viewed from the left side of an object (see Figure 7-2).

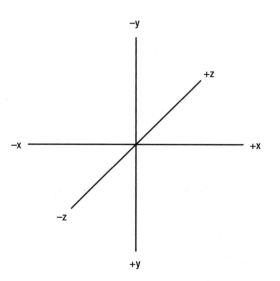

Figure 7-1. Flash 10 3D coordinates

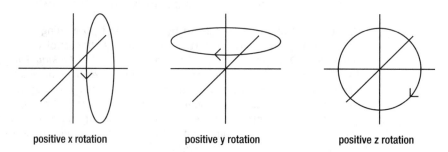

positive x rotation   positive y rotation   positive z rotation

Figure 7-2. Flash 10 3D rotations

Another important thing to realize is that for 3D rotation in Flash 10, angles are in degrees, not radians. This might seem odd if you've gotten used to programming 3D, in which you use a lot of trigonometric functions that operate on radians. But 3D in Flash is tied to the authoring tools, which are geared toward designers, not engineers. They want to put something at a 45-degree angle, not a Math.PI/4 radian angle. In case you need a reminder of how to convert between radians and degrees, here you go:

```
radians = degrees * PI / 180
degrees = radians * 180 / PI
```

Okay, now that we've defined our terms, let's look at what we have to work with in Flash 10 in terms of the 3D application programming interface (API). Although there is a lot more than these, the real meat of the whole new 3D API comes down to four new properties: z, rotationX, rotationY, and rotationZ. We'll cover the rest of the stuff, but these four properties will be your best friends while creating basic 3D effects.

Let's try it out. Create the following class and compile it. As with all files in this chapter and the rest of the book, you can find them at the book's download page on www.friendsofed.com. This file name is Test3D.as:

```
package {
    import flash.display.Shape;
    import flash.display.Sprite;
    import flash.display.StageAlign;
    import flash.display.StageScaleMode;
    import flash.events.Event;
    import flash.geom.PerspectiveProjection;
    import flash.geom.Point;

    [SWF(backgroundColor=0xffffff)]
    public class Test3D extends Sprite
    {
        private var _shape:Shape;

        public function Test3D()
        {
            stage.align = StageAlign.TOP_LEFT;
            stage.scaleMode = StageScaleMode.NO_SCALE;

            _shape = new Shape();
            _shape.graphics.beginFill(0xff0000);
            _shape.graphics.drawRect(-100, -100, 200, 200);
            _shape.x = stage.stageWidth / 2;
            _shape.y = stage.stageHeight / 2;
            addChild(_shape);
            addEventListener(Event.ENTER_FRAME, onEnterFrame);
        }

        private function onEnterFrame(event:Event):void
        {
            _shape.rotationY += 2;
        }
    }
}
```

Amazing! Native 3D in Flash!

Setting the vanishing point

I know you want to dive in and start making cool 3D stuff, but please read this section—there's some vital stuff here. Even if you know 3D, there are some quirks in Flash that will drive you crazy unless you know what's happening. Once you understand it, it will make sense, but otherwise you'll swear Flash is just plain broken.

If you used the last class as a document class for an FLA and compiled via Flash CS4, you probably saw something like Figure 7-3.

However, if you compiled for Flash 10 via Flex Builder or another setup using the Flex 4 SDK, you most likely saw something like Figure 7-4.

Figure 7-3. Rotation of a plane compiled in Flash CS4

Figure 7-4. Rotation of a plane compiled in Flex Builder

You see that it's kind of stretching off to the top left. The reason for this difference lies not in how the movies are compiled, but in the different ways they are published and how Flash sets the vanishing point. In 3D, the vanishing point is the point on which all objects converge as they move into the distance. I could insert a picture of a railroad track going off to the horizon, but you know what I'm talking about. When you code 3D from scratch, you have to manually choose a point to be the vanishing point and make sure that all objects converge on it. People usually choose the center of the stage as a vanishing point.

Flash 10 3D automatically sets the vanishing point for you and it will set it to the center of the stage. But it only does this a single time, the instant the SWF loads. When you test the movie from Flash, it pops up in a window based on the size set in the document properties panel. So the vanishing point is at its center, and that works out just fine.

However, in Flex Builder, the default size for a SWF is set to 500×375 pixels. Thus your vanishing point will be at 250, 187.5. But as soon as you set the stage.align to StageAlign.TOP_LEFT, and stage. scaleMode to StageScaleMode.NO_SCALE, it increases the size of the stage. (It's a common practice to set them so the SWF doesn't scale all its content if the display area increases—it just makes the stage larger.) You can see that by tracing out the stage width and height just before and after these calls:

```
trace(stage.stageWidth, stage.stageHeight); // 500, 375
stage.align = StageAlign.TOP_LEFT;
stage.scaleMode = StageScaleMode.NO_SCALE;
trace(stage.stageWidth, stage.stageHeight); // 1440, 794
```

You'll get a different value for the last trace, depending on the size of your browser. So, the stage size changes, and the sprite is then placed at the new center of the stage, which is something like 720, 397. But the vanishing point is still stuck at 250, 187.5. That's the problem right there.

The easiest way to fix this is to explicitly set a width and height in your SWF metadata:

```
[SWF(backgroundColor=0xffffff, width=800, height=800)]
```

This runs before the vanishing point is calculated, so it will be calculated as the center of 800, 800. The stage size won't change after the align and scaleMode are set, so your sprite gets placed at the same center.

But, perhaps you want to have a variable stage size, one that does fill the browser window no matter what size it is. Doing that is a bit more complex, but not too bad. You need to use a new class called PerspectiveProjection. This class controls various aspects about how 3D perspective is rendered, including the vanishing point. Each display object in Flash 10 now can now have a PerspectiveProjection assigned to it to control how it renders 3D. It is assigned to the perspectiveProjection property of the transform property. So, for a sprite named s, for example, you would access it like so:

```
s.transform.perspectiveProjection
```

The PerspectiveProjection class has a property named projectionCenter, which is an instance of the Point class. This is actually what we have been calling the vanishing point. Thus, to set the vanishing point for a display object to the center of the stage, you would do something like the following:

```
s.transform.perspectiveProjection.projectionCenter =
    new Point(stage.stageWidth / 2, stage.stageHeight / 2);
```

It sets the vanishing point for only that one object. But it also sets the vanishing point for any children of that object. If you want to set the vanishing point for all objects in the movie, set it on the root level, like so:

```
root.transform.perspectiveProjection.projectionCenter =
    new Point(stage.stageWidth / 2, stage.stageHeight / 2);
```

The following class does just that, right after setting the stage's align and scaleMode, which fixes the problem we saw earlier:

```
package {
    import flash.display.Shape;
    import flash.display.Sprite;
    import flash.display.StageAlign;
```

```
            import flash.display.StageScaleMode;
            import flash.events.Event;
            import flash.geom.PerspectiveProjection;
            import flash.geom.Point;

            [SWF(backgroundColor=0xffffff)]
            public class Test3D extends Sprite
            {
                private var _shape:Shape;

                public function Test3D()
                {
                    stage.align = StageAlign.TOP_LEFT;
                    stage.scaleMode = StageScaleMode.NO_SCALE;
                    root.transform.perspectiveProjection.projectionCenter =
                            new Point(stage.stageWidth / 2,
                                      stage.stageHeight / 2);

                    _shape = new Shape();
                    _shape.graphics.beginFill(0xff0000);
                    _shape.graphics.drawRect(-100, -100, 200, 200);
                    _shape.x = stage.stageWidth / 2;
                    _shape.y = stage.stageHeight / 2;
                    addChild(_shape);
                    addEventListener(Event.ENTER_FRAME, onEnterFrame);
                }

                private function onEnterFrame(event:Event):void
                {
                    _shape.rotationY += 2;
                }
            }
        }
```

You can go one step further and change the center point whenever the stage resizes by doing the following:

```
        package {
            import flash.display.Shape;
            import flash.display.Sprite;
            import flash.display.StageAlign;
            import flash.display.StageScaleMode;
            import flash.events.Event;
            import flash.geom.PerspectiveProjection;
            import flash.geom.Point;

            public class Test3D extends Sprite
            {
                private var _shape:Shape;
```

```
        public function Test3D()
        {
            stage.addEventListener(Event.RESIZE, onResize)
            stage.align = StageAlign.TOP_LEFT;
            stage.scaleMode = StageScaleMode.NO_SCALE;

            _shape = new Shape();
            _shape.graphics.beginFill(0xff0000);
            _shape.graphics.drawRect(-100, -100, 200, 200);
            _shape.x = stage.stageWidth / 2;
            _shape.y = stage.stageHeight / 2;
            addChild(_shape);

            addEventListener(Event.ENTER_FRAME, onEnterFrame);
        }

        private function onResize(event:Event):void
        {
            root.transform.perspectiveProjection.projectionCenter =
                    new Point(stage.stageWidth / 2,
                                stage.stageHeight / 2);
            if(_shape != null)
            {
                _shape.x = stage.stageWidth / 2;
                _shape.y = stage.stageHeight / 2;
            }
        }

        private function onEnterFrame(event:Event):void
        {
            _shape.rotationY += 2;
        }
    }
}
```

Because we listen for the resize event as a first action, the onResize method will be called as soon as we change the stage settings and the stage resizes, which will set the projection center immediately. It will also be called any other time the user changes the stage size by resizing the browser. I've also repositioned the shape to make sure it's always center stage as well. But onResize will be called the first time before the shape has been created, so we have to make sure it exists first. Hence the conditional in there.

For simplicity's sake, I'll go with the first solution of just setting the stage size with metadata in the rest of the chapter.

Okay, that's the vital stuff you need to know to keep your movies' perspectives looking good. Let's see what else we can do with 3D.

3D Positioning

This one is pretty obvious. I assume that you don't need to be told how to change an object's position on the x- and y-axis. Changing it on the z-axis is just as easy. The next class (found in the Position3D. as file) sets up a sine wave that swings a shape out into the distance and back, over and over. It also follows the mouse position on x and y:

```
package
{
    import flash.display.Shape;
    import flash.display.Sprite;
    import flash.events.Event;

    [SWF(width=800, height=800, backgroundColor=0xffffff)]
    public class Position3D extends Sprite
    {
        private var _shape:Shape;
        private var _n:Number = 0;

        public function Position3D()
        {
            _shape = new Shape();
            _shape.graphics.beginFill(0x00ff00);
            _shape.graphics.drawRect(-100, -100, 200, 200);
            _shape.graphics.endFill();
            addChild(_shape);

            addEventListener(Event.ENTER_FRAME, onEnterFrame);
        }

        private function onEnterFrame(event:Event):void
        {
            _shape.x = mouseX;
            _shape.y = mouseY;
            _shape.z = 10000 + Math.sin(_n += .1) * 10000;
        }
    }
}
```

I think the important thing to take away from this example is that once you change the z position, the x and y of a display object no longer directly refer to screen coordinates; they refer to 3D space coordinates. If you don't move your mouse, the x and the y of the shape do not change, but its x and y coordinates change onscreen. Only when z is equal to zero do the object's x and y match the screen x and y. This is because when z is less than zero, Flash scales the object up; when it's greater than zero, Flash scales the object down, but when z is exactly zero, the scale will be 100%.

Depth sorting

One thing you'll run into as soon as you start creating multiple objects and positioning in 3D space is that objects that are farther away (higher z value) sometimes appear in front of objects that are closer. I imagine you want to know the property or method. Unfortunately, there is no method or property you can set or call to ensure that objects are sorted correctly.

The 3D API in Flash 10 handles perspective scaling and distortion on an individual display object—and even that object's children if it has any—but it does not affect the order in which they are drawn to the screen. This is still handled the same way as for 2D objects in Flash 9: any object put on the display list via the addChild method will appear in front of previous objects added to the same container. The only ways to alter this are the various methods for managing the display list, such as addChild, addChildAt, swapChildren, removeChild, and so on. And because there is no sort method on a display object container, any depth sorting has to be done manually.

To look at how to solve the issue, let's first make an example that demonstrates the problem. How about a forest full of trees?

```
package
{
    import flash.display.Shape;
    import flash.display.Sprite;
    import flash.display.StageAlign;
    import flash.display.StageScaleMode;

    [SWF(width=800, height=800, backgroundColor = 0xccffcc)]
    public class DepthSort extends Sprite
    {
        public function DepthSort()
        {
            stage.align = StageAlign.TOP_LEFT;
            stage.scaleMode = StageScaleMode.NO_SCALE;

            for(var i:int = 0; i < 500; i++)
            {
                var tree:Shape = new Shape();
                tree.graphics.beginFill(Math.random() * 255 << 8);
                tree.graphics.lineTo(-10, 0);
                tree.graphics.lineTo(-10, -30);
                tree.graphics.lineTo(-40, -30);
                tree.graphics.lineTo(0, -100);
                tree.graphics.lineTo(40, -30);
                tree.graphics.lineTo(10, -30);
                tree.graphics.lineTo(10, 0);
                tree.graphics.lineTo(0, 0);
                tree.graphics.endFill();
```

```
                        tree.x = Math.random() * stage.stageWidth;
                        tree.y = stage.stageHeight - 100;
                        tree.z = Math.random() * 10000;
                        addChild(tree);
                    }
                }

            }
        }
```

Here we created a whole bunch of shapes and used the drawing API to draw a randomly shaded green tree in each one. Each one is randomly placed on x, y, and z. Not the high point in Flash design, but it serves the purpose. It doesn't look quite right, as you can see in Figure 7-5.

Figure 7-5. Perspective is fine, but no depth sorting

Again, we can't sort the display list, but we can sort an array. So instead of adding each tree to the display list as it's created, let's put it in an array. Then we can sort the array and add the trees to the display list in the right order—those with high z values first, lower z values later.

```
package
{
    import flash.display.Shape;
    import flash.display.Sprite;
```

```
import flash.display.StageAlign;
import flash.display.StageScaleMode;

[SWF(width=800, height=800, backgroundColor = 0xccffcc)]
public class DepthSort extends Sprite
{
    private var _trees:Array;

    public function DepthSort()
    {
        stage.align = StageAlign.TOP_LEFT;
        stage.scaleMode = StageScaleMode.NO_SCALE;

        _trees = new Array();

        for(var i:int = 0; i < 500; i++)
        {
            var tree:Shape = new Shape();
            tree.graphics.beginFill(Math.random() * 255 << 8);
            tree.graphics.lineTo(-10, 0);
            tree.graphics.lineTo(-10, -30);
            tree.graphics.lineTo(-40, -30);
            tree.graphics.lineTo(0, -100);
            tree.graphics.lineTo(40, -30);
            tree.graphics.lineTo(10, -30);
            tree.graphics.lineTo(10, 0);
            tree.graphics.lineTo(0, 0);
            tree.graphics.endFill();
            tree.x = Math.random() * stage.stageWidth;
            tree.y = stage.stageHeight - 100;
            tree.z = Math.random() * 10000;
            _trees.push(tree);
        }

        _trees.sortOn("z", Array.NUMERIC | Array.DESCENDING);
        for(i = 0; i < 500; i++)
        {
            addChild(_trees[i] as Shape);
        }
    }

}
```

Although this doesn't make the picture you see in Figure 7-6 any more artistic, at least the far away trees are behind the close ones, as you'd see them in a real forest.

Figure 7-6. Forest, now with depth sorting

3D containers

When I first started playing with the API, one of the things that made me really happy about 3D in Flash 10 was the realization that display object containers transform their children when they are transformed. In other words, when you add some display objects to a sprite and then move that container sprite around, it doesn't simply flatten the view of that sprite and move it around as a single object in 3D. No, it actually transforms each child so it looks like they are all moving individually in 3D space.

This is one of those things that's a lot easier to show than to describe. So the next class demonstrates it. Why don't we use something other than shapes with squares drawn in them this time? Text fields are display objects, too, and can be moved around in 3D exactly the same way. We'll make a sprite, throw a bunch of text fields in it with some random letters, and then move the sprite around. You can find the next example in the `Container3D.as` file:

```
package
{
    import flash.display.Sprite;
    import flash.display.StageAlign;
    import flash.display.StageScaleMode;
    import flash.events.Event;
    import flash.text.TextField;
    import flash.text.TextFormat;
```

```
[SWF(width=800, height=800, backgroundColor=0xffffff)]
public class Container3D extends Sprite
{
    private var _sprite:Sprite;
    private var _n:Number = 0;

    public function Container3D()
    {
        stage.align = StageAlign.TOP_LEFT;
        stage.scaleMode = StageScaleMode.NO_SCALE;

        _sprite = new Sprite();
        _sprite.y = stage.stageHeight / 2;

        for(var i:int = 0; i < 100; i++)
        {
            var tf:TextField = new TextField();
            tf.defaultTextFormat = new TextFormat("Arial", 40);
            tf.text = String.fromCharCode(65 +
                            Math.floor(Math.random() * 25));
            tf.selectable = false;
            tf.x = Math.random() * 300 - 150;
            tf.y = Math.random() * 300 - 150;
            tf.z = Math.random() * 1000;
            _sprite.addChild(tf);
        }

        addChild(_sprite);

        addEventListener(Event.ENTER_FRAME, onEnterFrame);
    }

    private function onEnterFrame(event:Event):void
    {
        _sprite.x = stage.stageWidth / 2 + Math.cos(_n) * 200;
        _n += .05;
    }
}
```

Each text field is randomly positioned in three dimensions within the parent sprite. Although the sprite is just moving back and forth on the x-axis, you can see the parallax effect as the letters move back and forth in 3D. See Figure 7-7.

Figure 7-7. 3D containers that look much better in motion!

3D Rotation

In addition to moving things around in 3D space, you can rotate any display object on any axis. We already saw a quick example of that at the beginning of the chapter, rotating a shape on the y-axis. I don't think I have to walk you through repeating this example on the x- and z-axis because you can probably figure that out on your own, and have probably gone way on ahead of the class and got something rotating on all three axes at once. (If you haven't, go ahead and try it.)

When you're ready, let's jump into rotating containers with display objects in them. First, we'll re-create that first experiment, but put the shape inside a sprite first. You can find the RotateAndPosition.as example file on the book's download page:

```
package {
    import flash.display.Shape;
    import flash.display.Sprite;
    import flash.events.Event;

    [SWF(width=800, height=800, backgroundColor = 0xffffff)]
    public class RotateAndPosition extends Sprite
    {
        private var _holder:Sprite;

        public function RotateAndPosition()
        {
```

```
            _holder = new Sprite();
            _holder.x = stage.stageWidth / 2;
            _holder.y = stage.stageHeight / 2;
            addChild(_holder);

            var shape:Shape = new Shape();
            shape.z = 200;
            shape.graphics.beginFill(0xff0000);
            shape.graphics.drawRect(-100, -100, 200, 200);
            _holder.addChild(shape);

            addEventListener(Event.ENTER_FRAME, onEnterFrame);
        }

        private function onEnterFrame(event:Event):void
        {
            _holder.rotationY += 2;
        }
    }
}
```

This just gives us a rotating square like before. But now let's move the square around within the container. First on the x-axis—add the line in bold in the constructor:

```
var shape:Shape = new Shape();
shape.x = 200;
shape.graphics.beginFill(0xff0000);
shape.graphics.drawRect(-100, -100, 200, 200);
_holder.addChild(shape);
```

Now instead of just rotating, it's kind of orbiting the center. We can get a different effect by moving the shape on the z-axis first:

```
var shape:Shape = new Shape();
shape.z = 200;
shape.graphics.beginFill(0xff0000);
shape.graphics.drawRect(-100, -100, 200, 200);
_holder.addChild(shape);
```

Well that's pretty cool. Let's make another square:

```
package {
    import flash.display.Shape;
    import flash.display.Sprite;
    import flash.events.Event;

    [SWF(width=800, height=800, backgroundColor = 0xffffff)]
    public class RotateAndPosition extends Sprite
    {
        private var _holder:Sprite;
```

```
public function RotateAndPosition()
{
    _holder = new Sprite();
    _holder.x = stage.stageWidth / 2;
    _holder.y = stage.stageHeight / 2;
    addChild(_holder);

    var shape1:Shape = new Shape();
    shape1.z = 200;
    shape1.graphics.beginFill(0xff0000);
    shape1.graphics.drawRect(-100, -100, 200, 200);
    _holder.addChild(shape1);

    var shape2:Shape = new Shape();
    shape2.z = -200;
    shape2.graphics.beginFill(0xff0000);
    shape2.graphics.drawRect(-100, -100, 200, 200);
    _holder.addChild(shape2);

    addEventListener(Event.ENTER_FRAME, onEnterFrame);
}

private function onEnterFrame(event:Event):void
{
    _holder.rotationY += 2;
}
}
}
```

We'll put one at a z of 200 and the other at −200. Now when we rotate the container, they'll kind of rotate around each other. But why limit it to y rotation? Change onEnterFrame to add some rotation on another axis:

```
private function onEnterFrame(event:Event):void
{
    _holder.rotationY += 2;
    _holder.rotationX += 1.5;
}
```

Heck, this is just too easy. Let's add some more squares! This time, we'll push them off to the left and right on the x-axis, but we'll also rotate them 90 degrees:

```
var shape3:Shape = new Shape();
shape3.x = 200;
shape3.rotationY = 90;
shape3.graphics.beginFill(0xff0000);
shape3.graphics.drawRect(-100, -100, 200, 200);
_holder.addChild(shape3);
```

```
var shape4:Shape = new Shape();
shape4.x = -200;
shape4.rotationY = -90;
shape4.graphics.beginFill(0xff0000);
shape4.graphics.drawRect(-100, -100, 200, 200);
_holder.addChild(shape4);
```

Now you have four walls orbiting each other. Why stop there? You're probably way ahead of me, but let's add a floor and ceiling (in a rough sense):

```
var shape5:Shape = new Shape();
shape5.y = 200;
shape5.rotationX = 90;
shape5.graphics.beginFill(0xff0000);
shape5.graphics.drawRect(-100, -100, 200, 200);
_holder.addChild(shape5);

var shape6:Shape = new Shape();
shape6.y = -200;
shape6.rotationX = -90;
shape6.graphics.beginFill(0xff0000);
shape6.graphics.drawRect(-100, -100, 200, 200);
_holder.addChild(shape6);
```

You can see the results in Figure 7-8.

Figure 7-8. Rotating cube!

Pretty neat, eh? And amazingly simple. Not even a single line of trig. I know exactly what you're thinking now, too: photo cube! Well, maybe that's not exactly what you're thinking, but I'm sure you're thinking that those red squares are getting a bit stale and they need *something* different. Of course, once you start changing colors and so forth, you'll ruin my carefully crafted illusion. Okay, go ahead and try it. Make each square a different color by changing the hex value in the beginFill call. You can even do it randomly if you want:

```
shape1.graphics.beginFill(Math.random() * 0xffffff);
```

You should see something like Figure 7-9.

Figure 7-9. Adobe, we have a problem.

Now that things aren't all red, you see the problem. If it's not clear in the screenshot here, what's happening is that parts of the cube that should be in back are now appearing in front. I'm hoping you've learned enough already to recognize instantly that this is a problem in depth sorting. Well, we've already learned about depth sorting and how to deal with that, so we can dive right in and apply it. The next class, available in the RotateAndPosition2.as file, attempts to solve the depth problem the way we just learned—by sorting the shapes by their z property and adding them to the display list in that order. I added a makeShape method to remove some of the duplication:

```
package {
    import flash.display.Shape;
    import flash.display.Sprite;
    import flash.events.Event;

    [SWF(width=800, height=800, backgroundColor = 0xffffff)]
    public class RotateAndPosition2 extends Sprite
    {
        private var _holder:Sprite;
        private var _shapes:Array;
```

```
public function RotateAndPosition2()
{
    _holder = new Sprite();
    _holder.x = stage.stageWidth / 2;
    _holder.y = stage.stageHeight / 2;
    addChild(_holder);

    var shape1:Shape = makeShape();
    shape1.z = 200;

    var shape2:Shape = makeShape();
    shape2.z = -200;

    var shape3:Shape = makeShape();
    shape3.x = 200;
    shape3.rotationY = 90;

    var shape4:Shape = makeShape();
    shape4.x = -200;
    shape4.rotationY = -90;

    var shape5:Shape = makeShape();
    shape5.y = 200;
    shape5.rotationX = 90;

    var shape6:Shape = makeShape();
    shape6.y = -200;
    shape6.rotationX = 90;

    _shapes = [shape1, shape2, shape3, shape4, shape5, shape6];
    sortShapes();

    addEventListener(Event.ENTER_FRAME, onEnterFrame);
}

private function makeShape():Shape
{
    var shape:Shape = new Shape();
    shape.graphics.beginFill(Math.random() * 0xffffff);
    shape.graphics.drawRect(-100, -100, 200, 200);
    _holder.addChild(shape);
    return shape;
}

private function sortShapes():void
{
    _shapes.sortOn("z", Array.NUMERIC | Array.DESCENDING);
    for(var i:int = 0; i < _shapes.length; i++)
```

```
            {
                _holder.addChildAt(_shapes[i] as Shape, i);
            }
        }

        private function onEnterFrame(event:Event):void
        {
            _holder.rotationY += 2;
            _holder.rotationX += 1.5;
            sortShapes();
        }
    }
}
```

In addition to the cleanup, we have an array called _shapes that contains all the shapes. The sort-Shapes method is called after each rotation. It sorts the shapes array on z and adds each one back on to the holder in the correct z order.

But, when you test it, it doesn't really do a darned thing. The problem is that we're sorting the elements on the z-axis internal to the container. So although they are correctly sorted on z, when the container is flipped around, they are suddenly completely backward. What we need to do is sort things in the order in which they appear from outside the holder. In other words, even if object A has a lower z depth than object B, it should appear behind object B when the container is rotated so that it is "backward" in respect to the z-axis.

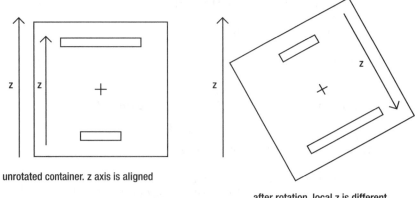

unrotated container. z axis is aligned

after rotation, local z is different than global z

Figure 7-10. The effects of rotating a 3D container

To do this, we need to write a custom sort function that transforms the local coordinates inside the container to the world (or stage or root) coordinates and then sorts based on it. The Array.sort method allows you to pass in a function as a parameter. This function is then called multiple times with pairs of objects during a sort. The function should return a negative number if the first object should be placed before the second in the array, a positive number if the first object should be placed after the second, and zero if they should be left as they are.

So now we need a way to convert the local coordinates to world coordinates. There are numerous ways to do this, including manually doing coordinate rotation that involves lots of complex trigonometry. Luckily, Flash 10 now has a new class, flash.geom.Matrix3D, which contains all kinds of useful methods for manipulating 3D coordinates. Even here, there are probably multiple ways of accomplishing what we are about to do. I don't know if the way I'm presenting is the best way, but it does get the job done and without too much pain.

This makes use of a method called deltaTransformVector on the Matrix3D class. Basically what this does is take a 3D point (stored in a Vector3D object) and applies the rotation and scaling portions of a 3D matrix to it. In simple terms, it rotates the positions of all our shapes according to the rotation of the container and lets us know where they sit in the global 3D space.

So first we need the Matrix3D that represents the rotation of the container. We can get that by typing the following:

```
container.transform.matrix3D
```

We can then call the deltaTransformVector method, passing in the 3D position of a point, and get its rotated position:

```
rotatedPosition = _holder.transform.matrix3D.deltaTransformVector(
                                        originalPosition)
```

If we do that to the positions of two separate shapes, we'll then know which one is farther away on the z-axis as seen from a global viewpoint. The last piece of the puzzle we need is how to get a Vector3D representation of the position of a display object. We could just create one on the fly by using the object's x, y, and z properties, but it happens that one already exists:

```
displayObject.transform.Matrix3D.position
```

Now we have everything we need to get the global coordinates of two display objects:

```
var posA:Vector3D = objA.transform.matrix3D.position;
posA = _holder.transform.matrix3D.deltaTransformVector(posA);
var posB:Vector3D = objB.transform.matrix3D.position;
posB = _holder.transform.matrix3D.deltaTransformVector(posB);
```

We can then make a sort compare function, which will determine which of two display objects is in front:

```
private function depthSort(objA:DisplayObject, objB:DisplayObject):int
{
    var posA:Vector3D = objA.transform.matrix3D.position;
    posA = _holder.transform.matrix3D.deltaTransformVector(posA);
    var posB:Vector3D = objB.transform.matrix3D.position;
    posB = _holder.transform.matrix3D.deltaTransformVector(posB);
    return posB.z - posA.z;
}
```

If object A is farther away than object B from a rotated, global viewpoint, this function will return a negative number, indicating that object A should be sorted before B in the array. We can then implement this in the sortShapes method quite easily:

```
private function sortShapes():void
{
    _shapes.sort(depthSort);
    for(var i:int = 0; i < _shapes.length; i++)
    {
        _holder.addChildAt(_shapes[i] as Shape, i);
    }
}
```

Now the rotating shapes should sort just fine, creating a nice 3D object, as you can see in Figure 7-11.

Figure 7-11. Correct depth sorting, even in a rotating container

By altering this slightly, we can get a carousel type of layout, often (maybe too often) used for navigation or for displaying galleries of images. I won't actually load any images in the next example, but you can easily modify the sprites to be loaders and supply them with a list of URLs. Anyway, here's the code, as found in the Carousel.as file:

```
package
{
    import flash.display.DisplayObject;
    import flash.display.Sprite;
    import flash.events.Event;
    import flash.geom.Vector3D;

    [SWF(width=800, height=800, backgroundColor = 0xffffff)]
    public class Carousel extends Sprite
    {
        private var _holder:Sprite;
        private var _items:Array;
```

```
private var _radius:Number = 200;
private var _numItems:int = 5;

public function Carousel()
{
    _holder = new Sprite();
    _holder.x = stage.stageWidth / 2;
    _holder.y = stage.stageHeight / 2;
    _holder.z = 0;
    addChild(_holder);

    _items = new Array();
    for(var i:int = 0; i < _numItems; i++)
    {
        var angle:Number = Math.PI * 2 / _numItems * i;
        var item:Sprite = makeItem();
        item.x = Math.cos(angle) * _radius;
        item.z = Math.sin(angle) * _radius;
        item.rotationY = -360 / _numItems * i + 90;
        _items.push(item);
    }
    sortItems();

    addEventListener(Event.ENTER_FRAME, onEnterFrame);
}

private function makeItem():Sprite
{
    var item:Sprite = new Sprite();
    item.graphics.beginFill(Math.random() * 0xffffff);
    item.graphics.drawRect(-50, -50, 100, 100);
    _holder.addChild(item);
    return item;
}

private function sortItems():void
{
    _items.sort(depthSort);
    for(var i:int = 0; i < _items.length; i++)
    {
        _holder.addChildAt(_items[i] as Sprite, i);
    }
}

private function depthSort(objA:DisplayObject,
                          objB:DisplayObject):int
{
    var posA:Vector3D = objA.transform.matrix3D.position;
    posA =
        _holder.transform.matrix3D.deltaTransformVector(posA);
```

```
        var posB:Vector3D = objB.transform.matrix3D.position;
        posB =
            _holder.transform.matrix3D.deltaTransformVector(posB);
        return posB.z - posA.z;
    }

    private function onEnterFrame(event:Event):void
    {
        _holder.rotationY += (stage.stageWidth / 2 - mouseX) * .01;
        _holder.y += (mouseY - _holder.y) * .1;
        sortItems();
    }
  }
}
```

The biggest changes are in bold: how the images get positioned and rotated originally, and how the container is moved in the onEnterFrame method. Instead of manually place each square, we do it in a loop this time, dividing Math.PI * 2 radians (360 degrees) by the number of items and multiplying it by the current item number. Using some trig on the resulting angle, along with a radius, gives us the x and z position for each item. We then do a similar calculation with the rotationY property, this time using degrees directly. Finally, in the enterFrame handler, we rotate the container on the y-axis based on the mouse position, as well as move it up and down on the y-axis to follow the mouse.

You can see how this looks in Figure 7-12.

Figure 7-12. A 3D carousel

Now that we have some basic ideas of how to position and rotate things in 3D, let's take a closer look at how to fine-tune the appearance of 3D.

Field of View and Focal Length

Obviously, when you are viewing any kind of image on a flat screen, you are actually viewing a two-dimensional image. Programs that render things in 3D use a number of tricks to give the illusion of a third dimension in a 2D plane. These various tricks come under the heading of perspective.

One trick of perspective is having things that are supposed to be in the distance appear behind things that are closer. We dealt with that in the last section when we did depth sorting. Another trick is making things in the distance somewhat faded out, like fog. Similarly, you can have objects at a certain depth in focus, and any objects closer or farther away out of focus. This is known as **depth of field**.

But the trick with the most impact by far is to make things that are farther away smaller, and have them approach a vanishing point as they go away and get smaller. Of course, depth sorting is pretty important for indicating a third dimension, too. Improper depth sorting will certainly ruin any illusion of 3D, as you have seen. But if you do only depth sorting and don't scale objects according to their depth, you don't really get much of a sense of 3D, either.

The big question is this: how much do you scale objects up and down as they get closer and farther away? Fortunately, this question has existed and been asked and answered by artists, engineers, and photographers long before personal computers existed. It all comes down to optics and the way the lens of either your eye or a camera works. If you've done any photography, you know that there are wide-angle lenses and telephoto lenses (and a whole range between). There are even "fish-eye" lenses that are essentially ultra-wide angle.

A wide-angle lens has a wide **field of view**. In other words, if you project an arc or cone out in front of the lens, covering the area it could "see," that cone would be very wide and cover a lot of area. A fish-eye lens can see almost 180 degrees. In a telephoto lens, this cone would be very narrow, covering a narrow sliver of the world in front of it.

Along with field of view is another concept, **focal length**, which is the distance from the center of the lens to its **focal point** (the point where the rays passing through it converge). See Figure 7-13.

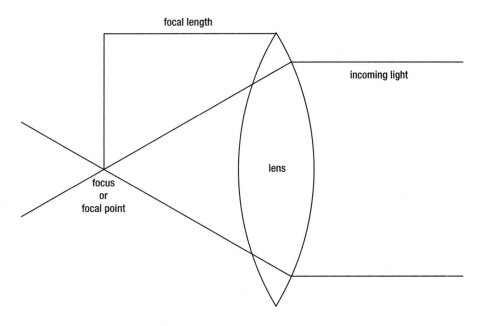

Figure 7-13. Focal length of a lens

Focal length is described a bit differently in the Adobe help files, but it still works out to be the same concept. Focal length and field of view are intimately related, and are also what determine how much scaling or distortion appears. A wider field of view, as in a wide-angle lens, results in a shorter focal length and a lot more scaling (which is why photos taken with a fish-eye lens often appear very distorted). A narrower field of view, as in a telephoto lens, results in a very long focal length and far less distortion. A good example of this includes photos from baseball games, taken from way back in the outfield where the pitcher and the batter appear almost the same size, despite the batter being farther away. In human perception, this kind of photo, with little or no distortion, can actually seem more distorted and give the impression that the batter is huge. You can see the relationship between field of view and focal length in Figures 7-14 and 7-15.

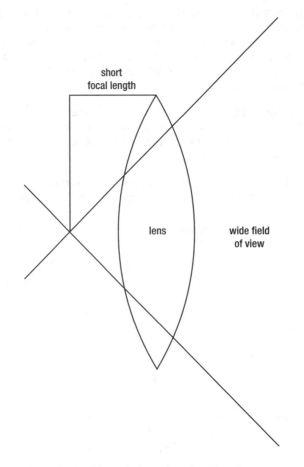

Figure 7-14. Wide angle lens, short focal length

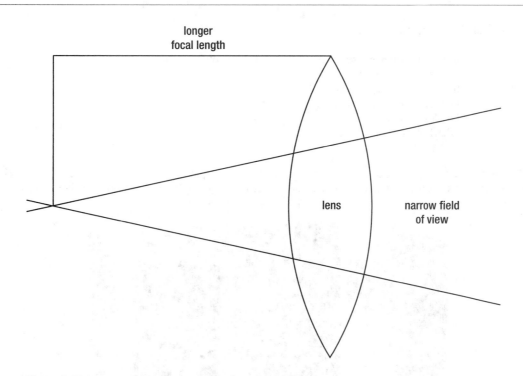

Figure 7-15. Narrow angle (telephoto) lens, long focal length

In Flash 10 3D, you can control this distortion by setting either focal length or field of view. Actually, setting either one will change the other, but you get to use the one that's most comfortable to you. This is done through two properties on the perspectiveProjection property of a display object's transform property: focalLength and fieldOfView. Generally, it's best to set these on the root of your movie unless you have some need to have different containers or objects have different perspectives (perhaps if viewing things in different windows).

The field of view is measured in terms of degrees, and it needs to be greater than 0 and less than 180, or else you will get an error. Setting a field of view of 0 means you wouldn't be able to see anything. Setting it to 180 would make your focal length 0, which I imagine would cause some problems in trying to calculate and render an image. You'll probably want to avoid numbers very close to these extremes, anyway. A field of view close to zero gives you a focal length close to infinity, which effectively cancels out any 3D perspective scaling. Fields of view close to 180 give you tiny focal lengths and a massive distortion of your rendered image. In the physical world, it is possible to get a field of view greater than 180. As far as I can tell, the widest angle lens ever made had a field of view of 220 degrees!

Anyway, getting back to Flash, it's a good thing to play around with these values and see what they do. You can do so right from the Carousel example in the last section. Just add the line in bold, right in the constructor:

```
public function Carousel()
{
    root.transform.perspectiveProjection.fieldOfView = 110;
    _holder = new Sprite();
    _holder.x = stage.stageWidth / 2;
    _holder.y = stage.stageHeight / 2;
    _holder.z = 0;
    addChild(_holder);
    ...
```

This gives you a very pronounced perspective. Because the squares closer to the "camera" are much larger now, this is probably a good setting for a photo gallery type of application. See Figure 7-16.

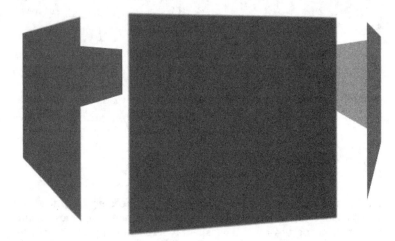

Figure 7-16. Wide field of view equals more perspective distortion

Try setting it down to 25, which narrows the field of view considerably. Now the perspective scaling is much less noticeable. See Figure 7-17.

Figure 7-17. Narrow field of view, less distortion

You should also try various high and low values for focal length, to see what they do, as in the following example:

```
root.transform.perspectiveProjection.focalLength = 300;
```

Again, short focal lengths result in more distortion; high values result in less distortion.

Screen and 3D Coordinates

Occasionally you might need to find out the screen coordinates that correspond to a point in 3D space. Or in reverse, you might need to take a point on the screen and figure out where it translates to in 3D space. Fortunately, display objects have two built-in methods just for that purpose: local3DToGlobal and globalToLocal3D. The first converts from a flash.geom.Vector3D object to a 2D flash.geom. Point object, and the second does the conversion the other way around.

First, let's see the local3DToGlobal method in action. We'll make a sprite and move it around in 3D. In that sprite there are some graphics, with a circle drawn at x=200, y=0, z=0. Then we'll create another sprite that will track that circle as it moves around by transforming the local 3D point (200, 0, 0) to global screen coordinates. Here's the class, which you can find in the LocalGlobal.as file:

```
package
{
    import flash.display.Sprite;
    import flash.events.Event;
    import flash.geom.Point;
    import flash.geom.Vector3D;

    [SWF(width=800, height=800)]
    public class LocalGlobal extends Sprite
    {
        private var _sprite:Sprite;
        private var _tracker:Sprite;
        private var _angle:Number = 0;


        public function LocalGlobal()
        {
            _sprite = new Sprite();
            _sprite.graphics.lineStyle(10);
            _sprite.graphics.lineTo(200, 0);
            _sprite.graphics.drawCircle(200, 0, 10);
            _sprite.x = 400;
            _sprite.y = 400;
            addChild(_sprite);
```

```
            _tracker = new Sprite();
            _tracker.graphics.lineStyle(2, 0xff0000);
            _tracker.graphics.drawCircle(0, 0, 20);
            addChild(_tracker);
            addEventListener(Event.ENTER_FRAME, onEnterFrame);
        }


        private function onEnterFrame(event:Event):void
        {
            _sprite.rotationX += 1;
            _sprite.rotationY+= 1.2;
            _sprite.rotationZ += .5;
            _sprite.x = 400 + Math.cos(_angle) * 100;
            _sprite.y = 400 + Math.sin(_angle) * 100;
            _sprite.z = 200 + Math.cos(_angle * .8) * 400;
            _angle += .05;
            var p:Point =
                    _sprite.local3DToGlobal(new Vector3D(200, 0, 0));
            _tracker.x = p.x;
            _tracker.y = p.y;
        }


    }
}
```

The constructor makes a 3D sprite and a tracker sprite, and puts some graphics in them. The enterFrame handler mostly consists of some code to move the sprite around in 3D space in a seemingly random fashion. It's moving and rotating on all three axes at once, using numbers I just kind of randomly threw in there. The important part is the local3DToGlobal line, in which it converts (200, 0, 0) to a 2D Point object, and then assigns that location to the tracker sprite. When you run this, you'll see that although the sprite is moving all over the place in all three dimensions, the tracker follows the circle with no problem at all. See Figure 7-18.

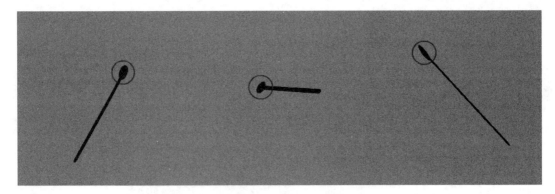

Figure 7-18. Multiple shots of tracking a 3D point in 2D

There are probably all kinds of uses for this, including knowing when a 3D object has gone off screen. Because a 3D object's x or y position might be much larger than the screen coordinates and still be visible if it is far back on the z-axis, it might be useful to know whether an object really was onscreen.

Going the other way, we can convert from a screen position to local 3D coordinates. I made a few changes to the last file, now class `GlobalLocal`, in the `GlobalLocal.as` file. The main changes are outlined in bold:

```
package
{
    import flash.display.Sprite;
    import flash.events.Event;
    import flash.geom.Point;
    import flash.geom.Vector3D;

    [SWF(width=800, height=800)]
    public class GlobalLocal extends Sprite
    {
        private var _sprite:Sprite;
        private var _tracker:Sprite;
        private var _angle:Number = 0;

        public function GlobalLocal()
        {
            _sprite = new Sprite();
            _sprite.graphics.lineStyle(5);
            _sprite.graphics.drawRect(-200, -200, 400, 400);
            _sprite.x = 400;
            _sprite.y = 400;
            addChild(_sprite);

            _tracker = new Sprite();
            _tracker.graphics.lineStyle(2, 0xff0000);
            _tracker.graphics.drawCircle(0, 0, 20);
            _sprite.addChild(_tracker);
            addEventListener(Event.ENTER_FRAME, onEnterFrame);
        }

        private function onEnterFrame(event:Event):void
        {
            _sprite.rotationX += 1;
            _sprite.rotationY+= 1.2;
            _sprite.rotationZ += .5;
            _sprite.x = 400 + Math.cos(_angle) * 100;
            _sprite.y = 400 + Math.sin(_angle) * 100;
            _sprite.z = 200 + Math.cos(_angle * .8) * 400;
            _angle += .05;
```

```
            var p:Vector3D =
                    _sprite.globalToLocal3D(new Point(mouseX, mouseY));
            _tracker.x = p.x;
            _tracker.y = p.y;
        }

    }
}
```

Here we draw a large square to the rotating sprite and put the tracker right inside of it. In the enterFrame handler, we call globalToLocal3D to get the 3D coordinates that relate to the current mouse position. This comes through as a Vector3D object. The z property of this Vector3D will always be 0 in this case, so we just use its x and y properties to set the position of the tracker within the rotating sprite. As you can see, it moves around in 3D but follows the mouse, which is moving in 2D. You can see this in Figure 7-19.

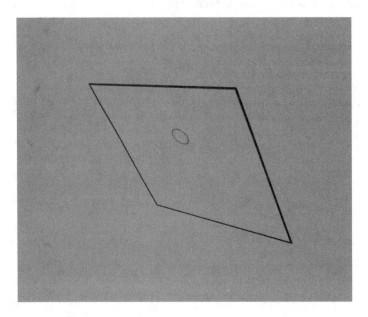

Figure 7-19. Tracking 2D coordinates in 3D

As cool as this is, though, I found a much simpler way to do the same thing: using local mouse coordinates of the rotated object. It turns out that if you access the mouseX and mouseY properties of a 3D transformed object, it will automatically do that global-to-local 3D conversion. So our onEnterFrame handler can become a bit simpler:

```
private function onEnterFrame(event:Event):void
{
    _sprite.rotationX += 1;
    _sprite.rotationY+= 1.2;
    _sprite.rotationZ += .5;
    _sprite.x = 400 + Math.cos(_angle) * 100;
    _sprite.y = 400 + Math.sin(_angle) * 100;
    _sprite.z = 200 + Math.cos(_angle * .8) * 400;
    _angle += .05;
    _tracker.x = _sprite.mouseX;
    _tracker.y = _sprite.mouseY;
}
```

This does exactly the same thing. Realize that it works only if you are converting mouse coordinates. If you want to convert the coordinates of an object on . stage to local 3D coordinates, you'll still need to use the conversion function.

Pointing at Something

Once you get comfortable with Flash 10 3D, you might want to start poking around the various related classes in the help files to see what's there. A good place to start is the flash.geom package, which contains stuff like Matrix3D, Orientation3D, PerspectiveProjection, Utils3D, and Vector3D. All those classes are chock-full of methods to help you do all kinds of 3D calculations. A rather neat one I dug up in the Matrix3D class is the pointAt method.

The pointAt method takes a Vector3D object as a target to point at. If called from the matrix3D object of a display object's transform property, it will rotate that display object in 3D to point at the specified location. The following class, found in the FollowMouse3D.as file, demonstrates this in action:

```
package
{
    import flash.display.Sprite;
    import flash.events.Event;
    import flash.events.MouseEvent;
    import flash.geom.Vector3D;

    [SWF(width=800, height=800, backgroundColor = 0xffffff)]
    public class FollowMouse3D extends Sprite
    {
        private var _sprite:Sprite;
        private var _angleX:Number = 0;
        private var _angleY:Number = 0;
        private var _angleZ:Number = 0;
```

```
public function FollowMouse3D()
{
    _sprite = new Sprite();
    _sprite.x = 400;
    _sprite.y = 400;
    _sprite.z = 200;
    _sprite.graphics.beginFill(0xff0000);
    _sprite.graphics.moveTo(0, 50);
    _sprite.graphics.lineTo(-25, 25);
    _sprite.graphics.lineTo(-10, 25);
    _sprite.graphics.lineTo(-10, -50);
    _sprite.graphics.lineTo(10, -50);
    _sprite.graphics.lineTo(10, 25);
    _sprite.graphics.lineTo(25, 25);
    _sprite.graphics.lineTo(0, 50);
    _sprite.graphics.endFill();
    addChild(_sprite);

    addEventListener(Event.ENTER_FRAME, onEnterFrame);
}

private function onEnterFrame(event:Event):void
{
    _sprite.x = 400 + Math.sin(_angleX += .11) * 200;
    _sprite.y = 400 + Math.sin(_angleY += .07) * 200;
    _sprite.z = Math.sin(_angleZ += .09) * 200;
    _sprite.transform.matrix3D.pointAt(new Vector3D(mouseX,
                                                    mouseY,
                                                    0));
}
}
}
```

The constructor consists mostly of a bunch of lineTos that draw an arrow in a sprite.

The onEnterFrame method consists mostly of some code to move that sprite all around in 3D, not unlike the LocalGlobal example. The last line calls the pointAt method on the matrix3D object on the transform property of the sprite. It passes in a new Vector3D object made up of the mouse x and y coordinates, plus 0 on the z-axis. And just like that, the sprite, with its drawn arrow, will point at the mouse on each frame. It's moving all over the place, and you can move the mouse all over the place, but it never loses track (see Figure 7-20).

Figure 7-20. Pointing at the mouse in 3D

I'm not sure how practical this example is in and of itself, but I can think of all kinds of uses for this technique in making 3D games: steering, aiming, and so on.

Summary

Although we covered a lot in this chapter, we really just barely scratched the surface of 3D in Flash 10. We'll be looking into a few more 3D topics in the next chapter on the new drawing API features, but hopefully this chapter has giving you a jump start on what's possible in this subject. Again, look through the documentation, specifically for `flash.display.DisplayObject` and all the stuff in the `flash.geom` package. I'm sure you're going to have fun with this

Chapter 8

FLASH 10 DRAWING API

If you've been involved in Flash for less than six years or so, you might not have a full appreciation of the ActionScript drawing application programming interface (API). From my viewpoint, its release in Flash MX in late 2002 revolutionized scripted graphics in Flash. Prior to Flash MX, there was no way to dynamically generate any graphic content at all. Even writing this now, it seems hard to believe, but it's true—if you wanted something visible to appear in your SWF, you had to draw it on stage or import it to the library at author time, or load it in at run time. Naturally, there were various tricks, such as keeping a movie clip in your library with a single line in it and attaching numerous instances of this line clip, scaling, and positioning them to create dynamic graphics.

But in Flash MX, for the first time, you could start out with a FLA and nothing but code, and then create all kinds of graphics content completely on the fly. Despite the fact that the API was unbelievably minimal (drawing commands were limited to moveTo, lineTo, and curveTo, and later a few commands were added for drawing rectangles, circles and ellipses), it has been responsible for a vast amount of the graphics created on the Flash platform. In fact, there are many complex applications whose entire interface is built up through drawing API commands.

So, with that background, let me introduce the Flash 10 upgrades to the drawing API, which are anything but minimal. In fact, these "additions" dwarf the original API itself, in the number of new methods, number of new objects, sheer power, and complexity. So let's dive in and see whether we can make some sense of it all.

Paths

The first topic we'll discuss is paths, so I get to define the term for the second time—with a totally different definition than the one used in Chapter 4. In terms of the new drawing API, a **path** is a series of points and an associated series of drawing commands (moveTo, lineTo, curveTo) that are used to draw a shape in a Graphics object. It's not unlike the "connect-the-dots" drawings you did as a kid.

In the old days (Flash MX through Flash CS3), you would individually make calls to the moveTo, lineTo, or curveTo methods, passing in appropriate values. At first, you probably hard-coded values in long lists of graphics method calls. Later you realized that you could store the numbers for locations in arrays and loop through the arrays calling lineTo repeatedly with the next values from the array. If you were really good, you might have even devised a way to encode the different drawing methods and store an array of them, so you could call moveTo, followed by a few lineTo methods, and then a curveTo method if you needed it. So you could have a list of commands and a list of points that made up a shape. If you made it that far, or at least understand how it would have worked if you had done it, you will have no problem understanding paths in the new drawing API because that's precisely what they are: a list of points and a list of drawing commands.

The first place where we run into paths is in the drawPaths method of the flash.display.Graphics class. Let's look at it in its simplest form:

```
drawPath(commands:Vector.<int>, data:Vector.<Number>)
```

We have a list of commands stored in a vector of ints and a list of data stored in a vector of Numbers. The commands are moveTo, lineTo, and curveTo (and a few others you'll see shortly). They are encoded as integers and stored as static constant members of the flash.display.GraphicsPathCommand class, as follows:

```
public static const NO_OP:int = 0;
public static const MOVE_TO:int = 1;
public static const LINE_TO:int = 2;
public static const CURVE_TO:int = 3;
public static const WIDE_MOVE_TO:int = 4;
public static const WIDE_LINE_TO:int = 5;
```

Numbers 1, 2, and 3 should be familiar to you. The 0 command, NO_OP, is like a null command and tells the drawing API to do nothing. We'll cover how that would be used along with what those last two wide commands are all about a bit later.

When you want to draw a line, you usually move to a certain point and draw a line to another point. To encode it in a vector of commands, you would do something like this:

```
var commands:Vector.<int> = new Vector.<int>();
commands[0] = GraphicsPathCommand.MOVE_TO;
commands[1] = GraphicsPathCommand.LINE_TO;
```

Alternately, you could use ints directly:

```
var commands:Vector.<int> = new Vector.<int>();
commands[0] = 1;
commands[1] = 2;
```

Of course, that doesn't communicate what you are doing and you lose any compile time checking as well. You could happily enter 17 as a command, thinking that it means something or merely as a slip of the hand. Flash would happily compile it because it is in fact an int, but your program certainly wouldn't do what you expected.

Now we need a data vector, which will contain the points we want to draw the line between. You might expect this to be a vector of Point objects, in which each element contained an x and a y value. However, as you can see, it is a vector of Numbers. So the first element represents the x value of the first point, and the second element represents the y value of the first point. The next two elements represent the next point, and so on. Although this is a bit confusing to grasp at first, it is more efficient both in terms of speed and memory to store and access a vector of primitive values such as Numbers instead of complex objects such as Points. And these new additions to the drawing API are built for speed. One thing you need to make sure of is that you always have enough data points to match the number of commands you have. If you run out of points before you use up your commands, Flash will wind up using zeros for data, which is generally pretty useless.

Let's draw a line from 100, 100 to 250, 200. Here's the data vector:

```
var data:Vector.<Number> = new Vector.<Number>();
data[0] = 100;
data[1] = 100;
data[2] = 250;
data[3] = 200;
```

Now we can call drawPath, passing in the commands and data, and see a line. Of course we'll need to set a lineStyle first. A path merely represents the points and type of the drawing operation. You still have to specify any fills or strokes the old-fashioned way. (Later you'll see how to encode line styles and fills as well.)

```
graphics.lineStyle(0);
graphics.drawPath(commands, data);
```

Now let's see the whole thing in a class you can actually execute. This one is available as the SingleLine. as file from the book's download page at www.friendsofed.com:

```
package
{
    import flash.display.GraphicsPathCommand;
    import flash.display.Sprite;
    import flash.display.StageAlign;
    import flash.display.StageScaleMode;

    [SWF(backgroundColor=0xffffff)]
    public class SingleLine extends Sprite
    {
        public function SingleLine()
        {
            stage.align = StageAlign.TOP_LEFT;
            stage.scaleMode = StageScaleMode.NO_SCALE;
```

```
var commands:Vector.<int> = new Vector.<int>();
commands[0] = GraphicsPathCommand.MOVE_TO;
commands[1] = GraphicsPathCommand.LINE_TO;

var data:Vector.<Number> = new Vector.<Number>();
data[0] = 100;
data[1] = 100;
data[2] = 250;
data[3] = 200;

graphics.lineStyle(0);
graphics.drawPath(commands, data);
            }
        }
    }
```

Now, you are probably thinking that's a lot of code to draw a single line. And it's true. If that's all you were doing, it would certainly be much easier to just call moveTo and lineTo and be done with it. As you'll see as we move through the examples, these new objects and methods are designed for far more complex drawing operations such as drawing very complex shapes. As a matter of fact, one of the main purposes of these additions is to enable the drawing of 3D forms. And yes, we'll get into a bit of that later in the chapter.

But first let's see a more practical use of drawPath.

A simple drawing program

If you are familiar with software design patterns, you might see a bit of the command pattern begin-ning to emerge here. In the command pattern, objects represent actions. You create a command object that encapsulates an action as well as the parameters that are used with that action. Here we are actually storing a list of actions (drawing commands) and their parameters (data).

In the next example, we'll create a small drawing program that lets the user sketch some shapes. It stores the drawing as a list of commands and data. This drawing can then be redrawn at any time just by calling drawPath again. In this case, we will allow the user to change the line width using the up and down keys, and set a random color using the space key. The program will then redraw the sketch using the new line style. Of course, in a real application you would provide more useful controls to allow selection of a line width and color, but we'll concentrate on the drawing API drawPath stuff. Here's the class itself, which you can find as the PathSketch.as file:

```
package
{
    import flash.display.GraphicsPathCommand;
    import flash.display.Sprite;
    import flash.display.StageAlign;
    import flash.display.StageScaleMode;
    import flash.events.KeyboardEvent;
    import flash.events.MouseEvent;
    import flash.ui.Keyboard;
```

```
[SWF(backgroundColor=0xffffff)]
public class PathSketch extends Sprite
{
    private var commands:Vector.<int> = new Vector.<int>();
    private var data:Vector.<Number> = new Vector.<Number>();

    private var lineWidth:Number = 0;
    private var lineColor:uint = 0;

    public function PathSketch()
    {
        stage.align = StageAlign.TOP_LEFT;
        stage.scaleMode = StageScaleMode.NO_SCALE;

        stage.addEventListener(MouseEvent.MOUSE_DOWN, onMouseDown);
        stage.addEventListener(KeyboardEvent.KEY_UP, onKeyUp);
    }


    private function onMouseDown(event:MouseEvent):void
    {
        commands.push(GraphicsPathCommand.MOVE_TO);
        data.push(mouseX, mouseY);
        stage.addEventListener(MouseEvent.MOUSE_MOVE, onMouseMove);
        stage.addEventListener(MouseEvent.MOUSE_UP, onMouseUp);
        draw();
    }

    private function onMouseMove(event:MouseEvent):void
    {
        commands.push(GraphicsPathCommand.LINE_TO);
        data.push(mouseX, mouseY);
        draw();
    }

    private function onMouseUp(event:MouseEvent):void
    {
        stage.removeEventListener(MouseEvent.MOUSE_MOVE,
                            onMouseMove);
        stage.removeEventListener(MouseEvent.MOUSE_UP, onMouseUp);
    }

    private function onKeyUp(event:KeyboardEvent):void
    {
        if(event.keyCode == Keyboard.DOWN)
        {
            lineWidth = Math.max(0, lineWidth -1);
        }
        else if(event.keyCode == Keyboard.UP)
```

```
            {
                lineWidth++;
            }
            else if(event.keyCode == Keyboard.SPACE)
            {
                lineColor = Math.random() * 0xffffff;
            }
            draw();
        }

        private function draw():void
        {
            graphics.clear();
            graphics.lineStyle(lineWidth, lineColor);
            graphics.drawPath(commands, data);
        }
    }
}
```

The program starts by making vectors for commands and data, and assigning listeners for mouseDown and keyUp. We'll walk through it from there. First we have the mouseDown handler:

```
private function onMouseDown(event:MouseEvent):void
{
    commands.push(GraphicsPathCommand.MOVE_TO);
    data.push(mouseX, mouseY);
    stage.addEventListener(MouseEvent.MOUSE_MOVE, onMouseMove);
    stage.addEventListener(MouseEvent.MOUSE_UP, onMouseUp);
    draw();
}
```

This method is called when the user pushes the mouse button on the stage. We want the drawing API to move to that point, so we push a MOVE_TO onto the commands vector, and push the mouse x and y position onto the data vector. We then listen for mouseMove and mouseUp events and call the draw method.

The onMouseUp handler merely removes the event listeners. But let's have another look at the onMouse-Move handler:

```
private function onMouseMove(event:MouseEvent):void
{
    commands.push(GraphicsPathCommand.LINE_TO);
    data.push(mouseX, mouseY);
    draw();
}
```

This is pretty similar to onMouseDown—it pushes a LINE_TO onto the commands vector and the mouse position onto the data vector. Now the commands vector will have a list of MOVE_TOs and LINE_TOs, and data will contain a long list of numbers representing x and y coordinates. We can then call draw. Note that when we first called draw in our onMouseDown method we pushed MOVE_TO onto the commands vector so the drawing API just moved to that point. Here, we're pushing LINE_TO, so the API is now drawing from that initial point to the position to which we moved the mouse. With that in mind, let's see what the draw method contains:

```
private function draw():void
{
    graphics.clear();
    graphics.lineStyle(lineWidth, lineColor);
    graphics.drawPath(commands, data);
}
```

This is pretty simple. Clear the graphics; set a line style based on the lineWidth and lineColor properties (both set to 0 initially); and call drawPath, passing in commands and data. I won't go into the onKeyUp method—it just checks what key was pressed and changes either the line width or color.

Now you can draw some lines on the stage and use the arrow keys to change the weight of the stroke of those lines and the space key to change their color. Now this isn't anything that you couldn't have done before, but it makes it a lot easier than having to figure out how to encode your moveTos and lineTos and creating loops for drawing.

You could go a lot further with this kind of thing—separating each set of lines into its own path, allowing for undo, redo, and so on. And in the last section of this chapter, you'll look at some additional tools that make that kind of thing even easier. But first let's look at the rest of the path-related functionality.

Drawing curves

Drawing curves with drawPath is not much different from drawing lines. Of course, you need to change the command from LINE_TO to CURVE_TO, and you'll also need to supply extra data—one pair of numbers for the control point and another for the end point. And like LINE_TO, you usually want to start with a MOVE_TO or other drawing operation to set the starting point of the curve.

We'll keep this example simple because there's more to cover in this chapter. We'll just make eight points and draw some curves between them. The next class can be downloaded as the CurveDrawing. as file:

```
package
{
    import flash.display.GraphicsPathCommand;
    import flash.display.Sprite;
    import flash.display.StageAlign;
    import flash.display.StageScaleMode;

    [SWF(backgroundColor=0xffffff)]
    public class CurveDrawing extends Sprite
    {
        private var commands:Vector.<int> = new Vector.<int>();
        private var data:Vector.<Number> = new Vector.<Number>();
```

```
        public function CurveDrawing()
        {
            stage.align = StageAlign.TOP_LEFT;
            stage.scaleMode = StageScaleMode.NO_SCALE;

            data.push(200, 200);

            data.push(250, 100);
            data.push(300, 200);

            data.push(400, 250);
            data.push(300, 300);

            data.push(250, 400);
            data.push(200, 300);

            data.push(100, 250);
            data.push(200, 200);

            commands.push(GraphicsPathCommand.MOVE_TO);
            commands.push(GraphicsPathCommand.CURVE_TO);
            commands.push(GraphicsPathCommand.CURVE_TO);
            commands.push(GraphicsPathCommand.CURVE_TO);
            commands.push(GraphicsPathCommand.CURVE_TO);

            graphics.lineStyle(0);
            graphics.drawPath(commands, data);
        }
    }
}
```

This class gives you the picture you see in Figure 8-1, which I've annotated to show the locations of the points and what the drawing commands are doing.

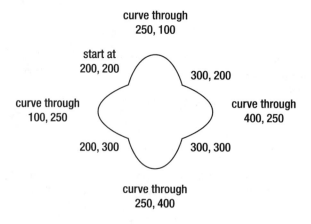

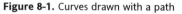

Figure 8-1. Curves drawn with a path

Again, this is nothing that might not be simpler with the old drawing API, but from the previous example, hopefully you can see how you could work this into a more complex drawing program. We'll see more real-life examples as time goes on.

Wide drawing commands and NO_OP

Suppose that you want to use the data set we created in the last example and draw some lines to further the shape. You might start out with creating a separate commands vector with LINE_TOs instead of CURVE_TOs, like so (class available in the LineAndCurveDrawing.as file):

```
package
{
    import flash.display.GraphicsPathCommand;
    import flash.display.Sprite;
    import flash.display.StageAlign;
    import flash.display.StageScaleMode;

    [SWF(backgroundColor=0xffffff)]
    public class LineAndCurveDrawing extends Sprite
    {
        private var commands:Vector.<int> = new Vector.<int>();
        private var lineCommands:Vector.<int> = new Vector.<int>();
        private var data:Vector.<Number> = new Vector.<Number>();


        public function LineAndCurveDrawing()
        {
            stage.align = StageAlign.TOP_LEFT;
            stage.scaleMode = StageScaleMode.NO_SCALE;

            data.push(200, 200);

            data.push(250, 100);
            data.push(300, 200);

            data.push(400, 250);
            data.push(300, 300);

            data.push(250, 400);
            data.push(200, 300);

            data.push(100, 250);
            data.push(200, 200);

            commands.push(GraphicsPathCommand.MOVE_TO);
            commands.push(GraphicsPathCommand.CURVE_TO);
            commands.push(GraphicsPathCommand.CURVE_TO);
            commands.push(GraphicsPathCommand.CURVE_TO);
            commands.push(GraphicsPathCommand.CURVE_TO);
```

```
lineCommands.push(GraphicsPathCommand.MOVE_TO);
lineCommands.push(GraphicsPathCommand.LINE_TO);
lineCommands.push(GraphicsPathCommand.LINE_TO);
lineCommands.push(GraphicsPathCommand.LINE_TO);
lineCommands.push(GraphicsPathCommand.LINE_TO);

graphics.lineStyle(0);
graphics.drawPath(commands, data);
graphics.lineStyle(0, 0x000000, .5);
graphics.drawPath(lineCommands, data);
        }
    }
}
```

However, that gives you the picture you see in Figure 8-2.

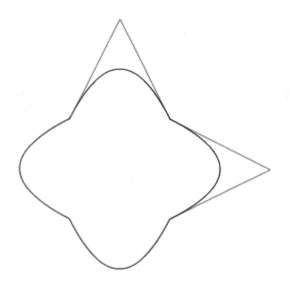

Figure 8-2. Curves and lines

The problem here is that CURVE_TOs consume two points whereas LINE_TOs consume only one. Because we put in only four LINE_TOs, we only make it halfway around. Push four more LINE_TOs onto the lineCommands vector and you have what we see in Figure 8-3.

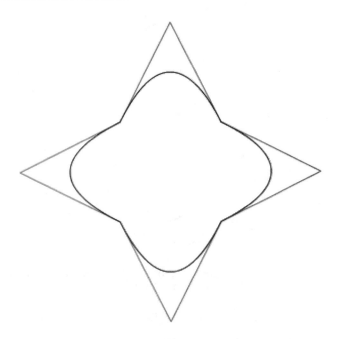

Figure 8-3. Curves and more lines

Good enough. But now say we wanted to simply replace each curve with a single line that went from one end point of each curve to the other, ignoring the control point. This would be impossible using the same data set with LINE_TO alone. You'd have to reconstruct a new data set pulling out every other value.

This is where the WIDE_LINE_TO command comes in. This command skips the next pair of numbers and draws a line to the following pair. Thus it can be directly substituted for a CURVE_TO command, ignoring the control point and drawing a line directly to the end point. Thus we can replace the four LINE_TO commands with WIDE_LINE_TO commands like so:

```
lineCommands.push(GraphicsPathCommand.MOVE_TO);
lineCommands.push(GraphicsPathCommand.WIDE_LINE_TO);
lineCommands.push(GraphicsPathCommand.WIDE_LINE_TO);
lineCommands.push(GraphicsPathCommand.WIDE_LINE_TO);
lineCommands.push(GraphicsPathCommand.WIDE_LINE_TO);
```

This will give us the picture shown in Figure 8-4.

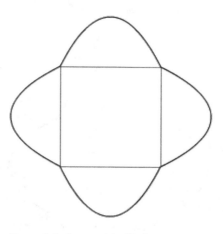

Figure 8-4. Curves and wide lines

Similarly, WIDE_MOVE_TO will skip the next pair of number in the data vector, and move to the following point (we can get away without an example for it).

You might expect that you can skip over the control points using a NO_OP command like so:

```
lineCommands.push(GraphicsPathCommand.MOVE_TO);
lineCommands.push(GraphicsPathCommand.NO_OP);
lineCommands.push(GraphicsPathCommand.LINE_TO);
lineCommands.push(GraphicsPathCommand.NO_OP);
lineCommands.push(GraphicsPathCommand.LINE_TO);
lineCommands.push(GraphicsPathCommand.NO_OP);
lineCommands.push(GraphicsPathCommand.LINE_TO);
lineCommands.push(GraphicsPathCommand.NO_OP);
lineCommands.push(GraphicsPathCommand.LINE_TO);
```

Unfortunately this does *not* work.

The NO_OP command is a noncommand; using it does nothing. It draws no lines or curves, and it does not move the drawing cursor. However, it doesn't consume any points from the data list, either. So the next LINE_TO command will continue to draw a line directly to the next point on the list. I don't have a practical example for when you'd actually need NO_OP, but I can imagine a few possibilities. For example, if you want to skip drawing a portion of a drawing, you could swap out drawing commands for those points with NO_OP commands, thus preserving the data in case you need to draw the full drawing again.

Winding

The last thing we'll cover with paths is **winding**, which refers to the direction that the points making up a shape are oriented. You know that a shape is drawn with lines or curves between points and should be able to see that as these points form a shape, they go around either clockwise or counterclockwise. A clockwise orientation is known as **positive winding**; a counterclockwise orientation is known as

negative winding. Of course, you could have a figure-eight shape, which has both positive and negative winding. This is not a problem because each part of the shape can be considered separately.

Now, for a single shape, the direction of its winding really doesn't make any difference. It becomes important when paths with the same fill intersect or overlap. When you are drawing two overlapping paths or a single path that overlaps itself between a single set of beginFill/endFill operations, there are two possibilities for that area of overlap— either it can be filled along with the rest of the shape, or the overlapping paths can cancel each other out—leaving an unfilled area. To see this in action, take a look at the next example, which you can find in the WindingDemo.as file:

```
package
{
    import flash.display.GraphicsPathCommand;
    import flash.display.GraphicsPathWinding;
    import flash.display.Sprite;
    import flash.display.StageAlign;
    import flash.display.StageScaleMode;

    [SWF(backgroundColor=0xffffff)]
    public class WindingDemo extends Sprite
    {
        private var commands:Vector.<int> = new Vector.<int>();
        private var data1:Vector.<Number> = new Vector.<Number>();
        private var data2:Vector.<Number> = new Vector.<Number>();


        public function WindingDemo()
        {
            stage.align = StageAlign.TOP_LEFT;
            stage.scaleMode = StageScaleMode.NO_SCALE;

            commands.push(GraphicsPathCommand.MOVE_TO);
            commands.push(GraphicsPathCommand.LINE_TO);
            commands.push(GraphicsPathCommand.LINE_TO);
            commands.push(GraphicsPathCommand.LINE_TO);
            commands.push(GraphicsPathCommand.LINE_TO);

            data1.push(150, 100);
            data1.push(200, 100);
            data1.push(200, 250);
            data1.push(150, 250);
            data1.push(150, 100);

            data2.push(100, 150);
            data2.push(250, 150);
            data2.push(250, 200);
            data2.push(100, 200);
            data2.push(100, 150);
```

```
                graphics.beginFill(0xff0000);
                graphics.drawPath(commands, data1);
                graphics.drawPath(commands, data2);
                graphics.endFill();
            }
        }
    }
```

Here we create two rectangles—one vertical, one horizontal—that overlap to form a cross. We draw them both using drawPath within a single set of beginFill and end-Fill statements, so they are being drawn with the same fill. By default, the intersecting area is unfilled, as you can see in Figure 8-5.

Note that a key point of this behavior is that it occurs when the paths are being drawn with the same fill. To see this, try changing the last few lines to the following:

```
graphics.beginFill(0xff0000);
graphics.drawPath(commands, data1);
graphics.endFill();
graphics.beginFill(0xff0000);
graphics.drawPath(commands, data2);
graphics.endFill();
```

Figure 8-5. An intersecting fill cancels itself out.

Because you ended the first fill and started a new one before drawing the second path, they overlap and the entire area of both rectangles is filled.

Also note that a single path can overlap itself very easily, as you can see in this slightly altered version:

```
package
{
    import flash.display.GraphicsPathCommand;
    import flash.display.GraphicsPathWinding;
    import flash.display.Sprite;
    import flash.display.StageAlign;
    import flash.display.StageScaleMode;

    [SWF(backgroundColor=0xffffff)]
    public class WindingDemo extends Sprite
    {
        private var commands:Vector.<int> = new Vector.<int>();
        private var data1:Vector.<Number> = new Vector.<Number>();


        public function WindingDemo()
        {
            stage.align = StageAlign.TOP_LEFT;
            stage.scaleMode = StageScaleMode.NO_SCALE;
```

```
                commands.push(GraphicsPathCommand.MOVE_TO);
                commands.push(GraphicsPathCommand.LINE_TO);
                commands.push(GraphicsPathCommand.LINE_TO);
                commands.push(GraphicsPathCommand.LINE_TO);
                commands.push(GraphicsPathCommand.LINE_TO);

                commands.push(GraphicsPathCommand.MOVE_TO);
                commands.push(GraphicsPathCommand.LINE_TO);
                commands.push(GraphicsPathCommand.LINE_TO);
                commands.push(GraphicsPathCommand.LINE_TO);
                commands.push(GraphicsPathCommand.LINE_TO);

                data1.push(150, 100);
                data1.push(200, 100);
                data1.push(200, 250);
                data1.push(150, 250);
                data1.push(150, 100);

                data1.push(100, 150);
                data1.push(250, 150);
                data1.push(250, 200);
                data1.push(100, 200);
                data1.push(100, 150);

                graphics.beginFill(0xff0000);
                graphics.drawPath(commands, data1);
                graphics.endFill();
            }
        }
    }
```

This gives you the exact same result as the first version.

Taking this last version, if you want to override the default behavior and fill the whole area, you can't just throw an endFill and new beginFill in the middle because there is only a single drawPath call happening. This is where the third optional parameter to drawPath comes in: winding. This winding parameter is a string and can be either "evenOdd" or "nonZero". They are provided as static constants of the flash.display.GraphicsPathWinding class: GraphicsPathWinding.EVEN_ODD and GraphicsPathWinding.NON_ZERO.

You can dig into this a bit more in the Flash CS4 help files to understand why they are called what they are called, and the theories behind them. But in simple terms, EVEN_ODD is the default behavior that does not fill any intersecting areas of shapes drawn with the same fill.

You can see this by changing the call to drawPath in the last example to the following and see that it still behaves the same way:

```
        graphics.drawPath(commands, data1, GraphicsPathWinding.EVEN_ODD);
```

The alternate winding option gives you a bit more control in how the shapes intersect. Go ahead and try it:

```
graphics.drawPath(commands, data1, GraphicsPathWinding.NON_ZERO);
```

Now the shape is completely filled again. But it's not as simple as saying, "EVEN_ODD doesn't fill intersections, and NON_ZERO does." Remember that positive/negative winding stuff? Here's the reason why I talked about it. When you specify NON_ZERO winding, Flash looks at the winding direction of the two overlapping paths (or path portions) to determine what to do with that intersecting area, and applies the following rules:

- If the winding directions of the two paths are the same direction (either positive or negative), the intersecting area will be filled.
- If the winding directions of the two paths are different (one positive, one negative), the intersecting area is not filled.

In the previous example, both rectangles were drawn in a clockwise direction, as you can see in Figure 8-6.

We can see this in action by switching a couple of the points in one of the rectangles like so:

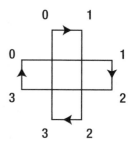

Figure 8-6. Two clockwise paths

```
data1.push(150, 100);
data1.push(200, 100);
data1.push(200, 250);
data1.push(150, 250);
data1.push(150, 100);

data1.push(100, 150);
data1.push(100, 200);
data1.push(250, 200);
data1.push(250, 150);
data1.push(100, 150);
```

By switching the second and fourth points of the second rectangle, you are changing its winding to be counterclockwise. Test that and you'll see that the middle area is no longer filled. Switch the same two points in the first rectangle and they'll both have counterclockwise winding. But then the winding will be the same, and the shape will be fully filled.

Okay, that's all we'll cover on drawPath, although paths will come up again in an even more powerful context. Next up, we'll take a look at triangles.

Triangles

Triangles are a pretty important concept in computer graphics. Two points form a line; three points are required to define a plane. Thus, three points are the minimum needed to do any kind of color or bitmap fill. Furthermore, triangles are often the basic building block of 3D modeling systems. Even when you model with splines or primitives, models are often broken down into triangles somewhere within the rendering process. And as a matter of fact, the new triangle drawing features in Flash 10 are primarily aimed at 3D effects. But they can be used for a lot more.

Let's start with the bare minimum case. We'll draw a single triangle. A triangle is made up of three points, right? So first we have to create a list of three x, y coordinates. Let's go with 100, 100 for the first point; 200, 100 for the second; and 150, 200 for the third.

So, to make a vector that contains the vertices to draw the single triangle we just described, we would write the following:

```
var vertices:Vector.<Number> = new Vector.<Number>();
vertices.push(100, 100);
vertices.push(200, 100),
vertices.push(150, 200);
```

Now, to draw this triangle, we simply pass it in to the drawTriangles method of a Graphics object, like so:

```
graphics.drawTriangles(vertices);
```

Again, you'll need to set a line style or some sort of fill in order to actually draw anything visible. The following class, Triangles1, demonstrates drawing this one triangle. You'll find it as the Triangles1. as file:

```
package
{
    import flash.display.Sprite;
    import flash.display.StageAlign;
    import flash.display.StageScaleMode;

    [SWF(backgroundColor=0xffffff)]
    public class Triangles1 extends Sprite
    {
        public function Triangles1()
        {
            stage.align = StageAlign.TOP_LEFT;
            stage.scaleMode = StageScaleMode.NO_SCALE;

            var vertices:Vector.<Number> = new Vector.<Number>();
            vertices.push(100, 100);
            vertices.push(200, 100);
            vertices.push(150, 200);

            graphics.lineStyle(0);
            graphics.drawTriangles(vertices);
        }
    }
}
```

And Figure 8-7 shows you the result.

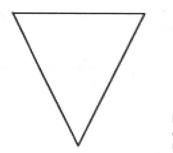

Figure 8-7. A single triangle
drawn with the `drawTriangles`
method

As you see, this is a bit easier than drawPath. No need for a moveTo or lineTo. You give it three points
and it knows what to do.

Next, let's draw two triangles. For that, we'll need 6 points, which means 12 numbers in the list. The
next class, Triangles2, available for download as Triangles2.as, shows this:

```
package
{
    import flash.display.Sprite;
    import flash.display.StageAlign;
    import flash.display.StageScaleMode;

    [SWF(backgroundColor=0xffffff)]
    public class Triangles2 extends Sprite
    {
        public function Triangles2()
        {
            stage.align = StageAlign.TOP_LEFT;
            stage.scaleMode = StageScaleMode.NO_SCALE;

            var vertices:Vector.<Number> = new Vector.<Number>();
            vertices.push(100, 100);
            vertices.push(200, 100);
            vertices.push(150, 200);

            vertices.push(250, 150);
            vertices.push(350, 175);
            vertices.push(200, 300);

            graphics.lineStyle(0);
            graphics.drawTriangles(vertices);
        }
    }
}
```

As you can see, the only thing we did here is add three more vertices, which draws the triangles seen
in Figure 8-8.

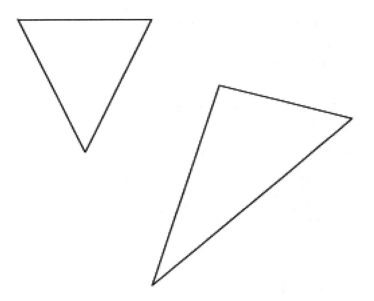

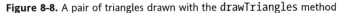

Figure 8-8. A pair of triangles drawn with the `drawTriangles` method

When used this way, `drawTriangles` absolutely expects to be given a list of numbers whose total is a multiple of six. For instance, try removing the last vertex from the list:

```
vertices.push(100, 100);
vertices.push(200, 100);
vertices.push(150, 200);
vertices.push(250, 150);
vertices.push(350, 175);
```

With only five vertices, Flash does not know how to construct two triangles and will complain that one of the parameters to `drawTriangles` is invalid.

Now this brings to mind two thoughts: drawing a bunch of individual triangles has limited usefulness, and I could draw two triangles with only four vertices by reusing two of the vertices. Fortunately, although the default behavior of `drawTriangles` is to draw a separate triangle with each triplet of vertices, the method has an optional second parameter, `indices`, that allows you to control which vertices are used to draw certain triangles.

The `indices` parameter is again a vector (this time, a vector of `int`s). Each index in the `indices` vector specifies an individual vertex in the `vertices` vector. Going back to the first example, drawing a single triangle, we had this:

```
var vertices:Vector.<Number> = new Vector.<Number>();
vertices.push(100, 100);
vertices.push(200, 100);
vertices.push(150, 200);
graphics.lineStyle(0);
graphics.drawTriangles(vertices);
```

329

Using an indices vector, we can do exactly the same thing:

```
var vertices:Vector.<Number> = new Vector.<Number>();
vertices.push(100, 100);
vertices.push(200, 100);
vertices.push(150, 200);
var indices:Vector.<int> = new Vector.<int>();
indices.push(0, 1, 2);
graphics.lineStyle(0);
graphics.drawTriangles(vertices, indices);
```

We tell Flash to use vertex 0 (100, 100) as the first corner of the triangle, vertex 1 (200, 100) as the second corner, and vertex 3 (150, 200) as the final corner. Now that's no different from what it was doing all by itself, but it shows you how it works in the simplest example possible. Now let's try to draw two triangles with just four points. The next example is in the Triangles3.as file:

```
package
{
    import flash.display.Sprite;
    import flash.display.StageAlign;
    import flash.display.StageScaleMode;

    [SWF(backgroundColor=0xffffff)]
    public class Triangles3 extends Sprite
    {
        public function Triangles3()
        {
            stage.align = StageAlign.TOP_LEFT;
            stage.scaleMode = StageScaleMode.NO_SCALE;

            var vertices:Vector.<Number> = new Vector.<Number>();
            vertices.push(100, 100);
            vertices.push(200, 100);
            vertices.push(200, 200);
            vertices.push(100, 200);

            var indices:Vector.<int> = new Vector.<int>();
            indices.push(0, 1, 2);
            indices.push(2, 3, 0);

            graphics.lineStyle(0);
            graphics.drawTriangles(vertices, indices);
        }
    }
}
```

We draw one triangle using vertices 0, 1, and 2, and another triangle using vertices 2, 3, and 0. This gives you the shape you see in Figure 8-9. I've annotated this one to label the four vertices so you can see what is being drawn.

Now, as we saw with drawPath, you don't see the full power of these new commands by meticulously hard-coding individual points and commands, or vertices and indices. But when you start getting into more complex shapes, keeping a vector or two around and passing it into a method to redraw that shape can be pretty powerful. Furthermore, the real power of triangles comes in when you start using it for bitmap fills, as discussed next.

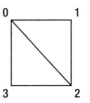

Figure 8-9. A connected pair of triangles

Bitmap fills and triangles

When drawing shapes with the drawing API, you have always had a few options for filling in the shape: a single color fill, a gradient fill, and a bitmap fill. As you'll see in the next chapter, there is now also a shader fill that works in conjunction with Pixel Bender.

But here we'll look at some very significant improvements to bitmap fills that are available when creating a shape using triangles.

First, you can use any type of fills with triangles, just as you would use them with a path or any of the older drawing API methods:

```
graphics.beginFill(0xFF0000);
graphics.drawTriangles(vertices, indices);
graphics.endFill();
```

This will fill in each triangle or the shape they make up as a whole, with the color of the fill. Overlapping triangles are rendered completely. There are no wrapping parameter or unfilled intersecting areas. Now let's see what we can do with a bitmap fill. The next class, available for download as BitmapTriangles. as, will demonstrate the basics of filling a set of triangles with a bitmap:

```
package
{
    import flash.display.Bitmap;
    import flash.display.Sprite;
    import flash.display.StageAlign;
    import flash.display.StageScaleMode;

    [SWF(backgroundColor=0xffffff)]
    public class BitmapTriangles extends Sprite
    {
        [Embed(source="image.jpg")]
        private var ImageClass:Class;

        public function BitmapTriangles()
        {
            stage.align = StageAlign.TOP_LEFT;
            stage.scaleMode = StageScaleMode.NO_SCALE;
            var vertices:Vector.<Number> = new Vector.<Number>();
            vertices.push(100, 100);
            vertices.push(200, 100);
            vertices.push(200, 200);
            vertices.push(100, 200);
```

331

```
            var indices:Vector.<int> = new Vector.<int>();
            indices.push(0, 1, 2);
            indices.push(2, 3, 0);

            var bitmap:Bitmap = new ImageClass() as Bitmap;
            graphics.beginBitmapFill(bitmap.bitmapData);
            graphics.drawTriangles(vertices, indices);
            graphics.endFill();
        }
    }
}
```

It's pretty much the same as the last example, but we are embedding an external JPG, creating an instance of it as a Bitmap, and using its bitmapData property to fill the triangles we draw. The image I used is also available for download, but any valid bitmap image will do (JPG, .tif, BMP, or GIF).

Now when you run this, you'll see only a black square. You might see something else if you used a different image file, but you won't be seeing the entire picture. The bitmap is displayed at full size, but the square we are drawing with our two triangles is only 100×100 pixels, so you see only the top-left corner of the bitmap.

You can try stretching out a couple of the vertices like so:

```
        vertices.push(100, 100);
        vertices.push(1000, 100);
        vertices.push(1000, 600);
        vertices.push(100, 200);
```

This will show a bit more of the bitmap (see Figure 8-10), but it's not really what we are after.

You could also try applying a transform matrix to the beginBitmapFill call, but that can get pretty complex, and still you wouldn't be able to do all you can with the new triangle bitmap fill feature. So let's look at that new feature.

Figure 8-10. A bitmap fill with triangles

uvtData

The third optional parameter to drawTriangles is another vector of Numbers, referred to as uvtData. The uvt part refers to three values that affect how the bitmap is mapped to the overall triangle shape. The u and v values map values on the x-axis and y-axis of the bitmap to individual vertices of the various triangles making up the shape. The t value is optional and allows you to do further scaling when using triangles for 3D. I'll discuss u and v now (and t a bit later in this section).

Figure 8-11 shows how the u and v values are mapped to a bitmap.

Figure 8-11. uv mapping of a bitmap

The top left of the bitmap corresponds to u, v values of 0, 0. The top right is 1, 0; and the bottom left and bottom right are 0, 1, and 1, 1. You can map fractional values, too, but let's just work with the four corners for now.

In our last example, we had four points forming two triangles, arranged to make a rectangle. We can now map those four points to the four corners of the bitmap. All we need to do is make a vector of Numbers and set a u and v value for each vertex in the vertices vector. The next class, downloadable as BitmapTrianglesUV1.as, shows this:

```
package
{
    import flash.display.Bitmap;
    import flash.display.Sprite;
    import flash.display.StageAlign;
    import flash.display.StageScaleMode;

    [SWF(backgroundColor=0xffffff)]
    public class BitmapTrianglesUV1 extends Sprite
```

```
        {
            [Embed(source="image.jpg")]
            private var ImageClass:Class;

            public function BitmapTrianglesUV1()
            {
                stage.align = StageAlign.TOP_LEFT;
                stage.scaleMode = StageScaleMode.NO_SCALE;
                var vertices:Vector.<Number> = new Vector.<Number>();
                vertices.push(100, 100);
                vertices.push(200, 100);
                vertices.push(200, 200);
                vertices.push(100, 200);

                var uvtData:Vector.<Number> = new Vector.<Number>();
                uvtData.push(0, 0);
                uvtData.push(1, 0);
                uvtData.push(1, 1);
                uvtData.push(0, 1);

                var indices:Vector.<int> = new Vector.<int>();
                indices.push(0, 1, 2);
                indices.push(2, 3, 0);

                var bitmap:Bitmap = new ImageClass() as Bitmap;
                graphics.beginBitmapFill(bitmap.bitmapData);
                graphics.drawTriangles(vertices, indices, uvtData);
                graphics.endFill();
            }
        }
    }
```

We make a uvtData vector and push eight values to it. These map to the eight values (four vertices) in the vertices vector; and correspond to the top left, top right, bottom right, and bottom left of the bitmap. We pass that in as a third parameter to drawTriangles, and the result is what you see in Figure 8-12.

It looks a bit squashed because the triangles are forming a square, but the bitmap itself is a rectangle. We can now move the vertices around and distort the image:

```
    vertices.push(150, 50);
    vertices.push(1000, 100);
    vertices.push(800, 600);`
    vertices.push(100, 200);
```

Figure 8-12. A bitmap fill with triangles and uvt data

These coordinates will give you something like what you can see in Figure 8-13.

Already, this is starting to look 3D. But before we dive deep into that subject, let's just play with 2D distortion a bit more.

Figure 8-13. Moving the points

The next example, in the `BitmapTrianglesUV2.as` file, extends the first one, making the vertices dynamic. I won't go into the class in too much detail, but essentially it creates four draggable handles. When the handles are moved, the vertices vector is filled with the handles' positions and the shape is redrawn:

```
package
{
    import flash.display.Bitmap;
    import flash.display.Sprite;
    import flash.display.StageAlign;
    import flash.display.StageScaleMode;
    import flash.events.MouseEvent;

    [SWF(backgroundColor=0xffffff)]
    public class BitmapTrianglesUV2 extends Sprite
    {
        [Embed(source="image.jpg")]
        private var ImageClass:Class;

        private var handle0:Sprite;
        private var handle1:Sprite;
        private var handle2:Sprite;
        private var handle3:Sprite;
        private var vertices:Vector.<Number> = new Vector.<Number>();
        private var uvtData:Vector.<Number> = new Vector.<Number>();
        private var indices:Vector.<int> = new Vector.<int>();
        private var bitmap:Bitmap;
```

```
public function BitmapTrianglesUV2()
{
    stage.align = StageAlign.TOP_LEFT;
    stage.scaleMode = StageScaleMode.NO_SCALE;

    handle0 = makeHandle(100, 100);
    handle1 = makeHandle(200, 100);
    handle2 = makeHandle(200, 200);
    handle3 = makeHandle(100, 200);

    uvtData.push(0, 0);
    uvtData.push(1, 0);
    uvtData.push(1, 1);
    uvtData.push(0, 1);

    indices.push(0, 1, 2);
    indices.push(2, 3, 0);

    bitmap= new ImageClass() as Bitmap;
    draw();
}

private function makeHandle(xpos:Number, ypos:Number):Sprite
{
    var handle:Sprite = new Sprite();
    handle.graphics.beginFill(0);
    handle.graphics.drawCircle(0, 0, 5);
    handle.graphics.endFill();
    handle.addEventListener(MouseEvent.MOUSE_DOWN,
                            onMouseDown);
    handle.x = xpos;
    handle.y = ypos;
    addChild(handle);
    return handle;
}

private function onMouseDown(event:MouseEvent):void
{
    event.target.startDrag();
    stage.addEventListener(MouseEvent.MOUSE_MOVE, onMouseMove);
    stage.addEventListener(MouseEvent.MOUSE_UP, onMouseUp);
}

private function onMouseMove(event:MouseEvent):void
{
    draw();
}
```

```
        private function onMouseUp(event:MouseEvent):void
        {
            stopDrag();
            stage.removeEventListener(MouseEvent.MOUSE_MOVE,
                                onMouseMove);
            stage.removeEventListener(MouseEvent.MOUSE_UP, onMouseUp);
        }

        private function draw():void
        {
            vertices[0] = handle0.x;
            vertices[1] = handle0.y;
            vertices[2] = handle1.x;
            vertices[3] = handle1.y;
            vertices[4] = handle2.x;
            vertices[5] = handle2.y;
            vertices[6] = handle3.x;
            vertices[7] = handle3.y;

            graphics.clear();
            graphics.beginBitmapFill(bitmap.bitmapData);
            graphics.drawTriangles(vertices, indices, uvtData);
            graphics.endFill();
        }
    }
}
```

You can drag around the four points interactively and see how the image distorts. This kind of thing was possible in earlier versions of Flash, but involved complicated setups and more complicated math. Here, we are doing the same thing without a single math operator!

More triangles!

So far we are dealing with just four points and two triangles, which limit us to four-sided shapes (quadrilaterals). If we add some more triangles, we have more points to move around and do interesting things with. We could painstakingly plot out each vertex and specify all the indexes for each triangle by hand. Or we could figure out an algorithm to do it all for us. The next class, found in the BitmapTriangleUV3.as file, does just that. I'll present it first and then explain it. Some of the more important points are in bold:

```
package
{
    import flash.display.Bitmap;
    import flash.display.Sprite;
    import flash.display.StageAlign;
    import flash.display.StageScaleMode;
    import flash.events.MouseEvent;
```

```
[SWF(backgroundColor=0xffffff)]
public class BitmapTrianglesUV3 extends Sprite
{
    [Embed(source="image.jpg")]
    private var ImageClass:Class;

    private var vertices:Vector.<Number> = new Vector.<Number>();
    private var uvtData:Vector.<Number> = new Vector.<Number>();
    private var indices:Vector.<int> = new Vector.<int>();
    private var bitmap:Bitmap;
    private var res:Number = 100;
    private var cols:int = 5;
    private var rows:int = 4;


    public function BitmapTrianglesUV3()
    {
        stage.align = StageAlign.TOP_LEFT;
        stage.scaleMode = StageScaleMode.NO_SCALE;

        bitmap= new ImageClass() as Bitmap;
        makeTriangles();

        graphics.beginBitmapFill(bitmap.bitmapData);
        graphics.drawTriangles(vertices, indices, uvtData);
        graphics.endFill();

        graphics.lineStyle(0);
        graphics.drawTriangles(vertices, indices);
    }

    private function makeTriangles():void
    {
        for(var i:int = 0; i < rows; i++)
        {
            for(var j:int = 0; j < cols; j++)
            {
                vertices.push(j * res, i * res);
                uvtData.push(j / (cols - 1), i / (rows - 1));

                if(i < rows - 1 && j < cols - 1)
                {
                    // first triangle
                    indices.push(i * cols + j,
                                 i * cols + j + 1,
                                 (i + 1) * cols + j);
```

```
                                    // second triangle
                                    indices.push(i * cols + j + 1,
                                                (i + 1) * cols + j + 1,
                                                (i + 1) * cols + j);
                            }
                        }
                    }
                }
            }
        }
```

First we set up three new variables: res (resolution) determines the size of the triangles, and rows and cols determine how many rows and columns of vertices there will be. In the makeTriangles method, we loop through rows and cols to make a grid of vertices. Each vertex is defined as j * res, i * res. The uvtData is defined as j / (cols - 1), i / (rows - 1). This will make it range from 0.0 to 1.0 on each axis.

Within this loop, if we are not at the last row or last column, we can make some triangles by taking the current point, the point to its right, and the point below it as the first triangle. Then the one to its right, the one down and to the right, and the one below it as the second triangle (see Figure 8-14).

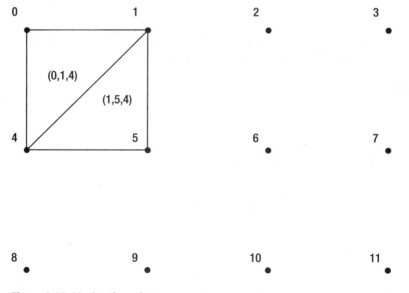

Figure 8-14. Moving the points

In this sample code, I not only drew the image using a bitmap fill with the triangles but also drew the triangles again with a stroke, so you can see how they are arranged. Try changing the values for res, rows, and cols to see how the layout and size of the final image change.

It is nice, but because we're still just drawing a rectangle, we're not really seeing much benefit from all those extra triangles. Once we start moving these vertices around, we can create all kinds of effects, including (drum roll, please) 3D!

Triangles and 3D

Here's the basic strategy behind using triangles for 3D:

1. Create a bunch of vertices and indices that form triangles.

2. Calculate the position of a 3D point that corresponds to each vertex.

3. Use perspective to calculate the 2D screen coordinates of that 3D point. This becomes the value of the vertex.

4. Use drawTriangles, passing in the vertices and indices.

Realize that this type of 3D is quite different from the DisplayObject 3D that was discussed in Chapter 7. In fact, you could almost say that Flash 10 has two separate 3D engines now, with drawTriangles being the second. The 3D calculations we'll be using to apply the perspective here are exactly as described in *Making Things Move*. You might want to review the 3D chapters of that book or otherwise brush up on basic perspective calculations. The basic formula for perspective is as follows:

```
perspectiveScale = focalLength / (focalLength + zPosition)
```

So, we have an x, y, and z position; we use the z position to find a scale. Then we multiply the x and y values by this scale to get their screen position, which becomes the position of each vertex in the vertices list.

The next class, which you can download as the ImageTube.as file, builds on the last example, but now arranges the vertices of the grid around in a tube shape. We'll put the bitmap fill on hold briefly and just draw triangles with strokes so we can see what we are drawing:

```
package
{
    import flash.display.Bitmap;
    import flash.display.Sprite;
    import flash.display.StageAlign;
    import flash.display.StageScaleMode;

    [SWF(backgroundColor=0xffffff)]
    public class ImageTube extends Sprite
    {
        [Embed(source="image.jpg")]
        private var ImageClass:Class;

        private var vertices:Vector.<Number> = new Vector.<Number>();
        private var indices:Vector.<int> = new Vector.<int>();
        private var uvtData:Vector.<Number> = new Vector.<Number>();
        private var bitmap:Bitmap;
        private var sprite:Sprite;
        private var res:Number = 60;
        private var cols:int = 20;
        private var rows:int = 6;
        private var centerZ:Number = 200;
```

```
private var focalLength:Number = 250;
private var radius:Number = 200;

public function ImageTube()
{
    stage.align = StageAlign.TOP_LEFT;
    stage.scaleMode = StageScaleMode.NO_SCALE;

    sprite = new Sprite();
    sprite.x = 400;
    sprite.y = 400;
    addChild(sprite);

    bitmap= new ImageClass() as Bitmap;
    makeTriangles();
    draw();
}

private function draw():void
{
    sprite.graphics.lineStyle(0, 0, .5);
    sprite.graphics.drawTriangles(vertices, indices);
}

private function makeTriangles():void
{
    for(var i:int = 0; i < rows; i++)
    {
        for(var j:int = 0; j < cols; j++)
        {
            var angle:Number = Math.PI * 2 / (cols - 1) * j;

            var xpos:Number = Math.cos(angle) * radius;
            var ypos:Number = (i - rows / 2) * res;
            var zpos:Number = Math.sin(angle) * radius;

            var scale:Number = focalLength /
                            (focalLength + zpos + centerZ);

            vertices.push(xpos * scale,
                        ypos * scale);
            uvtData.push(j / (cols - 1), i / (rows - 1));

            if(i < rows - 1 && j < cols - 1)
            {
                indices.push(i * cols + j,
                            i * cols + j + 1,
                            (i + 1) * cols + j);
```

```
                                  indices.push(i * cols + j + 1,
                                               (i + 1) * cols + j + 1,
                                               (i + 1) * cols + j);
                               }
                           }
                       }
                   }
               }
           }
```

The first difference you see is the introduction of the `radius` variable, which determines the radius of the tube. Then we add a sprite to the stage and position it at 400, 400 (because in calculating 3D, we need a vanishing point). We could set a vanishing point at 400, 400 and add this to each vertex, but it's simpler to leave the vanishing point as 0, 0; draw everything into a sprite; and move the sprite.

We moved the actual drawing code into its own method (you'll see the reason for this later).

Finally, in `makeTriangles`, we calculate an angle that will range from 0 to PI * 2. Taking the cosine and sine of this angle times the radius gives us the x and z position for each point. The y position will range from a negative value to a positive one, based on the number of rows and the resolution.

Now that we have an x, y, and z value for each point, we calculate a scale. Each vertex can now be defined as `xpos * scale`, `ypos * scale`, which is the screen position of the 3D point after perspective is applied. When this is run, you see the picture shown in Figure 8-15.

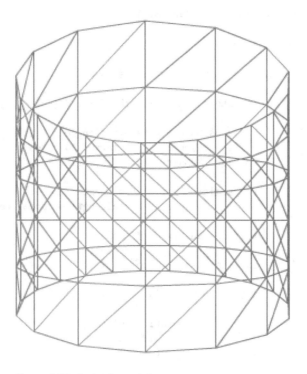

Figure 8-15. A wire frame tube

This is a wire frame representation of all the triangles—they form a tube that is distorted by 3D projection. So far, so good! Now we just need to add the bitmap fill back in, right? Well, yes and no. There's a bit more work to do. But let's go ahead and see what happens. Change the draw method to the following:

```
private function draw():void
{
    sprite.graphics.beginBitmapFill(bitmap.bitmapData);
    sprite.graphics.drawTriangles(vertices, indices, uvtData);
    sprite.graphics.endFill();

    sprite.graphics.lineStyle(0, 0, .5);
    sprite.graphics.drawTriangles(vertices, indices);
}
```

Hmmm. This doesn't look quite right (see Figure 8-16).

Figure 8-16. Something is wrong here.

What's happening is that we are drawing all the rectangles—the ones in back and the ones in front. Now if you read Chapter 7, you probably have your hand raised and are ready to shout out, "Depth sorting!" In a sense you are correct, but there's a slightly different concept at work when drawing triangles: **backface culling** (this was also covered in *Making Things Move*, and all worked out manually). The basic concept is this: draw all triangles that are formed in a clockwise direction and don't draw any that are counterclockwise. Or vice versa—it depends on how you made your triangles. In either case, if you made them consistently, the triangles facing you will be going one way (clockwise or counterclockwise), and the ones facing away from you will be going the opposite way. Those facing away are called **back faces** and do not need to be drawn.

Fortunately, this is now all built into Flash. When we call drawTriangles, the optional fourth parameter is culling, which is a string that can be equal to "positive", "negative", or "none". These values are provided as static constants of the flash.display.TriangleCulling class:

```
TriangleCulling.POSITIVE
TriangleCulling.NEGATIVE
TriangleCulling.NONE
```

You can read the Flash help file for this class for a more technical description of how culling works, but here's a simple way to think about it: **positive culling** draws only counterclockwise triangles, and **negative culling** draws only clockwise triangles. Setting culling to NONE results in all triangles being drawn. Because the triangles we set up are done in a clockwise direction, we need to use negative culling, like so:

```
private function draw():void
{
    sprite.graphics.beginBitmapFill(bitmap.bitmapData);
    sprite.graphics.drawTriangles(vertices, indices, uvtData,
                                  TriangleCulling.NEGATIVE);
    sprite.graphics.endFill();

    sprite.graphics.lineStyle(0, 0, .5);
    sprite.graphics.drawTriangles(vertices, indices, uvtData,
                                  TriangleCulling.NEGATIVE);
}
```

Now when you run the file, you'll see what is shown in Figure 8-17.

This actually looks like an image wrapped around a tube. You can remove the second drawTriangles call to see just the image without the triangle outlines.

Figure 8-17. Backface culling solved the problem.

The t in uvt

Now we come to that other part of the data: the t, which is specifically used for adjusting the scaling of the bitmap when drawing in 3D. In the last example, we calculated a scale value based on each point's z position. We used this scale value to adjust the x and y positions to project them to a screen position and create the vertices used in drawing each triangle. It turns out that this scale value is also the value we need to use for the t value of each vertex. This affects how the pixels between any two points are scaled and spaced out. If you can imagine a line of evenly spaced fence posts going off into the distance, the posts in the distance will appear closer together when seen in 3D perspective, whereas the ones in the foreground will seem farther apart. The t value does this for pixels instead of fence posts. Without the t, pixels between two points will be spaced evenly, which can result in an image looking distorted.

This t value is added right after the u and v values in the uvtData vector, like so:

```
var scale:Number = focalLength / (focalLength + zpos + centerZ);
vertices.push(xpos * scale, ypos * scale);
uvtData.push(j / (cols - 1), i / (rows - 1));
uvtData.push(scale);
```

Now you might think this would mess things up because previously every two values in uvtData referred to two values in the vertices vector. Now we have three values for each vertex. Luckily, drawTriangles is smart enough to figure this out. If uvtData is the same length as vertices, it assumes that it contains only u and v. If uvtData is 1.5 times the length of vertices, it remaps it so that each set of three values is interpreted as u, v, and t.

Go ahead and add that line. You probably won't see much of a difference in this example, but if you were to do screen captures and compare them side by side, you'd see a very subtle change in how the bitmap is stretched across the tube. Although it's not so noticeable in this example, it's good to get into the habit of using the extra scaling because it can make a significant difference in how realistic your 3D forms look, especially when perspective gets more pronounced.

Rotating the tube

Because the title of this book contains the word "animation," let's get this tube moving somehow. We can at least make it rotate.

We'll have an offset value that will continually change. We'll move all the vertex and uvtData creation into the draw method and update it each frame, adding the offset to the calculated angle. This will cause the vertices to rotate around the tube, dragging the bitmap with it. The illusion is a rotating tube:

```
package
{
    import flash.display.Bitmap;
    import flash.display.Sprite;
    import flash.display.StageAlign;
    import flash.display.StageScaleMode;
    import flash.display.TriangleCulling;
    import flash.events.Event;

    [SWF(backgroundColor=0xffffff)]
    public class ImageTube extends Sprite
    {
        [Embed(source="image.jpg")]
        private var ImageClass:Class;

        private var vertices:Vector.<Number> = new Vector.<Number>();
        private var indices:Vector.<int> = new Vector.<int>();
        private var uvtData:Vector.<Number> = new Vector.<Number>();
        private var bitmap:Bitmap;
        private var sprite:Sprite;
        private var res:Number = 60;
        private var cols:int = 20;
        private var rows:int = 6;
        private var centerZ:Number = 200;
        private var focalLength:Number = 250;
        private var radius:Number = 200;
        private var offset:Number = 0;
```

```
public function ImageTube()
{
    stage.align = StageAlign.TOP_LEFT;
    stage.scaleMode = StageScaleMode.NO_SCALE;

    sprite = new Sprite();
    sprite.x = 400;
    sprite.y = 400;
    addChild(sprite);

    bitmap= new ImageClass() as Bitmap;
    makeTriangles();
    draw();
    addEventListener(Event.ENTER_FRAME, onEnterFrame);
}

private function onEnterFrame(event:Event):void
{
    draw();
}

private function draw():void
{
    offset += .05;
    // clear out the data in vertices and uvtData
    vertices.length = 0;
    uvtData.length = 0;

    for(var i:int = 0; i < rows; i++)
    {
        for(var j:int = 0; j < cols; j++)
        {
            var angle:Number = Math.PI * 2 / (cols - 1) * j
                                + offset;

            var xpos:Number = Math.cos(angle) * radius;
            var ypos:Number = (i - rows / 2) * res;
            var zpos:Number = Math.sin(angle) * radius;

            var scale:Number = focalLength /
                                (focalLength + zpos + centerZ);

            vertices.push(xpos * scale,
                        ypos * scale);
            uvtData.push(j / (cols - 1), i / (rows - 1));
            uvtData.push(scale);
        }
    }
```

```
                    sprite.graphics.clear();
                    sprite.graphics.beginBitmapFill(bitmap.bitmapData);
                    sprite.graphics.drawTriangles(vertices, indices, uvtData,
                                            TriangleCulling.NEGATIVE);
                    sprite.graphics.endFill();

//              sprite.graphics.lineStyle(0, 0, .5);
//              sprite.graphics.drawTriangles(vertices, indices, uvtData,
//                                      TriangleCulling.NEGATIVE);
                }

            private function makeTriangles():void
            {
                for(var i:int = 0; i < rows; i++)
                {
                    for(var j:int = 0; j < cols; j++)
                    {
                        if(i < rows - 1 && j < cols - 1)
                        {
                            indices.push(i * cols + j,
                                        i * cols + j + 1,
                                        (i + 1) * cols + j);

                            indices.push(i * cols + j + 1,
                                        (i + 1) * cols + j + 1,
                                        (i + 1) * cols + j);
                        }
                    }
                }
            }
        }
    }
```

Note that the makeTriangles method contains only the code to create the indices. Indices need to be created only a single time and will not change. However, the vertices and uvtData have to be updated on every frame, so they are recalculated on every frame in the draw method.

Now that we have a tube, it's not too much of a reach to transform it into a globe. Let's try it.

Making a 3D globe

Our final exploration into 3D with triangles is creating a 3D rotating globe. I dug up a world map that will fit nicely here, but again you can use any image you want to map to a sphere. Most of the code will be the same as the tube example. We just need to adjust the vertex values so they join at the top and bottom, and form a circle in between. This took a bit of trigonometry, and a lot of trial and error, but here is the result, which you can find in the ImageSphere.as file:

```
package
{
    import flash.display.Bitmap;
```

```
import flash.display.Sprite;
import flash.display.StageAlign;
import flash.display.StageScaleMode;
import flash.display.TriangleCulling;
import flash.events.Event;

[SWF(backgroundColor=0x000000, width=800, height=800)]
public class ImageSphere extends Sprite
{
    [Embed(source="map.jpg")]
    private var ImageClass:Class;

    private var vertices:Vector.<Number> = new Vector.<Number>();
    private var indices:Vector.<int> = new Vector.<int>();
    private var uvtData:Vector.<Number> = new Vector.<Number>();
    private var bitmap:Bitmap;
    private var sprite:Sprite;
    private var centerZ:int = 500;
    private var cols:int = 20;
    private var rows:int = 20;
    private var focalLength:Number = 1000;
    private var radius:Number = 400;
    private var offset:Number = 0;

    public function ImageSphere()
    {
        stage.align = StageAlign.TOP_LEFT;
        stage.scaleMode = StageScaleMode.NO_SCALE;

        sprite = new Sprite();
        sprite.x = 400;
        sprite.y = 400;
        addChild(sprite);

        bitmap= new ImageClass() as Bitmap;
        makeTriangles();
        draw();
        addEventListener(Event.ENTER_FRAME, onEnterFrame);
    }

    private function onEnterFrame(event:Event):void
    {
        draw();
    }

    private function draw():void
    {
        offset -= .02;
        vertices.length = 0;
        uvtData.length = 0;
```

```
        for(var i:int = 0; i < rows; i++)
        {
            for(var j:int = 0; j < cols; j++)
            {
                var angle:Number = Math.PI * 2 / (cols - 1) * j;
                var angle2:Number = Math.PI * i / (rows - 1)
                                        - Math.PI / 2;

                var xpos:Number = Math.cos(angle + offset) * radius
                                    * Math.cos(angle2);
                var ypos:Number = Math.sin(angle2) * radius;
                var zpos:Number = Math.sin(angle + offset) * radius
                                    * Math.cos(angle2);

                var scale:Number = focalLength /
                                    (focalLength + zpos + centerZ);

                vertices.push(xpos * scale,
                                ypos * scale);
                uvtData.push(j / (cols - 1), i / (rows - 1));
                uvtData.push(scale);
            }
        }

        sprite.graphics.clear();
        sprite.graphics.beginBitmapFill(bitmap.bitmapData);
        sprite.graphics.drawTriangles(vertices, indices, uvtData,
                                    TriangleCulling.NEGATIVE);
        sprite.graphics.endFill();

//          sprite.graphics.lineStyle(0, 0, .4);
//          sprite.graphics.drawTriangles(vertices, indices, uvtData,
//                                    TriangleCulling.NEGATIVE);
        }

        private function makeTriangles():void
        {
            for(var i:int = 0; i < rows; i++)
            {
                for(var j:int = 0; j < cols; j++)
                {
                    if(i < rows - 1 && j < cols - 1)
                    {
                        indices.push(i * cols + j,
                                    i * cols + j + 1,
                                    (i + 1) * cols + j);
```

```
        indices.push(i * cols + j + 1,
                   (i + 1) * cols + j + 1,
                   (i + 1) * cols + j);
      }
     }
    }
   }
  }
 }
}
```

As you can see, there's not a huge difference between it and the tube: a different bitmap and a few more-complex formulas for creating the vertices on each frame. The angle2 variable will range from –Math.PI to +Math.PI. Taking the sine of this will position the y value of each vertex from the "North Pole" to the "South Pole" of the globe. The cosine of this angle will be used to smoothly vary the radius of the circle around the y-axis, turning the tube into a globe. You can see the result in Figure 8-18.

There's lots of room to play with this one. And this is only the beginning of showing you the types of things you can model. Of course, it's still not as powerful as PaperVision3D, which already has much of this functionality in it already. But I'm sure portions of this new API will find their way into the various Flash-based 3D packages out there because they are now part of the Player and operate at a lower level than compiled ActionScript.

Now we leave 3D behind and finish out the chapter with a discussion of graphics data.

Figure 8-18. A rotating globe

Graphics Data

So far we've covered drawing paths and drawing triangles, which are both powerful new aspects of the drawing API. But believe it or not, they are just building blocks that are part of an even more powerful aspect of the drawing API. This new power is accessed primarily by the new method on flash. display.Graphics called drawGraphicsData.

As you recall, you could draw lines or fills using drawPath or drawTriangles, but you had to specify the line or fill styles using the same old lineStyle and beginFill methods. With drawGraphicsData, you can specify paths, triangles, strokes (line styles), and any kind of fill.

The way it works is pretty simple: you pass the drawGraphicsData method a vector. This vector is filled with objects of IGraphicsData, which is an interface. This means that a number of different types of objects can go into this vector—anything that implements the IGraphicsData interface. The following classes implement it:

- GraphicsStroke
- GraphicsSolidFill
- GraphicsGradientFill
- GraphicsBitmapFill
- GraphicsShaderFill
- GraphicsEndFill
- GraphicsPath
- GraphicsTrianglePath

These classes are all in the flash.display package. I won't go into every single one in detail, but will cover a few of them well enough so you'll have an idea of how to use them in general. Let's start with GraphicsStroke and GraphicsPath, which will at least allow you to draw a line or several. Here's the constructor for GraphicsStroke:

```
GraphicsStroke(thickness:Number = NaN, pixelHinting:Boolean = false,
            scaleMode:String = "normal", caps:String = "none",
            joints:String = "round", miterLimit:Number = 3.0,
            fill:IGraphicsFill = null)
```

Anything you can specify in the Graphics.lineStyle method, you can also specify in a GraphicsStroke object in the constructor. All these constructor parameters are also public properties of the class, so you can just create a new GraphicsStroke object with the default parameters and then set the properties on it like so:

```
var stroke:GraphicsStroke = new GraphicsStroke();
stroke.thickness = 1;
```

The one thing that might be confusing is the fill property. Normally you think of drawing a shape with lines, and the fill is the color, gradient, or bitmap that fills up the space between those lines. In the case of a GraphicsStroke object, however, the fill refers to the color, alpha, gradient, and so on of the stroke itself. The fill is defined in another object of type IGraphicsFill. This again is an interface. The following types of graphics fills implement the IGraphicsFill interface:

- GraphicsSolidFill
- GraphicsGradientFill
- GraphicsBitmapFill
- GraphicsShaderFill

Let's just use a solid fill for now. The GraphicsSolidFill class constructor looks like this:

```
GraphicsSolidFill(color:uint = 0, alpha:Number = 1.0)
```

These parameters are also public properties on the class in case you want to change them on an existing fill object. With all this, you can now create a stroke object like so, which creates a five-pixel-wide red stroke:

```
var stroke:GraphicsStroke = new GraphicsStroke(5);
stroke.fill = new GraphicsSolidFill(0xff0000);
```

Now we can create a GraphicsPath object. The constructor for this is as follows:

```
GraphicsPath(commands:Vector.<int> = null,
             data:Vector.<Number> = null,
             winding:String = "evenOdd")
```

We already know all about paths, so we can throw this together pretty easily:

```
var commands:Vector.<int> = new Vector.<int>();
commands.push(GraphicsPathCommand.MOVE_TO);
commands.push(GraphicsPathCommand.LINE_TO);

var data:Vector.<Number> = new Vector.<Number>();
data.push(100, 100);
data.push(200, 200);

var path:GraphicsPath = new GraphicsPath(commands, data);
```

Here we have a commands vector and a data vector. We create a GraphicsPath object passing them into it.

Okay, now we have a stroke and a path. We just need to push them into a IGraphicsData vector, pass that vector to drawGraphicsData, and we should have a line. Here's the final test, available as the GraphicsDataDemo1.as file:

```
package
{
    import flash.display.GraphicsPath;
    import flash.display.GraphicsPathCommand;
    import flash.display.GraphicsSolidFill;
    import flash.display.GraphicsStroke;
    import flash.display.IGraphicsData;
    import flash.display.Sprite;
    import flash.display.StageAlign;
    import flash.display.StageScaleMode;

    [SWF(backgroundColor=0xffffff)]
    public class GraphicsDataDemo1 extends Sprite
    {
        public function GraphicsDataDemo1()
        {
            stage.align = StageAlign.TOP_LEFT;
            stage.scaleMode = StageScaleMode.NO_SCALE;

            var graphicsData:Vector.<IGraphicsData> =
                new Vector.<IGraphicsData>();

            var stroke:GraphicsStroke = new GraphicsStroke(5);
            stroke.fill = new GraphicsSolidFill(0xff0000);
```

```
        var commands:Vector.<int> = new Vector.<int>();
        commands.push(GraphicsPathCommand.MOVE_TO);
        commands.push(GraphicsPathCommand.LINE_TO);

        var data:Vector.<Number> = new Vector.<Number>();
        data.push(100, 100);
        data.push(200, 200);

        var path:GraphicsPath = new GraphicsPath(commands, data);

        graphicsData.push(stroke);
        graphicsData.push(path);
        graphics.drawGraphicsData(graphicsData);
      }
    }
  }
```

The lines in bold are the only important ones you didn't see before. Run it and you should get a red line on the stage. Amazing! Just 13 lines to do what you could do in about 3 lines with the old drawing API!

You know what I'm going to say: that this is suited for more complex drawings. Earlier I mentioned the command pattern, in which an action and its parameters are encapsulated in an object. This is exactly what's going on here. Instead of coding a long list of drawing methods, you create a vector of drawing commands. Because each of these commands is an object, you can add more to the list, remove them, rearrange them, alter them, and at any point draw the whole list. Let's take a look at how useful this can be.

In the final example of this chapter, we'll do something similar to the simple sketch program we created earlier, but we'll give it some history. Here's the strategy:

1. Each time the mouse button is pressed, choose a random stroke (thickness and color) and add it to a graphics data buffer.

2. When the mouse moves, add LINE_TOs and data points to a path as before.

3. When the mouse is released, create a GraphicsPath object based on the commands and data of the path just drawn. Push this GraphicsPath object into the buffer.

4. In the draw method, copy over the graphics data buffer into another vector of GraphicsData and draw it using drawGraphicsData.

The reason for the buffer is to enable a history. Pressing the left or right key on the keyboard will move an index variable up or down. The draw method actually copies over the commands from the buffer up to the index variable. Thus if you've drawn five lines, but then hit the left key, the index variable will be decremented. Then only the first four commands will be copied from the buffer into the commands vector. So only the first four lines will be drawn. Press the right key, and the index is increased. Now all five lines will be drawn. Here's the code, which you can also find as the HistoryDraw.as file:

```
package
{
    import flash.display.GraphicsPath;
    import flash.display.GraphicsPathCommand;
```

```
import flash.display.GraphicsSolidFill;
import flash.display.GraphicsStroke;
import flash.display.IGraphicsData;
import flash.display.Sprite;
import flash.display.StageAlign;
import flash.display.StageScaleMode;
import flash.events.KeyboardEvent;
import flash.events.MouseEvent;
import flash.ui.Keyboard;

[SWF(backgroundColor=0xffffff)]
public class HistoryDraw extends Sprite
{
    private var graphicsData:Vector.<IGraphicsData>;
    private var graphicsDataBuffer:Vector.<IGraphicsData>;
    private var commands:Vector.<int>;
    private var data:Vector.<Number>;
    private var index:int = 0;

    public function HistoryDraw()
    {
        stage.align = StageAlign.TOP_LEFT;
        stage.scaleMode = StageScaleMode.NO_SCALE;

        graphicsData = new Vector.<IGraphicsData>();
        graphicsDataBuffer = new Vector.<IGraphicsData>();

        stage.addEventListener(MouseEvent.MOUSE_DOWN, onMouseDown);
        stage.addEventListener(KeyboardEvent.KEY_UP, onKeyUp);
    }

    private function onMouseDown(event:MouseEvent):void
    {
        // create a random stroke, add it to buffer
        var stroke:GraphicsStroke = new GraphicsStroke();
        stroke.thickness = Math.random() * 10;
        stroke.fill = new GraphicsSolidFill(Math.random() *
                                            0xffffff);
        graphicsDataBuffer.push(stroke);

        // increment index
        // and make this the last command in the buffer
        index++;
        graphicsDataBuffer.length = index;

        // push a moveTo onto the commands
        commands = new Vector.<int>();
        commands.push(GraphicsPathCommand.MOVE_TO);
```

```
        // move to this point
        data = new Vector.<Number>();
        data.push(mouseX, mouseY);

        // draw a gray line for now
        graphics.lineStyle(0, 0, .5);
        graphics.moveTo(mouseX, mouseY);

        stage.addEventListener(MouseEvent.MOUSE_MOVE, onMouseMove);
        stage.addEventListener(MouseEvent.MOUSE_UP, onMouseUp);
    }

    private function onMouseMove(event:MouseEvent):void
    {
        // push a lineto onto the commands,
        // and current point to data
        commands.push(GraphicsPathCommand.LINE_TO);
        data.push(mouseX, mouseY);

        // draw temporary line
        graphics.lineTo(mouseX, mouseY);
    }

    private function onMouseUp(event:MouseEvent):void
    {
        // this line is done. push path onto buffer
        graphicsDataBuffer.push(new GraphicsPath(commands, data));

        // increment index and make this last command in buffer
        index++;
        graphicsDataBuffer.length = index;

        stage.removeEventListener(MouseEvent.MOUSE_MOVE,
                                 onMouseMove);
        stage.removeEventListener(MouseEvent.MOUSE_UP, onMouseUp);
        draw();
    }

    private function onKeyUp(event:KeyboardEvent):void
    {
        // go back two commands (path and stroke)
        if(event.keyCode == Keyboard.LEFT)
        {
            index -= 2;
        }
        // go forward two commands (stroke and path)
        else if(event.keyCode == Keyboard.RIGHT)
        {
            index += 2;
        }
```

```
        // limit index to sensible range
        index = Math.max(0, index);
        index = Math.min(graphicsDataBuffer.length, index);
        draw();
    }

    private function draw():void
    {
        // clear graphics data vector
        graphicsData.length = 0;

        // copy over data from buffer up to index
        for(var i:int = 0; i < index; i++)
        {
            graphicsData[i] = graphicsDataBuffer[i];
        }
        // draw graphics data
        graphics.clear();
        graphics.drawGraphicsData(graphicsData);
    }
  }
}
```

Note that in the onMouseUp handler we set the buffer length to the index, making the last path added to it the last element in the vector. This is the usual behavior in undoable operations. If you draw some lines, undo a few of them and draw some more; there is no way to redo the stuff that you just undid. Allowing this would result in unpredictable behavior because you just inserted some stuff in the middle of what was already there.

There you go—a drawing program with history. Of course, you could build this up to something more professional, with real controls for changing color and thickness instead of random values, and so on. And this is only the tip of the iceberg of graphics data. Remember that you can do any kind of fills: gradient, bitmap, and even shader fills (which we will cover in Chapter 9). You can even draw triangles. If you are really ambitious, you could redo the ImageSphere program to use drawGraphicsData instead of drawTriangles.

Summary

This chapter covered the features of the new drawing API, but pretty much just skimmed the surface of them. There's so much more you can do here that you could fill an entire book with it. In fact, you might want to take a look at *Foundation ActionScript 3.0 Image Effects* by Todd Yard (Apress, 2009).

Next up, we're going to take a look at another fantastic graphics tool added to Flash 10: Pixel Bender.

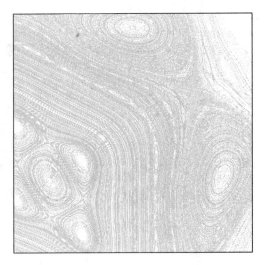

Chapter 9

PIXEL BENDER

This is an interesting chapter because it introduces not only a whole new tool that can be used in conjunction with Flash CS4 (or whatever you use to compile Flash 10 Player–based SWFs) but also a whole new language used by this tool. The Pixel Bender Toolkit was prereleased under the code name Hydra in late 2007. If features a simple integrated development environment (IDE) for coding and compiling pixel shaders, which are like miniprograms that you can use within Flash, PhotoShop, and After Effects to create very powerful image processing and animation effects. This subject deserves a whole book, but in this one chapter I'll try to give you at least enough info to get you up and running and hopefully inspired to go forward and learn more.

What Is Pixel Bender?

The Pixel Bender Toolkit refers to the IDE that is used to create, compile, test, and export pixel shaders for use in various CS4 products, including Flash. It's an extremely simple IDE featuring a bare-bones code editor, a preview area, and an area for setting parameters and viewing errors and warnings (see Figure 9-1).

Pixel Bender refers to the programming language you use to write pixel shaders in the Pixel Bender Toolkit. I'll start by assuming that you have a copy of the Pixel Bender Toolkit, have successfully installed it, have figured out how to run the program, and are ready to create some pixel shaders.

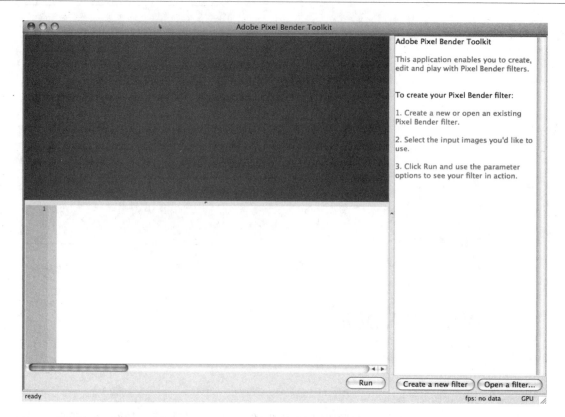

Figure 9-1. Pixel Bender Toolkit

Okay, but what is a **pixel shader**? Simply put, it is a small program that calculates the value of a single pixel. It sounds almost too simple when put that way, but that's essentially what it does. It can rely on various forms of input and make use of all kind of complex calculations, but in the end it says, "This pixel should have this value."

There are several reasons why this is a big deal and why people are excited about it. First, Pixel Bender can take a bitmap, fill, or other visual object and then run this pixel shader on each and every pixel in it. Not one by one, but in parallel. Yes, that's right; it calculates all the pixels in an area at the same time. They are compiled to be very optimized and run in a separate process from the Flash Player itself. All this adds up to the fact that pixel shaders are incredibly fast, compared with just about any other graphics process in Flash.

One of the disadvantages of having all this power is that Pixel Bender shaders must be created outside of Flash using the Pixel Bender Toolkit and written in the Pixel Bender language, which is based on C. Then they must be compiled, saved, and finally loaded or embedded into your Flash movie before they can be used. Yes, it's a bit of work, and yes, you are actually going to have to learn a bit of C. Don't worry; it will be good for you.

Pixel shaders exist in a very different paradigm than most ActionScript programs you are probably familiar with. Because the shader is interested in only a single pixel and is being run probably thousands of times in the same instant, all it inherently knows is the x, y value of the specific pixel it is being run on. You can assign variables and pass in parameters (including one or more input images), but when you first start coding these things, you might feel somewhat limited in what you can do. But soon you'll get a feel for the language and realize how to use the new capabilities Pixel Bender does give you.

Within Flash, you can use Pixel Bender shaders in four ways:

- *Custom filters*: Just as you have drop shadows, blurs, bevels, and so on, you can now assign a ShaderFilter to any display object. This is tied to a shader that you have written in Pixel Bender.

- *Fills*: In the drawing application programming interface (API) you've always been able to fill a shape with a solid color, a gradient, or a bitmap. Now you can fill it with a Pixel Bender shader with the beginShaderFill method.

- *Blend modes*: A pixel shader can also be used as a blend mode, affecting how a display object is composited on what is beneath it. This is done by assigning a shader to the blendShader property of a display object.

- *"Generic number crunching"*: This is a term given to using a shader's power and speed to perform fast mathematical operations on a set of data. Instead of using the shader to actually shade anything, you pass it in a byte array. It performs specified operations on the data in the byte array and returns the processed data. All you have to do is make the shader see the byte array as an image. This technique is beyond the scope of this book, but it is certainly an interesting topic to research on your own.

Writing a Pixel Shader

So you have the Pixel Bender Toolkit fired up and you're ready to write a pixel shader. Using the File menu, choose New Kernel Filter or press the button on the bottom of the screen that says Create New Filter. This should fill the editing area with something that looks like this:

```
<languageVersion : 1.0;>

kernel NewFilter
<   namespace : "Your Namespace";
    vendor : "Your Vendor";
    version : 1;
    description : "your description";
>
{
    input image4 src;
    output pixel4 dst;

    void
    evaluatePixel()
    {
        dst = sampleNearest(src,outCoord());
    }
}
```

If you want to see the result of a shader in the toolkit, you'll need to load an image. You do this through the File menu as well, and several sample images are included with the toolkit, just in case you don't have any pictures on your computer or can't find any on the Internet. Choose an image and you'll see it in the preview area. Press the Run button and you'll see the result of the shader being applied to the image.

And what do you see? Absolutely nothing; the image didn't change at all because the default shader is an identity shader. It just looks at the pixel in the source image that is in the same position as the pixel it is evaluating and outputs that pixel. So your output is exactly the same as your input.

Actually, I think this default example starts a bit higher than I'd like to for an introduction, so change the filter to the following:

```
<languageVersion : 1.0;>

kernel NewFilter
<    namespace : "Your Namespace";
     vendor : "Your Vendor";
     version : 1;
     description : "your description";
>
{
     input image4 src;
     output pixel4 dst;

     void
     evaluatePixel()
     {
         dst = pixel4(1, 0, 0, 1);
     }
}
```

You don't have to stop the shader from running and you don't have to save it at any point if you don't want to (although that's always a good practice). Just type the new lines of code and press the Run button when you see the changes. If you do this now, you'll see your picture change to a solid red rectangle (you'll see why in a moment).

This shader is about the most minimum one you could write, so it's a good place to start and examine the different pieces that go into writing a shader. Any pixel shader must have the following elements:

- Metadata specifying the language version of the file.
- The kernel definition, which contains the rest of the required elements (I'll cover exactly what a kernel is shortly).
- Required kernel metadata, consisting of namespace, vendor, and version (and optionally, description).
- An output property, which represents a pixel that you are shading.

- A function called evaluatePixel, which is the main function of a shader. In fact, when writing shaders for use in Flash, it's the only function you can have in your shader. So this is where *all* the code will go to calculate what the pixel value will be.

- Although it's not strictly required, you almost always want to specify an input property, which represents a source bitmap image. If you are using a shader for a fill in the drawing API, there might not be any input image. However, in order to see anything at all while developing the shader in the Pixel Bender Toolkit, you will need to specify an input image.

First, the language version metadata, which is the first line of the shader source file and looks like this:

```
<languageVersion : 1.0;>
```

There will be future versions of the tool with new capabilities, of course. So this lets the compiler and Flash know which features to expect in this shader.

Then there is the kernel definition. A kernel is the basic unit of a shader. It's pretty safe to regard a kernel just as you would regard a class: it's a single unit that defines a pixel shader object. It can have functions, variables, and constants. The functions can make calls to each other and access the variables and constants of the kernel, and call other built-in functions and libraries of functions.

There are quite a few limitations when creating shaders for use in Flash: the use of other libraries and calls to other functions outside of the main evaluatePixel function are not allowed. You can, however, call other built-in functions, as you'll see soon.

Like a class, a kernel is defined with the keyword kernel, followed by the name of the kernel. The body of the kernel is contained within brackets:

```
kernel NewFilter
{
    // kernel code
}
```

As you can see in the autogenerated shader code, just before the body of the kernel is another block of metadata:

```
kernel NewFilter
<   namespace : "Your Namespace";
    vendor : "Your Vendor";
    version : 1;
    description : "your description";
>
{
    // kernel code
}
```

The namespace, vendor, and version metadata are currently mandatory. You usually want to fill in the namespace with some unique identifier that nobody else will use. Your domain name is a good bet. The vendor is you or the company, and the version is the version of this specific shader. If you improve it later, update the version number so people know which version they are using. The description is optional, but it's a good idea to put something in there. You can access this metadata from within Flash after you have created the instance of the shader, as you'll see later in this chapter.

Within the kernel, we first have two special variables. These variables are specified with the keywords input and output. The input variable refers to the source image passed into the shader; the output variable refers to the pixel value that is being evaluated.

If you are only used to ActionScript, the syntax for defining these variables might look strange. In ActionScript we declare variables with the keyword var and specify the type with post-colon syntax like so:

```
var variableName:Type;
```

In C, on which Pixel Bender is based, you declare variables simply by stating their type and name:

```
Type variableName;
```

For these special variables, we have the additional input and output keywords tacked on in front, but from the following you can see that we have a variable named src (source) that is of type image4 and a variable named dst (destination) that is of type pixel4:

```
input image4 src;
output pixel4 dst;
```

I'll cover some of the different data types next, but image4 represents a four-channel (red, green, blue, alpha) bitmap image, and pixel4 represents a four-channel pixel.

As mentioned earlier, you always almost want to have an input image variable, at least when developing the shader in the toolkit. You also must have exactly one output pixel variable.

Next comes the evaluatePixel function. Like variables, functions in C are declared by stating the type they return, followed by the function name, and then like ActionScript, the body of the function in brackets:

```
void
evaluatePixel()
{
    dst = pixel4(1, 0, 0, 1);
}
```

In the autogenerated filter, this is formatted with the return type on one line and the function name on the next. This is no different from the following, which might seem more natural:

```
void evaluatePixel()
{
    dst = pixel4(1, 0, 0, 1);
}
```

The return type is void, so we don't need to return anything here. Whatever we do in the evaluatePixel method, however, it needs to result in the output variable dst being assigned a value. In this case, that's all we do. We assign it a pixel4 value directly. The constructor for pixel4 takes arguments for each of the four channels of the pixel: red, green, blue, and alpha. Each of these channels can be assigned a value from 0.0 to 1.0. Actually, you can assign it values higher or lower than that, but they will be truncated to values within that range. So assigning pixel4(100, 0, 0, 1) is no different from pixel4(1, 0, 0, 1). In this example, we are setting red to 1, green and blue to 0, and alpha to 1. This makes a solid opaque red pixel. This shader is run on every single pixel of the image in parallel, so every single pixel is colored red. That's why you wind up with a red rectangle.

Congratulations! You just made your first pixel shader; if you've followed along so far, you hopefully understand exactly what you did, which is pretty impressive.

Data Types

Before we go on, we should take a look at some of the different data types available within Pixel Bender. The basic types available are bool, int, and float, which correspond to Boolean, int, and Number in ActionScript. The bool type holds true/false values, int holds integers, and float holds floating-point numbers.

An important thing to remember is that when assigning constant float values, you must include the decimal part. Otherwise, the number is considered to be an int. For example, saying float num = 1; will give you a compile error; you need to say float num = 1.0;. You are almost certain to make this error countless times until you get used to the difference, so it's good to be able to recognize it. You also have to be careful about using an int in place of a float in various mathematical operations or as arguments to functions. Again, you'll probably do this many times and begin to recognize it quickly.

Then there are the various vector types, which are similar to vectors in ActionScript in that they hold multiple values of the same type. For example, the float2 type holds two float types, float3 holds three float types, and float4 holds four float types. Similar types exist for bool and int. Of all these types, you will probably use float2 most often because it can be used like a Point class.

Then there are values for holding pixel and image data. The pixel1 type holds a single channel of a single pixel. Similarly, there are pixel2, pixel3, and pixel4 vector types. This last one, pixel4, will be used most often because it can hold all four channels—red, green, blue, and alpha—of a pixel. And among the image1, image2, image3, and image4 types, image4 is most useful for the same reason.

In the ActionScript Vector type, you need to use array notation to get at the individual elements in the list, like so:

    myVector[2]

Pixel Bender vector types are much more user-friendly. For example, to get at the first element of a pixel4 value (the red channel), you don't have to write myPixel[0]; you just write myPixel.r. Similarly, the green, blue, and alpha channels can be accessed by the g, b, and a properties, respectively.

The values of a float2 variable can likewise be accessed with its x and y properties.

Actually, all four-element vector types have the following properties, regardless of what types they hold:

    r, g, b, a
    x, y, z, w
    s, t, p, q

These properties represent the four elements of the vector. So myPixel.x refers to the same thing as myPixel.r, or even myPixel.s. It makes more sense to use the rgba values when using pixel types and use the xyzw values when using floats.

You can rewrite the preceding example's evaluatePixel function as follows:

```
void
evaluatePixel()
{
    dst.r = 1.0;
    dst.g = 0.0;
    dst.b = 0.0;
    dst.a = 1.0;
}
```

Furthermore, you can access any two or more of the single element properties by combining them like so:

```
myPixel.rgb    // returns a pixel3 vector
               // containing red, green and blue channels
myPixel.ra     // returns a pixel2 vector
               // containing red and alpha channels
```

This lets you do complex combinations such as the following:

```
evaluatePixel()
{
    pixel3 pxl = pixel3(1, 0, 1);
    dst.rgb = pxl;
    dst.a = 1.0;
}
```

Here we make a pixel3 value consisting of 1 on the red channel, 0 on the green channel, and 1 on the blue channel—a purple color. We assign that to dst.rgb. But this leaves dst without any alpha channel, so we assign that directly.

Even more powerfully, you can mix and match the r, g, b, and a values any way you want. For example, in the following, I swapped the green and blue channels when assigning pxl to dst:

```
evaluatePixel()
{
    pixel3 pxl = pixel3(1, 0, 1);
    dst.rbg = pxl;
    dst.a = 1.0;
}
```

This results in dst getting 1, 1, 0 for its rgb, so you get a yellow rectangle. You can do the same thing another way:

```
evaluatePixel()
{
    pixel3 pxl = pixel3(1, 0, 1);
    dst.rgb = pxl.grb;
    dst.a = 1.0;
}
```

This swaps red and green on pxl before assigning it to rgb on dst, resulting in a cyan color. This swapping around of vector elements is known as **swizzling** and can be used with very simple syntax for powerful image processing.

Getting the Current Pixel Coordinates

One important bit of information that you do have when evaluating a pixel is the position of the pixel you are evaluating. You can get at that with the built-in function outCoord. This returns a float2 value, consisting of an x, y coordinate. Because every pixel will have a different coordinate, you can now use this data to color each pixel differently, instead of just assigning the same value to every pixel. You can download the following example from the book's website at www.friendsofed.com (it is available as the SineWave1.pbk file):

```
<languageVersion : 1.0;>
kernel SineWave1
<   namespace : "com.friendsofed";
    vendor : "Advanced ActionScript 3.0 Animation";
    version : 1;
    description : "draws vertical bands";
>
{
    input image4 src;
    output pixel4 dst;

    void
    evaluatePixel()
    {
        dst = pixel4(0, 0, 0, 1);
        float2 pos = outCoord();
        dst.r = sin(pos.x * .2) * .5 + .5;
    }
}
```

The important parts are in bold. First we color the pixel opaque black; then we get the current pixel coordinate as a float2 value named pos. In the last line, we multiply pos.x by .2 to slow down the wave a bit and then take the sine of that value. This will give us a value from –1.0 to +1.0. Multiply that by .5 to get a range from –0.5 to +0.5; then add .5 to get a range from 0.0 to 1.0, which is the correct range for a pixel channel value. Finally, assign that to dst.r. This will make the red value of each pixel vary smoothly according to the x position, giving you the picture you see in Figure 9-2.

Figure 9-2. Pixel Bender gradient bars

We can then do the same thing for the y-axis, as you can see in the next example, available as the SineWave2.pbk file:

```
<languageVersion : 1.0;>

kernel SineWave2
<   namespace : "com.friendsofed";
    vendor : "Advanced ActionScript 3.0 Animation";
    version : 1;
    description : "draws vertical and horizontal bands";
>
{
    input image4 src;
    output pixel4 dst;

    void
    evaluatePixel()
    {
        dst = pixel4(0, 0, 0, 1);
        float2 pos = outCoord();
        dst.r = sin(pos.x * .2) * .5 + .5;
        dst.b = sin(pos.y * .2) * .5 + .5;
    }
}
```

This gives you the image shown in Figure 9-3.

Figure 9-3. Double bars

Now, suppose that you want to change multiple channels at the same time. For example, you want to make black and white bars, so you want to the red, green, and blue channels to change equally. You might try something like this:

```
void
evaluatePixel()
{
    dst = pixel4(0, 0, 0, 1);
    float2 pos = outCoord();
    dst.r = sin(pos.x * .2) * .5 + .5;
    dst.g = sin(pos.x * .2) * .5 + .5;
    dst.b = sin(pos.x * .2) * .5 + .5;
}
```

This is pretty wasteful, so you could do something more like this:

```
void
evaluatePixel()
{
    dst = pixel4(0, 0, 0, 1);
    float2 pos = outCoord();
    pixel1 pxl = sin(pos.x * .2) * .5 + .5;
    dst.r = pxl;
    dst.g = pxl;
    dst.b = pxl;
}
```

369

This lets you do the calculation just once and then assign the output to each channel. But there's even a simpler way, as seen in the next example, available as SineWave3.pbk:

```
<languageVersion : 1.0;>

kernel SineWave3
<    namespace : "com.friendsofed";
     vendor : "Advanced ActionScript 3.0 Animation";
     version : 1;
     description : "draws vertical and horizontal bands";
>
{
     input image4 src;
     output pixel4 dst;

     void
     evaluatePixel()
     {
         dst = pixel4(0, 0, 0, 1);
         float2 pos = outCoord();
         dst.rgb = pixel3(sin(pos.x * .2) * .5 + .5);
         dst.a = 1.0;
     }
}
```

If you make a vector value, passing in only a single value, Pixel Bender will fill all the elements of the vector with that one value. Thus, the r, g, and b of dst get the same value, resulting in grayscale vertical bars, as you can see in Figure 9-4.

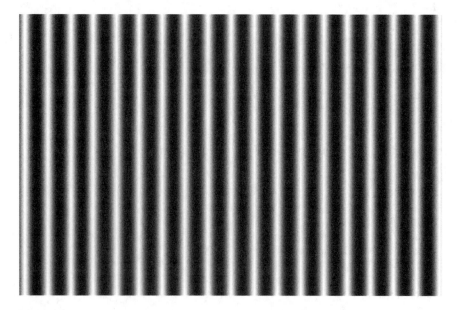

Figure 9-4. Grayscale bars

The Pixel Bender Language Reference, which should have been installed when you installed the Pixel Bender Toolkit, describes all the various built-in mathematical and geometric functions available to you. Play around with some of them and see what kind of interesting patterns you can make. Next we'll look at how to vary values at run time.

Parameters

A Pixel Bender shader that consists of completely hard-coded values would have limited usefulness. Suppose that you were making a shader that blurred an image. You would have to make one shader for a slight blur, another for a medium blur, and yet another for a strong blur. Fortunately, Pixel Bender allows you to vary certain values at run time. These special values are called **parameters**. In their simplest form, they are declared just like any other variable, with the added parameter keyword in front:

```
parameter float myParameter;
```

When you add a numeric parameter and run the shader within the Pixel Bender Toolkit, you'll see a slider appear in the top-right area of the toolkit. If you add a parameter of type bool, you'll see a check box. Let's try it. The next example is available in the SineWaveParam.pbk file:

```
<languageVersion : 1.0;>

kernel SineWaveParam
<   namespace : "com.friendsofed";
    vendor : "Advanced ActionScript 3.0 Animation";
    version : 1;
    description : "draws vertical bands";
>
{
    input image4 src;
    output pixel4 dst;

    parameter float mult;

    void
    evaluatePixel()
    {
        dst = pixel4(0, 0, 0, 1);
        float2 pos = outCoord();
        dst.r = sin(pos.x * mult) * .5 + .5;
    }
}
```

Running this should give you a slider like that shown in Figure 9-5.

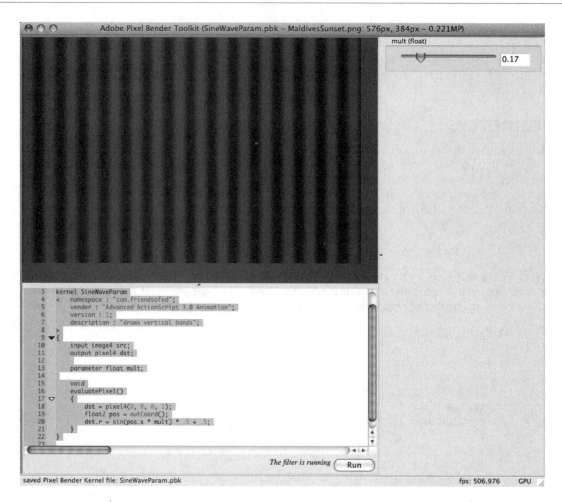

Figure 9-5. Parameter slider in the Pixel Bender Toolkit

Here we create a parameter called mult. We multiply pos.x by this value before feeding it to the Math.sin function to create the sine wave. Now you can adjust the size of the vertical bars by moving the slider back and forth.

If you make a parameter of a vector type, you will get multiple sliders grouped together, as you can see in the next example, available for download as ColorChooser.pbk:

```
<languageVersion : 1.0;>

kernel ColorChooser
<    namespace : "com.friendsofed";
     vendor : "Advanced ActionScript 3.0 Animation";
     version : 1;
     description : "shows a pixel4 parameter in action";
>
```

```
{
    input image4 src;
    output pixel4 dst;

    parameter pixel4 color;

    void
    evaluatePixel()
    {
        dst = color;
    }
}
```

Because the parameter color is a pixel4 value, you'll get four sliders, as you can see in Figure 9-6.

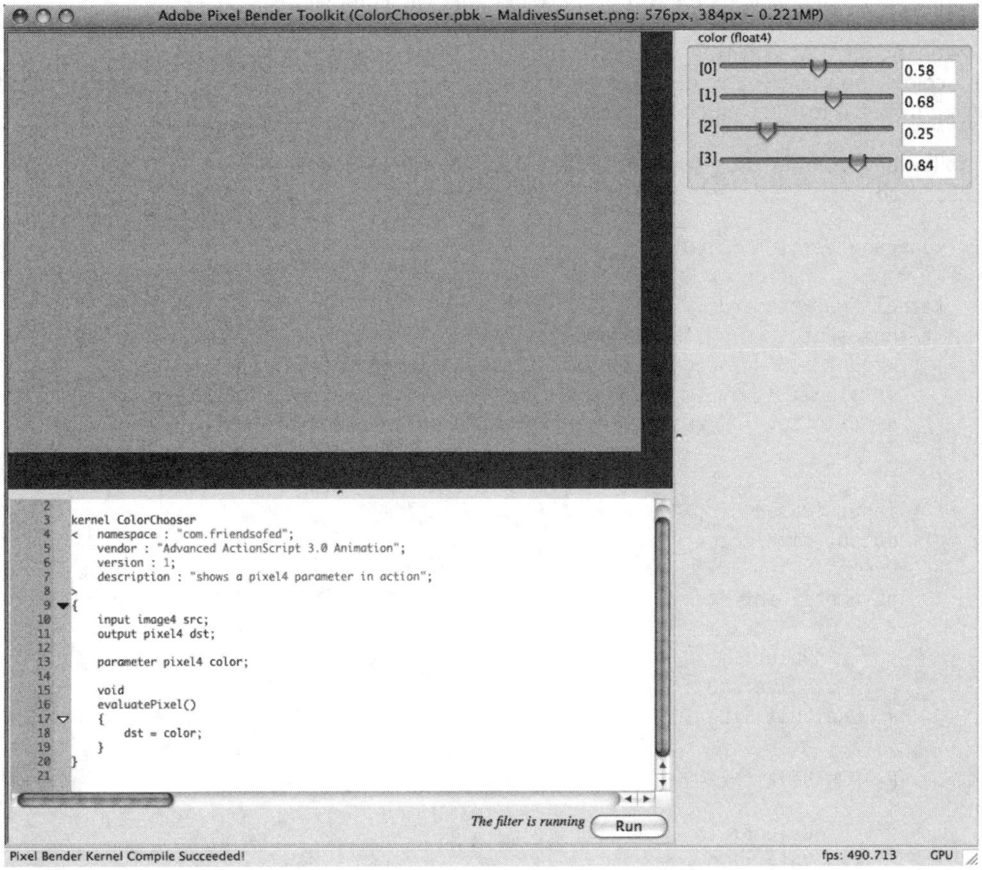

Figure 9-6. A four-channel slider

Move the sliders around to adjust the color of the resulting image. Of course, you'll need to move slider 3 (alpha) up at least a little bit to see any changes at all.

Advanced parameters

When you create a parameter, it will default to minimum and maximum values of 0.0 and 1.0, and a starting value of 0.0. For some parameters this might be fine, but in many cases you'll want to choose other values for maximum, minimum, and starting values. For this purpose, you can use parameter metadata to affect these settings to look like this:

```
parameter float myValue
<
    minValue:0.0;
    maxValue:100.0;
    defaultValue:50.0;
>;
```

Important syntax to note: the metadata comes directly after the variable name, and the semicolon goes after the metadata. Mess that up, and Pixel Bender will complain.

The settings consist of minValue, maxValue, and defaultValue, which are self-explanatory. Follow that with a colon, the value you want to set it, and then a semicolon. The preceding example makes the slider go from 0.0 to 100.0 and starts it out at 50.0.

The following example uses two int parameters to create a checkerboard pattern (the file is Checkerboard.pbk):

```
<languageVersion : 1.0;>

kernel Checkerboard
<   namespace : "com.friendsofed";
    vendor : "Advanced ActionScript 3.0 Animation";
    version : 1;
    description : "creates a checkerboard pattern";
>
{
    input image4 src;
    output pixel4 dst;

    parameter int xres
    <
        minValue:1;
        maxValue:200;
        defaultValue:50;
    >;
    parameter int yres
    <
        minValue:1;
        maxValue:200;
        defaultValue:50;
    >;
```

```
void
evaluatePixel()
{
    float2 pos = outCoord();
    float xpos = floor(pos.x / float(xres));
    float ypos = floor(pos.y / float(yres));
    if(mod(xpos, 2.0) > 0.0 ^^ mod(ypos, 2.0) > 0.0)
    {
        dst = pixel4(1, 1, 1, 1);
    }
    else
    {
        dst = pixel4(0, 0, 0, 1);
    }
}
}
```

First we get the current coordinate with outCoord. We divide it by xres and take the floor of that value. For example, if the width of the image is 500 and xres is 100, it results in values from 1 to 5. Note that we need to cast xres to a float in order to divide pos.x by it.

Then we do the same thing for the y-axis. We take the modulus of each value and 2.0 (**modulus** is what is left over if you divide a value by some other value). Taking the modulus of an integer and 2 results in 0 if the integer is even; it results in 1 if the integer is odd. The ^^ operator is an exclusive OR. It means that if either one of the conditions, but not both, is true, it will return true. If this condition is true, we color the pixel white; otherwise, we color it black. The result is a checkerboard pattern. You can adjust the slider to change the size of the squares (or rectangles) that make up the pattern.

Sampling the Input Image

So far we have been using the input image only to provide an area to work with. But at its heart, Pixel Bender is an image-processing language, meaning it processes images. (And they pay me to write this stuff!) So naturally it needs to provide a way to get at the data of the image. It does this through a couple of different sampling functions (**sampling** means to get the pixel value of an image at a specific location).

The simplest sampling function is sampleNearest. This takes an image and a float2 value that represents an x, y position in that image, finds the pixel in the image that is closest to that point, and returns its value.

So now we can go back to that original default shader code that Pixel Bender spit out, and actually understand it:

```
void
evaluatePixel()
{
    dst = sampleNearest(src, outCoord());
}
```

We are passing in src, which is the input image, as the first parameter; and passing in outCoord(), which returns the float2–based coordinates of the current pixel, as the second parameter. Suppose that we are evaluating pixel 100, 100. This will look at pixel 100, 100 in the source image and return its value. Thus, pixel for pixel, the output image is exactly the same as the input image. Of course, we can alter it to sample a different pixel from the current pixel we are evaluating. When we do this, we can start to move pixels around from their original positions and create various distortions. The next example, available as GlassTile.pbk, does just that:

```
<languageVersion : 1.0;>

kernel GlassTile
<    namespace : "com.friendsofed";
     vendor : "Advanced ActionScript 3.0 Animation";
     version : 1;
     description : "creates a glass tile refraction effect";
>
{
    input image4 src;
    output pixel4 dst;

    parameter float mult
    <
        minValue:0.0;
        maxValue:10.0;
        defaultValue:1.0;
    >;

    parameter float wave
    <
        minValue:0.0;
        maxValue:1.0;
        defaultValue:0.1;
    >;

    void
    evaluatePixel()
    {
        float2 pos = outCoord();
        pos += float2(sin(pos.x * wave) * mult,
                      sin(pos.y * wave) * mult);
        dst = sampleNearest(src, pos);
    }
}
```

Instead of simply sampling the current pixel, this shader offsets the x, y coordinates by a certain amount. This is done by taking the sine of the current x and y positions, reduced somewhat and multiplied by a certain amount. The reduction is done by the wave parameter, and the multiplication is done by the mult parameter. The result is what you see in Figure 9-7.

Figure 9-7. A glass tile effect

Linear sampling

I mentioned that there are a couple of different types of sampling. So far, we've just seen sampleNearest. Again, this takes the x, y coordinate that is passed in and finds the closest pixel to it. Take a look at Figure 9-8.

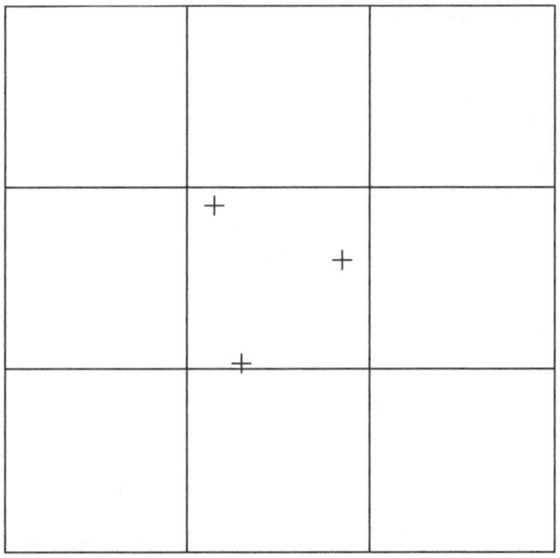

Figure 9-8. All three sampled points will get the value of the middle pixel.

The figure shows a closeup of a nine-pixel area. Suppose that the middle pixel is at location 100, 100. The three crosshairs show three different points passed in to sampleNearest. Maybe the top-left one is something like 99.7, 99.6; the one on the right is 100.4, 99.9; and the bottom one is 99.8, 100.5. All are nearest to pixel 100, 100, so they would get the same values. Although this is a pretty simple method of sampling and probably pretty quick, it can result in some blockiness (as you can see in Figure 9-9, which is a closeup of an image saved from the GlassTile shader).

Figure 9-9. Blockiness resulting from sampleNearest

If you are running into this kind of thing in your shaders, you can try the other sampling method: sampleLinear. Actually, if you look in the documentation, you'll see there are three sampling methods listed: sample, sampleLinear, and sampleNearest. But actually, sample is just an alternate name for sampleLinear; they are really the exact same function.

The way sampleLinear works is to take a sort of weighted average of the four nearest pixels. For example, in Figure 9-10 you can see the crosshair representing the point passed in.

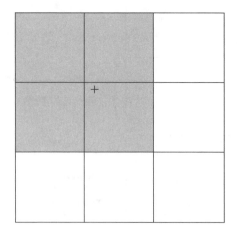

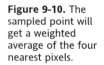

Figure 9-10. The sampled point will get a weighted average of the four nearest pixels.

The four gray pixels represent the four pixels that will be sampled. They aren't actually averaged per se, but bilinearly interpolated. In other words, the pixels that are closest to the sample point will be weighted more heavily in the average than the pixels that are farther from it. So you get a much smoother blend between similar sample points.

To see this in action, simply change the line in GlassTile.pbk from this:

```
dst = sampleNearest(src, pos);
```

to this:

```
dst = sampleLinear(src, pos);
```

or this:

```
dst = sample(src, pos);
```

This gets rid of the blockiness that was present before, and gives you smooth gradients, as you can see in Figure 9-11.

Figure 9-11. A smoother gradient produced by sampleLinear

Let's do one more deformation before looking at how to actually use shaders in Flash.

Twirl Shader for Flash

In the sample shaders included with the Pixel Bender Toolkit is a twirl filter that spins the pixels around a given point. Unfortunately, this is written using several features that are not available when exporting shaders for use in Flash. So let's make one that will work in Flash.

The file is TwirlFlash.pbk, and you can see it here:

```
<languageVersion : 1.0;>

kernel TwirlFlash
<   namespace : "com.friendsofed";
    vendor : "Advanced ActionScript 3.0 Animation";
    version : 1;
    description : "spins an image";
>
{
    input image4 src;
    output pixel4 dst;

    parameter float2 center
    <
        minValue:float2(0.0);
        maxValue:float2(1000.0);
        defaultValue:float2(200.0);
    >;

    parameter float twist
    <
        minValue:-10.0;
        maxValue:10.0;
        defaultValue:0.0;
    >;

    parameter float radius
    <
        minValue:0.0;
        maxValue:500.0;
        defaultValue:100.0;
    >;

    void
    evaluatePixel()
    {
        float2 pos = outCoord();
        float dist = distance(center, pos);
        float PI = 3.14159;

        if(dist < radius)
        {
            float dx = pos.x - center.x;
            float dy = pos.y - center.y;
            float angle = atan(dy, dx);
            angle += sin(dist / radius * PI) * twist;
            float2 newpos = center + float2(cos(angle) * dist,
                                            sin(angle) * dist);
            dst = sampleNearest(src, newpos);
```

```
        }
        else
        {
            dst = sampleNearest(src, pos);
        }
    }
}
```

There are three parameters:

- The center parameter specifies the point around which the twirl effect will take place. Remember that Pixel Bender does not have any information such as image size, so there is no concept of stage width and height as there is in Flash.

- The twist parameter determines how much the image will be twirled around the center point.

- The radius parameter determines how much of the image will be affected. The shader will affect only a circular area around the center point, defined by this radius.

In the evaluatePixel function, we get the position of the current pixel being evaluated and the distance from that pixel to the center parameter by using the built-in distance function. We also define a value for PI because it is not otherwise available within Pixel Bender:

```
float2 pos = outCoord();
float dist = distance(center, pos);
float PI = 3.14159;
```

Next we have an if statement, which is about the only real control structure available to you when creating shaders for use in Flash. There are no arrays, for or while loops, or switch statements. The limitations will make you more creative! Hopefully. Anyway, if the distance is less than the radius, we calculate the twirl. If not, we just pass through the source image pixel as is.

Then we get into some math. We get the component distances from center to pos on the x-axis and y-axis, and use that to get the angle between the two:

```
float dx = pos.x - center.x;
float dy = pos.y - center.y;
float angle = atan(dy, dx);
```

Now we want to add to that angle to perform the distortion. How much we add takes a bit of explanation. Here's the line again for reference:

```
angle += sin(dist / radius * PI) * twist;
```

First we take dist / radius * PI. The value of dist will be somewhere between 0.0 and radius, so dist / radius will range from 0.0 to 1.0. Multiply this by PI, and it will go from 0.0 to 3.1459. Taking the sine of this value gives us a smooth curve from 0.0 to 1.0 and back to 0.0. Finally we multiply it by the twist value and add it to the angle, which means that at the center of the effect there will be no distortion. Halfway out to the radius will be maximum distortion, and we'll be back to no distortion at the edge of the radius.

Now we have a distance and an angle. We then find the point located at that angle and that distance from the center and sample that point on the source image. This is the `pixel4` value that we use as an output. You can see the result in Figure 9-12.

Figure 9-12. The `TwirlFlash` shader in action

You now know the basics of how to create shaders and some of the techniques involved. Searching around the labs and developer center at www.adobe.com or even just a search on the Web should give you additional techniques and lots of sample Pixel Bender files to learn more from. Also, don't limit yourself to just Pixel Bender material. Pixel Bender is based on the Open GL shader language GLSL. Although there are some differences, you should be able to pick up some tips and techniques from reference materials on that language.

At any rate, I trust that you are on your way to creating some cool shaders with the Pixel Bender Toolkit. Now let's look at how to use them within Flash.

Using Pixel Bender Shaders in Flash

As covered in the introduction to this chapter, Pixel Bender shaders can be used in four possible ways within Flash:

- Filters
- Fills
- Blend modes
- "Generic number crunching"

We'll cover the first three here. Using shaders for high-speed generic math calculations is a bit too broad and is (as of this writing) very much an experimental subject.

Using shaders in Flash requires three basic steps:

1. Exporting the shader in a format Flash can read

2. Loading or embedding the shader into a Flash movie

3. Creating a shader instance within Flash and using that shader as a fill, filter, or blend mode

So let's go through the steps. First we'll export the shader from the Pixel Bender Toolkit. Open up the Checkerboard.pbk file created earlier for this example. Exporting the shader for Flash is as easy as going to the File menu and choosing Export Kernel Filter for Flash Player. Use the default name, which should be the same as the kernel file you just loaded. Save it in a location where your Flash movie can access it. It will be saved with a .pbj extension (which always makes me think "peanut butter and jelly," but that's another story).

Now we need to create a Flash movie to utilize this shader. We'll create a document class that can be used with Flex Builder, Flash CS4, or any other method of coding and compilation that you prefer.

Loading shaders versus embedding shaders

To use a shader in Flash, you'll need to either load it in at run time or embed it when compiling the movie. I prefer embedding for a few reasons. First, you don't need to provision the shader along with your SWF as it is compiled into the SWF. Second, you don't have to wait for it to load because it is available as soon as the SWF loads. This makes it a lot easier to code, at least when developing and testing. Of course, loading a shader in does have the benefit that if you change the shader at some point, you'll just need to replace the online version and will not need to recompile any SWFs that load it in.

At any rate, I'll show you how to load shaders first and then embed them.

We start by creating the basic framework you use to load other content in, such as XML, using a URLLoader and a COMPLETE event handler. You can download the completed file as ShaderFillDemo.as:

```
package {
    import flash.display.Sprite;
    import flash.events.Event;
    import flash.net.URLLoader;
    import flash.net.URLLoaderDataFormat;
    import flash.net.URLRequest;

    public class ShaderFillDemo extends Sprite
    {
        private var loader:URLLoader;
        private var shaderURL:String = "Checkerboard.pbj";

        public function ShaderFillDemo()
        {
            stage.align = StageAlign.TOP_LEFT;
            stage.scaleMode = StageScaleMode.NO_SCALE;
```

```
            loader = new URLLoader();
            loader.addEventListener(Event.COMPLETE, onLoadComplete);
            loader.dataFormat = URLLoaderDataFormat.BINARY;
            loader.load(new URLRequest(shaderURL));
        }

        private function onLoadComplete(event:Event):void
        {

        }
    }
}
```

One important thing to note is that we set the loader's data format to binary because we are loading in binary data. Also make sure that the `.pbj` shader file is in the same location as the final SWF so it can be loaded or adjust the path of the URL as necessary.

Now that the shader data is loaded in, we need to make a Shader object from it. This is an instance of the `flash.display.Shader` class. The loader's data property will contain the binary shader bytecode. You pass this into the constructor of the shader like so:

```
        private function onLoadComplete(event:Event):void
        {
            var shader:Shader = new Shader(loader.data);
        }
```

You need to do this step no matter what you are using the shader for: fill, filter, or blend mode. Let's use it as a fill.

Using a shader as a fill

We do this with the Graphics method, `beginShaderFill`, passing in the shader you want to use. You can then draw whatever you want, and—just like a solid fill, gradient fill, or bitmap fill—the shape you draw will be filled with the pattern created by your shader. Here's the completed class in full:

```
package {
    import flash.display.Shader;
    import flash.display.Sprite;
    import flash.display.StageAlign;
    import flash.display.StageScaleMode;
    import flash.events.Event;
    import flash.net.URLLoader;
    import flash.net.URLLoaderDataFormat;
    import flash.net.URLRequest;

    public class ShaderFillDemo extends Sprite
    {

        private var loader:URLLoader;
        private var shaderURL:String = "Checkerboard.pbj";
```

```
                public function ShaderFillDemo()
                {
                    stage.align = StageAlign.TOP_LEFT;
                    stage.scaleMode = StageScaleMode.NO_SCALE;

                    loader = new URLLoader();
                    loader.addEventListener(Event.COMPLETE, onLoadComplete);
                    loader.dataFormat = URLLoaderDataFormat.BINARY;
                    loader.load(new URLRequest(shaderURL));
                }

                private function onLoadComplete(event:Event):void
                {
                    var shader:Shader = new Shader(loader.data);
                    graphics.beginShaderFill(shader);
                    graphics.drawRect(0, 0, 400, 400);
                    graphics.endFill();
                }
            }
        }
```

If all goes well, you'll have drawn a rectangle filled with a checkerboard pattern.

Good enough. We'll look at how to set parameters and some other things soon, but first let's look at how to do the same thing with embedding. For this we will use the Embed metadata tag to compile the shader right into the SWF so it will not need to be loaded. This is the same as embedding an external bitmap, SWF, font, and so on. Here's the basic setup for that, available as ShaderFillEmbed.as:

```
    package {
        import flash.display.Shader;
        import flash.display.Sprite;
        import flash.display.StageAlign;
        import flash.display.StageScaleMode;

        public class ShaderFillEmbed extends Sprite
        {
            [Embed (source="Checkerboard.pbj",
                    mimeType="application/octet-stream")]
            private var ShaderClass:Class;

            public function ShaderFillEmbed()
            {
                stage.align = StageAlign.TOP_LEFT;
                stage.scaleMode = StageScaleMode.NO_SCALE;
            }
        }
    }
```

Note that you have to set the mimeType to "application/octet-stream". Also, don't forget to put the .pbj file in the same directory as the source document class or otherwise adjust the path to it so it can be found by the compiler.

Now you're ready to create a shader the same way you created one in the last example. But now the bytecode is contained in the ShaderClass class, so we make an instance of that and pass it to the shader constructor:

```
var shader:Shader = new Shader(new ShaderClass());
```

Now you can use the shader instance in a beginShaderFill, just like before. Here's the whole class again:

```
package {
    import flash.display.Shader;
    import flash.display.Sprite;
    import flash.display.StageAlign;
    import flash.display.StageScaleMode;

    public class ShaderFillEmbed extends Sprite
    {
        [Embed (source="Checkerboard.pbj",
                mimeType="application/octet-stream")]
        private var ShaderClass:Class;

        public function ShaderFillEmbed()
        {
            stage.align = StageAlign.TOP_LEFT;
            stage.scaleMode = StageScaleMode.NO_SCALE;

            var shader:Shader = new Shader(new ShaderClass());
            graphics.beginShaderFill(shader);
            graphics.drawRect(0, 0, 400, 400);
            graphics.endFill();
        }
    }
}
```

To me this is much easier than loading, which is why I prefer it. But at any rate, the rest of the techniques in this chapter can be used no matter which method of getting the shader into your SWF you use. First let's look at accessing shader metadata.

Accessing shader metadata in Flash

Once you have a shader instance in Flash, you can access the metadata that you set while creating the shader in the Pixel Bender Toolkit. You do this through the data property of the shader itself. This is an instance of the flash.display.ShaderData class. From this, you can access the namespace, vendor, version, and description metadata properties you set when creating the shader. You can also access the name of the shader itself, which is the name of the kernel you wrote. These all come through as strings. Just add the following lines to the last example to see this in action:

```
public function ShaderFillEmbed()
{
    stage.align = StageAlign.TOP_LEFT;
    stage.scaleMode = StageScaleMode.NO_SCALE;

    var shader:Shader = new Shader(new ShaderClass());
    trace(shader.data.name);
    trace(shader.data.namespace);
    trace(shader.data.vendor);
    trace(shader.data.version);
    trace(shader.data.description);

    graphics.beginShaderFill(shader);
    graphics.drawRect(0, 0, 400, 400);
    graphics.endFill();
}
```

This traces out like so:

```
Checkerboard
com.friendsofed
Advanced ActionScript 3.0 Animation
1
creates a checkerboard pattern
```

Although you won't always need this, it's good to know you have access to it. It could be very useful in creating a tool that allows you to load and apply different shaders because you could list this data out in the interface.

Setting shader parameters in Flash

In the Pixel Bender Toolkit, any time you created a parameter you were given sliders or perhaps a check box for altering those parameters in the toolkit itself and seeing the results. In Flash, of course, you won't see sliders or check boxes, but you do need some way to affect those parameters via code. This again is done through the shader's data property. But it's not quite as straightforward as you might hope.

Each parameter you created in your shader is a property on the shader's data property. So, for our checkerboard shader, there will be this:

```
shader.data.xres
```

and this:

```
shader.data.yres
```

Now you might think that you can just set them with a line of code like this:

```
shader.data.xres = 20;
```

Go ahead and try it if you want, but it won't work. It won't throw an error or anything, but it doesn't change the parameter, either. You need to go one step deeper into the value property of the parameter:

```
shader.data.xres.value
```

387

But wait, there's more! The value property wants an array of values, not just a single value. Remember that a parameter can be one of the vector types that could consist of up to four values. So even if you are passing just a single value, you need to pass it in as an array, like so:

```
shader.data.xres.value = [20];
```

Finally, this passes through the value to the parameter as expected. In the preceding example, this will result in something that looks like Figure 9-13.

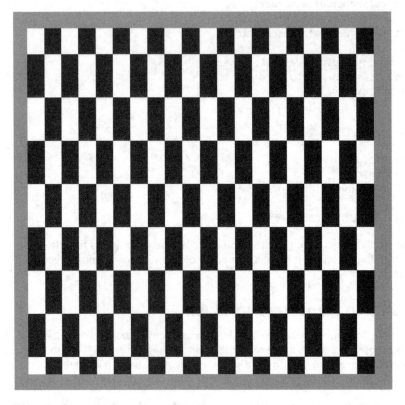

Figure 9-13. Checkerboard pattern produced with a fill

Try changing the yres parameter as well.

Transforming a shader fill

The beginShaderFill, like some of the other fill methods, has a second parameter of type flash.display.Matrix. You can use it to scale, rotate, or translate the shader as it is drawn. If you look up the Matrix class in the Flash help files, you'll see that you can rotate a matrix by a certain angle with the following parameters, where q is the angle you want to rotate, in radians:

```
new Matrix(cos(q), sin(q), -sin(q), cos(q), 0, 0);
```

Of course, as Seb (this book's tech reviewer) pointed out, you could just say this:

```
var m:Matrix = new Matrix();
m.rotate(q);
```

So now you know two ways of doing the same thing! Always good. Using this data, we can rotate the shader by any angle as we draw it like so:

```
public function ShaderFillEmbed()
{
    stage.align = StageAlign.TOP_LEFT;
    stage.scaleMode = StageScaleMode.NO_SCALE;

    var shader:Shader = new Shader(new ShaderClass());

    var angle:Number = Math.PI / 4; // 45 degrees in radians
    var cos:Number = Math.cos(angle);
    var sin:Number = Math.sin(angle);
    graphics.beginShaderFill(shader, new Matrix(cos, sin, -sin, cos));
    graphics.drawRect(0, 0, 400, 400);
    graphics.endFill();
}
```

This rotates the shader by 45 degrees (PI / 4 radians) as it draws it, displaying what you see in Figure 9-14.

Figure 9-14. Checkerboard pattern with a rotation matrix

You can, of course, similarly scale, translate, or even skew a shader fill by using different parameters for the matrix.

Animating a shader fill

Here's where you see the real power of parameters to make shaders dynamic. The idea is quite simple: draw a shader fill, change a parameter, apply it again on the next frame, and so on. The next example shows a very simple example, again using the checkerboard pattern (the file is available as ShaderFillAnim.as):

```
package {
    import flash.display.Shader;
    import flash.display.Sprite;
    import flash.display.StageAlign;
    import flash.display.StageScaleMode;
    import flash.events.Event;

    public class ShaderFillAnim extends Sprite
    {
        [Embed (source="Checkerboard.pbj",
                mimeType="application/octet-stream")]
        private var ShaderClass:Class;

        private var shader:Shader;
        private var xAngle:Number = 0;
        private var yAngle:Number = 0;
        private var xSpeed:Number = .09;
        private var ySpeed:Number = .07;

        public function ShaderFillAnim()
        {
            stage.align = StageAlign.TOP_LEFT;
            stage.scaleMode = StageScaleMode.NO_SCALE;

            shader = new Shader(new ShaderClass());

            addEventListener(Event.ENTER_FRAME, onEnterFrame);
        }

        private function onEnterFrame(event:Event):void
        {
            var xres:Number = Math.sin(xAngle += xSpeed) * 50 + 55;
            var yres:Number = Math.sin(yAngle += ySpeed) * 50 + 55;

            shader.data.xres.value = [xres];
            shader.data.yres.value = [yres];
            graphics.clear();
            graphics.beginShaderFill(shader);
```

```
                    graphics.drawRect(20, 20, 400, 400);
                    graphics.endFill();
                }
            }
        }
```

Here we create properties for an angle and speed on the x- and y-axis. We add the speed to the angle on each frame and take the sine of that value. Multiply it by 50 and add it to 55, and you get values ranging from 5 to 105. These are fed into the xres and yres parameters of the shader. Clear the graphics and redraw the shape with the shader fill and you have animation.

Specifying a shader input image

In the previous examples, the shaders produced a pattern based purely on mathematical formulas. But what if you want to use another shader like the TwirlFlash example? That shader really is an image-processing shader because its pixel outputs are directly dependent on an input image. Let's go ahead and see what happens if we try to use it. The next example can be found in the ShaderFillImage.as file:

```
package {
    import flash.display.Shader;
    import flash.display.Sprite;
    import flash.display.StageAlign;
    import flash.display.StageScaleMode;
    import flash.filters.ShaderFilter;

    public class ShaderFillImage extends Sprite
    {
        [Embed (source="TwirlFlash.pbj",
                mimeType="application/octet-stream")]
        private var ShaderClass:Class;

        public function ShaderFillImage()
        {
            stage.align = StageAlign.TOP_LEFT;
            stage.scaleMode = StageScaleMode.NO_SCALE;

            var shader:Shader = new Shader(new ShaderClass());
            shader.data.center.value = [400, 300];
            shader.data.twist.value = [-6];
            shader.data.radius.value = [300];

            graphics.beginShaderFill(shader);
            graphics.drawRect(20, 20, 800, 600);
            graphics.endFill();
        }
    }
}
```

If you run this program as is, you'll get an error message—The Shader input src is missing or an unsupported type—because the shader is trying to sample pixels on an image that doesn't exist. The good news is that we can simply pass it an image to use as a source image.

First we need to get a BitmapData into the file. I included a photo of a good friend of mine and embedded it in the class:

```
package {
    import flash.display.Bitmap;
    import flash.display.Shader;
    import flash.display.Sprite;
    import flash.display.StageAlign;
    import flash.display.StageScaleMode;
    import flash.filters.ShaderFilter;

    public class ShaderFillImage extends Sprite
    {
        [Embed (source="TwirlFlash.pbj",
                mimeType="application/octet-stream")]
        private var ShaderClass:Class;

        [Embed (source="john_davey.jpg")]
        private var JohnDavey:Class;

        public function ShaderFillImage()
        {
            stage.align = StageAlign.TOP_LEFT;
            stage.scaleMode = StageScaleMode.NO_SCALE;

            var shader:Shader = new Shader(new ShaderClass());
            shader.data.center.value = [400, 300];
            shader.data.twist.value = [-6];
            shader.data.radius.value = [300];

            var image:Bitmap = new JohnDavey();
            shader.data.src.input = image.bitmapData;

            graphics.beginShaderFill(shader);
            graphics.drawRect(20, 20, 800, 600);
            graphics.endFill();
        }
    }
}
```

We can then make an instance of this embedded image, which will be of type Bitmap. The BitmapData will be accessed through the bitmapData property of that Bitmap. We assign this to shader.data.src. input, and the shader now has an input image to sample. The results are shown in Figure 9-15.

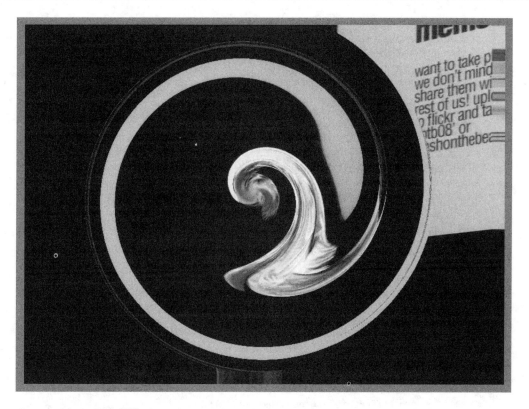

Figure 9-15. The TwirlFlash shader used as a fill

Note that the src in shader.data.src.input is not some magic value. It comes directly from this line in the shader kernel code:

```
input image4 src;
```

Had we named the input image with some other variable name such as source, we'd have to reflect this in the ActionScript:

```
shader.data.source.input = image.bitmapData;
```

And that covers just about all you need to know about shaders used as fills. As a matter of fact, I covered most of what you need to know about the Shader class in general. I'll cover using shaders as filters and blend modes next, but everything just covered is fully applicable to those subjects as well.

Using a Shader as a Filter

Using a shader as a filter is, if anything, easier than using it as a fill. Let's use the TwirlFlash shader again, but instead of an image, let's prove that we can use it on any display object, even a text field. The next file is called ShaderAsFilter.as:

```
package {
    import flash.display.Shader;
    import flash.display.Sprite;
    import flash.display.StageAlign;
    import flash.display.StageScaleMode;
    import flash.filters.ShaderFilter;
    import flash.text.TextField;
    import flash.text.TextFormat;

    [SWF(backgroundColor=0xFFFFFF)]
    public class ShaderAsFilter extends Sprite
    {
        [Embed (source="TwirlFlash.pbj",
                mimeType="application/octet-stream")]
        private var ShaderClass:Class;

        public function ShaderAsFilter()
        {
            stage.align = StageAlign.TOP_LEFT;
            stage.scaleMode = StageScaleMode.NO_SCALE;

            var shader:Shader = new Shader(new ShaderClass());
            shader.data.center.value = [200, 200];
            shader.data.twist.value = [-1];
            shader.data.radius.value = [200];

            var tf:TextField = new TextField();
            tf.width = 400;
            tf.height = 400;
            tf.wordWrap = true;
            tf.multiline = true;
            tf.border = true;
            tf.defaultTextFormat = new TextFormat("Arial", 24);
            addChild(tf);

            for(var i:int = 0; i < 340; i++)
            {
                tf.appendText(String.fromCharCode(65 +
                              Math.random() * 25));
            }
            tf.filters = [new ShaderFilter(shader)];
        }
    }
}
```

Here we create a text field and fill it with some random text. In the very last line, we set the text field's filters property to an array containing a new ShaderFilter, passing in the shader we just created. Couldn't be more simple!

Using a Shader as a Blend Mode

This final use case is a bit different from the others. In fact, we'll need to go back and make a new shader that will work correctly when used as a blend mode.

First of all, your blend mode shader needs to have two input images: one for the background and one for the foreground. You need to define them within the kernel, but on the Flash side of things it is handled automatically—whatever display object the shader is being applied to will be passed in as the foreground, and whatever display object it is on top of will be passed in as the background. Actually, what happens is this: when you apply a blend mode to any display object, that object's cacheAsBitmap property is set to true. This generates a bitmap representation of the display object as it exists and passes that through to the shader as a source image.

There are also some limitations of what you can do within the shader. You can't do fancy sine waves, checkerboard patterns, or distortions as with the other shaders. They will work in the Pixel Bender Toolkit, but won't do a thing once you use the shader as a blend mode. What you are basically left with is the ability to sample the current pixel from both input images and then combine them in whatever way you want. The following file (ChannelBlend.pbk) demonstrates this:

```
<languageVersion : 1.0;>

kernel ChannelBlend
<   namespace : "com.friendsofed";
    vendor : "Advamced ActionScript 3.0 Animation";
    version : 1;
    description : "blends the channels of two images";
>
{
    input image4 back;
    input image4 fore;

    output pixel4 dst;

    parameter float3 amt;

    void
    evaluatePixel()
    {
        pixel4 bg = sampleNearest(back, outCoord());
        pixel4 fg = sampleNearest(fore, outCoord());
        dst.r = fg.r * amt.r + bg.r * (1.0 - amt.r);
        dst.g = fg.g * amt.g + bg.g * (1.0 - amt.g);
        dst.b = fg.b * amt.b + bg.b * (1.0 - amt.b);
        dst.a = 1.0;
    }
}
```

First we declare two image4 variables, fore and back. It doesn't matter what you name them. The first variable declared will receive the background image, and the second one will receive the foreground image.

In the evaluatePixel function, we sample both images at the outCoord location. Up to this point is basically what you would probably do for any shader to be used as a blend mode. After that, you can combine those two pixels whatever way you want. In this case, I'm mixing the two based on the amt parameter, which allows you to mix all the channels separately. To test this in the Pixel Bender Toolkit, you'll have to load in two images via the File menu. The first image you load will be the background, and the second one will be the foreground. You can test the effect by playing with the sliders created by the amt parameter.

Now, back into Flash (this file is available as ShaderBlendMode.as):

```
package {
    import flash.display.Bitmap;
    import flash.display.Shader;
    import flash.display.Sprite;
    import flash.display.StageAlign;
    import flash.display.StageScaleMode;

    public class ShaderBlendMode extends Sprite
    {
        [Embed (source="ChannelBlend.pbj",
                mimeType="application/octet-stream")]
        private var ShaderClass:Class;

        [Embed (source="input1.jpg")]
        private var input1:Class;

        [Embed (source="input2.jpg")]
        private var input2:Class;

        public function ShaderBlendMode()
        {
            stage.align = StageAlign.TOP_LEFT;
            stage.scaleMode = StageScaleMode.NO_SCALE;

            var back:Bitmap = new input2();
            addChild(back);

            var fore:Bitmap = new input1();
            addChild(fore);

            var shader:Shader = new Shader(new ShaderClass());
            shader.data.amt.value = [1.0, 0.9, 0.0];
            fore.blendShader = shader;
        }
    }
}
```

Here we embed and instantiate two bitmap images and put them on stage. We create a new shader based on the ShaderBlend shader we just created, set some values, and assign that shader directly to the blendShader property of the topmost bitmap. You should see something like Figure 9-16.

Figure 9-16. Two images blended with the ChannelBlend shader

If you used blend modes before, you might be used to assigning a string value to the blendMode property. Actually, setting a shader to the blendShader property of a display object automatically sets the blendMode to "shader".

Try changing the parameters and see that the shader behaves the same way as in the toolkit.

Summary

This chapter covered a lot in a short space. At least enough to get you up and running with creating shaders and using them in Flash. Now it's up to you to come up with some cool and useful ones. I'm looking forward to seeing them.

Chapter 10

TWEEN ENGINES

In Chapter 8 of *Making Things Move* I wrote about a subject called **easing**. I called this type of easing **simple easing** because it was quite easy to implement and had limited power and flexibility. This type of easing consists of having an object and a target location for that object to move to. On each frame you calculate the distance between the object and the target and move it one-half (or some other fraction) of that distance. The object moves smoothly into place, slowing down as it arrives at the target.

In that chapter I made reference to Robert Penner's easing functions and suggested that you look into them, (referring to them as **advanced easing**). This was a subject I would have liked to write about back then, but we ran out of room in that book. So now I've finally gotten around to it. Robert Penner's easing formulas have been used extensively, not only in conjunction with the tweening classes provided with Flash and Flex builder but also with a number of tween engines that have popped up over the years.

As a quick note: from this point on in the chapter, when I refer to a **tween** or **tweening**, I am referring to moving an object or changing some property over time with code—usually by using some predefined tweening class. It has absolutely nothing to do with tweening using the timeline.

There are two separate Tween classes published by Adobe: `fl.transitions.Tween`, from the classes included with the Flash authoring environment; and `mx.effects.Tween`, included in the Flex framework. These classes do essentially the same thing:

they take a start value and an end value, and interpolate values between them over a specific time period. Both were built around Robert Penner's easing formulas and allow you to do complex eases, including easing in and out with different formulas, bouncing in and out, specifying the total time an ease should take from start to end, and so on.

Tweening engines are code frameworks, most of which (also using Robert Penner's easing formulas) aim to make tweening easier. I'm not sure how many ActionScript tweening engines there are out there. I made a list of some of the major ones when I started to write this book. By the time I got to this chapter, I had to add two or three new engines to that list.

Now, let me tell you what this chapter *isn't*.

First, it isn't meant to be a definitive guide to every ActionScript 3.0 tweening engine out there. Like so many other chapters in this book, that could be a whole book in itself. And such a book would be outdated as soon as it was published. Actually, if you want to know more about the background of tweening engines in Flash, take a look at Chapter 10 of *The Essential Guide to Open Source Flash Development* (Apress, 2008). In that chapter, Moses Gunesch gives a history of tweening engines leading up to his own enormously popular Fuse tweening kit. He then introduces his new project, GoASAP, which is a framework for creating tweening engines. I originally intended to write about Go in this chapter, but I think Moses covers it better than I could.

Neither is this chapter intended to be interpreted in any way as a list of the "best" tween engines, a list of my favorite ones, or any kind of endorsement for any particular engine. They all have strengths, weaknesses, and different ways of handling things.

Finally, this chapter is not a complete guide to any of the engines mentioned here.

This chapter *is* an introduction and overview of different types of tweening engines so you can decide which might be best for your purposes. I tried to get a bit of a range of the different engines in terms of their approaches to doing tweening, and I cover a few basic tasks using each one. Thus you can compare and contrast them, and see each one's strengths and weaknesses. In addition to the Adobe-provided classes, the engines I've chosen are the following:

- Tweener
- TweenLite/TweenGroup
- KitchenSync
- gTween

Let's start with the Adobe classes.

The Flash Tween Class

As mentioned, this Tween class is part of the library of classes that gets installed when you install the Flash authoring environment. It is in the `fl.transtions` package (along with some other interesting classes you might not be aware of—all sorts of crazy transitions). But for the purposes of this chapter, we're talking about the Tween class.

I assume that you are compiling via the Flash authoring tool, so the `fl.transitions` package will automatically be available for you. You can compile these examples using Flex Builder or another mxlmc-based method, but you need to add the flash.swc file (which can be found in the Flash installation directory) to your library path. I won't explain how to do that because it's different for each tool, and I don't think many of you will be going down this road.

The way this class works is that you create an instance of it, passing in an object reference and the name of some property on that object; an easing function (based on Robert Penner's easing formulas); a start and end value for that property; and a duration. Here's the constructor:

```
new Tween(object,
          property,
          easingFunction,
          begin,
          finish,
          duration,
          useSeconds)
```

The object can be just about any object that has at least one public numeric property. The property parameter is a string representing the name of the property you want to change. For example, if the object is a Sprite and you want to tween the x position of that sprite, you would pass in "x" as the property (including the quotes).

The easingFunction is a function defined in one of the classes in the flash.transitions.easing package. We'll take a look at these shortly.

The begin and finish properties are numeric values. When the tween starts, the object property specified will be set to the begin value. When the tween is complete, the property will be equal to the finish value.

By default, the duration specifies how many frames the tween will play across. But the final parameter is a Boolean value called useSeconds. It defaults to false, meaning that the tween will interpret duration as a number of frames. But if you set this last parameter to true, duration will be interpreted as a number of seconds.

Let's see it in action. The first example is in a file called FlashTween.as, available for download from the book's site at www.friendsofed.com:

```
package {
    import fl.transitions.Tween;
    import fl.transitions.easing.None;

    import flash.display.Sprite;
    import flash.display.StageAlign;
    import flash.display.StageScaleMode;

    [SWF(backgroundColor=0xffffff)]
    public class FlashTween extends Sprite
    {
        private var tween:Tween;
        private var sprite:Sprite;
```

```
        public function FlashTween()
        {
            stage.scaleMode = StageScaleMode.NO_SCALE;
            stage.align = StageAlign.TOP_LEFT;

            sprite = new Sprite();
            sprite.graphics.beginFill(0xff0000);
            sprite.graphics.drawRect(-50, -25, 100, 50);
            sprite.graphics.endFill();
            sprite.x = 100;
            sprite.y = 100;
            addChild(sprite);

            tween = new Tween(sprite, "x", None.easeIn,
                              100, 500, 1, true);
        }
    }
}
```

The important lines, which are in bold, are where the tween is created. Note that the moment it is created, it starts running. You do not have to do anything to make it start. The sprite (which has a red rectangle drawn in it) moves from an x position of 100 to an x position of 500 in 1 second.

Easing functions

In the example just created, the easing function is defined as None.easeIn. You might be wondering what that is all about. The easing function parameter determines what formula is used to ease in and out of the animation. In other words, if you are tweening an object's position, how quickly does it go from 0 to full speed, and how quickly does it "brake" to arrive at the target point and stop?

In the fl.transitions.easing package are a number of classes:

- Back
- Bounce
- Elastic
- None
- Regular
- Strong

Each of these classes has three methods:

- easeIn
- easeOut
- easeInOut

The None class also has an easeNone method.

The easeIn methods control how the tween starts and builds up to full speed.

The easeOut methods control how the tween slows down and stops as it approaches its target.

The easeInOut methods control both of these things.

These methods are called internally by the Tween class itself. You never have to call them yourself. You just pass the method in as a parameter to the Tween constructor. These methods are what contain the easing formulas written by Robert Penner.

The example used the easeIn method of the None easing class. This class creates a linear ease that is not really an ease at all. The tween starts out at full speed and maintains that speed until the target is reached—where it stops abruptly. Actually, it doesn't matter which method of the None class you use—they all result in the same linear behavior.

Well, that's not too exciting. Let's see what some of these other methods do. We'll try Regular first. This class creates eases that are the same as the eases you get when doing an old-school timeline tween in Flash and choosing 100% ease in or out. Change the line that creates the tween to the following:

```
tween = new Tween(sprite, "x", Regular.easeIn, 100, 500, 1, true);
```

Now you see that the sprite starts out slowly, builds up speed, and stops abruptly. If you try Regular. easeOut, you'll see that the sprite starts out quickly and slows down as it approaches its target, roughly the same way as the simple easing described in *Making Things Move*. Try Regular.easeInOut, which combines easing in and out. This is a pretty professional effect, great for moving all kinds of interface elements around smoothly. Of course, play around with some of the other parameters. Change the duration or start and end properties. Try tweening a property other than x, such as y or rotation. Try easing alpha from 0 to 1 like so:

```
tween = new Tween(sprite, "alpha", Regular.easeInOut, 0, 1, 1, true);
```

The Strong ease class does the same thing as Regular, but with a more pronounced effect. Elastic performs a bit of a springy oscillation while easing in or out. You might want to increase the duration to see it more clearly:

```
tween = new Tween(sprite, "x", Elastic.easeInOut, 100, 800, 3, true);
```

The Bounce class also performs a bit of a bounce, but like the object bounces off a hard surface. Finally, the Back class goes a bit in the opposite direction before beginning to move, shoots slightly past the target, and then eases back to it. Try them out to get a feel for them. Now you know what you need to know about the easing functions—at least for the Flash Tween class.

Combining tweens

The first example works just fine, but tweens only a single property on a single object. If you're tweening only one property on an object, and all your tweens are completely independent, you're all set. But you'll probably want to change more than one property of an object at the same time (at least the x and y position). And sometimes you might want to tween one thing and then start another one as soon as that tween is done.

Multiple tweens happening at the same time are known as **parallel tweens** or groups, and tweens that occur one after the other are called **tween sequences**.

Parallel tweens n the Flash Tween class are pretty simple. Just make a new tween for each property and object you want to tween. Say you want to move something on the x- and y-axis. Make two tweens like so:

```
tween1 = new Tween(sprite, "x", Regular.easeInOut, 100, 800, 3, true);
tween2 = new Tween(sprite, "y", Regular.easeInOut, 100, 400, 3, true);
```

You can make as many of these as you want. They don't need to use the same easing function or the same duration, as you can see here:

```
tween1 = new Tween(sprite, "x", Regular.easeInOut, 100, 800, 3, true);
tween2 = new Tween(sprite, "y", Regular.easeInOut, 100, 400, 3, true);
tween3 = new Tween(sprite, "rotation", Strong.easeInOut,
                   0, 360, 4, true);
```

Note that the rotation ease uses the Strong ease class and takes four seconds, whereas x and y use Regular and three seconds. Note that in these cases, I made additional tween properties to hold these new tweens:

```
private var tween1:Tween;
private var tween2:Tween;
private var tween3:Tween;
```

Sequences are a bit more complex: you need to wait for one ease to finish before starting the next. To do this, listen for an event that tells you when the tween has completed (the TweenEvent.MOTION_ FINISH event). Suppose that you want the three tweens from the last example to run one after another instead of all at once. The next class, available in the FlashTweenSequence.as file, gives a simple example of how to do this:

```
package {
    import fl.transitions.Tween;
    import fl.transitions.TweenEvent;
    import fl.transitions.easing.Regular;
    import fl.transitions.easing.Strong;

    import flash.display.Sprite;
    import flash.display.StageAlign;
    import flash.display.StageScaleMode;

    [SWF(backgroundColor=0xffffff)]
    public class FlashTweenSequence extends Sprite
    {
        private var tween1:Tween;
        private var tween2:Tween;
        private var tween3:Tween;
        private var sprite:Sprite;
```

```
        public function FlashTweenSequence()
        {
            stage.scaleMode = StageScaleMode.NO_SCALE;
            stage.align = StageAlign.TOP_LEFT;

            sprite = new Sprite();
            sprite.graphics.beginFill(0xff0000);
            sprite.graphics.drawRect(-50, -25, 100, 50);
            sprite.graphics.endFill();
            sprite.x = 100;
            sprite.y = 100;
            addChild(sprite);

            tween1 = new Tween(sprite, "x",
                            Regular.easeInOut,
                            100, 800, 3, true);
            tween1.addEventListener(TweenEvent.MOTION_FINISH,
                            onTween1Finish);
        }

        private function onTween1Finish(event:TweenEvent):void
        {
            tween2 = new Tween(sprite, "y",
                            Regular.easeInOut,
                            100, 400, 3, true);
            tween2.addEventListener(TweenEvent.MOTION_FINISH,
                            onTween2Finish);
        }

        private function onTween2Finish(event:TweenEvent):void
        {
            tween3 = new Tween(sprite, "rotation",
                            Strong.easeInOut,
                            0, 360, 4, true);
        }
    }
}
```

Here we create the first tween and immediately add an event listener for the MOTION_FINISH event. When this completes, we create the second tween and listen for the same event on that. When that fires, we create the final tween. I kept it simple here, but in a more complete application you'd also want to manage your event listeners, removing them if you were done with them, and so on.

If you have a complex interface with lots of things moving around, you can wind up with lots of event handlers and a nightmare of logic to keep track of. Of course, there are other ways of structuring something like that, maybe with a single event handler that checks the target of the event and acts accordingly. But no matter what you do, it will get complicated.

It was the desire to solve problems like this that gave rise to the various tween engines discussed later in the chapter. But before we do that, let's take a quick look at the Tween class that comes with the Flex framework.

Flex Tween Class

Although the Flex Tween class is part of the Flex framework, you don't need to create a Flex project to use it; you can use it directly in an ActionScript 3.0 project, or even from a Flash CS4–based movie. However, to use this in a non–Flex-based project, you need to add the framework.swc file to your library path. This SWC is located in the folder where your Flex framework is installed. Within that folder, it's in the frameworks/libs/framework.swc path.

In Flex Builder, you add SWCs through the Project Properties panel, ActionScript Build Path section, and Library Path tab (see Figure 10-1).

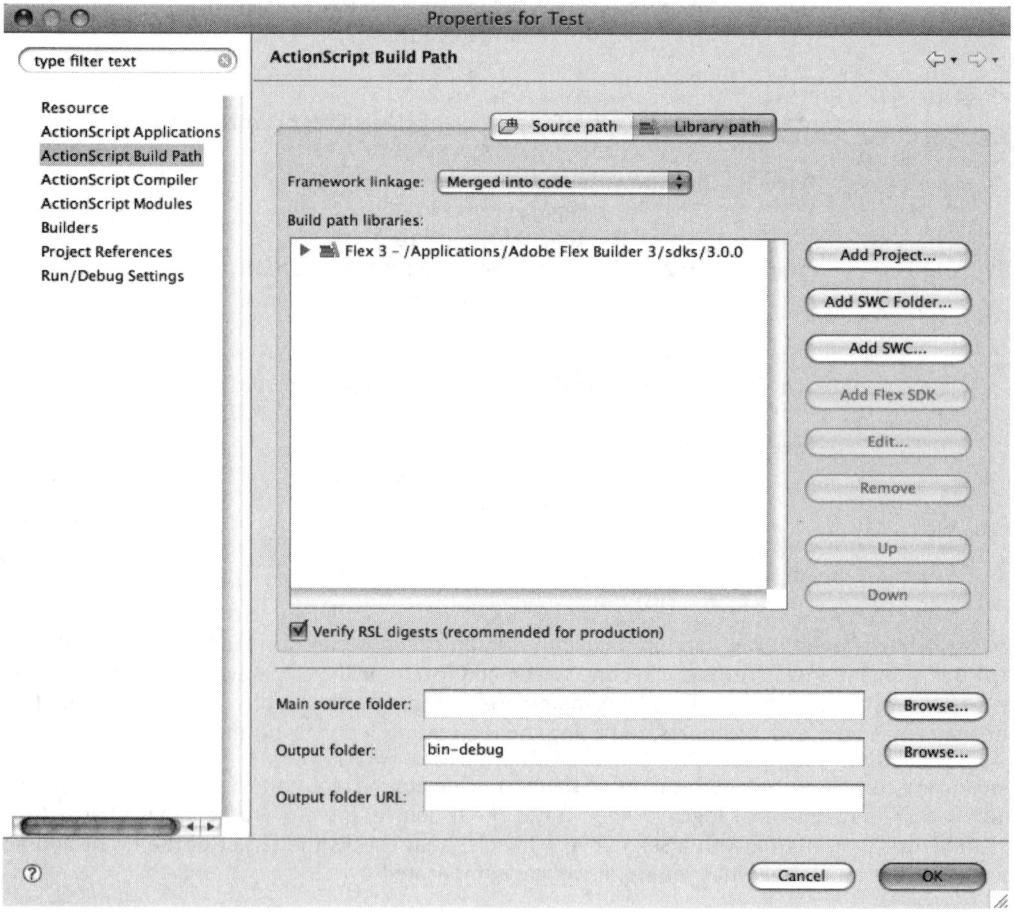

Figure 10-1. Add SWCs in this dialog box

Click Add SWC and browse to the framework.swc file. See Figure 10-2.

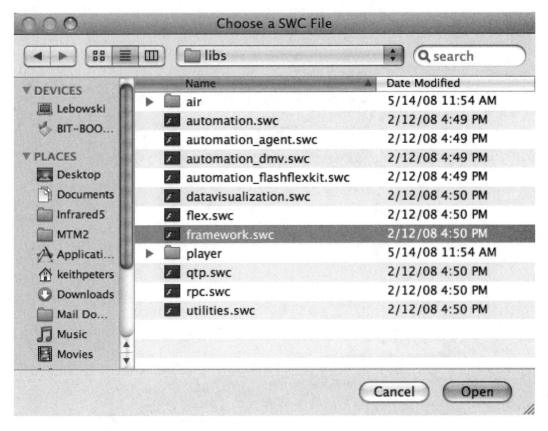

Figure 10-2. Adding the file

In Flash CS4, open up the Publish Settings panel, click the ActionScript 3.0 Settings button, and go to the Library Path section. See Figure 10-3.

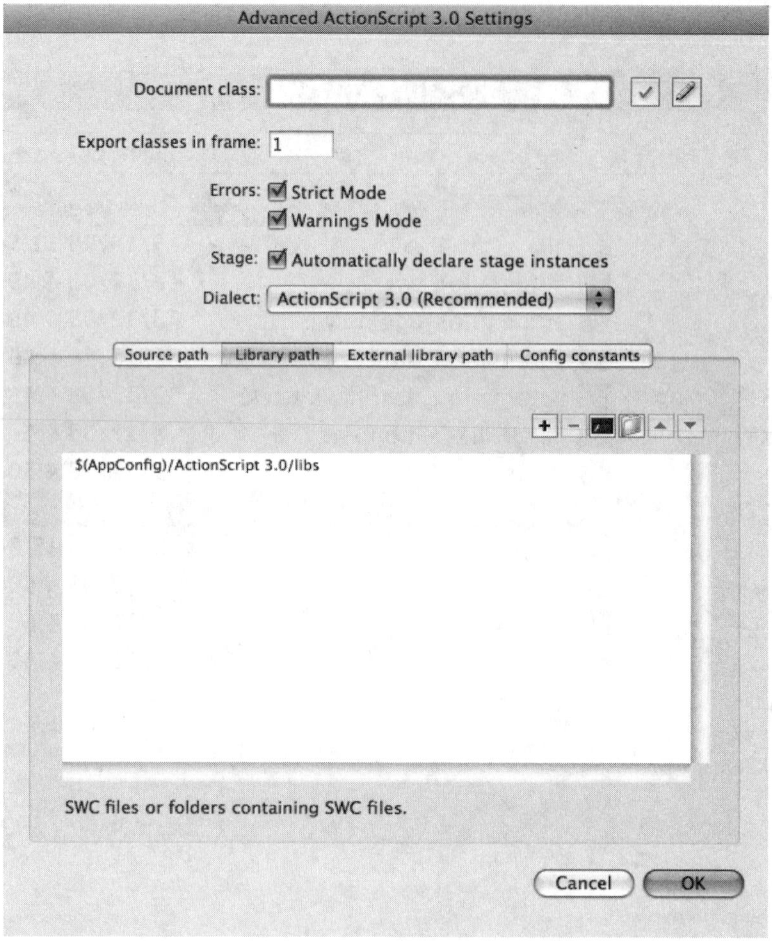

Figure 10-3. Library Path section

Click the + icon to add a new entry to the list, and then click the red icon two spots over to browse to the framework.swc file. When you are done, the panel should look something like Figure 10-4.

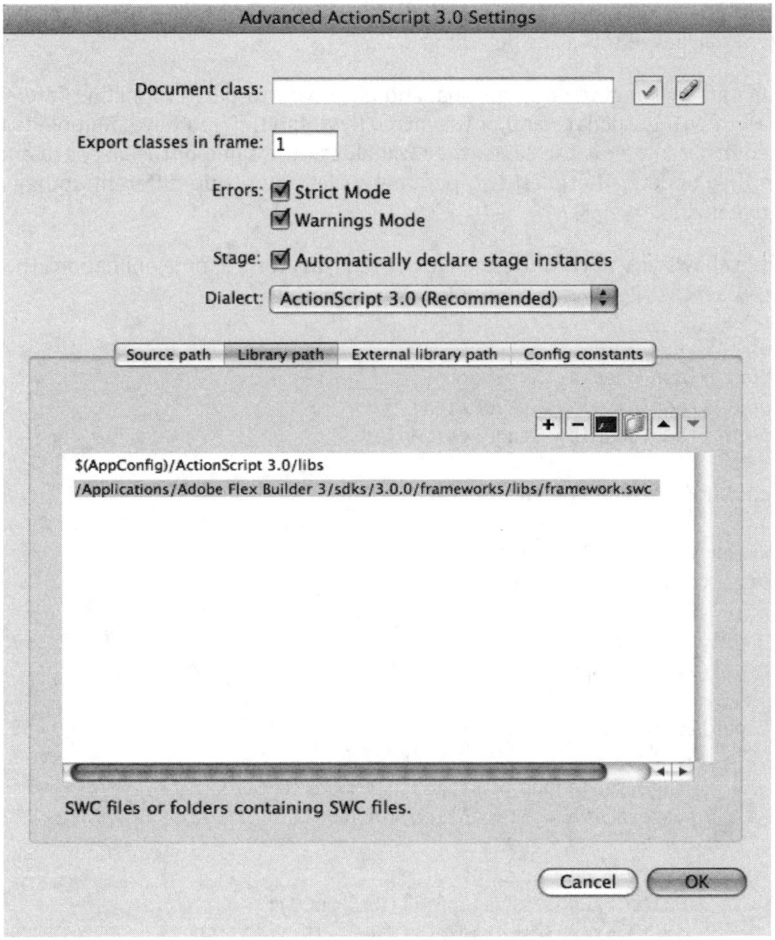

Figure 10-4. The file added to the library path

Adding this SWC to your project does not put the entire Flex framework into your final SWF—only the classes you reference in your code and any dependent classes (which are not many in the case of Tween).

The Flex Tween class is a bit different from the Flash one. You don't supply an object and property to the tween itself, just a listener object, start and end values, and duration. The listener object should have methods on it that will be called as the tween updates and when it finishes. These methods should be named onTweenUpdate and onTweenEnd. Both should take a single argument of type Object. Here is the full constructor for mx.effects.Tween:

```
new Tween(listener, startValue, endValue, duration,
          minFps, updateFunction, endFunction);
```

The minFPS parameter is optional, and it sets a minimum number of times per second the tween will run. You can generally leave this at its default value of −1.

updateFunction and endFunction are optional and allow you to pass in function references that will be called instead of onTweenUpdate and onTweenEnd. By default, if you have multiple tweens running, and their listener parameter is the same, they will all call the same onTweenUpdate and onTweenEnd functions when they update. These last two parameters let you set up different update and end handlers for each tween.

The next example shows you how to use the Flex Tween class for a simple animation. The class is available in the FlexTween.as file:

```
package {
    import flash.display.Sprite;
    import flash.display.StageAlign;
    import flash.display.StageScaleMode;

    import mx.effects.Tween;

    [SWF(backgroundColor=0xffffff)]
    public class FlexTween extends Sprite
    {
        private var tween:Tween;
        private var sprite:Sprite;

        public function FlexTween()
        {
            stage.scaleMode = StageScaleMode.NO_SCALE;
            stage.align = StageAlign.TOP_LEFT;

            sprite = new Sprite();
            sprite.graphics.beginFill(0xff0000);
            sprite.graphics.drawRect(-50, -25, 100, 50);
            sprite.graphics.endFill();
            sprite.x = 100;
            sprite.y = 100;
            addChild(sprite);

            tween = new Tween(this, 100, 800, 1000);
        }

        public function onTweenUpdate(value:Object):void
        {
            sprite.x = value as Number;
        }
```

```
        public function onTweenEnd(value:Object):void
        {
            sprite.x = value as Number;
        }
    }
}
```

Here we create the new Tween passing in this as the listener. Doing so makes the tween look at the FlexTween class itself for the update and end handlers. We set a start value of 100, an end value of 800, and a duration of 1000. Here's another difference between the Flash and Flex Tween classes. Although the flash Tween class interprets duration in terms of frames by default but can be forced to use seconds, the Flex Tween class simply uses milliseconds (1000 milliseconds is 1 second).

Also note that the start and end values are simply numeric values; they don't yet relate to any property, position, or anything else. They simply get passed through to the update and end handlers, and it's up to you to do what you want with them there.

In the handler functions, these values get passed through as objects instead of numbers, and you'll see why in a moment. The first time onTweenUpdate is called, the value passed through will be slightly more than the start value. The last time it is called, it will be slightly less than the end value. When onTweenEnd is finally called, its value parameter will be exactly equal to the end value. Here, we simply cast value as a Number and assign it to sprite.x. A bit more complex than the Flash Tween class, but it has a bit more power, too.

Easing functions for the Flex Tween class

Like its Flash cousin, the Flex Tween class allows you to specify an easing function. Here, though, you don't do this in the constructor, but instead on the instance after it has been created. Similar to Flash, these easing functions are methods (easeIn, easeOut, easeInOut) on a set of classes in an easing package. The package is mx.effects.easing, and the classes are as follows:

- Back
- Bounce
- Circular
- Cubic
- Elastic
- Exponential
- Linear
- Quadratic
- Quartic
- Quintic
- Sine

These classes are a bit more mathematically oriented than the Flash classes. The Back, Bounce, and Elastic classes are essentially the same as those with the same name in Flash. Linear is equivalent to None in Flash. This leaves us with Circular, Cubic, Exponential, Quadratic, Quartic, Quintic, and Sine. Probably the easiest way to explain these classes is to point you to Robert Penner's site, where he has an easing equation visualizer, which lets you choose an equation and move an object with that formula. It also gives a visual graph of how the velocity will change over time. The URL for the demo is the following:

```
http://www.robertpenner.com/easing/easing_demo.html
```

Incidentally, if you do not assign an easing function, the default one is Sine.easeInOut. So now let's try some other ones. Right after you create the tween, assign an easing function:

```
tween = new Tween(this, 100, 800, 1000);
tween.easingFunction = Linear.easeIn;
```

Don't forget to import whatever easing class you are using. I just tried Linear in the last example, which is the same as None in Flash. So this performs a constant speed motion from start to end. Try a few others and see how they work. Here's Quintic.easeInOut, which has a very sharp acceleration curve:

```
tween.easingFunction = Quintic.easeInOut;
```

It is different from Sine or Quadratic, which have much more gradual changes in speed.

Multiple tweens

In the Flash Tween class, if you wanted to tween multiple properties of a single object, you had to make multiple tweens. In the Flex version, you can use the same tween-to-tween multiple values. The way this works is that instead of assigning single numerical values for the start and end values, you assign an array of values. Now you see why these parameters, as well as the value parameters passed to the update and end event handlers, are typed as objects: they can be simple numbers or arrays of numbers. This is shown in the next class, available for download as FlexTweenXY.as:

```
package {
    import flash.display.Sprite;
    import flash.display.StageAlign;
    import flash.display.StageScaleMode;

    import mx.effects.Tween;
    import mx.effects.easing.Quintic;

    [SWF(backgroundColor=0xffffff)]
    public class FlexTweenXY extends Sprite
    {
        private var tween:Tween;
        private var sprite:Sprite;

        public function FlexTweenXY()
        {
            stage.scaleMode = StageScaleMode.NO_SCALE;
            stage.align = StageAlign.TOP_LEFT;
```

```
            sprite = new Sprite();
            sprite.graphics.beginFill(0xff0000);
            sprite.graphics.drawRect(-50, -25, 100, 50);
            sprite.graphics.endFill();
            sprite.x = 100;
            sprite.y = 100;
            addChild(sprite);

            tween = new Tween(this, [100, 100], [800, 400], 1000);
        }

        public function onTweenUpdate(value:Object):void
        {
            sprite.x = value[0];
            sprite.y = value[1];
        }

        public function onTweenEnd(value:Object):void
        {
            sprite.x = value[0];
            sprite.y = value[1];
        }
    }
}
```

In the constructor we pass in an array of two values for both start and end values. Again, they don't inherently have any meaning; they are just two numerical values. The Tween class will interpolate between all elements of the arrays smoothly, and the interpolated values will come in as an array in the handlers. In the handlers, we can interpret them whichever way we want. In this case, I'm taking the first element as the x position and the second element as the y position. So I want the sprite to move from 100 to 800 on x and 100 to 400 on y. Now we are tweening in two dimensions.

Another way of using this Tween class is to simply pass 0 and 1 as start and end values, and do your own calculations within the handlers. Something like this:

```
package {
    import flash.display.Sprite;
    import flash.display.StageAlign;
    import flash.display.StageScaleMode;

    import mx.effects.Tween;

    [SWF(backgroundColor=0xffffff)]
    public class FlexTweenXY extends Sprite
    {
        private var tween:Tween;
        private var sprite:Sprite;

        public function FlexTweenXY()
        {
```

```
                    stage.scaleMode = StageScaleMode.NO_SCALE;
                    stage.align = StageAlign.TOP_LEFT;

                    sprite = new Sprite();
                    sprite.graphics.beginFill(0xff0000);
                    sprite.graphics.drawRect(-50, -25, 100, 50);
                    sprite.graphics.endFill();
                    sprite.x = 100;
                    sprite.y = 100;
                    addChild(sprite);

                    tween = new Tween(this, 0, 1, 1000);
                }

                public function onTweenUpdate(value:Object):void
                {
                    sprite.x = 100 + 700 * (value as Number);
                    sprite.y = 100 + 300 * (value as Number);
                }

                public function onTweenEnd(value:Object):void
                {
                    sprite.x = 100 + 700 * (value as Number);
                    sprite.y = 100 + 300 * (value as Number);
                }
            }
        }
```

The value parameter will now be something between 0 and 1. We multiply that by the total distance we want it to move and add it to the starting position. This is not quite as straightforward as passing in direct values, but this method can be extremely useful when you need a lot of flexibility. For example, say you wanted to have one object fade in while another fades out. Do a 0 to 1 tween and do this in the handler:

```
public function onTweenUpdate(value:Object):void
{
    obj1.alpha = value as Number;
    obj2.alpha = 1.0 - value as Number;
}
```

As the value goes from 0 to 1, so does the obj1 alpha. But the obj2 alpha will go from 1 to 0. Single tween, dual fade.

Tween sequences

Unfortunately, sequences are not much simpler with the Flex Tween than they are in Flash. The mx.effects package does have additional classes for doing parallel and sequential tweens, but they are much more tied to the Flex framework itself and are really meant to be used within a Flex-based application (unlike Tween, which can easily be used by itself).

When sequencing tweens with the Flex Tween class, you need to wait for the onTweenEnd handler to fire; if you have specified another handler, you also need to wait for it to fire. The next class, as seen in the FlexTweenSequence.as file, demonstrates this. This class essentially duplicates the functionality of the earlier example class FlashTweenSequence. The key points are in bold:

```
package {
    import flash.display.Sprite;
    import flash.display.StageAlign;
    import flash.display.StageScaleMode;

    import mx.effects.Tween;

    [SWF(backgroundColor=0xffffff)]
    public class FlexTweenSequence extends Sprite
    {
        private var tween1:Tween;
        private var tween2:Tween;
        private var tween3:Tween;
        private var sprite:Sprite;

        public function FlexTweenSequence()
        {
            stage.scaleMode = StageScaleMode.NO_SCALE;
            stage.align = StageAlign.TOP_LEFT;

            sprite = new Sprite();
            sprite.graphics.beginFill(0xff0000);
            sprite.graphics.drawRect(-50, -25, 100, 50);
            sprite.graphics.endFill();
            sprite.x = 100;
            sprite.y = 100;
            addChild(sprite);

            tween1 = new Tween(this, 100, 800, 3000,
                            -1, onTween1Update, onTween1End);
        }

        public function onTween1Update(value:Object):void
        {
            sprite.x = value as Number;
        }

        public function onTween1End(value:Object):void
        {
            sprite.x = value as Number;
            tween2 = new Tween(this, 100, 400, 3000,
                            -1, onTween2Update, onTween2End);
        }
```

```
        public function onTween2Update(value:Object):void
        {
            sprite.y = value as Number;
        }

        public function onTween2End(value:Object):void
        {
            sprite.y = value as Number;
            tween3 = new Tween(this, 0, 360, 4000,
                                -1, onTween3Update, onTween3End);
        }

        public function onTween3Update(value:Object):void
        {
            sprite.rotation = value as Number;
        }

        public function onTween3End(value:Object):void
        {
            sprite.rotation = value as Number;
        }
    }
}
```

The first tween update handler changes the x value, the second changes the y value, and the third changes the rotation of the sprite. As each tween ends, it creates the next tween.

This code is not too pretty and is for a relatively simple three-part motion. Some fancy interfaces might have dozens of these synchronized and sequenced tweens. Of course, I didn't go out of my way to make the code pretty. There are various improvements you can make and patterns you can apply that make the code a bit clearer, more concise, and even reusable. And going down this road is how you end up with a tween engine, which is what I'll discuss next.

Tween Engines

By now, I think you know why a tween engine is a good thing: it can make coding complex multiple tweens of multiple properties on multiple objects a lot more manageable. Again, I chose a number of different engines to take a look at, not because they are my favorite or "the best," but because they are fairly popular and demonstrate a range of different approaches to the problems. Some of them are very developer-oriented and require a fair bit of code to get working. Others are more designer-oriented and are easy to work with, but some of the coding conventions would make a hard-core developer cry: untyped parameters, generic objects, "magic strings," function callbacks in lieu of events, and so on. The engine you use ultimately depends on which one fits best with your workflow and team and gives you the functionality you need.

Again, the engines covered are as follows:

- Tweener
- TweenLite/TweenGroup

- KitchenSync
- gTween

Let's get started with Tweener.

Tweener

The Tweener tween engine has gained a fair amount of popularity over the years. It started as an ActionScript 2.0 engine and was ported to ActionScript 3.0. Both versions are still available. In fact, Tweener is at least in part based on an earlier ActionScript 1.0 engine called MC Tween, which was released in 2003. Tweener was originally written by Zeh Fernando (http://zehfernando.com), but has had contributions from several others.

To install Tweener, download the source files from the Google code repository: http://code.google.com/p/tweener/. The top-level folder of the package is named caurina. Put that folder in the same folder as the rest of the source files for your project (or in a location where your development environment can find it). The main class for the engine is caurina.transitions.Tweener.

The Tweener syntax is pretty easy to get used to. Unlike the Adobe Tween classes, you never make an instance of the main class, Tweener. Instead, you call static methods on Tweener. The main method is addTween; it looks like this:

```
Tweener.addTween(target, tweeningParameters);
```

Both target and tweeningParameters are typed as Objects. The target is the object you want to affect—usually a movie clip, sprite, or some other display object (although it can be anything with at least one numeric public property that can be changed). The tweeningParameters parameter is a generic object with various properties that allow you to specify the tween values, easing function, duration, and so on. So you might call it something like this, which moves the object named sprite to an x location of 800 in 3 seconds:

```
Tweener.addTween(sprite, {x:800, time:3});
```

Or this, which moves the sprite to an x, y position of 800, 400:

```
Tweener.addTween(sprite, {x:800, y:400, time:3});
```

Obviously, this procedure is far simpler than either of the Adobe Tween classes. Any properties you add to the tweeningParameters object will be tweened on the target object. Notice that there is no starting value. The starting values are presumed to be the target object's current values for each tweened property. Also important to realize is that the values specified in tweeningParameters are absolute target values. In other words, the sprite will *not* move 800 pixels on the x-axis and 400 pixels on the y-axis. Instead, it will move *to* location 800, 400.

The generic object tweeningParameters is one of Tweener's strengths and one of the reasons why many more serious developers might not like it. On one hand, it gives you enormous flexibility, allowing you to tween just about any public numeric property on any type of object. For example, even though Tweener was written long before Flash 10 was released, you can use it to tween the 3D properties of a sprite in Flash 10 with no problems whatsoever:

```
Tweener.addTween(sprite, {x:800, z:800,
                          rotationX:180, rotationY:270,
                          time:3});
```

On the other hand, because a generic object is used, and you can put any property of any type on a generic object, you can do all kinds of crazy things that will never work. The compiler will happily compile it, and you'll only notice when you start throwing run-time errors—if you have the debug player installed. For example, you could try a tween like this:

```
Tweener.addTween(sprite, {dog:800, time:3});
```

Obviously, dog is not a property of the Sprite class and has no business being there. It will blow up when you run the SWF, of course, but this will compile without any warning. Furthermore, you can start passing wrong types in, like so:

```
Tweener.addTween(sprite, {x:"dog", time:3});
```

Now we all know x should be a number, but if for some reason a string winds up getting in there, you lose all compile time type-checking. This won't even complain at run time. The sprite simply disappears off screen to whatever numerical x location the string "dog" resolves to. On the other hand, Tweener is smart enough to convert a number formatted as a string to a number. So the following works just fine:

```
Tweener.addTween(sprite, {x:"800", time:3});
```

Easing functions in Tweener

Easing functions are also specified in the tweeningParameters object. And not surprisingly, they are based on Robert Penner's equations. However, the classes and methods themselves are hidden. You just pass in a string describing the type of ease you want; for example:

```
Tweener.addTween(sprite, {x:800, time:3, transition:"easeInOutCubic"});
```

See the Tweener documentation for a full list of transition strings.

Again, this is probably much easier for a designer who just needs to remember a name, not the classpath, class name, and method name. But what if you accidentally misspell it: "easeInOutCubix"? It would compile just fine, and even run just fine, but the easing formula would revert to the default value, "easeOutExpo", which you might not notice until several weeks later when the client says that something about the interface just doesn't "look as nice" as it used to.

I'm not saying these types of issues are reasons why you should not use Tweener; I'm just pointing them out as things to be aware of when evaluating the various engines. (Note that Tweener is not the only engine that uses this type of syntax.)

Multiple tweens in Tweener

Tweens in Tweener are added on a per-object basis. So if you want to tween multiple objects, make multiple tweens:

```
Tweener.addTween(spriteA, {x:"800", time:3});
Tweener.addTween(spriteB, {x:"300", time:3});
```

I think this is offset by the fact that you can so easily tween multiple properties on a single object.

Sequences in Tweener

Another benefit of using Tweener is that it starts to make sequences much easier. There are actually two ways to run one tween after another has completed. First, you can set up an onComplete callback in the tweeningParams object. This is simply a function reference; the function will be called when the tween is complete. It looks like this:

```
Tweener.addTween(spriteA, {x:"800", time:3, onComplete:tweenEnd});
```

Here, tweenEnd is a reference to a function that will be called when the tween is done. So when one tween is done, you might want to add another. I did this in the next demo, which you can download as the TweenerSequence.as file:

```
package {
    import caurina.transitions.Tweener;

    import flash.display.Sprite;
    import flash.display.StageAlign;
    import flash.display.StageScaleMode;

    [SWF(backgroundColor=0xffffff)]
    public class TweenerSequence extends Sprite
    {
        private var sprite:Sprite;

        public function TweenerSequence()
        {
            stage.scaleMode = StageScaleMode.NO_SCALE;
            stage.align = StageAlign.TOP_LEFT;

            sprite = new Sprite();
            sprite.graphics.beginFill(0xff0000);
            sprite.graphics.drawRect(-50, -25, 100, 50);
            sprite.graphics.endFill();
            sprite.x = 100;
            sprite.y = 100;
            addChild(sprite);

            Tweener.addTween(sprite,
                        {x:800, time:3,
                         transition:"easeInOutCubic",
                         onComplete:tween1End});
        }
```

```
            private function tween1End():void
            {
                Tweener.addTween(sprite,
                            {y:400, time:3,
                             transition:"easeInOutCubic",
                             onComplete:tween2End});
            }

            private function tween2End():void
            {
                Tweener.addTween(sprite,
                            {rotation:360, time:4,
                             transition:"easeInOutCubic"});
            }
        }
    }
```

When the first tween is complete, tween1End is called, which sets up another tween. When that's done, tween2End is called, which sets up the last tween. This is a bit easier than setting up sequences in the Adobe Tween classes, but Tweener offers another way that is even easier: the delay property.

Another property you can add to tweeningParameters is delay. This is a number in terms of seconds that Tweener should wait before executing that tween. So you can set up something like it in the next example (download TweenerDelay.as):

```
package {
    import caurina.transitions.Tweener;

    import flash.display.Sprite;
    import flash.display.StageAlign;
    import flash.display.StageScaleMode;

    [SWF(backgroundColor=0xffffff)]
    public class TweenerDelay extends Sprite
    {
        private var sprite:Sprite;

        public function TweenerDelay()
        {
            stage.scaleMode = StageScaleMode.NO_SCALE;
            stage.align = StageAlign.TOP_LEFT;

            sprite = new Sprite();
            sprite.graphics.beginFill(0xff0000);
            sprite.graphics.drawRect(-50, -25, 100, 50);
            sprite.graphics.endFill();
            sprite.x = 100;
            sprite.y = 100;
            addChild(sprite);
```

```
Tweener.addTween(sprite,
                 {x:800, time:3,
                  transition:"easeInOutCubic"});
Tweener.addTween(sprite,
                 {y:400, time:3,
                  transition:"easeInOutCubic",
                  delay:3});
Tweener.addTween(sprite,
                 {rotation:360, time:4,
                  transition:"easeInOutCubic",
                  delay:6});
        }
    }
}
```

Here you just set up all your tweens directly. The first one will take three seconds, so we tell the second one to wait that long before starting. Likewise, we tell the last one to wait six seconds. The result is that all three tweens play out perfectly in sequence.

One situation to be careful of when using a delay is tweening the same property of the same object twice with a delay. As long as the delay of the second tween is at least as long as the time of the first tween, both will play out. In this case the sprite will move over to 800 on the x-axis and then move to 100:

```
Tweener.addTween(sprite, {x:800, time:3});
Tweener.addTween(sprite, {x:100, time:3, delay:3});
```

But if the delay of the second tween causes it to cut into the time of the first one, the first tween will simply be overwritten by the second and not play at all.

```
Tweener.addTween(sprite, {x:800, time:3});
Tweener.addTween(sprite, {x:100, time:3, delay:2.5});
```

Here, the sprite does not move at all for 2.5 seconds and then moves to 100 on the x-axis.

That should give you a pretty good idea of what Tweener is all about. As you can see, it provides some nice shortcuts to making complex tweens with minimal code and with easy-to-understand syntax. And there are plenty of other useful features available—just browse through the documentation on the site listed previously. Some of the more hard-core developers might wince a bit at the looseness of data types, but for many Tweener is an improvement over the Adobe classes.

TweenLite/TweenGroup

The next package consists of a couple of classes written by Jack Doyle of www.greensock.com. You can get the code from http://blog.greensock.com/tweenliteas3/ and, like Tweener, simply add the top-level folder, gs, to your project directory or somewhere else where your compiler can to find it. The main class is in the top level of that package: gs.TweenLite.

If you followed along with the previous section or are already familiar with Tweener, TweenLite should be very easy for you. According to its author, the goal was to make TweenLite more compact, faster, and more efficient than tween engines such as Tweener. This chapter also takes a look at TweenGroup, which is a dedicated class for making parallel tweens, tween sequences, and other coordinated groups of tweens.

Like Tweener, you can create a tween by calling a static method on the TweenLite class; in this case, TweenLite.to:

```
TweenLite.to(sprite, 3, {x:800});
```

Here, you pass in the target object as a first parameter and the duration of the tween as the second parameter. The third parameter is variables, and like Tweener's tweeningParameters object, it is a generic object with properties that you want to tween. So the preceding example will move the object named sprite to an x position of 800 in 3 seconds.

Calling this to method will return an instance of the TweenLite class. You can then use this instance to further tweak the tween:

```
var tween1:TweenLite = TweenLite.to(sprite, 3, {x:800});
```

But even more intuitively, you can just make a new instance of the class. The constructor has the same syntax as the to method:

```
var tween1:TweenLite = new TweenLite(sprite, 3, {x:800});
```

Let's put that all together in a class you can actually run (available as the TweenLiteDemo1.as file):

```
package {

    import flash.display.*;

    import gs.TweenLite;

    [SWF(backgroundColor=0xffffff)]
    public class TweenLiteDemo1 extends Sprite
    {
        private var sprite:Sprite;
        private var tween:TweenLite;

        public function TweenLiteDemo1()
        {
            stage.scaleMode = StageScaleMode.NO_SCALE;
            stage.align = StageAlign.TOP_LEFT;

            sprite = new Sprite();
            sprite.graphics.beginFill(0xff0000);
            sprite.graphics.drawRect(-50, -25, 100, 50);
            sprite.graphics.endFill();
```

```
        sprite.x = 100;
        sprite.y = 100;
        addChild(sprite);

        tween = new TweenLite(sprite, 3, {x:800});
    }
  }
}
```

The key lines are in bold. You can easily tween multiple properties by adding them to the variables object:

```
tween = new TweenLite(sprite, 3, {x:800, y:400, rotation:360});
```

Like Tweener, this again opens up the possibility of passing in nonexistent properties or incorrect data types in the variables object. So be careful.

Easing functions in TweenLite

Here's where TweenLite gets a little more programmer-ish. Instead of magic strings for easing functions, it does use method names on various classes, just like the Adobe Tween classes.

Not surprisingly, these easing classes are directly based on Robert Penner's easing equations (are you bowing down to him yet?) and are in the gs.easing package:

- Back
- Bounce
- Circ
- Cubic
- Elastic
- Expo
- Linear
- Quad
- Quart
- Quint
- Sine
- Strong

Each has three methods: easeIn, easeOut, and easeInOut. Like the Adobe Tween classes, you choose the type of ease by specifying the class and the method. This goes in the variables object, assigned to the ease property:

```
tween = new TweenLite(sprite, 3, {x:800, y:400, rotation:360,
                            ease:Elastic.easeInOut});
```

Make sure to import any easing classes you are using or the entire gs.easing.* package.

Alternately, because you now have a reference to the tween, you can specify the ease type there:

```
tween = new TweenLite(sprite, 3, {x:800, y:400, rotation:360});
tween.ease = Elastic.easeInOut;
```

Multiple tweens in TweenLite

Again, tweening multiple objects generally means making multiple tweens:

```
tween1 = new TweenLite(spriteA, 3, {x:800});
tween2 = new TweenLite(spriteB, 3, {x:100});
```

This tweens one sprite to 800 on the x-axis, while simultaneously tweening another to 100.

However, you can use TweenGroup to do this in a much more concise manner. The TweenGroup class is also in the gs package and should be installed when you install TweenLite. It's a pretty powerful class that can be used several ways. If you are tweening a number of objects on the same properties, you can tween them all at once with the TweenGroup.allTo static method. This works just like the TweenLite. to method, but accepts an array of objects as the first parameter, instead of just a single object:

```
TweenGroup.allTo([s1, s2, s3, s4], 3, {x:800});
```

Here, s1, s2, s3, and s4 (presumably 4 different sprites) will all be tweened to an x position of 800 over the next 3 seconds. Here's a full class so you can see it in action (you can download this class as TweenGroupDemo1.as):

```
package {

    import flash.display.*;

    import gs.TweenGroup;

    [SWF(backgroundColor=0xffffff)]
    public class TweenGroupDemo1 extends Sprite
    {
        private var sprite:Sprite;
        private var group:TweenGroup;

        public function TweenGroupDemo1()
        {
            stage.scaleMode = StageScaleMode.NO_SCALE;
            stage.align = StageAlign.TOP_LEFT;

            var s1:Sprite = makeSprite(100, 100, 0xff0000);
            var s2:Sprite = makeSprite(100, 200, 0x00ff00);
            var s3:Sprite = makeSprite(100, 300, 0x0000ff);
            var s4:Sprite = makeSprite(100, 400, 0xffff00);

            TweenGroup.allTo([s1, s2, s3, s4], 3, {x:800});
        }
```

```
                private function makeSprite(xpos:Number,
                                            ypos:Number,
                                            color:uint):Sprite
        {
            var s:Sprite = new Sprite();
            s.graphics.beginFill(color);
            s.graphics.drawRect(-50, -25, 100, 50);
            s.graphics.endFill();
            s.x = xpos;
            s.y = ypos;
            addChild(s);
            return s;
        }
    }
}
```

I added a makeSprite method that allows us to easily create any number of sprites, and then position and color them in a single line of code. We make four sprites and position them vertically. Then we pass them all into TweenGroup.allTo to start them moving.

Note that TweenGroup.allTo returns an instance of TweenGroup, which you can then keep track of and alter as needed:

```
var tg:TweenGroup = TweenGroup.allTo([s1, s2, s3, s4], 3, {x:800});
```

Sequences in TweenLite/TweenGroup

I think that the sequencing capabilities in TweenLite and TweenGroup are what make this package really shine.

Like Tweener, TweenLite has a delay property that can be used to delay a tween. But there is a major difference that actually gives you a bit more flexibility. First, going back to an example with a single sprite, we sequence three tweens like so (TweenLiteSequence1.as):

```
package {

    import flash.display.*;

    import gs.TweenLite;
    import gs.easing.Elastic;

    [SWF(backgroundColor=0xffffff)]
    public class TweenLiteSequence1 extends Sprite
    {
        private var sprite:Sprite;
        private var tween1:TweenLite;
        private var tween2:TweenLite;
        private var tween3:TweenLite;

        public function TweenLiteSequence1()
        {
```

```
        stage.scaleMode = StageScaleMode.NO_SCALE;
        stage.align = StageAlign.TOP_LEFT;

        sprite = new Sprite();
        sprite.graphics.beginFill(0xff0000);
        sprite.graphics.drawRect(-50, -25, 100, 50);
        sprite.graphics.endFill();
        sprite.x = 100;
        sprite.y = 100;
        addChild(sprite);

        tween1 = new TweenLite(sprite, 3, {x:800});
        tween2 = new TweenLite(sprite, 3, {y:400, delay:3});
        tween3 = new TweenLite(sprite, 3, {rotation:360, delay:6});
      }
    }
  }
```

When you run this, nothing happens for six seconds and then the final tween runs. In TweenLite, any tween on an object overwrites any previous tween by default—even if you are tweening different properties and have sufficient delay between the tweens. You'll remember that Tweener overwrites only if two tweens share the same property and overlap in time.

Fortunately, you can control this behavior with the overwrite property on the variables object. This takes a number from 0 to 4, meaning the following:

- 0: NONE mode. No tweens are overwritten.
- 1: ALL mode. All tweens are overwritten by any new tween on the same object.
- 2: AUTO mode. This works like Tweener's overwrite logic. Only overlapping tweens of the same property are overwritten.
- 3: CONCURRENT mode. Overwrites any overlapping tweens on the same object, regardless of property.

Unfortunately, the concept of overlapping does not seem to take into account the delay. So even if you set overwrite to 2 or 3 for tween2 and tween3 in the previous example, it would still result in only the last tween running because the first two will be overwritten.

So, to fix the previous file, set the overwrite property to 0, which will ensure that none of the tweens is ever overwritten:

```
tween1 = new TweenLite(sprite, 3, {x:800});
tween2 = new TweenLite(sprite, 3, {y:400, delay:3, overwrite:0});
tween3 = new TweenLite(sprite, 3,
                    {rotation:360, delay:6, overwrite:0});
```

Note that there is also a class called OverwriteManager in the TweenLite package that includes these values as static properties (that is, OverwriteManager.NONE, OverwriteManager.ALL, and so on). Although it's a bit more wordy, it does give you some compile-time checking and documentation of your intentions.

Another way to sequence is to wait for each tween to finish before starting the next one, which is almost exactly the same thing done in the earlier example, TweenerSequence:

```
package {

    import flash.display.*;

    import gs.TweenLite;
    import gs.easing.Elastic;

    [SWF(backgroundColor=0xffffff)]
    public class TweenLiteSequence2 extends Sprite
    {
        private var sprite:Sprite;
        private var tween1:TweenLite;
        private var tween2:TweenLite;
        private var tween3:TweenLite;

        public function TweenLiteSequence2()
        {
            stage.scaleMode = StageScaleMode.NO_SCALE;
            stage.align = StageAlign.TOP_LEFT;

            sprite = new Sprite();
            sprite.graphics.beginFill(0xff0000);
            sprite.graphics.drawRect(-50, -25, 100, 50);
            sprite.graphics.endFill();
            sprite.x = 100;
            sprite.y = 100;
            addChild(sprite);

            tween1 = new TweenLite(sprite, 3,
                            {x:800,
                                onComplete:onTween1End});
        }

        private function onTween1End():void
        {
            tween2 = new TweenLite(sprite, 3,
                            {y:400,
                                onComplete:onTween2End});
        }

        private function onTween2End():void
        {
            tween3 = new TweenLite(sprite, 3, {rotation:360});
        }
    }
}
```

We create the first tween and set the onComplete callback. When that fires, we create the next tween and set its onComplete callback. In the final callback we create the final tween. Of course, this is more complex than using a delay, but in cases when you might need to perform other actions as each tween finishes, it can be quite powerful. For example, when a navigation element finishes tweening on the stage, it then needs to populate itself with a callback.

Finally, TweenGroup gives us even more powerful ways to synchronize and sequence tweens. The first way to do this is to use the align property of a TweenGroup object, which can be set to a number of different modes and affects how the different tweens in a group play out together. For creating sequences, the most useful one is ALIGN_SEQUENCE. Going back to the TweenGroupDemo1 class we created a bit earlier in the section, we can turn the group into a sequence quite easily (the file for this example is TweenGroupDemo2.as):

```
package {

    import flash.display.*;

    import gs.TweenGroup;

    [SWF(backgroundColor=0xffffff)]
    public class TweenGroupDemo2 extends Sprite
    {
        private var sprite:Sprite;
        private var group:TweenGroup;

        public function TweenGroupDemo2()
        {
            stage.scaleMode = StageScaleMode.NO_SCALE;
            stage.align = StageAlign.TOP_LEFT;

            var s1:Sprite = makeSprite(100, 100, 0xff0000);
            var s2:Sprite = makeSprite(100, 200, 0x00ff00);
            var s3:Sprite = makeSprite(100, 300, 0x0000ff);
            var s4:Sprite = makeSprite(100, 400, 0xffff00);

            var tg:TweenGroup = TweenGroup.allTo([s1, s2, s3, s4],
                                                 1, {x:800});
            tg.align = TweenGroup.ALIGN_SEQUENCE;;
        }

        private function makeSprite(xpos:Number,
                                    ypos:Number,
                                    color:uint):Sprite
        {
            var s:Sprite = new Sprite();
            s.graphics.beginFill(color);
            s.graphics.drawRect(-50, -25, 100, 50);
            s.graphics.endFill();
            s.x = xpos;
            s.y = ypos;
```

```
                addChild(s);
                return s;
            }
        }
    }
```

Here we save the TweenGroup in the variable tg. We can then set the align property of the group to TweenGroup.ALIGN_SEQUENCE. This causes each tween in the group to happen only when the previous one has completed. When you run this, you'll see that as a group the four sprites go one by one instead of moving across the stage.

Now that's fine if we have several objects to tween in a sequence, but what if we want to have a single object tween in several different ways in a sequence (move on the x-axis, move on the y-axis, and then rotate)?

We can make tweens for all these actions and then make a group that runs them in sequence. You can see this in the next example, available as the TweenGroupDemo3.as file:

```
    package {

        import flash.display.*;

        import gs.TweenGroup;
        import gs.TweenLite;

        [SWF(backgroundColor=0xffffff)]
        public class TweenGroupDemo3 extends Sprite
        {
            private var sprite:Sprite;
            private var tween1:TweenLite;
            private var tween2:TweenLite;
            private var tween3:TweenLite;

            public function TweenGroupDemo3()
            {
                stage.scaleMode = StageScaleMode.NO_SCALE;
                stage.align = StageAlign.TOP_LEFT;

                sprite = new Sprite();
                sprite.graphics.beginFill(0xff0000);
                sprite.graphics.drawRect(-50, -25, 100, 50);
                sprite.graphics.endFill();
                sprite.x = 100;
                sprite.y = 100;
                addChild(sprite);

                tween1 = new TweenLite(sprite, 3, {x:800});
                tween2 = new TweenLite(sprite, 3, {y:400, overwrite:0});
                tween3 = new TweenLite(sprite, 3, {rotation:360,
                                            overwrite:0});
```

```
                    var tg:TweenGroup = new TweenGroup([tween1, tween2, tween3]);
                    tg.align = TweenGroup.ALIGN_SEQUENCE;
            }
        }
    }
```

At first glance, this seems a bit more complex than just using a delay because you're creating an extra object and setting a property on it. But it is so much more flexible. With a delay you have to keep track of the duration of all the tweens in a sequence and make sure that each delay adds up to the duration of all the tweens before it. Very easy to make an error! Of course, you could use variables for the durations and add the variables together to get a delay, but once you start doing that, it starts getting just as complex as using a group.

What we've touched on here is really only the tip of the iceberg of what is available with TweenLite and TweenGroup. And we haven't even looked at TweenLite's big brother, TweenMax, which adds a whole bunch of additional features. If you are doing a lot of complex sequenced tweens, these classes could save you.

KitchenSync

Our next tweening engine is KitchenSync, written by Mims Wright. You can download the project at the Google code site (http://code.google.com/p/kitchensynclib/) as either a source directory package or an SWC library. I trust that you know how to add source directories and/or SWC libraries to your build path. If not, see the installation notes page available on the KitchenSync site just mentioned.

The main class of the package is org.as3lib.kitchensync.KitchenSync. As a first action in the main document class of any KitchenSync project, you need to call KitchenSync.initialize(this). The use of this passes in a reference to the document class itself, but really you can pass in a reference to any display object. KitchenSync uses the display object passed in to listen for enterFrame events, which it uses to update the progress of any tweens or time-based actions.

After you initialize the engine, you can make a tween, which is an instance of org.as3lib.kitchensync.action.KSTween. The constructor looks like this:

```
    new KSTween(target, property, startValue, endValue, duration);
```

You can probably guess at most of these, but target is the object that you want to tween; property is a string representing the property you want to tween, such as "x", "y", "rotation"; start and end values are numeric values specifying where the property will start and end; and duration is how long the tween will last.

An interesting thing about the duration property is that it can take a number or a string. If you pass in a number, it is interpreted as milliseconds (so 3000 would be 3 seconds). However, you can pass in a string like "3sec" to represent the number of seconds the tween should last. That should be enough to get by for now, but check the documentation to see the various strings you can use.

Another thing that is different about KSTween from all the other tween classes we've looked at so far is that it does not start as soon as you create it. You'll need to call the start method on the KSTween instance, or else your tweened object will just sit there doing nothing.

Well, that's enough to get started. Let's make a KitchenSync tween (the next example is available as KitchenSyncDemo1.as):

```
package {
    import flash.display.Sprite;
    import flash.display.StageAlign;
    import flash.display.StageScaleMode;

    import org.as3lib.kitchensync.KitchenSync;
    import org.as3lib.kitchensync.action.KSTween;

    [SWF(backgroundColor=0xffffff)]
    public class KitchenSyncDemo1 extends Sprite
    {
        private var sprite:Sprite;

        public function KitchenSyncDemo1()
        {
            stage.scaleMode = StageScaleMode.NO_SCALE;
            stage.align = StageAlign.TOP_LEFT;

            sprite = new Sprite();
            sprite.graphics.beginFill(0xff0000);
            sprite.graphics.drawRect(-50, -25, 100, 50);
            sprite.graphics.endFill();
            sprite.x = 100;
            sprite.y = 100;
            addChild(sprite);

            KitchenSync.initialize(this);
            var tween:KSTween = new KSTween(sprite, "x",
                                    100, 800, 3000);
            tween.start();
        }
    }
}
```

The important lines are in bold. We initialize the engine, create a new tween that will move the sprite from 100 to 800 on the x-axis over 3 seconds, and start the tween. Magic.

Easing functions in KitchenSync

Guess who wrote the easing equations used by KitchenSync? Robert Penner! Yes, but in addition to the standard functions you've seen several times already, Mims has also included a few new classes of his own:

- Oscillate
- Random
- Sextic
- Stepped

Feel free to experiment with them, but now let's see how to specify an easing function. Basically, you just pass it in as the last argument to the KSTween constructor. However, there is one more, second-to-last optional argument: delay. If you are not using a delay, you can just pass in 0 and then the easing function. The easing classes are in the org.as3lib.kitchensync.easing package and, similar to the other implementations, they each have an easeIn, easeOut, and easeInOut method. So to use the Quartic.easeInOut function, do the following:

```
var tween:KSTween = new KSTween(sprite, "x", 100, 800, 3000,
                                0, Quartic.easeInOut);
```

Tweening multiple objects/properties with KitchenSync

Unlike Tweener or TweenLite, which allow you to tween several properties with one tween, with KitchenSync you have to create a new tween for each property. There is a shortcut for making a new tween: cloneWithTarget. You take an existing tween and call cloneWithTarget on it, passing in another (or the same) target object, and a property string. So you can do something like this:

```
var tween1:KSTween = new KSTween(sprite, "x", 100, 800, 3000,
                                 0, Quartic.easeInOut);
var tween2:KSTween = tween1.cloneWithTarget(sprite, "y");
tween1.start();
tween2.start();
```

But this will copy the start and end values as well. In almost all cases, you'll be using different values when tweening multiple properties of the same object. So this clone method seems to have limited usefulness in this case, and you are probably better off just creating a new tween:

```
var tween1:KSTween = new KSTween(sprite, "x", 100, 800, 3000,
                                 0, Quartic.easeInOut);
var tween2:KSTween = new KSTween(sprite, "y", 100, 400, 3000,
                                 0, Quartic.easeInOut);

tween1.start();
tween2.start();
```

Similarly, you'll need to create multiple tweens to tween multiple objects. Here cloneWithTarget might be more useful. See the next example (KitchenSyncMultiple.as):

```
package {
    import flash.display.Sprite;
    import flash.display.StageAlign;
    import flash.display.StageScaleMode;

    import org.as3lib.kitchensync.KitchenSync;
    import org.as3lib.kitchensync.action.KSTween;
    import org.as3lib.kitchensync.easing.Quartic;

    [SWF(backgroundColor=0xffffff)]
    public class KitchenSyncMultiple extends Sprite
    {
        private var sprite:Sprite;
```

```
        public function KitchenSyncMultiple()
        {
            stage.scaleMode = StageScaleMode.NO_SCALE;
            stage.align = StageAlign.TOP_LEFT;

            var s1:Sprite = makeSprite(100, 100, 0xff0000);
            var s2:Sprite = makeSprite(100, 200, 0x00ff00);
            var s3:Sprite = makeSprite(100, 300, 0x0000ff);
            var s4:Sprite = makeSprite(100, 400, 0xffff00);

            KitchenSync.initialize(this);
            var tween1:KSTween = new KSTween(s1, "x", 100, 800, 3000,
                                             0, Quartic.easeInOut);
            var tween2:KSTween = tween1.cloneWithTarget(s2, "x");
            var tween3:KSTween = tween1.cloneWithTarget(s3, "x");
            var tween4:KSTween = tween1.cloneWithTarget(s4, "x");
            tween1.start();
            tween2.start();
            tween3.start();
            tween4.start();
        }

        private function makeSprite(xpos:Number,
                                    ypos:Number,
                                    color:uint):Sprite
        {
            var s:Sprite = new Sprite();
            s.graphics.beginFill(color);
            s.graphics.drawRect(-50, -25, 100, 50);
            s.graphics.endFill();
            s.x = xpos;
            s.y = ypos;
            addChild(s);
            return s;
        }
    }
}
```

Each additional tween is a clone of the first with a different target.

Notice that you have to start each tween separately. Some of the more powerful features of KitchenSync are its action groups, which are similar to the TweenGroup class that's part of the TweenLite package. Using an action group, you can synchronize the action of multiple tweens. There are several types of action groups. To start several tweens at the same time, use the org.as3lib.kitchensync.action. KSParallelGroup class. Pass in any tweens you want to group together in the constructor and then call start on the group, like so:

```
        var tween1:KSTween = new KSTween(s1, "x", 100, 800, 3000,
                                         0, Quartic.easeInOut);
```

```
    var tween2:KSTween = tween1.cloneWithTarget(s2, "x");
    var tween3:KSTween = tween1.cloneWithTarget(s3, "x");
    var tween4:KSTween = tween1.cloneWithTarget(s4, "x");

    var pg:KSParallelGroup = new KSParallelGroup(tween1,
                                                 tween2,
                                                 tween3,
                                                 tween4);

    pg.start();
```

Again, at first this looks more complex than just calling start four times. However, the action groups make up a lot of the power of KitchenSync. When creating an action group such as KSParallelGroup, you can pass in not only instances of KSTween but also other instances of KSParallelGroup or any other action group. Thus, you can create complex nested, sequenced animations that you can replay any time just by calling start on the group. You'll see more of this in the next section.

Tween sequences in KitchenSync

Similar to the other engines you've looked at so far, you can create sequences using delay or by listening for the completion of a tween before starting the next one. I won't go through this again because it's not too different from the other engines. Far more interesting is using another action group, KSSequenceGroup, to create sequences.

Using KSSequenceGroup is just as easy as using KSParallelGroup. The next class, available as KitchenSyncSequence.as, demonstrates this:

```
    package {
        import flash.display.Sprite;
        import flash.display.StageAlign;
        import flash.display.StageScaleMode;

        import org.as3lib.kitchensync.KitchenSync;
        import org.as3lib.kitchensync.action.KSSequenceGroup;
        import org.as3lib.kitchensync.action.KSTween;
        import org.as3lib.kitchensync.easing.Quartic;

        [SWF(backgroundColor=0xffffff)]
        public class KitchenSyncSequence extends Sprite
        {
            private var sprite:Sprite;

            public function KitchenSyncSequence()
            {
                stage.scaleMode = StageScaleMode.NO_SCALE;
                stage.align = StageAlign.TOP_LEFT;

                sprite = new Sprite();
                sprite.graphics.beginFill(0xff0000);
                sprite.graphics.drawRect(-50, -25, 100, 50);
                sprite.graphics.endFill();
```

```
    sprite.x = 100;
    sprite.y = 100;
    addChild(sprite);

    KitchenSync.initialize(this);
    var tween1:KSTween = new KSTween(sprite, "x", 100, 800,
                                     3000, 0,
                                     Quartic.easeInOut);
    var tween2:KSTween = new KSTween(sprite, "y", 100, 400,
                                     3000, 0,
                                     Quartic.easeInOut);
    var tween3:KSTween = new KSTween(sprite, "rotation", 0,
                                     360, 3000, 0,
                                     Quartic.easeInOut);

    var sg:KSSequenceGroup = new KSSequenceGroup(tween1,
                                                 tween2,
                                                 tween3);
    sg.start();
  }
 }
}
```

Here we create the three tweens for three different properties and feed them into a KSSequenceGroup instance. Start that group, and the whole thing plays out in order.

Remember that you can add a sequence group to a new parallel group to have that sequence run alongside some other tweens, and vice versa. It can be quite powerful.

KitchenSync is probably a bit more developer-oriented than the two packages you've looked at so far. Whereas with Tweener, you can do just about everything with a single class, and TweenLite has a few more, KitchenSync is a large framework with dozens of classes, packages, and interfaces. It requires a bit more of a learning curve, but might fit in well with your workflow and is flexible enough to do just about anything you want.

gTween

The last engine is gTween by Grant Skinner. Grant is a well-known Flash developer and a good friend (I've mentioned his work several times in this book). As of this writing, gTween has just recently been released as a public beta, so its application programming interface (API) and workflow might change by the time you read this, but I think it's still worth getting a quick overview of the engine.

You can download gTween here: http://gskinner.com/libraries/gtween/.

The whole of gTween exists in a single class: com.gskinner.motion.GTween. The constructor for this class is as follows:

```
new GTween(target, duration, properties, tweenProperties);
```

Like the other engines you've seen, target is the object you'll be tweening, and duration is how long the tween will last. The properties parameter contains the properties of the object that you want to tween. This is a generic object and works the same way that Tweener and TweenLite do. However, in gTween there is a separate parameter, tweenProperties, that lets you customize other aspects of the tween, such as a delay or an easing function.

This is enough to get us started. The next example is available as GTweenDemo.as:

```
package {
    import com.gskinner.motion.GTween;

    import flash.display.Sprite;
    import flash.display.StageAlign;
    import flash.display.StageScaleMode;

    [SWF(backgroundColor=0xffffff)]
    public class GTweenDemo extends Sprite
    {
        private var sprite:Sprite;

        public function GTweenDemo()
        {
            stage.scaleMode = StageScaleMode.NO_SCALE;
            stage.align = StageAlign.TOP_LEFT;

            sprite = new Sprite();
            sprite.graphics.beginFill(0xff0000);
            sprite.graphics.drawRect(-50, -25, 100, 50);
            sprite.graphics.endFill();
            sprite.x = 100;
            sprite.y = 100;
            addChild(sprite);

            var tween:GTween = new GTween(sprite, 3, {x:800});
        }
    }
}
```

Pretty simple. If you've followed along with the other engine descriptions in this chapter, there's really no explanation needed here. Like Tweener and TweenLite, you can tween multiple properties on an object just by adding them to the properties object:

```
var tween:GTween = new GTween(sprite, 3, {x:800, y:400});
```

Easing functions in gTween

One thing I admire about gTween is that it doesn't try to reinvent what already exists. As you can guess, the engine uses Robert Penner's equations. But unlike the other engines that copy over all these classes and functions into new, virtually identical classes and functions, gTween just uses the ones that come with Flash and the Flex framework: the ones in the `fl.transitions.easing` package for Flash and `mx.effects.easing` in the Flex framework.

You pass the easing function to the ease property of the tween either in the `tweeningProperties` parameter of the constructor or directly on the tween instance after it is created. Both of the following examples set the ease function to `mx.effects.easing.Circular.easeInOut` (make sure that you import whatever class you are using). Here's the first one:

```
var tween:GTween = new GTween(sprite, 3, {x:800, y:400},
                                {ease:Circular.easeInOut});
```

Here's the second:

```
var tween:GTween = new GTween(sprite, 3, {x:800, y:400});
tween.ease = Circular.easeInOut;
```

Tweening multiple objects with gTween

As is the norm for most tween engines, using multiple objects means creating multiple tweens. The GTween class includes a clone method to make creating multiple tweens easier. You can pass in a new target to the clone method, and the tween will be duplicated for that new target object. The next class, as the file GTweenMulti.as, demonstrates this:

```
package {
    import com.gskinner.motion.GTween;

    import flash.display.Sprite;
    import flash.display.StageAlign;
    import flash.display.StageScaleMode;

    import mx.effects.easing.Quadratic;

    [SWF(backgroundColor=0xffffff)]
    public class GTweenMulti extends Sprite
    {

        public function GTweenMulti()
        {
            stage.scaleMode = StageScaleMode.NO_SCALE;
            stage.align = StageAlign.TOP_LEFT;

            var s1:Sprite = makeSprite(100, 100, 0xff0000);
            var s2:Sprite = makeSprite(100, 200, 0x00ff00);
            var s3:Sprite = makeSprite(100, 300, 0x0000ff);
            var s4:Sprite = makeSprite(100, 400, 0xffff00);

            var tween1:GTween = new GTween(s1, 3, {x:800},
                                        {ease:Quadratic.easeInOut});
            var tween2:GTween = tween1.clone(s2);
```

```
                    var tween3:GTween = tween1.clone(s3);
                    var tween4:GTween = tween1.clone(s4);
            }

            private function makeSprite(xpos:Number,
                                        ypos:Number,
                                        color:uint):Sprite
            {
                var s:Sprite = new Sprite();
                s.graphics.beginFill(color);
                s.graphics.drawRect(-50, -25, 100, 50);
                s.graphics.endFill();
                s.x = xpos;
                s.y = ypos;
                addChild(s);
                return s;
            }
        }
    }
```

Tween sequences in gTween

Like the other tween engines, you can set up sequences by using the delay property or by listening for the completion of one tween to start another one. I demonstrated this enough already and it wouldn't be much different here. Some engines have group classes that you can fill with tweens to create groups. The gTween class takes quite another approach to sequences, however, through the nextTween property.

Simply put, you can create two tweens and pause the second one. Pass a reference to the second tween to the first tween's nextTween property. When the first one is done, the second will start. This is probably much better shown than described, so here's the next example, as seen in the GTweenSequence.as file:

```
package {
    import com.gskinner.motion.GTween;

    import flash.display.Sprite;
    import flash.display.StageAlign;
    import flash.display.StageScaleMode;

    import mx.effects.easing.Circular;
    import mx.effects.easing.Quadratic;

    [SWF(backgroundColor=0xffffff)]
    public class GTweenSequence extends Sprite
    {
        private var sprite:Sprite;

        public function GTweenSequence()
        {
```

```
stage.scaleMode = StageScaleMode.NO_SCALE;
stage.align = StageAlign.TOP_LEFT;

sprite = new Sprite();
sprite.graphics.beginFill(0xff0000);
sprite.graphics.drawRect(-50, -25, 100, 50);
sprite.graphics.endFill();
sprite.x = 100;
sprite.y = 100;
addChild(sprite);

var tween1:GTween = new GTween(sprite, 3,
            {x:800}, {ease:Quadratic.easeInOut});
var tween2:GTween = new GTween(sprite, 3,
            {y:400}, {ease:Quadratic.easeInOut});
var tween3:GTween = new GTween(sprite, 3,
            {rotation:180}, {ease:Quadratic.easeInOut});

tween2.pause();
tween3.pause();

tween1.nextTween = tween2;
tween2.nextTween = tween3;
        }
    }
}
```

Here we create the three tweens and then pause the second and third. Set the tween1 nextTween property to tween2, set tween2.nextTween to tween3, and they all play out perfectly.

Like just about everything else covered in this chapter, this discussion barely scratches the surface of the full capabilities of gTween, which has a lot of functionality in a single class. Look through the documentation, which I'm sure will be evolving, to see all the other stuff you can do with it. As a matter of fact, between the time I wrote this chapter and the time I gave it a final review, another build of gTween was released. So take this as the briefest of introductions and go to the source to find out what it's capable of at the time you read this.

Summary

This chapter has hopefully given you a decent overview of the tween engine landscape. Perhaps you have a better idea of the different approaches to tweening that have been taken and found one that suits your needs. Or maybe you even think you can do better and create your own tween engine! Go for it!

And, although I'm guessing that you haven't been reading this book linearly, this chapter also brings us to the end of the book. I hope you have. nearly as much fun exploring the different topics we've covered here as I did when researching them, coming up with fun examples for them, and writing them. At the very least, I trust that one or two of these chapters led you to a research project of your own.

INDEX

Numbers and Symbols

2D distortion, playing with, 335–337

2D flash.geom.Point object, converting to flash.geom.Vector3D object, 303

3D
  basics in Flash 10, 276–281
  carousel, example, 298
  containers, 286–287, 294
  coordinates and screen coordinates, 303–307
  depth sorting, 283–285
  engines for Flash, 275
  field of view and focal length, 298–303
  isometric block, creating, 119–121
  pointing at something, 307–309
  positioning, 282–287
  rotation of display objects, 288–298
  screen coordinates and, 303–307
  setting the vanishing point, 278–281
  triangles and, 340–344

3D positioning
  depth sorting, 283–285
  in Flash, 282–287

3D rotating globe, creating, 348–351

2001: A Space Odyssey, computer control in, 198

\# (hash sign), preceding tile definitions, 151

// (double slash), preceding comments in code with, 151

A

A* (A-Star) algorithm, 157–181
  basics, 157
  closed list in, 158
  common heuristics, 176–181
  cost, 157
  description, 158
  f used in, 157
  g used in, 158
  getting into the code, 164–176
  heuristics, common, 176–181
  heuristic function in, 158
  node, 157
  open list in, 158
  parent node in, 158
  pathfinding with, 157–181
  starting coding of, 164–181
  terms defined, 157–158
  visualizing, 160–181

acceleration, 52

acceleration method, calling in Eular.as file, 244

ActionScript, Vector types, 365

ActivityEvent.ACTIVITY, adding listener for, 209

ActivityEvent class
  as a noise-activated switch, 206–207
  dispatched by Microphone class, 206

activity level, visually graphing. 202–203

activityLevel property, for Camera class, 209

addChildToFloor method, 130

addChildToWorld method, 130

Adobe labs and developer center, web site address, 382

advanced terrain, 193–194

alignment behavior, 51
  in flocking, 93

angle, performing distortion with, 381

arrays, sorting by depth property, 125–127

arrivalThreshold, adding setter and getter to, 76

arrive behavior, 51
  slowing things down with, 75–77

artificial intelligence, 49

artificial life, 49

assignBallsToGrid method, 24–25

AStar.as file, AStar class in, 168–171

AStar class, 167–171
  implementing, 181–189

properties and default constructor, 171–172

refining the path: corners, 185–189

using in a game, 189–192

avoid method, using with object avoidance behavior, 85–87

AvoidTest.as file, 87–88

Away3D, in ActionScript for Flash, 275

axonometric projection, types of, 102

B

Back class, 403
  in mx.effects.easing package, 411

back faces, 344

backface culling, 344

Ball class
  collision detection with BEG, 20
  collision detection with END, 22

ball objects, hit testing an array of, 19–20

basicCheck() method, 29–31

Battat, James, 240

beginFill/endFill operations, 323

beginShadeFill method, filling Pixel Bender shader with, 361

beginShaderFill class, using shader instance in, 386

behaviors
  applying multiple to a single vehicle, 73–75
  overview of basic, 51

Bitmap class, in ActionScript, 2

BitmapCollision2 class, hit testing with semitransparent shapes, 9–11

BitmapCollision3 class, 12–13

BitmapCompare class, 3–4

BitmapData class, 2, 212
  drawing video to, 209
  getting into ShaderFillImage.as file, 392–393

BitmapData.hitTest
  comparing two BitmapData objects with, 2